Architecture of Advanced Numerical Analysis Systems

Designing a Scientific Computing System using OCaml

Liang Wang
Jianxin Zhao

Architecture of Advanced Numerical Analysis Systems: Designing a Scientific Computing System using OCaml

Liang Wang
Helsinki, Finland

Jianxin Zhao
Bejing, China

ISBN-13 (pbk): 978-1-4842-8852-8
https://doi.org/10.1007/978-1-4842-8853-5

ISBN-13 (electronic): 978-1-4842-8853-5

Managing Director, Apress Media LLC: Welmoed Spahr
Acquisitions Editor: Steve Anglin
Development Editor: James Markham
Coordinating Editor: Mark Powers

Cover designed by eStudioCalamar

Cover image by Lukasz Niescioruk on Unsplash (www.unsplash.com)

Distributed to the book trade worldwide by Apress Media, LLC, 1 New York Plaza, New York, NY 10004, U.S.A. Phone 1-800-SPRINGER, fax (201) 348-4505, e-mail orders-ny@springer-sbm.com, or visit www.springeronline.com. Apress Media, LLC is a California LLC and the sole member (owner) is Springer Science + Business Media Finance Inc (SSBM Finance Inc). SSBM Finance Inc is a Delaware corporation.

For information on translations, please e-mail booktranslations@springernature.com; for reprint, paperback, or audio rights, please e-mail bookpermissions@springernature.com.

Apress titles may be purchased in bulk for academic, corporate, or promotional use. eBook versions and licenses are also available for most titles. For more information, reference our Print and eBook Bulk Sales web page at http://www.apress.com/bulk-sales.

Any source code or other supplementary material referenced by the author in this book is available to readers on GitHub (https://github.com/Apress). For more detailed information, please visit http://www.apress.com/source-code.

Printed on acid-free paper

To my wife Maria, our daughters Matilda and Sofia,
and my beloved family.

—Liang

To my parents and sister; to their unyielding love and support.
To all those who are fighting for freedom and righteousness against the
unleashing evil from hell.

"Namárië, ar nai aistalë Eldar ar Atani ar ilyë Léralieron hilya le. Eleni
sílar antalyannar."

—Jianxin

Table of Contents

TABLE OF CONTENTS

About the Authors

Liang Wang is the Chief AI Architect at Nokia, the Chief Scientific Officer at iKVA, a Senior Researcher at the University of Cambridge, and an Intel Software Innovator. He has a broad research interest in artificial intelligence, machine learning, operating systems, computer networks, optimization theory, and graph theory.

Jianxin Zhao is a PhD graduate from the University of Cambridge. His research interests include numerical computation, artificial intelligence, decentralized systems, and their application in the real world.

Acknowledgments

Developing a full-featured numerical-analysis system is very complicated. Writing a book to dive deep into its architecture is an even more challenging task. It not only requires skills, enthusiasm, persistence, but also needs strong support from families, colleagues, and communities. For years, we have received so much help from so many individuals and organizations that it is almost impossible to make an exhaustive list. Nonetheless, we would particularly like to emphasize that Owl is developed on top of an enormous amount of previous work. Without the continuous efforts of these projects and the intellectual contributions of these people over the years, it would be impossible for us to create this system and deliver this book.

We give our most hearty thanks to those who contribute to the Owl project. Marcello Seri and Ta-Chu Kao developed owl-ode, an Ordinary Differential Equation solver library based on Owl. Pierre Vandenhove worked on the memory optimization of the computation graph module during his internship at the OCaml Labs in Cambridge. Tudor Tiplea participated in developing the base library in Owl so that it could run on various backends such as browsers. Ben Catterall's thesis work on the PSP provided a theoretical foundation for the Actor system.

We would like to express our sincerest gratitude and appreciation to the OCaml Software Foundation[1] and Ahrefs[2] for fully sponsoring this open access book as well as their long-term support to the Owl project.

---

[1] http://ocaml-sf.org/
[2] https://ahrefs.com/

CHAPTER 1

Introduction

This book introduces Owl, a numerical library we have been developing and maintaining for years. We develop Owl for scientific and engineering computing in the OCaml language. It focuses on providing a comprehensive set of high-level numerical functions so that developers can quickly build up any data analytical applications. Over years of intensive development and continuous optimization, Owl has evolved into a powerful software system with competitive performance compared to mainstream numerical libraries. Meanwhile, Owl's overall architecture remains simple and elegant. Its small codebase can be easily managed by a small group of developers.

In this book, we are going to introduce the design and architecture of Owl, from its designers' perspective. The target audience is anyone who is interested in not only how to use mathematical functions in numerical applications but also how they are designed, organized, and implemented from scratch. Some prerequisites are needed though. We assume the readers are familiar with basic syntax of the OCaml language. We recommend [38] as a good reference book on this matter. Also note that this book focuses on introducing core parts of the Owl codebase, such as the implementation and design of various key modules. If you are more interested in how to use the functionalities provided in Owl to solve numerical problems, such as basic mathematical calculation, linear algebra, statistics, signal processing, etc., please refer to our book *OCaml Scientific Computing: Functional Programming in Data Science and Artificial Intelligence* [26].

1.1 Numerical Computing in OCaml

Scientific computing is a rapidly evolving multidisciplinary field that uses advanced computing capabilities to understand and solve complex problems in the real world. It is widely used in various fields in research and industry, for example, simulations in biology and physics, weather forecasting, revenue optimization in finance, etc. One

L. Wang and J. Zhao, *Architecture of Advanced Numerical Analysis Systems*,
https://doi.org/10.1007/978-1-4842-8853-5_1

1

most recent hot topic in scientific computing is machine learning. Thanks to the recent advances in machine learning and deep neural networks, there is a huge demand on various numerical tools and libraries in order to facilitate both academic researchers and industrial developers to fast prototype and test their new ideas, then develop and deploy analytical applications at a large scale.

Take deep neural networks as an example; Google invests heavily in TensorFlow, while Facebook promotes their PyTorch. Beyond these libraries focusing on one specific numerical task, the interest on general-purpose tools like Python and Julia also grows fast. Python has been one popular choice among developers for fast prototyping analytical applications. One important reason is SciPy and NumPy libraries, tightly integrated with other advanced functionality such as plotting, offer a powerful environment which lets developers write very concise code to finish complicated numerical tasks. As a result, most frameworks provide Python bindings to take advantage of the existing numerical infrastructure in NumPy and SciPy.

On the other hand, back before Owl was developed, the support of basic scientific computing in OCaml was rather fragmented. There had been some initial efforts (e.g., Lacaml, Oml, Pareto, etc.), but their APIs were either too low level to offer satisfying productivity or the designs overly focused on a specific problem domain. Moreover, inconsistent data representation and excessive use of abstract types made it difficult to exchange data across different libraries. Consequently, developers often had to write a significant amount of boilerplate code just to finish rather trivial numerical tasks. There was a severe lack of a general-purpose numerical library in the OCaml ecosystem. However, we believe OCaml is a good candidate for developing such a general-purpose numerical library for two important reasons:

- We can write functional code as concise as that in Python with type-safety.

- OCaml code often has much superior performance compared to dynamic languages such as Python and Julia.

1.2 Architecture

Designing and developing a full-fledged numerical library is a nontrivial task, despite that OCaml has been widely used in system programming such as MirageOS. The key difference between the two is fundamental and interesting: system libraries provide a lean set of APIs to abstract complex and heterogeneous physical hardware, while numerical libraries offer a fat set of functions over a small set of abstract number types.

When the Owl project started in 2016, we were immediately confronted by a series of fundamental questions like: "what should be the basic data types", "what should be the core data structures", "what modules should be designed", etc. In the following development and performance optimization, we also tackled many research and engineering challenges on a wide range of different topics such as software engineering, language design, system and network programming, etc. As a result, Owl is a rather complex library, arguably one of the most complicated numerical software system developed in OCaml. It contains about 269K lines of OCaml code, 142K lines of C code, and more than 6500 functions. We have strived for a modular design to make sure that the system is flexible and extendable.

We present the architecture of Owl briefly as in Figure 1-1. It contains two subsystems. The subsystem on the left part is Owl's numerical subsystem. The modules contained in this subsystem fall into four categories:

- Core modules contain basic data structures, namely, the n-dimensional array, including C-based and OCaml-based implementation, and symbolic representation.

- Classic analytics contains basic mathematical and statistical functions, linear algebra, signal processing, ordinary differential equation, etc., and foreign function interface to other libraries (e.g., *CBLAS* and *LAPACKE*).

- Advanced analytics, such as algorithmic differentiation, optimization, regression, neural network, natural language processing, etc.

- Service composition and deployment to multiple backends such as to the browser, container, virtual machine, and other accelerators via a computation graph.

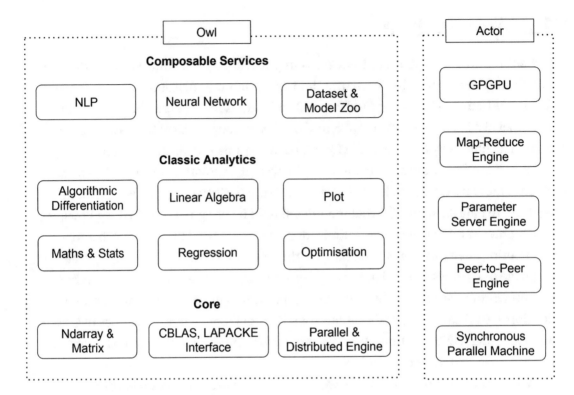

Figure 1-1. *The whole system can be divided into two subsystems. The subsystem on the left deals with numerical computation, while the one on the right handles the related tasks in a distributed and parallel computing context including synchronization, scheduling, etc*

In the rest of this chapter, we give a brief introduction about these various components in Owl and set a road map for this book.

Basic Computing and Analytics with Owl

In a numerical library or software such as NumPy, MATLAB, TensorFlow, and Owl, the *N*-dimensional array (ndarray) is the most fundamental data type for building scientific computing applications. In most such applications, solely using scalar values is insufficient. Both matrices and vectors are special cases of ndarray. Owl provides the Ndarray module, the usability and performance of which are essential to the whole architecture in Owl. In Chapter 2, we will introduce this module, including how it is designed and its performance optimization.

Owl supports a wide variety of classic numerical analytics methods, including basic mathematical functions, statistics, linear algebra, ordinary differential equation, and signal processing. The functions in each field are included in a corresponding module. Their design is similar to that of Ndarray module, which is mainly interfacing to existing tools in C code, such as OpenBLAS. The Ndarray module partly relies on these functions, especially the ones that operate on scalars. For example, Ndarray provides a sin function. What it does is actually calling the scalar version sin function in the Maths module and mapping them on all its elements. Since this book mainly focuses on the architectural design of Owl, we will not introduce in detail how to apply Owl in these fields; instead, we will briefly give some examples in Appendix A.

Advanced Design in Owl

We have introduced the various classic analytics fields that are supported in Owl. What makes Owl more powerful are a series of advanced analytics. At the heart of them lies algorithmic differentiation (AD), which will be introduced in Chapter 3. Performing differentiation is so crucial to modern numerical applications that it is utilized almost everywhere. Moreover, it is proven that AD provides both efficient and accurate differentiation computations that are not affected by numerical errors.

One of the prominent analytics that benefit from the power of AD is optimization (Chapter 4), which is about finding minima or maxima of a function. Though optimization methods do not necessarily require computing differentiation, it is often a key element in efficient optimization methods. One most commonly used optimization method is gradient descent, which iteratively applies optimization on a complex object function by small steps until it is minimized by some standard. It is exactly how another type of advanced application, regression, works. Regression covers a variety of methods, including linear regression, logistic regression, etc. Each can be applied to different scenarios and can be solved by various methods, but they share a similar solution method, namely, iterative optimization.

Depending on applications, the computation generated from AD can be quite complex. They often form a directed acyclic graph, which can be referred to as a computation graph. Based on the computation graph, we can perform various optimizations to improve the execution speed, reduce memory usage, etc. A computation graph plays a critical role in our system, and we introduce it in Chapter 6.

Finally, neural networks, as complex as their architectures can be, are in essence also an extension of regression and therefore are also trained by iterative optimization. We cover this topic in Chapter 5. With the popularity of machine learning and neural networks, this series of advanced analytics, especially the core technique AD, has become increasingly essential in modern numerical analysis library stacks. In this book, we will briefly introduce these topics and their architecture in design in Owl.

Hardware and Deployment

In the next part, we discuss the execution backends Owl executes on in Chapter 7. The first important backend we consider is hardware accelerators such as GPUs. Scientific computing often involves intensive computations, and a GPU is important to accelerate these computations by performing parallel computation on its massive cores. Besides, there are growingly more types of hardware accelerators. For example, Google develops the Tensor Processing Unit (TPU), specifically for neural network machine learning. It is highly optimized for large batches in using TensorFlow. To improve performance of a numerical library such as Owl, it is necessary to support multiple hardware platforms.

One idea is to "freeride" existing libraries that already support various hardware platforms. We believe that a computation graph is a suitable intermediate representation (IR) to achieve interoperability between different libraries. Along this line, we develop a prototype symbolic layer system by using which the users can define a computation in Owl and then turn it into an ONNX structure, which can be executed on many different platforms such as TensorFlow. By using the symbolic layer, we show the system workflow and how powerful features of Owl, such as algorithmic differentiation, can be used in TensorFlow.

Besides aiming for maximal performance on accelerators, sometimes a numerical library also targets to run in a wide range of environments, for example, to execute on web browsers based on JavaScript for ease of access to many end users. Besides, with the trending of edge computing and the Internet of Things, it is also crucial for numerical libraries to support running on computation resource–limited devices. One approach is to construct *unikernel*, a specialized minimal virtual machine image that only contains necessary libraries and modules to support an application. In this book, we also introduce Owl's support for execution in this environment.

Research on Owl

In the last part of this book, we introduce two components in Owl: *Zoo*, for service composition and deployment, and *Actor*, for distributed computing. The focus of these two chapters is to present two pieces of research based on Owl.

In Chapter 9, we introduce the Zoo subsystem. It was originally developed to share OCaml scripts. It is known that we can use OCaml as a scripting language as Python (at certain performance cost because the code is compiled into bytecode). Even though compiling into native code for production use is recommended, scripting is still useful and convenient, especially for light deployment and fast prototyping. In fact, the performance penalty in most Owl scripts is almost unnoticeable because the heaviest numerical computation part is still offloaded to Owl which runs native code. While designing Owl, our goal is always to make the whole ecosystem open, flexible, and extensible. Programmers can make their own "small" scripts and share them with others conveniently, so they do not have to wait for such functions to be implemented in Owl's master branch or submit something "heavy" to OPAM. Based on these basic functionalities, we extend the Zoo system to address the computation service composition and deployment issues.

Next, we discuss the topic of distributed computing. The design of distributed and parallel computing module essentially differentiates Owl from other mainstream numerical libraries. For most libraries, the capability of distributed and parallel computing is often implemented as a third-party library, and the users have to deal with low-level message passing interfaces. However, Owl achieves such capability through its Actor subsystem. Distributed computing includes techniques that combine multiple machines through a network, sharing data and coordinating progresses. With the fast-growing number of data and processing power they require, distributed computing has been playing a significant role in current smart applications in various fields. Its application is extremely prevalent in various fields, such as providing large computing power jointly, fault-tolerant databases, file system, web services, and managing large-scale networks, etc.

In Chapter 10, we give a brief bird's-eye view of this topic. Specifically, we introduce an OCaml-based distributed computing engine, Actor. It has implemented three mainstream programming paradigms: parameter server, map-reduce, and peer-to-peer. Orthogonal to these paradigms, Actor also implements all four types of synchronization barriers. We introduce four different types of synchronization methods or "barriers" that are commonly used in current systems. We further elaborate how these barriers are designed and provide illustrations from the theoretical perspective. Finally, we use evaluations to show the performance trade-offs in using different barriers.

1.3 Summary

In this chapter, we introduced the theme of this book, which centers on the design of Owl, a numerical library we have been developing. We briefly discussed why we build Owl based on the OCaml language. And then we set a road map for the whole book, which can be categorized into four parts: basic building block, advanced analytics, execution in various environments, and research topics based on Owl. We hope you will enjoy the journey ahead!

CHAPTER 2

Core Optimizations

Perhaps one of the most important questions in a numerical library or software is, "how to make it run faster?" You can never have a piece of scientific computation program that runs too fast or takes too little memory. That is surely also the primary concern when we are designing Owl. In this chapter, we discuss the optimization of the Ndarray module, the core module that underlies almost all computation in Owl. We first introduce this module and how it interfaces to C code. Next, we briefly introduce the basic principles in optimizing numerical code, including some common techniques. Then we use the code examples in Owl to demonstrate how these techniques are applied in Owl. We finish this chapter with a bit of touch on the topic of automatic performance tuning in numerical libraries.

2.1 N-Dimensional Array in Owl

Owl numerical functions are organized in multiple modules, such as linear algebra, signal processing, statistics, optimization, etc. In real-world applications though, it is quite rare for users to only deal with scalar values in data analytics. In linear algebra, matrices are a common data object. In a neural network, the input images are often represented by three-dimensional arrays, each element being in the range of $[0, 255]$. Indeed, a solid implementation of n-dimensional array, or ndarray, lies at the heart of any industry-level numerical library, such as NumPy, Julia, MATLAB, etc.

The Ndarray module provides this core data structure in Owl. It relies on the Bigarray module provided in OCaml. Compared to normal OCaml arrays, a Bigarray is not limited in size, supports up to 16 dimensions, and supports more space-efficient storage. Here shows the definition of an Ndarray type:

```
type ('a, 'b) t = ('a, 'b, c_layout) Genarray.t
```

© Liang Wang, Jianxin Zhao 2023
L. Wang and J. Zhao, *Architecture of Advanced Numerical Analysis Systems*,
https://doi.org/10.1007/978-1-4842-8853-5_2

Here, the GADT type 'b is an element kind, such as single-precision (32 bits) floating-point numbers, 8-bit integers, etc. Type 'a represents the type of OCaml values that can be written into Bigarray or read back from it. The Bigarrays can contain various types, and in Ndarray we mainly support four:

```
type ('a, 'b) kind =
  | Float32 : (float, float32_elt) kind
  | Float64 : (float, float64_elt) kind
  | Complex32 : (Complex.t, complex32_elt) kind
  | Complex64 : (Complex.t, complex64_elt) kind
```

Namely, Owl mainly supports single-precision float (S), double precision (D), single-precision complex (C), and double-precision complex (Z). Supporting complex data types is essential to applications such as signal processing using Fourier transform.

Besides the ('a, 'b) part, the definition also includes a c_layout parameter. Bigarray supports two different memory layouts. In Owl, we stick with the C-style data layout, which means that indices start at 0 and in row-major format. Initially, Owl aims to support both layouts, but it soon turns out that would just open the jar of worm without much benefit.

As an example, if we need to create an ndarray of shape 2x3, elements of which are all 0s of type single-precision float, we can use

```
Dense.Ndarray.S.ones [|2;3|]
```

In this naming of modules, Dense indicates the data is densely stored instead of using sparse structure. Owl also supports Sparse ndarray types, and its API is quite similar to that of the dense type. It also contains the four different kinds of data types as stated earlier. Indeed, if you call Dense.Ndarray.S.ones [|2;3|], you can get sparsely stored zero ndarrays. There are two popular formats for storing sparse matrices, the Compressed Sparse Column (CSC) format and the Compressed Sparse Row (CSR) format. Owl uses the Compressed Sparse Row format. Compared to the dense ndarray, the definition of sparse ndarray contains some extra information:

```
type ('a, 'b) t =
  { mutable s : int array
  ; mutable h : (int array, int) Hashtbl.t
  ; mutable d : ('a, 'b, c_layout) Array1.t
  }
```

In this chapter, we focus on the optimization of dense ndarray structures and will not further discuss details in the sparse ndarray.

The second part of the name is Ndarray, which is of course the topic of this chapter, but it should be noted that we also support matrix data types. Implemented based on Ndarray, the Matrix supports operations that work solely on matrices, such as row_num, and can interoperate with ndarrays if the dimension is two. For example, we can perform

```
let x = Dense.Ndarray.S.ones [|2;3|];;
let a = Dense.Matrix.S.row_num x;;
```

Besides the core implementation of data structure, the importance of the Ndarray module lies in the various operations it supports. They can be categorized into multiple types:

- Creation functions that generate dense data structures, such as empty, create, zeros, and ones. These functions return ndarrays of the specified shape and content.

- Mathematical operations. Many of them can be categorized into three generic operation patterns: map, fold, and scan. For example, the map function transforms one ndarray to another by applying the provided function to every element in the original ndarray, and operations such as sin and log belong to this pattern.

- Slicing operation that extracts part of an ndarray or a matrix according to certain slice definition, an index list that indicates which indices should be accessed and in what order for each dimension of the value being sliced. Indexing and slicing are perhaps the most important ndarray functions in any numerical library.

- Other calculation or manipulation functions: comparison, tile or repeat an ndarray, serialization, iterate over all the elements, etc.

It is always a good idea to push the performance of these operations forward, especially the mathematical functions. Contrary to many people's impression on functional language, OCaml is actually quite fast.[1] That being said, it is unreasonable to

---

[1] OCaml documentation: Profiling. https://ocaml.org/docs/profiling

claim that solely using OCaml can satisfy all the performance requirements of numerical computing. More often than not, we still need to rely on the power of C or FORTRAN, as in many other numerical computing libraries such as NumPy.

Therefore, in Owl we interface most ndarray operations to C implementation. In the next several sections, we first explain how to interface OCaml code to C and then introduce in detail the principles and techniques that are commonly applied to optimize the performance of computations.

2.2 Interface OCaml to C

To ensure its performance, we implement the core computation in the Ndarray module mostly in the C language and then interface them to OCaml. In this section, we briefly introduce how it is done. The corresponding code is mostly included in the src/owl/ core/ directory in the source code. Let's use the sine function in the Ndarray module as an example. This OCaml function is a wrapper of another OCaml function _owl_sin:

```
let _owl_sin : type a b. (a, b) kind -> int ->
  (a, b) owl_arr -> (a, b) owl_arr -> unit =
  fun k l x y ->
    match k with
    | Float32   -> owl_float32_sin l x y
    | Float64   -> owl_float64_sin l x y
    | Complex32 -> owl_complex32_sin l x y
    | Complex64 -> owl_complex64_sin l x y
```

This function serves as an entrance to implementations of different sine functions. As we have introduced, Owl provides four data types: float, double, complex float, and complex double. This function takes a data type as input and applies the sine function on l elements in input array x, and the output is stored in array y. One of the called functions, for example, owl_float32_sin, is declared as an external function that interfaces from outside the OCaml world, a C function called "float32_sin".

```
external owl_float32_sin : int
  -> (`a, `b) owl_arr
  -> (`a, `b) owl_arr -> unit = "float32_sin"
```

We do not implement the C function float32_sin directly, since we observe that the implementations of four different types of sine functions are mostly the same. Therefore, we utilize C macros. Here is the template (FUN4) that can be used to implement a series of mathematical functions:

```
#ifdef FUN4

CAMLprim value FUN4(value vN, value vX, value vY)
{
  CAMLparam3(vN, vX, vY);
  int N = Long_val(vN);
  INIT;

  struct caml_ba_array *X = Caml_ba_array_val(vX);
  NUMBER *X_data = (NUMBER *) X->data;
  struct caml_ba_array *Y = Caml_ba_array_val(vY);
  NUMBER *Y_data = (NUMBER *) Y->data;
  NUMBER *start_x, *stop_x;
  NUMBER *start_y;

  caml_release_runtime_system();  /* Allow other threads */

  start_x = X_data;
  stop_x = start_x + N;
  start_y = Y_data;

  while (start_x != stop_x) {
    NUMBER x = *start_x;
    *start_y = (MAPFN(x));

    start_x += 1;
    start_y += 1;
  };

  caml_acquire_runtime_system();  /* Disallow other threads */

  CAMLreturn(Val_unit);
}

#endif /* FUN4 */
```

This C function should satisfy certain specifications. The returned value of `float32_sin` must be of `CAMLprim value` type, and its parameters are of type `value`. Several macros can be used to convert these `value` types into the native C types. These macros are included in the `<caml/mlvalues.h>` header file. For example, we use `Long_val` to cast a parameter into an integer value and `Caml_ba_array_val` from an OCaml `Bigarray` type to an array of numbers. Finally, the computation itself is straightforward: apply the function `MAPFN` on every element in the array x in a for-loop, and the output is saved in array y. Since the returned value of the OCaml function `_owl_sin` is `unit`, this C function also needs to return the macro `Val_unit`.

Notice that we haven't specified several macros in this template yet: the number type and the function to be applied on the array. For that, we use

```
#define FUN4 float32_sin
#define NUMBER float
#define MAPFN(X) (sinf(X))
#include OWL_NDARRAY_MATHS_MAP
```

Here, we specify a function of name `float32_sin` that uses the aforementioned template, where its number type is `float`, and the function to be applied on each element in the input array is `sinf` from standard C library `<math.h>`. We can easily change the macros here to use other functions to get the sine function of other precisions or other mathematical functions such as `exp`, `log`, etc.

To sum it up, when we call `Dense.Ndarray.S.sin x` in Owl, it ends up calling the `sinf` function on all float numbers in x. In this design, we can choose implementation in other libraries, such as the Intel Math Kernel Library (MKL), which can achieve superior performance on Intel-based machines. Actually, that's indeed what we do for many other modules. Instead of handcrafting all the highly sophisticated linear algebra functions, etc., we interface their implementation to libraries such as OpenBLAS (linear algebra routines), SMTF (random number generator), FFTPack (fast Fourier transform), Cephes (special mathematical functions), etc. But we try to reduce reliance on third-party libraries to the minimum while avoiding reinventing wheels.

Except for the interface mechanism we have introduced, we can also utilize the *foreign function interface* to invoke routines in a different programming language from OCaml. This approach is nicely explained in *Real World OCaml* [38]. This book is recommended for anyone who wants to dig deep in the OCaml world.

Implementing the core code enables multiple optimization opportunities: single-instruction-multiple-data (SIMD), parallel processing on multicore hardware [4], loop unrolling, using tile to improve efficiency of cache [48], etc. Besides, we can also build systems to automatically choose suitable parameters in the Owl system to fit the hardware/software platform it runs on. We will talk about these topics in detail in the rest of this chapter.

2.3 Core Optimization of Computation

Ever since the creation of computers, one question kept resurfacing from time to time: "How to improve the performance of a piece of code?" Back in the early days of computers, using computers was a privilege, and users had to utilize every second of their limited computing time to the utmost. And nowadays, every PC gamer wants high-quality visual effects. Not to mention those scientific researchers who would be overjoyed if their simulation program running time can be cut by half.

In the good old days, the answer was simple. We can simply freeride Moore's Law: "the number of transistors in a dense integrated circuit doubles about every two years." A similar exponential increase shows in quite a lot of related areas. With more CPU clock speed, any code can automatically run faster, not to mention the dramatic increase of memory and storage capacity. All you need to do is to wait for a while.

However, the free lunch is over, and the clock speed has stagnated for years.[2] Faced with this situation, programmers need to achieve performance gains in fundamentally different ways on modern hardware. It generally includes two aspects: utilizing parallel computing mechanisms provided in processors and reducing accessing data from slow storage media.

Figure 2-1 shows a much simplified and yet thorough architecture illustration of a quad-core CPU.[3] It shows some of the core components in a processor. The CPU follows a "fetch-decode-execute" cycle to process instructions. It basically goes as described as follows. When the program counter indicates the next instruction to be executed, the *Fetch/Decode* fetches the instruction value from memory and decodes it into actions the computer can understand. Next, the *Arithmetic Logic Unit* (ALU) is invoked to

---

[2] *Microprocessor chronology*, Wikipedia, URL: https://en.wikipedia.org/wiki/Microprocessor_chronology

[3] This figure is inspired by the CMU 15-418/15-618 course *Parallel Computer Architecture and Programming*, which is recommended to anyone who is serious about learning parallel computing.

perform required computation operations. This process repeats until the program stops. During this process, the *Execution Context* contains necessary state information, such as computing results, program counter, registers, etc. Besides these parts, the CPU also contains several levels of cache, which finally connect to memory. This model provides a quite good approximation to real CPUs. In the rest of this section, we will explain these different parts and how they benefit the performance of computation in detail.

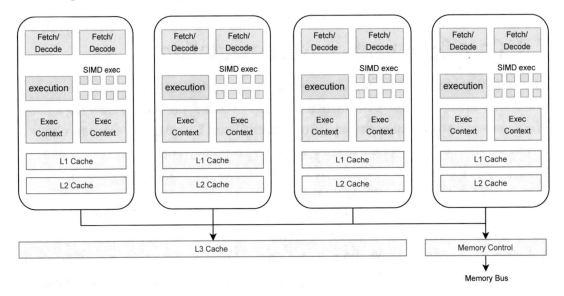

Figure 2-1. *Architectural illustration of a quad-core CPU*

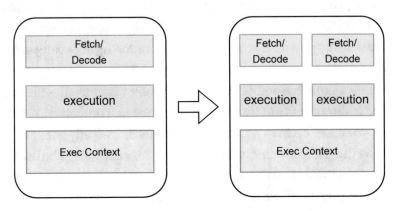

Figure 2-2. *Processor parallelism: multiple fetch and decode modules*

CPU Support of Parallel Computing

Instruction-Level Parallelism

A program consists of a stream of instructions. In a basic processor model, it executes one instruction in one clock cycle. But instructions do not strictly sequentially depend on one another. Instead, some of them can be executed in parallel without interference. Architecture that exploits such instruction-level parallelism (ILP) is called *superscalar*, which can date back to the 1960s. It can execute more than one instruction per clock cycle by dispatching multiple instructions at the same time. Therefore, the processor contains multiple fetch/decode and ALU modules, as Figure 2-2 shows. The parallelism among an instruction stream is automatically and dynamically discovered by the hardware during execution and thus is not visible to programmers.

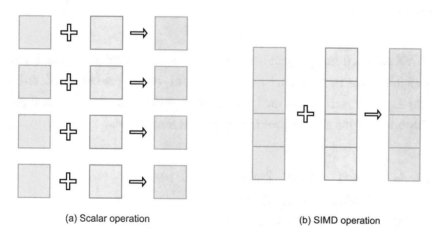

(a) Scalar operation   (b) SIMD operation

Figure 2-3. *Comparison of computing conventional and SIMD*

Vectorization

The ALU also has the potential to provide more than one piece of data in one clock cycle. The *single instruction multiple data* (SIMD) refers to a computing method that uses one single instruction to process multiple data. It is in contrast with the conventional computing method that processes one piece of data, such as load, add, etc., with one construction. The comparison of these two methods is shown in Figure 2-3. In this example, one instruction processes four float numbers at the same time.

SIMD is now widely supported on various hardware architectures. Back in 1996, Intel's *MMX* instruction set was the first widely deployed SIMD, enabling processing four 16-bit numbers at the same time. It is then extended to more instruction sets, including SSE, AVX, AVX2, etc. In *AVX2*, users can process 16 16-bit numbers per cycle. Similarly, the ARM architecture provides NEON to facilitate SIMD. Next is a simple example that utilizes Intel AVX2 instructions to add eight integers to another eight integers:

```
#include <immintrin.h>

int main(int argc, char* argv[]) {
    __m256i a = _mm256_set_epi32(1, 2, 3, 4, 5, 6, 7, 8);
    __m256i b = _mm256_set_epi32(10, 20, 30, 40, 50, 60, 70, 80);
    __m256i c = _mm256_add_epi32(a, b);

    return 0;
}
```

To use AVX instructions, programmers need to use the Intel intrinsics, included in header files such as immintrin .h. Here, _mm256_set_epi32 packed eight 32-bit integers together into a group, and _mm256_add_epi32 adds packed 32-bit integers. If you look at the assembly code in this simple program, part of it looks like

```
...
vpunpcklqdq    %xmm3, %xmm0, %xmm0
vpunpcklqdq    %xmm2, %xmm1, %xmm1
vinserti128    $0x1, %xmm1, %ymm0, %ymm0
vmovdqa    %ymm0, 8(%rsp)
vmovdqa    -24(%rsp), %ymm0
vmovdqa    %ymm0, 72(%rsp)
vmovdqa    8(%rsp), %ymm0
vmovdqa    %ymm0, 104(%rsp)
vmovdqa    72(%rsp), %ymm1
vmovdqa    104(%rsp), %ymm0
vpaddd    %ymm0, %ymm1, %ymm0
...
```

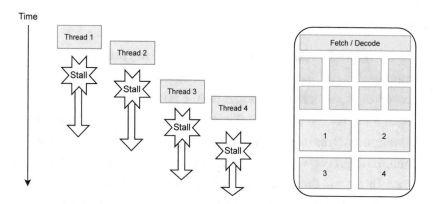

Figure 2-4. *Switching context based on hardware threads to hide latency*

It can be seen that instead of normal instructions such as add, AVX2 uses vpaddd to add two packed doubleword integers and also utilizes special registers such as ymm0, etc. In general, using SIMD can significantly improve the performance of computations.

Context Switching

As we have explained, the execution context in a processor contains necessary state information when executing instructions. But that does not mean one processor can only have one execution context. For example, the Intel Core i9-9900K contains two execution contexts, or "hardware threads." That provides the possibility of concurrent processing. Specifically, a core can apply *context switching* to store execution state in one context while running instructions on the other if possible.

Note that unlike previous methods we have introduced, context switching does not enable parallel processing at exactly the same cycle; a core still has one ALU unit to process instructions. Instead, at each clock a core can choose to run an instruction on an available context. This is especially useful to deal with instruction streams that contain high-latency operations such as memory read or write. As shown in Figure 2-4, while one instruction is executing, perhaps waiting for a long while to read some data from memory, the core can switch to the other contexts and run another set of instructions. In this way, the execution latency is hidden and increases overall throughput.

Multicore Processor

What we have introduced so far focuses on one single core. But another idea about improving computation performance is more straightforward to a wider audience: multicore processor. It means integrating multiple processing units, or cores, on one single processor and enables the possibility of parallel processing at the same time. The processor development trend is to add more and more cores in a processor. For example, Apple M1 contains eight cores, with four high-performance cores and four high-efficiency cores. Intel Core i9-12900HX processor contains 16 cores.

Similar to previous mechanisms, just because a processor provides the possibility of parallel processing does not mean a piece of code can magically perform better by itself. The challenge is how to utilize the power of multiple cores properly from the OS and applications' perspective. There are various approaches for programmers to take advantage of the capabilities provided by multicore processors. For example, on Unix systems the IEEE *POSIX* 1003.1c standard specifies a standard programming interface, and its implementations on various hardware are called POSIX threads, or Pthreads. It manages threads, such as their creation and joining, and provides synchronization primitives such as mutex, condition variable, lock, barrier, etc. The OCaml language is also adding native support for multicore, including parallelism via the shared memory parallel approach and concurrency. It will be officially supported in the OCaml 5.0 release.

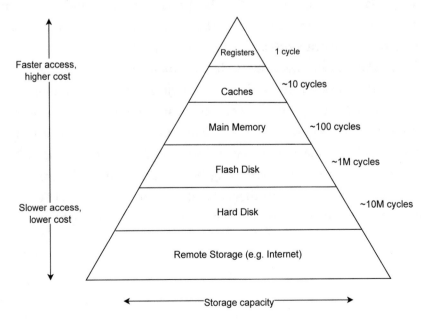

Figure 2-5. *Memory hierarchy*

Memory

Besides the processor architecture, another core component, memory, also plays a pivotal role in the performance of programs. In the rest of this section, we introduce several general principles to better utilize memory properties. For more detailed knowledge about this topic, we highly recommend the article by U. Drepper [18].

Ideally, a processing unit only needs to access one whole memory, as the Von Neumann architecture indicates. However, such a universal memory would struggle to meet various real-world requirements: permanent storage, fast access speed, cheap, etc. Modern memory design thus has adopted the "memory hierarchy" approach which divides memory into several layers, each layer being a different type of memory, as shown in Figure 2-5. Broadly speaking, it consists of two categories: (1) internal memory that is directly accessible by the processor, including CPU registers, cache, and main memory; (2) external memory that is accessible to the processor through the I/O module, including flash disk, traditional disk, etc. As the layer goes down, the storage capacity increases, but the access speed and cost also decrease significantly.

The register is the closest to a computer's processor. For example, an Intel Xeon Phi processor contains 16 general-purpose registers and 32 floating-point registers, each of 64-bit size. It also contains 32 registers for AVX instructions; the size of each is 256 or 512 bits. The access speed to registers is the fastest in the memory hierarchy, only taking one processor cycle. The next level is caches of various levels. In Figure 2-1, we have seen how a processor core connects directly to the various levels of caches. On an Intel Core i9-9900K, the cache size is 64KB (L1, each core), 256KB (L2, each core), and 16MB (shared), respectively. Its access speed is about ten cycles, with L1 being the fastest.

Cache

Due to the fast access time of cache compared to memory, utilizing cache is key to improving performance of computing. Imagine that if only all a program's data accesses are directly from cache, its performance will reach orders of magnitude faster. Short of reaching that ideal scenario, one principle is to utilize cache as much as possible. Specifically, we need to exploit the *locality* of data access in programs, which means that a program tends to reuse data that is "close" to what it has already used. The meaning of "close" is twofold: first, recently used data is quite likely to be used again in the near future, called *temporal locality*; second, data with nearby addresses are also likely to be used recently. Later, we will discuss techniques based on these principles.

As a sidenote, due to the importance of caches, it is necessary to know the cache size on your computer. You can surely go through its manual or specification documentation or use commands such as lscpu. In the Owl codebase, we have employed the same approach as used in Eigen,[4] which is to use the cpuid instruction provided on x86 architectures. It can be used to retrieve CPU information such as the processor type and if features such as AVX are included. Overall, the routine query_cache_size first checks whether the current CPU vendor is x86 or x64 architecture. If not, it means cpuid might not be supported, and it only returns a conservative guess. Otherwise, it retrieves information depending on if the vendor is AMD or Intel. Here, the macros OWL_ARCH_x86_64 and OWL_ARCH_i386 are implemented by checking if predefined system macros such as __x86_64__, _M_X64, __amd64, __i386, etc. are defined in the compiler. The CPUID macro is implemented using assembly code utilizing the cpuid instruction.

```
void query_cache_sizes(int* 11p, int* 12p, int* 13p) {
  if (OWL_ARCH_i386 || OWL_ARCH_x86_64) {
    int cpuinfo[4];
    CPUID(cpuinfo, 0x0, 0);

    if (cpu_is_amd(cpuinfo)) {
      query_cache_sizes_amd(11p, 12p, 13p);
      return;
    }
    int highest_func = cpuinfo[1];
    if (highest_func >= 4)
      query_cache_sizes_intel(11p, 12p, 13p);
    else {
      *11p = 32 * 1024;
      *12p = 256 * 1024;
      *13p = 2048 * 1024;
    }
  } else {
    *11p = 16 * 1024;
    *12p = 512 * 1024;
    *13p = 512 * 1024;
```

---

[4] Eigen: A C++ template library for linear algebra. The Eigen project. https://eigen.tuxfamily.org/

```
  }
}

OWL_INLINE void query_cache_sizes_intel(int* 11p, int* 12p, int* 13p) {
  int cpuinfo[4];
  int 11 = 0, 12 = 0, 13 = 0;
  int cache_id = 0;
  int cache_type = 0;
  do {
    cpuinfo[0] = cpuinfo[1] = cpuinfo[2] = cpuinfo[3] = 0;
    CPUID(cpuinfo, 0x4, cache_id);
    cache_type = (cpuinfo[0] & 0x0F) >> 0;

    if(cache_type == 1 || cache_type == 3) {
      int cache_level = (cpuinfo[0] & 0xE0) >> 5;
      int ways        = (cpuinfo[1] & 0xFFC00000) >> 22;
      int partitions  = (cpuinfo[1] & 0x003FF000) >> 12;
      int line_size   = (cpuinfo[1] & 0x00000FFF) >>  0;
      int sets        = (cpuinfo[2]);

      int cache_size = (ways + 1) * (partitions + 1)
        * (line_size + 1) * (sets + 1);
      switch(cache_level) {
        case 1: 11 = cache_size; break;
        case 2: 12 = cache_size; break;
        case 3: 13 = cache_size; break;
        default: break;
      }
    }
    cache_id++;
  } while(cache_type > 0 && cache_id < 16);

  if (11 == 0) 11 = 32 * 1024;
  if (12 == 0) 12 = 256 * 1024;
  if (13 == 0) 13 = 2048 * 1024;

  *11p = 11; *12p = 12; *13p = 13;
  return;
}
```

Prefetching

To mitigate the long loading time of memory, *prefetching* is another popular approach. As the name suggests, the processor fetches data into cache before it is demanded, so that when it is actually used, the data can be accessed directly from the cache. Prefetching can be triggered in two ways: via certain hardware events or explicit request from the software.

Naturally, prefetching faces challenges from two aspects. The first is to know what content should be prefetched from memory. A cache is so precious that we don't want to preload useless content, which leads to a waste of time and resources. Secondly, it is equally important to know when to fetch. For example, fetching content too early risks getting it removed from the cache before even being used.

For hardware prefetching, the processor monitors memory accesses and makes predictions about what to fetch based on certain patterns, such as a series of cache misses. The predicted memory addresses are placed in a queue, and the prefetch would look just like a normal READ request to the memory. Modern processors often have different prefetching strategies. One common strategy is to fetch the next N lines of data. Similarly, it can follow a stride pattern: if currently the program uses data at address x, then prefetch that at x+k, x+2k, x+3k, etc.

Compared with the hardware approach, software prefetching allows control from programmers. For example, a GCC intrinsics is for this purpose:

```
void __builtin_prefetch (const void *addr, ...)
```

It contains three arguments. The first is the data address to be prefetched; the second is a compile-time integer that indicates if the prefetch is preparing for a read from or write to memory; and the final one indicates the temporal locality of fetched data to decide if it should be evicted from cache once accessed.

The programmer can insert `__builtin_prefetch` into code if the corresponding data is anticipated to be accessed soon. This intrinsic will be compiled into data prefetch instructions via the compiler. If the prefetch is executed at a proper moment before the access, ideally the required data will be already in the cache by the time it is used. The following code is a simple example to demonstrate how it works in a C code:

```
for (i=0; i < n; ++i)
  for (j=0; j < m; ++j) {
    __builtin_prefetch(&x[i+1][j]);
    c += x[i][j]
  }
```

There are also other approaches for software control on prefetching, such as the `_mm_prefetch (char const* p, int i)` intrinsics from the SSE instruction set on Intel. It prefetches a line of data from memory that contains address p to a location in the cache hierarchy; argument i indicates the level of locality of cached data.

However, it is still tricky to do it right; sometimes, improper prefetching can even make the execution slower. For one thing, it is normally difficult for us to know exactly how far ahead the data should be fetched, especially in applications that access memory irregularly. Frequent early prefetch actually reduces cache hit accuracy. Besides, the locality pattern of different chunks of data is also complex to manage for programmers. That's why this approach should be used with caution.

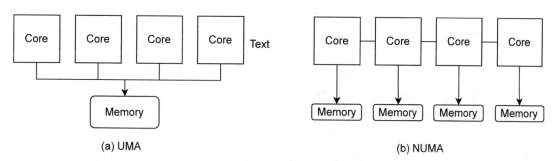

Figure 2-6. *Changing from uniform memory access to non-uniform memory access*

NUMA

Finally, we briefly talk about non-uniform memory access (NUMA), since it demonstrates the hardware aspect of improving memory access efficiency. We have mentioned the multicore design of processors. While improving parallelism in processors, it has also brought challenges to memory performance. When an application is processed on multiple cores, only one of them can access the computer's memory at a time, since they access a single entity of memory uniformly. In a memory-intensive application, this leads to a contention for the shared memory and a bottleneck. One approach to mitigate this problem is the non-uniform memory access (NUMA) design.

Compared with the uniform access model we have introduced, NUMA separates memory for each processor, and thus each processor can access its own share of memory at a fairly low cost, as shown in Figure 2-6. However, the performance of NUMA depends on the task being executed. If one processor needs to frequently access memory of the other processors, that would lead to undesirable performance.

2.4 Optimization Techniques

The topic of computation optimization is a classic topic in computer science, and there is still a lot of work about it in both academia and industry. Explaining even only a part of them in detail requires a whole book. Instead, in this section we give some optimization technique examples to demonstrate how the principles in the previous sections are implemented.

Hardware Parallelization

Utilizing multicore is a straightforward way to improve computation performance, especially complex computation on arrays with a huge amount of elements. Except for the Pthread we have introduced, Open Multi-Processing (OpenMP) is another tool that is widely used. OpenMP is a library that provides APIs to support shared memory multiprocessing programming in C/FORTRAN languages on many platforms. An OpenMP program uses multiple threads in its parallel section, and it also sets up the environment in the sequential execution section at the beginning. The parallel section is marked by the OpenMP directive omp pragma. Each thread executes the parallel section and then joins together after finishing. Here is an example:

```
#include <omp.h>

int main(int argc, char **argv) {
    int x[200000];

    #pragma omp parallel for
    for (int i = 0; i < 100000; i++) {
        x[i] = sinf(i);
    }
    return 0;
}
```

Here, in a big array of 200000 elements, for each element we compute the `sin` function on its index number. To apply multicore computing, we simply add one line of derivative on the for-loop. Without specifying the number of threads, it divides the whole workload, the array, onto all available cores.

In Owl, we have also applied OpenMP to improve computation performance. For example, we have introduced the template to map a single function on all elements in an array. We can now change part of the template as follows. Here, `caml_release_runtime_system` releases the master lock in a calling thread, enabling other threads to run code in parallel with the execution of the current thread:

```
...
caml_release_runtime_system();
start_x = X_data;
stop_x = start_x + N;
start_y = Y_data;

#pragma omp parallel for schedule(static)
for (int i = 0; i < N; i++) {
  NUMBER x = *(start_x + i);
  *(start_y + i) = (MAPFN(x));
}
caml_acquire_runtime_system();
...
```

We can also benefit from SIMD. For example, instead of interfacing to standard C math library functions, we can implement our own SIMD version of math functions. It is unfortunately not as simple as adding one line of derivative, since the SIMD intrinsics do not include complex computations. Even for one sine function, for example, we need to carefully implement the Taylor expansion–based algorithm using various existing intrinsics. Not to mention that we need to always think about different versions of SIMD: SSE, AVX2, AVX512, etc., or different hardware vendors. In summary, the performance boost using SIMD requires a significant amount of engineering work.

Cache Optimization

There are numerous cache optimization techniques, but most of them share the same theme: improve data locality (both spatial and temporal) and align the code and data.

If you put something into cache, you'd better make it count: reusing cached data as much as possible. Next, we will use matrix multiplication as an example. Matrix multiplication is one of the center pieces in scientific computing. Its basic algorithm is simple:

```
for (i = 0; i < N; ++i)
  for (j = 0; j < N; ++j)
    for (k = 0; k < N; ++k)
      r[i][j] += mul1[i][k] * mul2[k][j];
```

The way the data is read is from left to right: $(0, 0)$, $(0,1)$, ... $(0, n)$, $(1, 0)$, $(1, 1)$, ... $(1, n)$, ... While the element $(0, 0)$ is loaded, the next several elements are also saved in the cache so that $(0, 1)$, $(0, 2)$, etc. are all loaded from cache instead of memory. However, the elements in mul2 are not accessed this way. After $(0, 1)$, the elements $(1, 0)$, $(2, 0)$, ... are required. That means the cached elements are all wasted. One approach to deal with this problem is to transpose mul2 before multiplication:

```
double tmp[N][N];

for (i = 0; i < N; ++i)
  for (j = 0; j < N; ++j)
    tmp[i][j] = mul2[j][i];

for (i = 0; i < N; ++i)
  for (j = 0; j < N; ++j)
    for (k = 0; k < N; ++k)
      r[i][j] += mul1[i][k] * tmp[j][k];
```

Another approach even utilizes L1 cache better. First, it "cuts" a large matrix into multiple smaller square ones. Each line of such a square matrix can be fit into an L1 cache. These multiple smaller matrix multiplications are iterated in an outer loop. This technique is sometimes called *tiling*. The algorithm can be demonstrated using Figure 2-7. In a smaller matrix multiplication $ab = c$, a row of a is stored in L1 cache (Step ①). The column number moves in matrix b to compute the corresponding output in c (Step ②). Only after this step the cached line will be evicted and a new row in a will be retrieved into the cache (Step ③). The previous rows in a will not be used again. The algorithm is implemented as follows. Here, E is the number of elements in a row of the small matrix:

```
for (i = 0; i < N; i += E)
  for (j = 0; j < N; j += E)
    for (k = 0; k < N; k += E)
      for (ii = 0, rr = &r[i][j],
          am = &mul1[i][k]; ii < E;
          ++ii, rr += N, am += N)
        for (kk = 0, bm = &mul2[k][j];
            kk < E; ++kk, bm += N)
          for (jj = 0; jj < E; ++jj)
            rr[jj] += am[kk] * bm[jj];
```

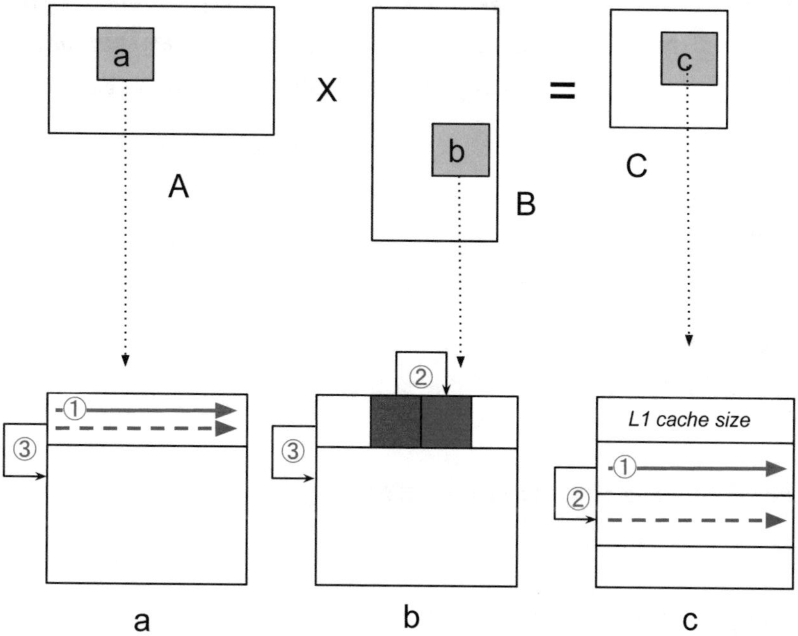

Figure 2-7. *Illustration of a matrix multiplication algorithm that utilizes L1 cache*

Another technique that utilizes cache is **loop merging**. We can merge consecutive loops that sweep through data into one loop to reuse data in the cache, reducing memory access. The following code shows a simple example:

```
for (i = 0; i < N; i++) {
    x[i] = buf[i]
}
```

29

```
for (i = 0; i < N; i++) {
    y[i] = i * x[i] + bias
}
```

Obviously, these two loops can be fused into one single loop:

```
for (i = 0; i < N; i++) {
    x[i] = buf[i]
    y[i] = i * x[i] + bias
}
```

By fusing two loops into one, the access order of the x elements changed, increasing temporal locality. It can further be accelerated using techniques such as parallel computing techniques we have mentioned. For some of the cases that loop merging cannot be directly applied, the *loop alignment* technique may help. For example, the two for-loops

```
for (i=0; i<n; i++) {
    x[i] = y[i] + a
}

for (i=0; i<n; i++) {
    z[i] = x[i+1] + b
}
```

can be fused after aligning the x and z arrays:

```
x[0] = y[0] + a

for (i=1; i<n; i++) {
    x[i] = y[i] + a
    z[i-1] = x[i] + b
}

z[n-1] = x[n] + b
```

Other Techniques

Besides processor parallelism and cache utilization, there are still many techniques to improve code performance. We will only briefly introduce some of them in this part.

Compilers surely have a great impact on the code performance. For example, compilers such as LLVM or GCC can be configured with plenty of options and flags. Choosing the most suitable options can actually be a challenging task. Besides, programmers can add inline assembly code to C to further increase the execution speed. Another optimization technique, *unrolling*, is also partly about understanding how compilers work. For example, we can unroll the for-loop into eight parts:

```
for(i=0;i<n;i++) {
    a[i] = b[i] + 1
}
for(i=0; i<n; i+=8) {
    a[i] = b[i] + 1
    a[i] = b[i+1] + 1
    a[i] = b[i+2] + 1
    a[i] = b[i+3] + 1
    a[i] = b[i+4] + 1
    a[i] = b[i+5] + 1
    a[i] = b[i+6] + 1
    a[i] = b[i+7] + 1
}
```

It allows the compiler to decrease the number of conditional branches, thus reducing potential branch mispredictions and condition evaluations.

Despite what we have explained, note that cache is not always helping. Sometimes, the data is put into cache, but won't be used again in a short while. That means the cache is just wasting time on writing without being read. In that case, it is necessary to bypass the caching phase. Processors support nontemporal write directly to memory. SIMD also provides intrinsics to do that, such as the following intrinsics.

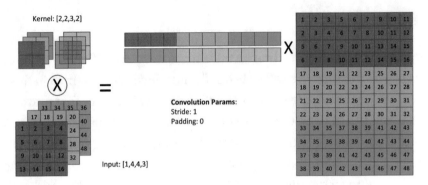

Figure 2-8. *Convolution algorithm illustration*

```
#include <ammintrin.h>
void _mm_stream_sd(double *p, __m128d a);
void _mm_stream_ss(float *p, __m128 a);
```

2.5 Example: Convolution

Convolution is a family of mathematical operations that is arguably the most important operation in deep neural networks. It makes up the backbone of a majority of deep neural network architectures and takes up a large part of computation resources involved in their training and inference. According to the shape of input, convolution operations can be categorized into one dimensional, two dimensional, and three dimensional. It can also be categorized according to usage in the forward or backward propagation phase as normal convolution, backward convolution on kernel, and backward convolution on input. There are special operations such as transpose convolution, dilated convolution, etc. But their implementation principles are quite similar. There is a lot of work on optimizing convolution operations due to their importance [55]. It takes significant engineering effort to implement only part of them. In this section, we use the two-dimensional convolution operation Conv2D as an example to demonstrate how we apply various optimization techniques on convolution operations in Owl.

A convolution operation takes two ndarrays as input: image (I) and kernel (F). In a two-dimensional convolution, both ndarrays are of four dimensions. The image ndarray has B batches; each image has size $H \times W$ and has IC channels. The kernel ndarray has R rows, C columns, the same input channel IC, and output channel K. The convolution can then be expressed as in Eq. 2.1.

$$CONV_{b,h,w,k} = \sum_{ic=1}^{IC}\sum_{r=1}^{R}\sum_{c=1}^{C} I_{b,h+r,w+c,ic} F_{r,c,ic,k}. \tag{2.1}$$

The convolution operation is first implemented in Owl by interfacing to the Eigen library, which is also used in TensorFlow for convolution implementation on the CPU. However, interfacing to this C++ library proves to be problematic and leads to a lot of installation issues. That is why we turn to handcrafting convolution operations. They consist of three types: Conv, ConvBackwardKernel, and ConvBackwardInput. The Conv operation calculates the output given the input image and kernel. Similarly, ConvBackwardKernel calculates the kernel given the input and output ndarrays, and ConvBackwardInput gets input ndarray from the kernel and output. The last two are mainly used in the backpropagation phase in training a DNN, but all three operations share a similar calculation algorithm.

A naive convolution algorithm is to implement Eq. 2.1 with nested for-loops. It is easy to see that this approach does not benefit from any parallelization and thus is not suitable for production code.

The next version of implementation uses the im2col algorithm. This algorithm is illustrated in Figure 2-8. In this example, we start with an input image of shape 4x4 and three output channels. Each channel is denoted by a different color. Besides, the index of each element is also shown in the figure. The kernel is of shape 2x2 and has three input channels as the input image. Each channel has the same color as the corresponding channel of the input image. The two output channels are differentiated by various levels of transparency in the figure. According to the definition of convolution operation, we use the kernel to slide over the input image step by step, and at each position, an element-wise multiplication is applied. Here, in this example, we use a stride of 1 and a valid padding. In the first step, the kernel starts with the position where the element indices are [1,2,5,6] in the first input channel, [17,18,21,22] in the second input channel, and [33,34,37,38] in the third input channel. The element-wise multiplication result is filled into the corresponding position in the output ndarray. Moving on to the second position, the input indices become [2,3,6,7,18,19,22,23,34,35,38,39], so on and so forth. It turns out that this process can be simplified as one matrix multiplication. The first matrix is just the flattened kernel. The second matrix is based on the input ndarray. Each column is a flattened subblock of the same size as one channel of the kernel. This approach is the basic idea of the im2col algorithm. Since the matrix multiplication is a highly optimized operation in linear algebra packages such as OpenBLAS, this algorithm can be executed efficiently. Here, we show its implementation code:

```
CAMLprim value FUN_NATIVE (spatial) (
  value vInput_ptr, value vKernel_ptr, value vOutput_ptr,
  value vBatches, value vInput_cols, value vInput_rows, value vIn_channel,
  value vKernel_cols, value vKernel_rows,
  value vOutput_cols, value vOutput_rows, value vOut_channel,
  value vRow_stride,  value vCol_stride,
  value vPadding, value vRow_in_stride, value vCol_in_stride
) {
  struct caml_ba_array *IN = Caml_ba_array_val(vInput_ptr);
  struct caml_ba_array *KE = Caml_ba_array_val(vKernel_ptr);
  struct caml_ba_array *OU = Caml_ba_array_val(vOutput_ptr);
  TYPE *input_ptr  = (TYPE *) IN->data;
  TYPE *kernel_ptr = (TYPE *) KE->data;
  TYPE *output_ptr = (TYPE *) OU->data;

  int batches       = Long_val(vBatches);
  int input_cols    = Long_val(vInput_cols);
  int input_rows    = Long_val(vInput_rows);
  int in_channel    = Long_val(vIn_channel);
  int kernel_cols   = Long_val(vKernel_cols);
  int kernel_rows   = Long_val(vKernel_rows);
  int output_cols   = Long_val(vOutput_cols);
  int output_rows   = Long_val(vOutput_rows);
  int out_channel   = Long_val(vOut_channel);
  int row_stride    = Long_val(vRow_stride);
  int col_stride    = Long_val(vCol_stride);
  int padding       = Long_val(vPadding);
  int row_in_stride = Long_val(vRow_in_stride);
  int col_in_stride = Long_val(vCol_in_stride);

  const int input_cri  = in_channel  * input_rows  * input_cols;
  const int input_ri   = in_channel  * input_rows;
  const int output_cri = out_channel * output_rows * output_cols;
  const int output_cr  = output_rows * output_cols;
  const int output_crb = output_rows * output_cols * batches;
  const int kernel_cri = kernel_cols * kernel_rows * in_channel;
```

```
const int kernel_cr  = kernel_cols * kernel_rows;
const int kernel_ri  = kernel_rows * in_channel;

memset(output_ptr, 0, batches * output_cri * sizeof(TYPE));
INIT;

int pr = 0, pc = 0;
if (padding != 1) {
  pr = (row_stride * ( output_rows - 1) + kernel_rows - input_rows) / 2;
  pc = (col_stride * ( output_cols - 1) + kernel_cols - input_cols) / 2;
  if (pr < 0) pr = 0;
  if (pc < 0) pc = 0;
}

TYPE *inpt2d = (TYPE *) calloc(mat_size, sizeof(TYPE));
if (inpt2d == NULL) exit(1);

...
```

The code starts by locating the starting pointers of inputs (input and kernel) and the various metadata about inputs: input channel, row/column numbers, output channel, stride, padding size, etc. Besides, it also assigns memory space for outputs and intermediate buffers. The code next implements what we have introduced. Using three for-loops, we fill in the intermediate input buffer inpt2d, which is one matrix, and multiply it with the kernel matrix using the GEMM routine provided by OpenBLAS.

```
...

for (int i = 0; i < output_crb; ++i) {
  int bt = i / output_cr;
  int cr = i % output_cr;
  int c = cr / output_rows;
  int r = cr % output_rows;

  const int cstart = c * col_stride - pc;
  const int rstart = r * row_stride - pr;
  const int cend = cstart + kernel_cols;
  const int rend = rstart + kernel_rows;
  const int input_idx_base = bt * input_cri;
```

```
    int cnt = 0;
    for (int a = cstart; a < cend; ++a) {
      for (int b = rstart; b < rend; ++b) {
        for (int h = 0; h < in_channel; ++h) {
          if (a < input_cols && a >= 0 &&
              b < input_rows && b >= 0) {
            int input_idx =
                input_idx_base + a * input_ri + b * in_channel + h;
            inpt2d[i * kernel_cri + cnt] = input_ptr[input_idx];
          }
          ++cnt;
        }
      }
    }
  }

  GEMM(CblasRowMajor, CblasNoTrans, CblasNoTrans,
    output_crb, out_channel, kernel_cri, ALPHA,
    inpt2d, kernel_cri, kernel_ptr, out_channel,
    BETA, output_ptr, out_channel);

  free(inpt2d);

  return Val_unit;

}
```

However, this algorithm requires generating a large temporary intermediate matrix. Depending on the input image size, this matrix can take gigabytes of memory in applications such as FST. If you look closely at the intermediate matrix, you will find that it contains a lot of redundant information. Algorithms such as memory-efficient convolution [11] aim to reduce the size of this intermediate matrix, but still fail with large input or kernel sizes.

To reduce the memory usage, we apply the method proposed in [25], which is to cut matrices into small blocks so as to fit into the L1/L2 cache of the CPU to do high-performance computation while reducing the memory usage, regardless of the input size. The multiplication of two matrices can be divided into a multiplication of small blocks. It still generally follows the previous matrix multiplication approach, but instead of generating the whole intermediate matrix, it cuts the input and kernel matrices into small blocks one at a time so that the memory usage is limited no matter how large the input and kernel are. Next, we show the code:

```
int mat_size = kernel_cri * output_crb;
if (mat_size / kernel_cri == output_crb && mat_size < IM2COL_THRESHOLD) {
  // if generated input matrix is small enough, use im2col implementation
}

int mc = output_crb;
int kc = kernel_cri;
int nc = out_channel;
compute_block_sizes(&kc, &nc, &mc, sizeof(TYPE));
```

Suitable implementations can be chosen depending on the input size. Here, we use the intermediate matrix size to decide if we need the memory-efficient implementation or not. If it is sufficiently small, we use the previous im2col implementation. It is still straightforward and fast with small input sizes. Otherwise, we compute the suitable small block sizes as in [25].

```
#if defined(AVX_PSIZE) && defined(_WIN32)
  int fast_flag = (in_channel % AVX_PSIZE == 0);
  TYPE *temp_mk = _aligned_malloc(mc * kc * sizeof(TYPE), ALIGN_SIZE);
  if (temp_mk == NULL) exit(1);
#elif defined(AVX_PSIZE)
  int fast_flag = (in_channel % AVX_PSIZE == 0);
  TYPE *temp_mk = NULL;
  if (posix_memalign((void**) &temp_mk, ALIGN_SIZE, mc * kc *
  sizeof(TYPE)))
    exit(1);
#else
  TYPE *temp_mk = (TYPE *) calloc(mc * kc, sizeof(TYPE));
  if (temp_mk == NULL) exit(1);
#endif
TYPE *temp_kn = (TYPE *) calloc(nc * kc, sizeof(TYPE));
if (temp_kn == NULL) exit(1);
TYPE *temp_mn = (TYPE *) calloc(mc * nc, sizeof(TYPE));
if (temp_mn == NULL) exit(1);
```

To further improve the performance, we use the SIMD intrinsics in filling the temporary matrix from input ndarray. For one thing, depending on whether the input channel is divisible by the supported data length AVX_PSIZE of SIMD (e.g., 8 float numbers for AVX), we provide two sets of implementations for filling the temporary blocks. We then assign space for the small blocks that can be fit into cache accordingly.

```
...
for (int m = 0; m < output_crb; m += mc) {
  int actual_mc = fminf(m + mc, output_crb) - m;
  for (int k = 0; k < kernel_cri; k += kc) {
    memset(temp_mk, 0, mc * kc * sizeof(TYPE));
    int actual_kc = fminf(k + kc, kernel_cri) - k;
    #ifdef AVX_PSIZE
    int kc_strip = (actual_kc / AVX_PSIZE) * AVX_PSIZE;
    #endif

    // iterate along each row of the generated input matrix.
    ...

    int idx_kn_base = k * out_channel;
    for (int n = 0; n < out_channel; n += nc) {
      int actual_nc = fminf(n + nc, out_channel) - n;
      idx_kn_base += n;

      // fill in the kernel matrix
      int cnk = 0;
      for (int ik = 0; ik < actual_kc; ik++) {
        for (int jn = 0; jn < actual_nc; jn++) {
          int index_kn = idx_kn_base + ik * out_channel + jn;
          temp_kn[cnk++] = kernel_ptr[index_kn];
        }
      }

      GEMM(CblasRowMajor, CblasNoTrans, CblasNoTrans,
        actual_mc, actual_nc, actual_kc, ALPHA,
        temp_mk, actual_kc, temp_kn, actual_nc,
        BETA, temp_mn, actual_nc);
```

```
        int cmn = 0;
        for (int ix = 0; ix < actual_mc; ix++) {
          for (int iy = 0; iy < actual_nc; iy++) {
            int index_mn = (ix + m) * out_channel + (iy + n);
            output_ptr[index_mn] += temp_mn[cmn++];
          }
        }
      }
    }
  }
  free(temp_mk);
  free(temp_kn);
  free(temp_mn);

  return Val_unit;
}
```

The code next follows a similar pattern as the previous method, filling in the input and kernel matrices and multiplying them to get the output, only that both need more detailed control to get smaller matrices to fit into cache. Specifically, here is the code to get the input matrix:

```
  int cmk = 0;
  for (int im = 0; im < actual_mc; im += 1) {
    int b  = (m + im) / output_cr;
    int cr = (m + im) - b * output_cr;
    int c = cr / output_rows;
    int r = cr - c * output_rows;

    const int cstart = c * col_stride - pc;
    const int rstart = r * row_stride - pr;
    const int idx_base = b * input_cri;

    // fill in the sub input matrix
#ifdef AVX_PSIZE
    if (fast_flag) {
      ACX_FUN_LOAD (load_sub_matrix_fast, spatial) (
        input_ptr, temp_mk, &cmk, kc_strip, k, kernel_ri, input_ri,
```

```
        in_channel, idx_base, cstart, rstart, input_cols, input_rows, 0);
    }
    else {
      ACX_FUN_LOAD (load_sub_matrix, spatial) (
        input_ptr, temp_mk, &cmk, kc_strip, actual_kc,
        k, kernel_ri, input_ri, in_channel, idx_base,
        cstart, rstart, input_cols, input_rows, kernel_rows, 0);
    }
#else
    for (int ik = 0; ik < actual_kc; ik += 1) {
      int kc  = (k + ik) / kernel_ri;
      int kri = (k + ik) - kc * kernel_ri;
      int kr  = kri / in_channel;
      int ki  = kri - kr * in_channel;

      int input_col = kc + cstart;
      int input_row = kr + rstart;
      if (input_col < input_cols && input_col >= 0 &&
        input_row < input_rows && input_row >= 0) {
        int input_index = idx_base + input_col * input_ri
          + input_row * in_channel + ki;
        temp_mk[cmk] = input_ptr[input_index];
      }
      cmk++;
    }
#endif
}
```

To maximize the performance of caching, we need to make the memory access as consecutive as possible. Depending on whether the input channel is divisible by the supported data length of SIMD (e.g., 8 float numbers for AVX), we provide two sets of implementations for filling the temporary blocks. If the input channel is divisible by data length, the input matrix can always be loaded consecutively at a step of data length with the AVX intrinsics; otherwise, I have to build the temporary matrix blocks with less AVX intrinsics, on only part of the matrix, and then take care of the edge cases. During loading data from input ndarrays to these matrix blocks, we also use AVX intrinsics such as _mm256_load_ps to improve performance.

```
#define FUN_NATIVE(dim) stub_float32_ndarray_conv ## _ ## dim  ## _ ## native
#define FUN_BYTE(dim) stub_float32_ndarray_conv ## _ ## dim  ## _ ## bytecode
#define TYPE float
#define INIT
#define ALPHA 1.
#define BETA 0.
#define GEMM cblas_sgemm
#ifdef OWL_AVX
  #define AVX_PSIZE 8
  #define AVX_TYPE  __m256
  #define ACX_FUN_LOAD(prefix, dim) prefix ## _ ## float32 ## _ ## dim
  #define AVX_STOREA _mm256_store_ps
  #define AVX_STOREU _mm256_storeu_ps
  #define AVX_LOADA  _mm256_load_ps
  #define AVX_LOADU  _mm256_loadu_ps
  #define AVX_ADD     _mm256_add_ps
#endif
#include "owl_ndarray_conv_impl.h"
#undef GEMM
#undef BETA
#undef ALPHA
#undef INIT
#undef TYPE
#undef FUN_BYTE
#undef FUN_NATIVE
#ifdef OWL_AVX
  #undef AVX_PSIZE
  #undef AVX_TYPE
  #undef ACX_FUN_LOAD
  #undef AVX_STOREA
  #undef AVX_STOREU
  #undef AVX_LOADA
  #undef AVX_LOADU
  #undef AVX_ADD
#endif
```

Finally, we reduce the implementation complexity by applying templates, abstracting elements such as function names, SIMD functions to be used, GEMM routines, etc. These implementations can then be easily extended to the three-dimensional and one-dimensional cases. Besides, the transpose convolutions and diluted convolutions are only variations of normal convolution, and the code only needs to be slightly changed. Above this C implementation level, mutable convolution operations are also provided, so as to further improve performance by utilizing existing memory space.

2.6 Automated Empirical Optimization of Software

We have introduced various optimization techniques so far, and together they comprise a very large optimization space. For example, we can apply both multicore and SIMD parallelism while utilizing certain cache techniques. We need to consider many different methods to apply, each with numerous possible parameters to tune. Sometimes, these techniques even conflict with each other, for example, each trying to take as much processor resource as possible. Worse still, with the heterogeneity of hardware devices, an "optimal" configuration on one machine may lead to degraded performance. It is thus of utmost importance for a numerical library to provide good performance on all devices it supports. For example, ATLAS and the recent Intel Math Kernel Library both provide optimized mathematical routines for science and engineering computations. They are widely used in many popular high-level platforms such as Matlab and TensorFlow. One of the reasons these libraries can provide good performance is that they have adopted the paradigm of *Automated Empirical Optimization of Software*, or AEOS. That is, a library chooses the best method and parameter to use on a given platform to do a required operation. One highly optimized routine may run much faster than a naively coded one. Optimized code is usually platform and hardware specific, so an optimized routine on one machine could perform badly on the other. Though Owl currently does not plan to improve the low-level libraries it depends on, as an initial endeavor to apply the AEOS paradigm in Owl, one ideal tuning point is the parameters of OpenMP used in Owl.

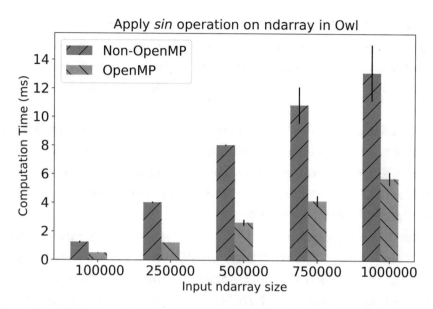

Figure 2-9. *Parallel execution of the sin operation on ndarray using OpenMP*

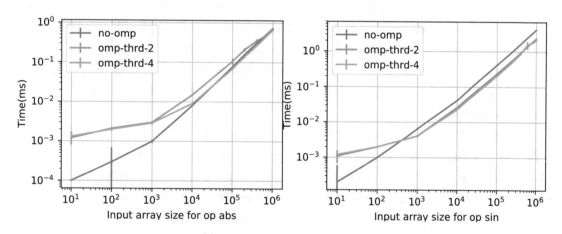

Figure 2-10. *Compare the behavior of abs and sine when using OpenMP*

Currently, many computers contain shared memory multiprocessors. OpenMP is used in key operations in libraries such as Eigen and MKL. Owl has also utilized OpenMP on many mathematical operations to boost their performance by threading calculation. For example, Figure 2-9 shows that when we apply the sine function on an ndarray in Owl, on a 4-core CPU MacBook, the OpenMP version only takes about a third of the execution time compared with the non-OpenMP version.

However, performance improvement does not come for free. The overhead of using OpenMP comes from time spent on scheduling chunks of work to each thread, managing locks on critical sections, startup time of creating threads, etc. Therefore, when the input ndarray is small enough, these overheads might overtake the benefit of threading.

What is a suitable input size to use OpenMP then? This question would be easy to solve if there is one single suitable input size threshold for every operation, but that is not the case. In a small experiment, we compare the performance of two operations, abs (absolute value) and sin, in three cases: running them without using OpenMP, with two-thread OpenMP, and with four-thread OpenMP.

The result in Figure 2-10 shows that, with growing input size, for the sine operation, the OpenMP version outperforms the non-OpenMP version at a size of less than 1000, but when using abs operation, that cross point is at about 1,000,000. The complexity of math operations varies greatly, and the difference is even starker when we compare their performance on different machines. Note that both axes use a log scale, and that is why a small deviation when the input array size is small looks large in the figure.

This issue becomes more complex when considered in real applications such as DNN, where users need to deal with operations of vastly different complexity and input sizes. Thus, one fixed threshold for several operations is not an ideal solution. Considering these factors, we need a fine-grained method to decide a suitable OpenMP threshold for each operation.

Toward this end, we implement the AEOS module in Owl. The idea is to add a tuning phase before compiling and installing Owl, so that each operation learns a suitable threshold parameter to decide if OpenMP should be used or not, depending on the input size. The key idea of parameter tuning is simple. We implement two versions of each operation, one using OpenMP and the other not. We then measure their execution time for various sizes of input. Each measurement is repeated multiple times, and, to reduce the effect of outliers, only the values that are within the first and the third quartiles are used. After removing outliers, regression is performed to find a suitable input size threshold. According to our initial experiment, linear regression is fit to estimate the OpenMP parameters here. Since this tuning phase is executed before compiling Owl, the AEOS module is independent of Owl, and all necessary implementation is coded separately to ensure that future changes of Owl do not affect the AEOS module itself.

The tuned parameters then need to be passed to Owl. When the OpenMP switch is turned on, the AEOS module generates a C header file which contains the definition of macros, each of which defines a threshold for one operation. When this header file is not generated, predefined default macro values are used instead. After that, Owl is compiled with this header file and uses these tuned parameters in its math operations. The tuning phase only needs to be performed once on each machine during installation.

The design of the AEOS module focuses on keeping tuning simple, effective, and flexible. Each operation is implemented as a single OCaml module, so that support for new operations can be easily added. The interface of such a module is shown as follows. We expect that tuning does not have to be only about OpenMP parameters and that different regression methods could be used in the future. For example, the Theil-Sen estimator can be plugged in for parameter estimation if necessary. In each module, arbitrary tuning procedures can be plugged in as long as the interface is satisfied.

```
module Sin = struct

(** Tuner type definition. *)
type t = {
    mutable name  : string;
    mutable param : string;
    mutable value : int;
    mutable input : int array array;
    mutable y     : float array
}

val make : unit -> t (** Create the tuner. *)
val tune : t -> unit (** Tuning process. *)
val save_data : t -> unit
(** Save tuned data to csv file for later analysis. *)
val to_string : t -> string
(** Convert the tuned parameter(s) to string to be written on file *)
end
```

The AEOS module is implemented in such a way that brings little interference to the main Owl library. Code can be viewed in this pull request and has been merged into the main branch of Owl. You only need to switch the ENABLE_OPENMP flag from 0 to 1 in the dune file to try this feature.

To evaluate the performance of tuned OpenMP thresholds, we need a metric to compare them. One metric to compare two thresholds is proposed as follows. I generate a series of ndarrays, whose sizes grow by certain steps until they reach a given maximum number, for example, 1,000,000, used in the following experiment. Note that only input sizes that fall between these two thresholds are chosen to be used. I then calculate the performance improvement ratio of the OpenMP version function over the non-OpenMP version on these chosen ndarrays. The ratios are added up and then amortized by the total number of ndarrays. Hereafter, I use this averaged ratio as a performance metric.

Table 2-1. *Tuned Parameters Using the AEOS Module*

Platform	tan	sqrt	sin	exp	sigmoid
Laptop	1632	max_int	1294	123	1880
Raspberry Pi	1189	209	41	0	0

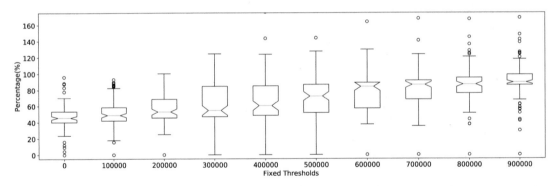

Figure 2-11. *Improvement of the square root operation after applying parameter tuning*

Table 2-1 presents the tuned threshold values of five operations on a MacBook with a 1.1GHz Intel Core m3 CPU and a Raspberry Pi 3B. We can see that they vary across different operations and different machines, depending on their computational complexity. For example, on MacBook, the tuning result is "max_int", which means that for the relatively simple square root calculation, OpenMP should not be used, but that is not the case on Raspberry Pi. Also, note that the less powerful Raspberry Pi tends to get lower thresholds.

We also compare the tuned thresholds with a series of regular thresholds. Specifically, for each operation, we choose ten different thresholds with a fixed interval: 0, 100000, 200000... 900000. For each generated threshold, we use 100 numbers between 0 and 1E6 as ndarray sizes. They are also generated with a fixed interval. The execution time on the ndarrays of given sizes for each threshold are then compared with that of the tuned threshold, and the element-wise ratios between these two arrays can be plotted as a bar plot for each threshold. For example, the comparison for the square root operation on the MacBook is shown in Figure 2-11. Here, each bar indicates the ratio between the tuned and the chosen threshold. One hundred percent means these two are of the same effect on performance, and lower percentage means the tuned threshold leads to faster execution time. This figure shows that regardless of the choice of fixed thresholds, the tuned parameter can always lead to similar or better execution time of operations in the AEOS module.

Note that we cannot claim that the tuned parameters are always optimal, since the figure shows that in some rare cases where the improvement percentages are negative, the randomly found values indeed perform better. Also, the result seems to suggest that AEOS can provide a certain bound, albeit a loose one, on the performance improvement, regardless of the type of operation.

2.7 Summary

In this chapter, we focused on the optimization of core ndarray operations in Owl. We started by introducing the Ndarray module in Owl and its pivotal role in a numerical library and then introduced how we interface the OCaml code to the C language. The rest of this chapter mostly focused on optimizations at the C level. As an important background, we explained the principles in optimizing scientific computing code, such as utilizing parallelism of processors and locality of caches. Next, we briefly introduced some techniques based on these principles. As an example, we demonstrated how we apply some of them to optimize one of the most important operations in deep neural networks: the convolution. Finally, we briefly introduced the automatic tuning approach to optimize library performance across various platforms, using multicore parallel computing on Owl as an example.

CHAPTER 3

Algorithmic Differentiation

Differentiation is key to numerous scientific applications including maximizing or minimizing functions, solving systems of ODEs, physical simulation, etc. Of existing methods, algorithmic differentiation, or AD, is a computer-friendly technique for performing differentiation that is both efficient and accurate. AD is a central component of the architecture design of Owl. In this chapter, we will show, with hands-on examples, how the AD engine is designed and implemented in Owl. AD will be used in some of the other chapters to show its application in optimization and machine learning.

3.1 Introduction

Assume an object moves a distance of Δs in a time Δt, the average velocity of this object during this period can be defined as the ratio between Δs and Δt. As both values get smaller and smaller, we can get the instantaneous velocity:

$$v = \lim_{\Delta t \to 0} \frac{\Delta s}{\Delta t} = \frac{ds}{dt} \tag{3.1}$$

The term $\frac{ds}{dt}$ is referred to as "the **derivative** of s with respect to t."

Differentiation is the process of finding a derivative in mathematics. It studies the functional relationship between variables, that is, how much one variable changes when the value of another variable changes. Differentiation has many important applications, for example, finding minimum and maximum values of a function, finding the rate of change of quantity, computing linear approximations to functions, and solving systems of differential equations. Its critical roles in these key mathematical fields mean it is widely used in various fields. One example is calculating marginal cost and revenue in economics.

© Liang Wang, Jianxin Zhao 2023
L. Wang and J. Zhao, *Architecture of Advanced Numerical Analysis Systems*,
https://doi.org/10.1007/978-1-4842-8853-5_3

In computer science, differentiation also plays a key role. Machine learning techniques, such as deep neural networks, have been gaining more and more momentum. The most important step in training a deep neural network module is called "backpropagation," which in essence is calculating the gradient of a very complicated function.

Three Ways of Differentiating

If we are to support differentiation at a scale as large as a deep neural network, manual calculation based on the chain rule in Calculus 101 is far from being enough. To do that, we need the power of automation, which is what a computer is good at. Currently, there are three ways to calculate differentiation: numerical differentiation, symbolic differentiation, and algorithmic differentiation.

The first method is **numerical differentiation**. Derived directly from the definition, numerical differentiation uses a small step δ to compute an approximate value toward the limit, as shown in Eq. 3.2.

$$f'(x) = \lim_{\delta \to 0} \frac{f(x+\delta) - f(x)}{\delta}. \qquad (3.2)$$

By treating the function f as a black box, this method is straightforward to implement as long as f can be evaluated. However, this method is unfortunately subject to multiple types of errors, such as the round-off error. It is caused by representing numbers with only a finite precision during the numerical computation. The round-off error can be so large as to that the computer thinks $f(x + \delta)$ and $f(x)$ are identical.

The second is **symbolic differentiation**. By manipulating the underlying mathematical expressions, symbolic differentiation obtains analytical results without numerical approximation, using mathematical derivative rules. For example, consider the function $f(x_0, x_1, x_2) = x_0 * x_1 * x_2$. Computing ∇f symbolically, we end up with

$$\nabla f = \left(\frac{\partial f}{\partial x_0}, \frac{\partial f}{\partial x_1}, \frac{\partial f}{\partial x_2} \right) = \left(x_1 * x_2, x_0 * x_2, x_1 * x_2 \right)$$

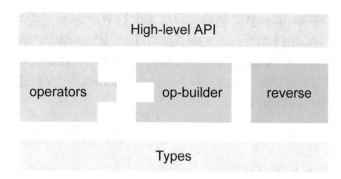

Figure 3-1. *Architecture of the AD module*

This process completely eliminates the impact of numerical errors, but the complexity of symbolic manipulation quickly grows as expressions become more complex. Just imagine computing the derivative of a simple calculation $f(x) = \prod_{i=0}^{n-1} x_i$: the result would be terribly long, if not that complex. As a result, symbolic differentiation can easily consume a huge amount of computing resource and becomes impractically slow in the end. Besides, unlike in numerical differentiation, we must know how a function is constructed to use symbolic differentiation.

Finally, there is the **algorithmic differentiation** (AD). It is a chain rule–based technique for calculating derivatives with respect to input variables of functions defined in a computer program. Algorithmic differentiation is also known as automatic differentiation, though strictly speaking it does not fully automate differentiation and can sometimes lead to inefficient code. In general, AD combines the best of both worlds: on one hand, it efficiently generates exact results and so is highly applicable in many real-world applications; on the other hand, it does not rely on listing all the intermediate results, and its computing process can be efficient. Therefore, it is the mainstream implementation of many numerical computing tools and libraries, such as JuliaDiff in Julia, ad in Python, ADMAT, etc. The rest of this chapter focuses mainly on algorithmic differentiation.

Architecture of Algodiff Module

The Algodiff module plays a pivotal role in the whole Owl library stack. It unifies various fundamental data types in Owl and is the most important functionality that serves the advanced analytics such as regression, neural networks, etc. Its design is elegant thanks to OCaml's powerful module system.

In this chapter, we assume you are familiar with how differentiation works mathematically, so we can focus on the design and implementation details of the AD module in Owl. But first, let's take a look at a simple example to see how the AD module is used in Owl. In this example, we simply calculate the first-order and second-order derivatives of the function tanh.

```
module AD = Algodiff.D
```

```
let f x = AD.Maths.(tanh x);;
let f1 = AD.diff f;;
let f2 = AD.diff f1;;
```

```
let eval_flt h x = AD.(pack_flt x |> h |> unpack_flt);;
let r1 = eval_flt f1 1.
let r2 = eval_flt f2 1.
```

That's all it takes. We define the function and apply diff on it to acquire its first-order derivative, on which the diff function can be directly applied to get the second-order derivative. We then evaluate and get the function value at point $x = 1$ on these two derivative functions.

Figure 3-1 shows the various components in the AD module. Let us inspect how they fit into the example code. First, we cannot directly use the basic data types, such as ndarray and float number. Instead, they need to be first "packed" into a type that the AD module understands. In this example, pack_flt is used to wrap a normal float number into an AD type float. After calculation finishes, assuming we still get an AD type float as output, it should be unpacked into a normal float number using the function unpack_flt. The **type system** is the most fundamental building block in AD. Second, to construct a computation in the AD system, we need to use **operators**, such as tahn used in this example. AD provides a rich set of operators that are generated from the op_builder module. After constructing a graph by stacking the operators, the AD engine starts to let the input data "flow," or "propagate," twice in this graph, once forward and once backward. The key function that is in charge of this process is the **reverse** function. Based on the aforementioned process, we can calculate the differentiation of various sorts. To simplify coding, a series of **high-level APIs** are constructed. The diff function used in this example is one such API. It applies differentiation on a function that accepts a float number as input and outputs a float number. These high-level APIs lead to extremely elegant code. As shown in this example, we can simply apply the differentiation function on the original tanh function iteratively to get its first-order, second-order, and any other higher-order derivatives. In the next several sections, we will explain these building blocks in detail and how these different pieces are assembled into a powerful AD module.

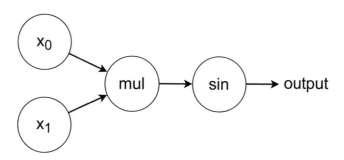

Figure 3-2. *Computation graph in the example calculation*

3.2 Types

We start with type definition. The data type in AD is defined in the `owl_algodiff_types.ml` file, as shown in the following. Even if you are familiar with the type system in OCaml, it may still seem a bit confusing. The essence of AD type is to express the forward and reverse differentiation modes. So first, we use an example to demonstrate how these two AD modes work.

```
module Make (A : Owl_types_ndarray_algodiff.Sig) = struct
  type t =
    | F   of A.elt
    | Arr of A.arr
    | DF  of t * t * int
    | DR  of t * t ref * op * int ref * int * int ref

  and adjoint = t -> t ref -> (t * t) list -> (t * t) list
  and register = t list -> t list
  and label = string * t list
  and op = adjoint * register * label
end
```

Forward and Reverse Modes

In this part, we illustrate the two modes of differentiation with an example, which is based on this simple function:

$$y(x_0, x_1) = (\sin x_0 x_1)$$
(3.3)

This function takes two inputs, and our aim is to compute $\nabla y = \left(\dfrac{\partial y}{\partial x_0}, \dfrac{\partial y}{\partial x_1} \right)$.

Computations can be represented as a graph shown in Figure 3-2. Each node represents either an input/output or intermediate variables generated by the corresponding mathematical function. Each node is named v_i. Herein, the input $v_0 = x_0$ and $v_1 = x_1$. The output $y = v_4$.

Both the forward and reverse modes rely on basic rules to calculate differentiation. On one hand, there are the basic forms of derivative equations, such as $\dfrac{d}{dx}\sin(x) = \cos(x)$,

$\dfrac{d}{dx}u(x)v(x) = u'(x)v(x) + u(x)v'(x)$, etc. On the other is the *chain rule*. It states that, suppose we have two functions f and g that can be composed to create a function $F(x) = f(g(x))$, then the derivative of F can be calculated as

$$F'(x) = f'(g(x))g'(x)$$
(3.4)

Table 3-1. *The Computation Process of Forward Differentiation, Shown to Three Significant Figures*

	Primal Computation	Tangent Computation
0	$v_0 = x_0 = 2$	$\dot{v}_0 = 1$
1	$v_1 = x_1 = 2$	$\dot{v}_1 = 0$
2	$v_2 = v_0 v_1 = 4$	$\dot{v}_2 = v_0 \dot{v}_1 + v_1 \dot{v}_0 = 2*0 + 2*1 = 2$
3	$v_3 = \sin(v_2) = -0.757$	$\dot{y} = \dot{v}_3 = \cos(v_2) * \dot{v}_2 = -0.654 * 2 = -1.308$

The question is how to implement them in a differentiation system.

Forward Mode

Let's look at the first way, namely, the "forward" mode, to calculate derivatives. We ultimately wish to calculate $\frac{\partial y}{\partial x_0}$ (and $\frac{\partial y}{\partial x_1}$, which can be calculated in a similar way). We begin by calculating some intermediate results that will prove to be useful. Using the labels v_i to refer to the intermediate computations, we have $\frac{\partial v_0}{\partial x_0} = 1$ and $\frac{\partial v_1}{\partial x_0} = 0$ immediately, since $v_0 = x_0$ and $v_1 = x_1$ actually.

Next, consider $\frac{\partial v_2}{\partial x_0}$, which requires us to use the derivative rule on multiplication. It is a bit trickier and requires the use of the chain rule:

$$\frac{\partial v_2}{\partial x_0} = \frac{\partial (x_0 x_1)}{\partial x_0} = x_1 \frac{\partial (x_0)}{\partial x_0} + x_0 \frac{\partial (x_1)}{\partial x_0} = x_1$$

After calculating $\frac{\partial v_2}{\partial x_0}$, we proceed to compute partial derivatives of v_4 which is the final result $\frac{\partial y}{\partial x_0}$ we are looking for. This process starts with the input variables and ends with the output variables, and that's where the name "forward differentiation" comes from. We can simplify the notation by letting $\dot{v}_i = \frac{\partial v_i}{\partial x_0}$. The $\dot{v}_i$ is called the *tangent* of function $v_i(x_0, x_1, \ldots, x_n)$ regarding the input variable x_0, and the results of evaluating the function at each intermediate point are called the *primal value*.

Let's calculate $\dot{y}$ when setting $x_0 = 2$ and $x_1 = 2$. The full forward differentiation calculation process is shown in Table 3-1 where two simultaneous computation processes take place in the two computation columns: the primal just performs computation following the computation graph; the tangent gives the derivative for each intermediate variable with regard to x_0.

Two things need to be noted in this calculation process. The first is that in algorithmic differentiation, unlike symbolic differentiation, the computation is performed step by step, instead of after the whole computation is unwrapped into one big formula following the chain rule. Second, in each step, we only need to keep two values: **primal** and **tangent**. Besides, each step only needs to have access to its "parents," using graph theory's term. For example, to compute v_2 and $\dot{v}_2$, we need to know the primal and tangent of v_0 and v_1; to compute that of $v3$, we need to know the primal and tangent of v_2; etc. These observations are key to our implementation.

Reverse Mode

Now let's rethink about this problem from the other direction: from outputs to inputs. The problem remains the same, that is, to calculate $\dfrac{\partial y}{\partial x_0}$. We still follow the same "step-by-step" procedure as in the previous forward mode. The only difference is that this time we calculate it backward. For example, in our example $y = v_3 = \sin(v2)$, so if only we know $\dfrac{\partial y}{\partial v_2}$, we would move a step closer to our target solution.

We first observe that $\dfrac{\partial y}{\partial v_3} = 1$, since y and v_3 are the same. We then compute $\dfrac{\partial y}{\partial v_2}$ by applying the chain rule:

$$\frac{\partial y}{\partial v_2} = \frac{\partial y}{\partial v_3} * \frac{\partial v_3}{\partial v_2} = 1 * \frac{\partial \sin(v_2)}{\partial v_2} = \cos(v_2). \tag{3.5}$$

We can simplify it by applying a substitution:

Table 3-2. *The Forward Pass in Reverse Mode*

	Primal Computation
0	$v_0 = x_0 = 2$
1	$v_1 = x_1 = 2$
2	$v_2 = v_0 * v1 = 4$
3	$y = \sin(v_2) = v_0\, v_1 = -0.757$

Table 3-3. *The Backward Pass in Reverse Mode*

	Adjoint Computation
4	$\bar{v}_3 = 1$
5	$\bar{v}_2 = \bar{v}_3 \dfrac{\partial v_3}{\partial v_2} = \bar{v}_3 \dfrac{\partial\left(\sin(v2)\right)}{\partial v_2} = 1 * \cos(v_2) = -0.654$
6	$\bar{v}_1 = \bar{v}_2 \dfrac{\partial v_2}{\partial v_1} = \bar{v}_2 \dfrac{\partial\left(v_0 v_1\right)}{\partial v_1} = -0.654 * v_0 = -1.308$
7	$\bar{v}_0 = \bar{v}_2 \dfrac{\partial v_2}{\partial v_1} = \bar{v}_2 \dfrac{\partial\left(v_0 v_1\right)}{\partial v_0} = -0.654 * v_1 = -1.308$

$$\bar{v}_i = \frac{\partial y}{\partial v_i}$$

for the derivative of output variable y with regard to intermediate node v_i. $\bar{v}_i$ is called the "*adjoint* of variable v_i with respect to the output variable y." Using this notation, Eq. 3.5 can be rewritten as

$$\bar{v}_2 = \bar{v}_3 * \frac{\partial v_3}{\partial v_2} = 1 * \cos(v_2)$$

Note the difference between tangent and adjoint. In forward mode, we know $\dot{v}_0$ and $\dot{v}_1$ and then calculate $\dot{v}_2$, $\dot{v}_3$, ... until we get the target. In reverse mode, we start with $\bar{v}_n = 1$ and calculate $\bar{v}_{n-1}$, $\bar{v}_{n-2}$, ... until we have our target $\bar{v}_0 = \dfrac{\partial y}{\partial v_0} = \dfrac{\partial y}{\partial x_0}$. $\dot{v}_3 = \bar{v}_0$ in this example, given that we are talking about derivatives with respect to x_0 when we use $\dot{v}_3$. As a result, the reverse mode is also called the *adjoint mode*.

Following this procedure, we can now perform the complete reverse mode differentiation. Note one major difference compared to the forward mode. In Table 3-1, we can compute the primal and tangent in one pass, since computing one of them does not require the other. However, as shown in the previous analysis, it is possible to require the value of v_2 and possibly other previous primal values to compute $\bar{v}_2$. Therefore, a *forward pass*[1] is first required, as shown in Table 3-2, to compute the required intermediate values. They are actually identical to those in the Primal Computation column of Table 3-1. We put it here again to stress our point about this stand-alone forward computing pass.

Table 3-3 shows the *backward pass* in the reverse differentiation process, starting from the very end, and calculates all the way up to the beginning. A short summary: To compute differentiation using reverse mode, we need a forward pass to compute **primal** and next a backward pass to compute **adjoint**.

Both the forward and reverse modes are equivalent in computing differentiation. So you might wonder, since the forward mode looks more straightforward, why don't we just stick with it all along? Note that we obtained $\frac{\partial y}{\partial x_1}$ "for free" while calculating $\frac{\partial y}{\partial x_0}$.

But in the forward mode, to calculate the derivative regarding another input, we have to calculate all the intermediate results again. So here lies one of the most significant strengths of the reverse mode: no matter how many inputs there are, a single reverse pass gives us all the derivatives of the inputs.

This property is extremely useful in neural networks. The computation graph constructed in neural networks tend to be quite complex, often with more than one input. The target of using AD is to find the derivative of the output – probably a scalar value of a loss function – regarding inputs. Thus, using the reverse mode AD is more efficient.

Data Types

Now that we understand the basic elements in computing a derivative, let's turn to the data type used in the AD system. It is built upon two basic types: scalar number F and ndarray Arr. They are of type A.elt and A.arr. Here, A presents an interface that mostly resembles that of an ndarray module. It means that their specific types, such as single or double precision, C implementation or base implementation, etc., all depend on this A ndarray module. Therefore, the AD module does not need to deal with all the lower-level details. We will talk about how the AD module interacts with the other modules later in this chapter. For now, it suffices to simply understand them as, for example, single-precision float number and ndarray with single-precision float as elements, so as to better grasp the core ideas in AD.

---

[1] Not to be confused with the "forward differentiation mode" introduced before.

```
module Make (A : Owl_types_ndarray_algodiff.Sig) = struct
  type t =
    | F    of A.elt
    | Arr of A.arr
    (* primal, tangent, tag *)
    | DF  of t * t * int
    (* primal, adj accu, op, fanout, tag, tracker *)
    | DR  of t * t ref * op * int ref * int * int ref

  and adjoint = t -> t ref -> (t * t) list -> (t * t) list

  and register = t list -> t list

  and label = string * t list

  and op = adjoint * register * label
end
```

The other two types are compounded types, each representing one differentiation mode. The DF type contains three parts, and the most important ones are the first two: primal and tangent. The DR type contains six parts, and the most important ones are the first, primal, and the third, op. op itself consists of three parts: adjoint, register, and label, of which adjoint is the most important component. The DR type also contains an adjoint accumulator (the second parameter), a fanout flag, and a tracker flag. The accumulator is of reference type since it needs to be updated during the propagation process. Both DF and DR types contain a tag of integer type. Later, we will discuss how these extra parts work in an AD engine. To focus on the core idea in AD, for now we introduce the most important elements: primal, tangent, and adjoint.

In essence, the computation graph in AD is constructed by building a list. Each element of this list contains two elements: the partial derivative computation and the original type t data. In the data type, the adjoint is a function. For each t type data, it specifies how to construct this list. Though the derivative computation rule of different operators varies, the adjoint generally falls into several patterns. For example, here is what the adjoint function looks like for an operation/function that takes one input and produces one output, such as sin, exp, etc.

```
let r a =
  let adjoint cp ca t = (dr (primal a) cp ca, a) :: t in
  let register t = a :: t in
  let label = S.label, [ a ] in
  adjoint, register, label
```

Here, the r function returns an op type, which consists of the adjoint function, the register function, and the label tuple. First, let's look at the adjoint function. The first two variables cp and ca will be used in the derivative function dr. We will talk about it later in Section 3.3. For now, we only need to know that the reverse derivative computation dr calculates something; we put it together with the original input operator a into a tuple and add them to the existing list t, which is the third argument. The other two components are supplementary. The register function actually is an adjoint function without really calculating adjoints; it only stacks a list of original operators. The third one, label, puts together a string such as "sin" or "exp" to the input operator.

Next, let's see another example in an operator that takes multiple inputs, such as add, mul (multiplication), etc. It's a bit more complex:

```
let r_d_d a b =
  let adjoint cp ca_ref t =
    let abar, bbar = dr_ab (primal a) (primal b) cp ca_ref in
    (abar, a) :: (bbar, b) :: t
  in
  let register t = a :: b :: t in
  let label = S.label ^ "_d_d", [ a; b ] in
  adjoint, register, label
```

The difference is that one such operator needs to push two items into the list. So here dr_ab is still a function that calculates derivatives reversely, and it returns the derivatives on its two parents, noted by abar and bbar, which are both pushed to the adjoint list. The register and label follow a similar pattern. In fact, in an operator that takes multiple inputs, we should consider other options, which is that one of the inputs is just a constant element. In that case, only one element should be put into the list:

```
let r_d_c a b =
  let adjoint cp ca_ref t = (S.dr_a (primal a) b cp ca_ref, a) :: t in
  let register t = a :: t in
  let label = S.label ^ "_d_c", [ a; b ] in
  adjoint, register, label
```

Operations on AD Type

After understanding the data type defined in AD, let's take a look at what sorts of
operations can be applied to them. They are defined in the owl_algodiff_core.ml
file. The most notable ones are the "get" functions that retrieve certain information
from an AD type data, such as its primal, tangent, and adjoint values. In the following
code, the primal' is a "deep" function that recursively finds the primal value as float or
ndarray format.

```
let primal = function
  | DF (ap, _, _)          -> ap
  | DR (ap, _, _, _, _, _) -> ap
  | ap                     -> ap

let rec primal' = function
  | DF (ap, _, _)          -> primal' ap
  | DR (ap, _, _, _, _, _) -> primal' ap
  | ap                     -> ap

let tangent = function
  | DF (_, at, _) -> at
  | DR _          -> failwith "error: no tangent for DR"
  | ap            -> zero ap

let adjval = function
  | DF _                   -> failwith "error: no adjval for DF"
  | DR (_, at, _, _, _, _) -> !at
  | ap                     -> zero ap
```

And the zero function resets all elements to the zero status:

```
let rec zero = function
  | F _                     -> F A.(float_to_elt 0.)
  | Arr ap                  -> Arr A.(zeros (shape ap))
  | DF (ap, _, _)           -> ap |> primal' |> zero
  | DR (ap, _, _, _, _, _) -> ap |> primal' |> zero
```

Another group of important operations are those that convert the AD type to and from ordinary types such as float and ndarray:

```
let pack_elt x = F x

let unpack_elt x =
  match primal x with
  | F x -> x
  | _   -> failwith "error: AD.unpack_elt"

let pack_flt x = F A.(float_to_elt x)

let _f x = F A.(float_to_elt x)

let pack_arr x = Arr x

let unpack_arr x =
  match primal x with
  | Arr x -> x
  | _     -> failwith "error: AD.unpack_arr"
```

There are also operations that provide helpful utilities. One of them is the zero we have seen, and also some functions show type information:

```
let shape x =
  match primal' x with
  | F _    -> [||]
  | Arr ap -> A.shape ap
  | _      -> failwith "error: AD.shape"
```

3.3 Operators

The graph is constructed with a series of operators that can be used to process AD type data as well as building up a computation graph that is differentiable. They are divided into submodules: Maths is the most important component, and it contains a full set of mathematical functions to enable constructing various computation graphs; Linalg contains a subset of linear algebra functions; NN contains functions used in neural networks, such as two-dimensional convolution, dropout, etc.; Mat is specifically for matrix operations, such as eye that generates an identity matrix; and Arr provides functions such as shape and numel for ndarrays.

As shown in Figure 3-1, the implementation of an operation can be abstracted into two parts: (a) what the derivative and calculation rules of it are and (b) how these rules are applied into the AD system. The first part is defined in the owl_algodiff_ops.ml, and the latter is in owl_algodiff_ops_builder.ml.

Calculation Rules

Let's look at some examples from the first to see what these calculation rules are and how they are expressed in OCaml. We can use the sine function as an example. It takes an input and computes its sine value as output. This module specifies four computing rules, each corresponding to one type of AD data. Here, module A is the underlying "normal" ndarray module that implements functions for ndarray and scalar values. It can be single precision or double precision, implemented using OCaml or C. For the F scalar type, ff_f specifies using the sin function from the Scalar submodule of A. If the data is an AD ndarray, ff_arr states that the sine functions should be applied on all of its elements by using the A.sin function. Next, if the data is of type DF, the df function is used. As shown in the example in Table 3-1, it computes *tangent (at) * derivative of primal (ap)*. In the case of the sine function, it computes at * cos ap. Finally, the dr computes what we have shown in Table 3-3. It computes *adjoint (ca) * derivative of primal (a)*. Therefore, here it computes !ca * cos a. Using the get reference operator !ca is because the adjoint value in the DR type is a reference that can be updated.

```
module struct
  let label = "sin"
  let ff_f a = F A.Scalar.(sin a)
  let ff_arr a = Arr A.(sin a)
```

```
  let df _cp ap at = at * cos ap
  let dr a _cp ca = !ca * cos a
end
```

The similar template can be applied to other operators that take one input and produce one output, such as the square root (sqrt), as shown in the next module. The derivative rule for the square root is $\left(\sqrt{x}\right)' = \dfrac{1}{2\sqrt{x}}$.

```
module struct
  let label = "sqrt"
  let ff_f a = F A.Scalar.(sqrt a)
  let ff_arr a = Arr A.(sqrt a)
  let df cp _ap at = at / (pack_flt 2. * cp)
  let dr _a cp ca = !ca / (pack_flt 2. * cp)
end
```

However, things get more complicated once an operator needs to deal with more than one input. The problem is that for each of these four computation rules, we need to consider multiple possible cases. Take the divide operation as an example. For a simple primal value computation, we need to consider four cases: both inputs are scalar, both are ndarray, and one of them is ndarray and the other is scalar. It corresponds to four rules: ff_aa, ff_bb, ff_ab, and ff_ba. For the forward computation of tangent regarding $\dfrac{a}{b}$, we also need to consider three cases:

- df_da corresponds to the derivative when the second input is constant:

$$\left(\frac{a(x)}{b}\right)' = \frac{a'(x)}{b} \tag{3.6}$$

- In code, it is at / bp. Here, at is the tangent of the first input $a'(x)$, and bp is the primal value of the second input b.

- df_db corresponds to the derivative when the first input is constant:

$$\left(\frac{a}{b(x)}\right)' = -\frac{a}{b(x)^2}b'(x) = -b'(x)\frac{a}{b(x)}\frac{1}{b(x)}, \tag{3.7}$$

- And thus, it can be represented by neg bt*cp/bp. Here, neg is the negative operator, and cp represents the original input $\dfrac{a}{b(x)}$.

- df_dab is for the case that both inputs are of nonconstant AD type, that is, DF or DR. It thus calculates

$$\left(\frac{a(x)}{b(x)}\right)' = \frac{a'(x) - \dfrac{a(x)}{b(x)}b'(x)}{b(x)}, \tag{3.8}$$

- And the corresponding code is (at-(bt*cp))/bp.

Expressing the rules in computing the reverse mode is more straightforward. If both inputs a and b are nonconstant, then the function dr_ab computes $\bar{a}\dfrac{\partial y}{\partial a}$ and $\bar{b}\dfrac{\partial y}{\partial b}$, where $y = \dfrac{a}{b}$. Thus, dr_ab returns two values; the first is $\bar{a}/b$ (!ca / b), and the second is $-\dfrac{a}{b^2}$ (!ca * (neg a / (b * b))). In the code, squeeze_broadcast x s is an internal helper function that squeezes array x so that it has shape s. If one of the inputs is constant, then we can just omit the corresponding result, as shown in dr_a and dr_b.

```
module struct
  let label = "div"
  let ff_aa a b = F A.Scalar.(div a b)
  let ff_ab a b = Arr A.(scalar_div a b)
  let ff_ba a b = Arr A.(div_scalar a b)
  let ff_bb a b = Arr A.(div a b)
  let df_da _cp _ap at bp = at / bp
  let df_db cp _ap bp bt = neg bt * cp / bp
  let df_dab cp _ap at bp bt = (at - (bt * cp)) / bp
  let dr_ab a b _cp ca =
    ( _squeeze_broadcast (!ca / b) (shape a)
    , _squeeze_broadcast (!ca * (neg a / (b * b))) (shape b) )
  let dr_a a b _cp ca = _squeeze_broadcast (!ca / b) (shape a)
  let dr_b a b _cp ca = _squeeze_broadcast
    (!ca * (neg a / (b * b))) (shape b)
end
```

A similar example is the operator pow that performs a^b calculation. It implements calculation rules that are similar to those of div.

```
module struct
  let label = "pow"
  let ff_aa a b = F A.Scalar.(pow a b)
  let ff_ab a b = Arr A.(scalar_pow a b)
  let ff_ba a b = Arr A.(pow_scalar a b)
  let ff_bb a b = Arr A.(pow a b)
  let df_da _cp ap at bp = at *
    (ap ** (bp - pack_flt 1.)) * bp
  let df_db cp ap _bp bt = bt * cp * log ap
  let df_dab cp ap at bp bt =
    ((ap ** (bp - pack_flt 1.)) * (at * bp)) +
      (cp * bt * log ap)
  let dr_ab a b cp ca =
    ( _squeeze_broadcast (!ca *
      (a ** (b - pack_flt 1.)) * b) (shape a)
    , _squeeze_broadcast (!ca * cp * log a) (shape b) )
  let dr_a a b _cp ca =
    _squeeze_broadcast (!ca *
      (a ** (b - pack_flt 1.)) * b) (shape a)
  let dr_b a b cp ca = _squeeze_broadcast
    (!ca * cp * log a) (shape b)
end
```

Generalize Rules into Builder Template

So far, we have talked about the calculation rules, but there is still a question: how to utilize these rules to build an operator of type t that we have described in Section 3.2. To do that, we need to use the power of functor in OCaml. In the AD module in Owl, the operators are categorized according to the number of inputs and outputs, each with its own template. Let's take the "single-input-single-output" (SISO) operators such as sine as an example. This template takes a module of type Siso as input, as shown in the following. Notice that the calculation rules of the sine function shown in the previous section exactly forms such a module.

```
module type Siso = sig
  val label : string
  val ff_f : A.elt -> t
  val ff_arr : A.arr -> t
  val df : t -> t -> t -> t
  val dr : t -> t -> t ref -> t
end
```

In the end, we need to build a sin : t -> t operator, which accepts a data of AD type t and returns output of type t. This function is what we need:

```
let op_siso ~ff ~fd ~df ~r a =
  match a with
  | DF (ap, at, ai) ->
    let cp = fd ap in
    DF (cp, df cp ap at, ai)
  | DR (ap, _, _, _, ai, _) ->
    let cp = fd ap in
    DR (cp, ref (zero cp), r a, ref 0, ai, ref 0)
  | ap -> ff ap
```

These names may seem enigmatic. Here, the fd x function calculates the primal value of x. ff x performs forward computation on the two basic types: scalar and ndarray. The df cp ap at function computes the tangents in forward mode. Finally, the function r computes the op part in the type, which "remembers" how to build up the graph in the form of a list. To put them together, the basic logic of this function goes like this:

- If the input is a DF type, produce a new DF type after calculating the primal and tangent in forward mode.

- If the input is a DR type, produce a new DR type, with its knowledge about how to compute adjoints and how to build up the list.

- Otherwise, it's the basic type, scalar or ndarray; perform simple forward computation on it.

Note that the newly constructed DR type, aside from its primal value and op being updated, the rest values, including adjoint, label, etc., are all set to 0. That is because a computation graph is constructed in the forward pass, and the calculation of adjoints does not happen in this step.

So the next question is: for the sine function, how can we get the fd, ff, etc.? Luckily, from the previous Siso module that specifies various calculation rules, we have already had all the ingredients required. Assume we have named this Siso sine module S, then we have the forward computation on the two basic types:

```
let ff = function
  | F a   -> S.ff_f a
  | Arr a -> S.ff_arr a
  | _     -> error_uniop label a
```

And the r function looks like what we have introduced in Section 3.2, using the dr function from module S to specify how to construct the list.

```
let r a =
  let adjoint cp ca t = (S.dr (primal a) cp ca, a) :: t in
  let register t = a :: t in
  let label = S.label, [ a ] in
  adjoint, register, label
```

So now we have the function:

```
let rec f a =
  let open S in
  (* define ff and r as stated above *)
  let fd a = f a in
  op_siso ~ff ~fd ~df:S.df ~r a
```

Put them together, and here is the final function that accepts a module and builds an operator:

```
let build_siso =
  (* define op_siso *)
  fun (module S : Siso) ->
    (* define f *)
    f
```

To build a `sin` operator, we use the following code:

```
let sin = build_siso (
  module struct
    let label = "sin"
    let ff_f a = F A.Scalar.(sin a)
    let ff_arr a = Arr A.(sin a)
    let df _cp ap at = at * cos ap
    let dr a _cp ca = !ca * cos a
  end : Siso)
```

The code is concise, easy to read, and less prone to various possible errors in coding. To build another "siso" operator, such as a square root, we only need to change the rules:

```
let sqrt = build_siso (
  module struct
    let label = "log"
    let ff_f a = F A.Scalar.(log a)
    let ff_arr a = Arr A.(log a)
    let df _cp ap at = at / ap
    let dr a _cp ca = !ca / a
  end : Siso)
```

Here, we only use the most simple SISO type builder template as an example. We also include the other templates:

- SIPO: Single input and pair outputs, such as the linear algebra operation qr for QR factorization

- SITO: Single input and three outputs, such as the SVD factorization

- SIAO: Single input and array outputs, such as the `split` function that splits input ndarray into multiple ones

- PISO: Pair inputs and single output, such as `add` and `mul`

- AISO: Array input and single output, such as `concatenate`, the inverse operation of `split`

These templates can become quite complex. For example, in building the add function, to choose from different combinations of possible input types, the builder function can be as complex as

```
op_piso ~ff ~fd ~df_da ~df_db ~df_dab ~r_d_d ~r_d_c ~r_c_d a b
```

But the principles are the same.

3.4 API

The previous section introduces AD operators, the building blocks to construct an AD computation graph. The next thing we need is an "engine" that begins the differentiation process. For that purpose, we first introduce several low-level APIs provided by the AD module and explain how they are used to build up user-friendly advanced APIs such as diff and grad.

Low-Level APIs

We differentiate between the two differentiation modes: forward mode and backward mode. As explained in the previous section, if an input x is of type DF, then by applying operations such as sin x, a computation graph is constructed, and the primal and tangent values are also computed during this process. All we need to do is to retrieve the required value once this process is finished. To start a forward mode differentiation, we need to create a DF type data as initial input, using the primal value, the initial tangent (equals to 1), and an integer tag as arguments:

```
let make_forward p t i = DF (p, t, i)
```

For example, if we are to calculate the derivative of $f = sin(x^2)$ at $x = 2$, we can first create an initial point as

```
let x = make_forward (pack_flt 2.) (pack_flt 1.) 1
let y = Maths.(pow x (pack_flt 2.) |> sin)
let t = tangent y
```

That's it. Once the computation y is constructed, we can directly retrieve the tangent value using the tangent function.

The backward mode is a bit more complex. Remember that it consists of two passes: one forward and one backward. From the previous section, we know that once the graph is constructed, the primal data are calculated, but the adjoint values are all set to zero. Therefore, we need some extra mechanism to pump the computation flow backward to calculate adjoint values. Here is an example to use low-level APIs to compute derivatives in the reverse mode:

```
open AD

let f x = Maths.(pow x (pack_flt 2.) |> sin)
let x = 2.;
let x' = make_reverse x (tag ());
let y = f x';
let _ = reverse_prop (F 1.) y;
let y' = adjval x';;
```

The problem to solve is still the same: calculate the derivative of $f = sin(x^2)$ at $x = 2$; the only difference is that we use the reverse mode this time. Let's explain this example line by line. First, we still need to build an initial operator with make_reverse.

```
let make_reverse p i =
  let adjoint _cp _ca t = t in
  let register t = t in
  let label = "Noop", [] in
  DR (p, ref (zero p), (adjoint, register, label), ref 0, i, ref 0)
```

The make_reverse function constructs a DR type data with a given primal value. The rest of its fields are all set to zero. It does two things: first, it wraps input x into a value of type t for Algodiff to process; second, it generates a unique tag for the input so that input numbers can be nested. Next, calling f x' constructs the computation graph of f, capturing the primal values and knowledge about how to calculate adjoints all in the DR type data y.

Next, reverse_prop propagates the error back to the inputs:

```
let reverse_prop v x =
    reverse_reset x;
    reverse_push v x
```

It consists of two steps: first, reset all values in this graph to initial status (reverse_reset); second, perform backward propagation (reverse_push). Both follow a recursive process.

```
let reverse_reset x =
  let rec reset xs =
    match xs with
    | []      -> ()
    | x :: t ->
      (match x with
       | DR (_cp, aa, (_, register, _), af, _ai, tracker) ->
         aa := reset_zero !aa;
         af := !af + 1;
         tracker := succ !tracker;
         if !af = 1 && !tracker = 1 then reset (register t) else reset t
       | _ -> reset t)
  in
  reset [ x ]
```

The next function is reverse_push that is the core engine that drives the backward propagation process. Its core idea is simple. It maintains a stack t of (adjoint value, AD value) pairs. At each iteration, the push function takes one pair out of the head of stack. The adjoint value v is added to the adjoint accumulator aa in the DR type node |x|. The node also specifies an adjoint function that knows how to calculate adjoint values of its parents, in the form of one or more (adjoint value, AD value) pairs. This process starts with only one pair, which is the output DR type value of a whole computation. It finishes when stack t is empty.

```
let reverse_push =
  let rec push xs =
    match xs with
    | []          -> ()
    | (v, x) :: t ->
      (match x with
       | DR (cp, aa, (adjoint, _, _), af, _ai, tracker) ->
         aa := reverse_add !aa v;
         (af := Stdlib.(!af - 1));
```

```
      if !af = 0 && !tracker = 1
      then push (adjoint cp aa t)
      else (
        tracker := pred !tracker;
        push t)
    | _ -> push t)
  in
  fun v x -> push [ v, x ]
```

After this step, the gradient of f is stored in the adjacent value of x', and we can retrieve the value using the adjval function.

High-Level APIs

Based on the basic low-level APIs, we are able to build more high-level and easy-to-access differentiation functions. The most commonly used function for differentiating is diff in the AD module. Given a function f that maps one scalar value to another, we can calculate its derivative at point x by diff f x. For example, given the triangular function tanh, we can easily calculate its derivative at position $x = 0.1$, as follows:

```
open Algodiff.D
let f x = Maths.(tanh x);;
let d = diff f (F 0.1);;
```

Its implementation using the forward mode low-level API is quite simple:

```
let diff' f x =
    if not (is_float x) then
      failwith "input must be a scalar";
    let x = make_forward x (pack_flt 1.) (tag ()) in
    let y = f x in
    primal y, tangent y

let diff f x = diff' f x |> snd
```

Next, we can generalize derivatives of scalar functions to gradients of multivariate functions. For a function that maps a vector input to a scalar, the grad function calculates its gradient at a given point. For example, in a three-dimensional space, the gradient at each point on a surface consists of three elements representing the partial derivative along the x, y, and z axes. This vector indicates the direction in which the function has the largest magnitude change. Its implementation uses the standard reverse mode:

```
let grad' f x =
    let x = make_reverse x (tag ()) in
    let y = f x in
    assert (is_float y);
    reverse_reset y;
    reverse_push (pack_flt 1.) y;
    primal y, x |> adjval

let grad f x = grad' f x |> snd
```

One important application of gradient is in gradient descent, a widely used technique for finding the minimum value of a function. We will discuss it in more detail in Chapter 4.

Just as gradient generalizes derivatives from scalars to vectors, the *Jacobian* function generalizes gradient from vectors to matrices. In other words, grad is applied to functions mapping vectors to scalars, while jacobian is applied to functions that map vectors to vectors. If we assume the function f takes an input vector of length n and produces an output vector of length m, then the Jacobian is defined as

$$\mathbf{J}(y) = \begin{bmatrix} \dfrac{\partial y_0}{\partial x_0} & \dfrac{\partial y_0}{\partial x_1} & \cdots & \dfrac{\partial y_0}{\partial x_{n-1}} \\[2ex] \dfrac{\partial y_2}{\partial x_0} & \dfrac{\partial y_2}{\partial x_1} & \cdots & \dfrac{\partial y_2}{\partial x_{n-1}} \\[2ex] \vdots & \vdots & \cdots & \vdots \\[2ex] \dfrac{\partial y_{m-1}}{\partial x_0} & \dfrac{\partial y_{m-1}}{\partial x_1} & \cdots & \dfrac{\partial y_{m-1}}{\partial x_{n-1}} \end{bmatrix}$$

The intuition behind the Jacobian is similar to that of the gradient. At a particular point in the domain of the target function, the Jacobian shows how the output vector changes given a small change in the input vector. Its implementation is as follows:

```
let jacobianv' f x v =
    if shape x <> shape v
    then failwith "jacobianv': vector not the same dimension as input";
    let x = make_forward x v (tag ()) in
```

CHAPTER 3   ALGORITHMIC DIFFERENTIATION

```
  let y = f x in
  primal y, tangent y

let jacobianv f x v = jacobianv' f x v |> snd
```

The advanced APIs support convenient composition and can be used to build more complex ones. For example, the second-order derivative of function *f* can be implemented as g = f |> diff |> diff. Another example is the hessian API. Given a multivariate function that maps *n* input variables to a scalar, this function calculates its second-order derivatives as a matrix. Its implementation is based on Jacobian:

```
let hessian f x = (f |> grad |> jacobian) x
```

In most applications, we use these high-level APIs to support more advanced applications, such as optimization, regression, neural network, etc. One good example is to implement Newton's method for finding the minimum value of a function. Rather than moving only in the direction of the gradient, Newton's method combines the gradient with the second-order gradients of a function, $\dfrac{\nabla f(x_n)}{\nabla^2 f(x_n)}$, starting from a random position and iterating until convergence according to Eq. 3.9. Its implementation in OCaml is shown as follows:

$$x_{n+1} = x_n - \alpha \mathbf{H}^{-1} \nabla f(x_n) \tag{3.9}$$

```
open Algodiff.D

let rec newton ?(eta=F 0.01) ?(eps=1e-6) f x =
  let g = grad f x in
  let h = hessian f x in
  if (Maths.l2norm' g |> unpack_flt) < eps then x
  else newton ~eta ~eps f Maths.(x - eta * g *@ (inv h))
```

As an example, we can apply this method to a two-dimensional triangular function, starting from a random initial point, to find a local minimum. Note that the newton function takes a vector as input and outputs a scalar.

```
let _ =
  let f x = Maths.(cos x |> sum') in
  newton f (Mat.uniform 1 2)
```

Besides what we have mentioned, Owl also implements other high-level differentiation functions, such as `laplacian`, which calculates the Laplacian operator $\nabla^2 f$, or the trace of a Hessian matrix. In essence, they are all built upon a concise set of low-level APIs or other high-level APIs. We will see more applications of the AD module in later chapters.

3.5 More Implementation Details

Besides the main structure we have mentioned so far, there are some other details that should be mentioned to build an industry-grade AD module. We introduce them in this section.

Perturbation Confusion and Tag

We have explained some of the fields in the DR type. But one of them is not covered yet: tag of type `int`, which is used to solve a particular problem when calculating higher-order derivatives with nested forward and backward modes. This problem is referred to as *perturbation confusion*. It is crucial for an AD engine to function properly to handle this problem. Here, we only scratch the surface of it. Let's look at an example. Suppose we want to compute the derivative of

$$f(x) = x\frac{d(x+y)}{dy}$$

that is, a function that contains another derivative function. It initially seems straightforward, and we don't even need a computer's help: as $\frac{d(x+y)}{dy} = 1$ so $f(x) = x' = 1$. Unfortunately, applying the simple implementation without `tag` leads to wrong answer.

```
# let diff f x =
    match x with
    | DF (_, _)    ->
      f x |> tangent
    | DR (_, _, _) ->
      let r = f x in
```

```
        reverse_push [(1., r)];
        !(adjoint x);;
val diff : (t -> t) -> t -> float = <fun>

# let f x =
        let g = diff (fun y -> add_ad x y) in
        mul_ad x (make_forward (g (make_forward 2. 1.)) 1.);;
val f : t -> t = <fun>

# diff f (make_forward 2. 1.);;
- : float = 4.
```

The result is 4 at point $(2, 2)$, but we have previously calculated, and the result should be 1 at any point. What has gone wrong? The answer is a bit tricky. Note that x=DF(2,1). The tangent value equals to 1, which means that $\dfrac{dx}{dx} = 1$. Now if we continue to use this same x value in function g, whose variable is y, the same x=DF(2,1) can be incorrectly translated by the AD engine as $\dfrac{dx}{dy} = 1$. Therefore, when used within function g, x should actually be treated as DF(2,0). That's where tagging comes to help. It solves the nested derivative problem by distinguishing derivative calculations and their associated attached parameters with a unique tag for each usage of the derivative operator.

Lazy Evaluation

We have seen how separating building template and operation definitions makes it convenient to add new operations, simplifying code and improving productivity. But it comes with a price: efficiency. Imagine a large calculation that contains thousands of operations, with one operation occurring many times. Such situations are actually quite common when using AD with neural networks where large computation graphs are created that use functions such as add and mul many hundreds of times. With the Builder approach described earlier, the operation will be recreated every time it is used, which is rather inefficient. Fortunately, we can simply use OCaml's lazy evaluation mechanism to perform caching.

```
val lazy: 'a -> 'a lazy_t
```

```
module Lazy : sig
  type 'a t = 'a lazy_t
  val force : 'a t -> 'a
end
```

OCaml provides a built-in function `lazy` that accepts an input of type `'a` and returns a value of type `'a lazy_t` where the computation of the value of type `'a` has been delayed. This lazy expression won't be evaluated until it is called by `Lazy.force`, and the first time it is called, the expression is evaluated and the result is cached. Subsequent applications of `Lazy.force` will simply return the cached result without further reevaluation. Here is an example of lazy evaluation in OCaml:

```
# let x = Printf.printf "hello world!"; 42
hello world!
val x : int = 42
# let lazy_x = lazy (Printf.printf "hello world!"; 42)
val lazy_x : int lazy_t = <lazy>
# let _ = Stdlib.Lazy.force lazy_x
hello world!
- : int = 42
# let _ = Stdlib.Lazy.force lazy_x
- : int = 42
# let _ = Stdlib.Lazy.force lazy_x
- : int = 42
```

In this example, we can see that building `lazy_x` does not evaluate the content, which is delayed to the first `Lazy.force`. After that, every time `force` is called, only the value is returned; the `x` itself, including the `printf` function, will not be evaluated. Now come back to the AD module in Owl. Imagine that we need to add support for the `sin` operation. The definition of `sin` remains the same:

```
open Algodiff.D

module Sin = struct
  let label = "sin"
  let ff_f a = F A.Scalar.(sin a)
  let ff_arr a = Arr A.(sin a)
  let df _cp ap at = Maths.(at * cos ap)
```

```
 let dr a _cp ca = Maths.(!ca * cos (primal a))
end
```

However, we can instead use lazy evaluation to actually build the implementation and benefit from the efficiency gain of the caching it provides.

```
let _sin_ad = lazy Builder.build_siso (module Sin : Builder.Siso);;
let new_sin_ad = Lazy.force _sin_ad;;
```

In this way, regardless of how many times this sin function is called in a massive computation graph, the Builder.build_siso process is only evaluated once.

Extending AD

A significant benefit of the module design described earlier is that it can be easily extended by providing modules representing new functions. For example, suppose that the AD system did not support the natural logarithm, $\sin x$, whose derivative is $\sin' x = \cos x$. Including this function is a simple matter of defining the necessary functions for calculating primal, tangent, and adjoint values in a module and applying the relevant function from the Builder module – in this case, build_siso for building "single input, single output" functions.

```
open Algodiff.D

module Sin = struct
  let label = "sin"
  let ff_f a = F A.Scalar.(sin a)
  let ff_arr a = Arr A.(sin a)
  let df _cp ap at = Maths.(at * cos ap)
  let dr a _cp ca = Maths.(!ca * cos (primal a))
end

let new_sin_ad = Builder.build_siso (module Sin : Builder.Siso)
```

We can directly use this new operator as if it is a native operation in the AD module. For example:

```
# let f x1 x2 =
    let x1 = F. x1 in
    let x2 = F. x2 in
    Maths.(div (cos x1) (new_sin_ad x2));;
val f : t -> t = <fun>
```

Graph Utility

Though not core functions, various utility functions provide convenience to users, for example, tools to visualize the computation graph built up by AD. They come in handy when we are trying to debug or understand how AD works. The core of the visualization function is a recursive traverse routine:

```
let _traverse_trace x =
    let nodes = Hashtbl.create 512 in
    let index = ref 0 in
    (* local function to traverse the nodes *)
    let rec push tlist =
      match tlist with
      | []        -> ()
      | hd :: tl ->
        if Hashtbl.mem nodes hd = false
        then (
          let op, prev =
            match hd with
            | DR (_ap, _aa, (_, _, label), _af, _ai, _) -> label
            | F _a -> Printf.sprintf "Const", []
            | Arr _a -> Printf.sprintf "Const", []
            | DF (_, _, _) -> Printf.sprintf "DF", []
          in
          (* check if the node has been visited before *)
          Hashtbl.add nodes hd (!index, op, prev);
          index := !index + 1;
          push (prev @ tl))
        else push tl
      in
```

```
(* iterate the graph then return the hash table *)
push x;
nodes
```

The _traverse_trace and its related functions are used to convert the computation graph generated in backward mode into human-readable format. It initializes variables for tracking nodes and indices, then iterates the graph and puts required information into a hash table. With some extra code, the parsed information can be displayed on a terminal or be converted into other formats that are suitable for visualization, such as the dot format by Graphviz.

3.6 How AD Is Built upon Ndarray

We have been saying how the AD does not need to deal with the details of computation implementation and thus can focus on the logic of differentiation. In previous examples, we assume the A module to be any Ndarray module. In the final section of this chapter, we will explain how the AD module is built upon the Ndarray modules. We hope to illustrate the power of the functor system in promoting a modular style system design.

First, the Ndarray module used in the AD module is not purely Ndarray as introduced in Chapter 2, but also contains several other modules, including the scalar functions, the ones that are specific to matrix and linear algebra. Together, they are called the Owl_algodiff_primal_ops module. Based on the specific precision of the modules included, it also divides the S and D submodules. For example, here are the components of Owl_algodiff_primal_ops.S:

```
module S = struct
  include Owl_dense_ndarray.S

  module Scalar = Owl_maths

  module Mat = struct
    let eye  = Owl_dense_matrix_s.eye
    let tril = Owl_dense_matrix_s.tril
    let triu = Owl_dense_matrix_s.triu
    ...
  end

  module Linalg = struct
    include Owl_linalg_s
```

```
    let qr a =
      let q, r, _ = qr a in
      q, r

      ...
  end
end
```

By replacing the single-precision modules used in it, such as `Owl_dense_ndarray.S` and `Owl_dense_matrix_s`, with their double-precision counterparts, we can get the `Owl_algodiff_primal_ops.D` module. Moreover, by replacing them with the base Ndarray modules, such as `Owl_base_dense_ndarray.S`, we can acquire AD modules the calculation of which is based on pure OCaml. Actually, the implementation is not limited to these types. The interface of the `Owl_algodiff_primal_ops` module is specified in the `Owl_types_ndarray_algodiff.Sig` module. As long as a module implements all the required functions and modules, it can be plugged into AD. For example, we can utilize the computation graph module in Owl and build a symbolic Ndarray module. An AD module built on this module can provide powerful symbolic computation functionality. It means that the execution of both forward and reverse differentiation modes can benefit from various optimization opportunities, such as graph and memory optimizations. We will explain the computation graph module in Chapter 6.

To build an AD module, we use code similar to the following:

```
module S = Owl_algodiff_generic.Make (Owl_algodiff_primal_ops.S)
module D = Owl_algodiff_generic.Make (Owl_algodiff_primal_ops.D)
```

So next, let's take a look at the `Owl_algodiff_generic.Make` functor. It includes all the existing submodules we have introduced so far: the core module, the operators, and the differential API functions such as `make_forward` and `diff`, as follows:

```
module Make (A : Owl_types_ndarray_algodiff.Sig) = struct
  module Core = Owl_algodiff_core.Make (A)
  include Core

  module Ops = Owl_algodiff_ops.Make (Core)
  include Ops
```

```
  let make_forward p t i = DF (p, t, i)
  let make_reverse p i = ...
  let diff f x = ...
  let grad f x = ...
end
```

These components all rely on the fundamental computation module A. The Core module itself is built using a functor, with the ndarray module as the parameter. Its interface is specified in Owl_algodiff_core_sig.ml, as follows. It includes the basic type definition of types and the operations that can be applied on them.

```
module type Sig = sig
  module A : Owl_types_ndarray_algodiff.Sig

  include Owl_algodiff_types_sig.Sig
    with type elt := A.elt and type arr := A.arr

  val primal  : t -> t
  val tangent : t -> t
  val adjref  : t -> t ref
  ...
end
```

Next, the operators such as sin are built using the Core module as a parameter. As we have explained, first the Builder module works as a factory that assembles various operators by providing different templates such as siso, including a type definition of the template and the function to build operators.

```
module Make (Core : Owl_algodiff_core_sig.Sig) = struct
  open Core

  module type Siso = sig
    val label : string
    val ff_f : A.elt -> t
    val ff_arr : A.arr -> t
    val df : t -> t -> t -> t
    val dr : t -> t -> t ref -> t
```

```
  end

  let build_siso =
    ...
```

Then in the operator module, based on `Core` and `Builder`, this module contains all the operators which are built from the builder functions. They are categorized into different modules such as `Maths` and `Linalg`.

```
module Make (Core : Owl_algodiff_core_sig.Sig) = struct
  open Core
  module Builder = Owl_algodiff_ops_builder.Make (Core)
  open Builder

  module Maths = struct
    let cos = (build_siso
      (module struct
        let label = "cos"
        let ff_f a = F A.Scalar.(cos a)
        let ff_arr a = Arr A.(cos a)
        let df _cp ap at = neg (at * sin ap)
        let dr a _cp ca = !ca * neg (sin a)
      end : Siso))

    and sin = (build_siso ...)
    ...
  end

  module Linalg = struct
  ...
  end

  module NN = struct
  ...
  end

  ...
end
```

3.7 Summary

In this chapter, we discussed the design of one of the core modules in Owl: the algorithmic differentiation module. We started from its basic theory and difference among three types of differentiations. Then we presented the overall architecture of the AD module in Owl. We explained several parts in detail in the following sections: the definition of types in this system, the operators, and the APIs built on existing mechanisms. We also discussed more subtle issues that should be paid attention to when building an industry-level AD engine, such as avoiding the perturbation confusion issue and using lazy evaluation to improve performance, graph visualization, etc. Finally, we explained how the AD system is built upon the `Ndarray` module in Owl.

CHAPTER 4

Mathematical Optimization

Mathematical optimization is the process of searching for optimal values from a selection of parameters, based on a certain metric. It can be formalized as follows:

$$\begin{aligned} \text{minimise} \quad & f(x) \\ \text{subject to} \quad & g_i(x) \le b_i, i = 1, 2, \ldots, n. \end{aligned} \tag{4.1}$$

Here, vector $\mathbf{x} = \{x_1, x_2, \ldots, x_n\}$ is the optimization variables, and function $f : \mathcal{R}^n \to \mathcal{R}$ is the target function. The functions $g_i : \mathcal{R}^n \to \mathcal{R}, i = 1, 2, \ldots, n$ are the constraints, with constants b_i being the constraint boundaries. The target of solving optimization problems is to find $\mathbf{x}*$ to minimize f.

An optimization problem aims to find a solution that minimizes some quantity; therefore, it arises in a wide range of disciplines, such as finance, engineering, computer science, etc. For example, in portfolio management in the finance industry, an optimal solution is required to divide the given total capital into n types of investments, where x_i is the amount of capital invested in financial asset i. The target might be to maximize to the expected return or to minimize the risk. The constraints might be requiring that the smallest return be larger than a predefined value, etc.

An optimization problem can be categorized into multiple types. The general form in Eq. 4.1 contains several constraints. If there are no constraints, the problem is called an *unconstrained optimization*; otherwise, it's a constrained optimization problem. From another perspective, some optimization target is to find the global minimal point (e.g., minimize $f(x) = x^2$), while the others only need to find the optimum in a certain range (e.g., minimize $f(x) = \sin(x)$ in the range of $[0, 2\pi]$). In this chapter, and in the implemented module in Owl, we focus on the unconstrained and local optimization problems. Specifically, we have implemented one of the most important optimization methods: gradient descent.

© Liang Wang, Jianxin Zhao 2023
L. Wang and J. Zhao, *Architecture of Advanced Numerical Analysis Systems*,
https://doi.org/10.1007/978-1-4842-8853-5_4

4.1 Gradient Descent

The gradient descent method is one of the most commonly used family of iterative optimization processes. Its basic idea is to start from an initial value and then find a certain search direction along a function to decrease the value by a certain step size until it converges to a local minimum. We can thus describe the nth iteration of the descent method as follows:

1. Calculate a descent direction d.

2. Choose a step size μ.

3. Update the location: $x_{n+1} = x_n + \mu\, d$.

Repeat this process until a stopping condition is met, such as the update being smaller than a threshold. Among the descent methods, *gradient descent* is one of the most widely used algorithms to perform optimization and the most common way to optimize neural networks. Based on the preceding descent process, a gradient descent method uses the function gradient to decide its direction d and can be described as follows:

1. Calculate a descent direction $-\nabla f(x_n)$.

2. Choose a step size μ.

3. Update the location: $x_{n+1} = x_n + \mu \nabla f(x_n)$.

Here, ∇ denotes the gradient. The distance μ along a certain direction is also called the *learning rate* of this iteration. In a gradient descent process, when searching for the minimum, it always follows the direction that is against the direction represented by the negative gradient. The gradient can be calculated based on the algorithm differentiation module we have introduced in Chapter 3. That's why the whole `Optimisation` module is built on `Algodiff`.

The implementation of gradient descent according to this definition is plain enough. For example, for a certain differentiable function f that does have one global minimal point, the following simple Owl code would do:

```
module n = Dense.Ndarray.D
open Algodiff.D
```

```
let _ =
  for i = 1 to n - 1 do
    let u = grad f !x |> unpack_arr in
    x := N.(sub !x (scalar_mul alpha u))
  done;;
```

It's basically a line-to-line translation of the process described before. You should be familiar with the functions from the AD module, such as grad for calculating gradients and unpack_arr for converting an AD type ndarray into a normal one. However, there are a lot of details that should be attended to if we need to implement a robust gradient descent method, such as how the learning rate should change, how other variant methods should be incorporated, etc. Next, we will introduce several building blocks for this method and the structure of the Optimise module in Owl.

4.2 Components

The core of the Optimise module in Owl abstracts several aspects of the gradient descent method in applications: learning rate, gradient method, momentum, etc. Each of them is represented as a submodule. All computation in these modules relies on the AD module. The following code shows an outline of this optimization module. It is designed as a functor parameterized by the AD module. In this section, we introduce a part of these submodules and how they implement different methods.

```
module Make (Algodiff : Owl_algodiff_generic_sig.Sig) = struct
  module Algodiff = Algodiff
  open Algodiff

  module Learning_Rate = struct
    ...
  end

  module Gradient = struct
    ...
  end

  ...

end
```

Learning Rate

When training a machine learning model, the learning rate is arguably the most important hyperparameter that affects the training speed and quality. It specifies how much the model weight should be changed given the estimated error in each training round. A large learning rate may lead to suboptimal solutions and unstable training processes, whereas a small rate may result in a long training time. That's why choosing a proper learning rate is both crucial and challenging in model training. There exist various methods to decide the learning rate, and we have incorporated them in the Learning_rate module, as follows:

```
module Learning_Rate = struct
    type typ =
        | Adagrad    of float
        | Const      of float
        | Decay      of float * float
        | RMSprop    of float * float

    let run = function
        | Adagrad a -> fun _ _ c ->
          Maths.(_f a / sqrt (c.(0) + _f 1e-32))
        | Const a -> fun _ _ _ -> _f a
        | Decay (a, k) -> fun i _ _ ->
          Maths.(_f a / (_f 1. + (_f k * _f (float_of_int i))))
        | RMSprop (a, _)   -> fun _ _ c ->
          Maths.(_f a / sqrt (c.(0) + _f 1e-32))

    let default = function
        | Adagrad _    -> Adagrad 0.01
        | Const _      -> Const 0.001
        | Decay _      -> Decay (0.1, 0.1)
        | RMSprop _    -> RMSprop (0.001, 0.9)

    let update_ch typ g c =
      match typ with
        | Adagrad _ -> [| Maths.(c.(0) + (g * g)); c.(1) |]
        | RMSprop (_, k) -> [| Maths.(
          (_f k * c.(0)) + ((_f 1. - _f k) * g * g)); c.(1) |]
        | _ -> c
```

```
let to_string = function,
   | Adagrad a        -> Printf.sprintf "adagrad %g" a
   | Const a          -> Printf.sprintf "constant %g" a
   | Decay (a, k)     -> Printf.sprintf "decay (%g, %g)" a k
   | RMSprop (a, k) -> Printf.sprintf "rmsprop (%g, %g)" a k
end
```

This module consists of the type definitions of learning rate methods and the functions that can be applied on it. The Learning_Rate.typ consists of four different types of algorithms.[1] For each type, it specifies parameters it requires.

Let's look at how these methods are implemented to better understand the code. The Const method is the most straightforward: just using a constant learning rate value throughout the whole training process,. In typ, its only parameter is this learning rate as a float number. Next, the run function takes in a learning rate type as input and returns a function that accepts three inputs: the iteration number i, the gradient g, and the parameters used in this method c (an array of floats). This function specifies how the learning rate should be changed. In the case of the Const method, the rate does not change. So it simply returns the previous learning rate itself. Recall from Chapter 3 that _f wraps a float number into an AD scalar type. The default and to_string are helper functions. The first generates a learning rate method with default parameters, and the second prints parameter information of a given method.

The Adagrad method is a bit more complex. As the name suggests, it changes the learning rate adaptively: a larger update step size for parameters associated with infrequent features and small learning rate otherwise. Its parameter update at the t's iterate follows the following rules:

$$\theta_{t+1} = \theta_t - \mu \frac{g_t}{\sqrt{G_t} + \epsilon} \tag{4.2}$$

Here, G is the sum of the squares of the corresponding gradients g_t's up to time step t. This equation consists of two parts. The first is how the learning rate should be updated. It is specified in the run function. The following code:

```
fun _ _ c ->
  Maths.(_f a / sqrt (c.(0) + _f 1e-32))
```

---

[1] Actually, there are more learning methods implemented, e.g., Adam optimization; they are omitted here for the purpose of keeping code demonstration clear.

corresponds to $\dfrac{\mu}{\sqrt{G+\epsilon}}$. The c array contains parameters that are utilized in updating μ,

which in this case is G. The second part is how to update this parameter. It is specified in

the update_ch function. In this case, the rule is $G_t = \displaystyle\sum_{i=1}^{t} g_i^2$, or

$$G_t = G_{t-1} + g_i^2.$$

Therefore, the code is

```
[| Maths.(c.(0) + (g * g)); c.(1) |]
```

at each iteration. The second element in this array is not used, so it remains the same.

The RMSprop method, is an adaptive learning rate method proposed by Geoff Hinton. It is an extension of Adagrad. It follows the update rule in Eq. 4.2. Only that here

$$G_t = kG_{t-1} + (1-k)g_t^2 \tag{4.3}$$

Note that k is a factor that is normally set to 0.9. Therefore, the run function keeps the same; the update_ch function for RMSprop becomes

```
(_f k * c.(0)) + ((_f 1. - _f k) * g * g)
```

Compared with Adagrad, by using a decaying moving average of previous gradients, RMSprop enables forgetting early gradients and focuses on the most recently observed gradients.

To demonstrate how this seemingly simple framework can accommodate more complex methods, let's consider the implementation of the Adam optimizer [33]. Its parameters are two decaying rates β_1 and β_2. Updating its learning rate requires two values: the estimated mean m_t and uncentered variance v_t of the gradients. They are updated according to the following rules:

$$\begin{aligned} m_t &= \beta_1 m_{t-1} + (1-\beta_1)g_t \\ v_t &= \beta_2 v_{t-1} + (1-\beta_2)g_t^2 \end{aligned}$$

Accordingly, its update_ch can be implemented as

```
let update_ch typ g c =
  match typ with
  | Adam (_, b1, b2) ->
```

```
let m = Maths.((_f b1 * c.(0)) + ((_f 1. - _f b1) * g)) in
let v = Maths.((_f b2 * c.(1)) + ((_f 1. - _f b2) * g * g)) in
[| m; v |]
| ...
```

Note the meaning of c is not the same as that in the Adagrad and RMSprop methods. The next thing is to specify how to update the learning rate. Adam's update rule is

$$\theta_t = \theta_{t-1} - \mu \frac{\bar{m}_t}{\sqrt{\bar{v}_t} + \epsilon},$$ (4.4)

where

$$\bar{m}_t = \frac{m_t}{1-\beta_1^t}, \bar{v}_t = \frac{v_t}{1-\beta_2^t}.$$

Therefore, the run function of Adam returns a function that utilizes all three parameters:

```
let run = function
  | Adam (a, b1, b2) ->
    fun i g c ->
      Maths.(
        let m = c.(0) /
          (_f 1. - (_f b1 ** _f (float_of_int i))) in
        let v = c.(1) /
          (_f 1. - (_f b2 ** _f (float_of_int i))) in
        (_f a) * m / (sqrt v + _f 1e-8)
        / (g + _f 1e-32))
  | ...
```

Note the final item / (g + _f 1e-32). You might notice that this item is not in Eq. 4.4. The reason we put it here is that our framework follows this update pattern:

$$\theta_t = \theta_{t-1} - \text{run}(\mu,\ldots)g.$$

But the final g multiplication item is not in the end of Eq. 4.4. That's why we divide it back in the run function.

So far, we have introduced multiple aspects in a learning rate method, most notably run and update_cn, but we have not yet explained how they will be used in an optimization process. We will show that in the next section. For now, let's move on to another aspect of optimization: the gradient descent algorithm.

Gradient

We have provided the framework of gradient methods in Section 4.1. However, there exist many variants of gradient descent algorithms. They are included in the Gradient module. The code is shown as follows. Its structure is similar to that of Learning_rate. The typ contains all the supported gradient methods; these methods do not carry type parameters. The to_string function prints helper information for each method.

```
module Gradient = struct
    type typ =
      | GD (* classic gradient descent *)
      | CG (* Hestenes and Stiefel 1952 *)
      | CD (* Fletcher 1987 *)
      | NonlinearCG (* Fletcher and Reeves 1964 *)
      | DaiYuanCG (* Dai and Yuan 1999 *)
      | NewtonCG (* Newton conjugate gradient *)
      | Newton

    let run = function
      | GD            -> fun _ _ _ g' -> Maths.neg g'
      | CG            ->
        fun _ _ g p g' ->
          let y = Maths.(g' - g) in
          let b = Maths.(sum' (g' * y) / (sum' (p * y) + _f 1e-32)) in
          Maths.(neg g' + (b * p))
      | CD            ->
        fun _ _ g p g' ->
          let b = Maths.(l2norm_sqr' g' / sum' (neg p * g)) in
          Maths.(neg g' + (b * p))
      | NonlinearCG ->
        fun _ _ g p g' ->
```

```
    let b = Maths.(l2norm_sqr' g' / l2norm_sqr' g) in
    Maths.(neg g' + (b * p))
  | DaiYuanCG   ->
    fun _ _ g p g' ->
      let y = Maths.(g' - g) in
      let b = Maths.(l2norm_sqr' g' / sum' (p * y)) in
      Maths.(neg g' + (b * p))
  | NewtonCG    ->
    fun f w _ p g' ->
      let hv = hessianv f w p |> Maths.transpose in
      let b = Maths.(hv *@ g' / (hv *@ p)) in
      Maths.(neg g' + (p *@ b))
  | Newton      ->
    fun f w _ _ _ ->
      let g', h' = gradhessian f w in
      Maths.(neg (g' *@ inv h'))

let to_string = function
  | GD            -> "gradient descent"
  | CG            -> "conjugate gradient"
  | CD            -> "conjugate descent"
  | NonlinearCG -> "nonlinear conjugate gradient"
  | DaiYuanCG    -> "dai & yuan conjugate gradient"
  | NewtonCG     -> "newton conjugate gradient"
  | Newton       -> "newton"
end
```

The key component is the run function. Remember that the descent optimization method is all about the process:

$$x_{n+1} = x_n + \mu \, d_n,$$

which shows the exploration direction at the next step. The `run` function specifies the form of d_n. Take the classic gradient descent method as an example; the direction is just the opposite of gradient. Therefore, $d_n = -g_n$, and thus the `run` function returns another function:

```
fun _f _w _g _p g' -> Maths.neg g'
```

This function takes five parameters as inputs, and the last one is the current gradient, which is the only parameter used in this case.

Conjugate gradient descent: A problem with gradient descent is that it may perform badly on certain types of functions. For example, if a function is steep and narrow, then gradient descent will take many very small steps to reach the minimum, bouncing back and forth, even if the function is in quadratic form. This can be fixed by the *conjugate gradient* (CG) method, which is first proposed by Hestenes and Stiefel [29].

The CG method is similar to gradient descent, but the new direction at each step does not completely follow the new gradient, but is somehow conjugated to the old gradients and to all previous directions traversed. If both methods start from the same position, gradient descent would follow the direction of the descent, which could be a blunt one since this function is steep. But the conjugate method would prefer following the previous momentum a little bit. As a result, the conjugate method follows a direction in between. The new direction finds the minimum more efficiently than the gradient descent method.

The conjugate gradient descent is also a family of optimization methods. Instead of using the opposite of gradient $-\nabla f(x_n)$ as a direction, they follow the procedure in the nth iteration:

1. Calculate the steepest direction, that is, negative gradient
   $-g_n = -\nabla f(x_n)$.

2. Calculate a certain parameter β_n; this parameter varies among different conjugate gradient methods.

3. Apply the conjugate direction $d_n = -g_n + \beta\, d_{n-1}$.

4. Update the optimization process $x_n = x_{n-1} + \mu_n\, d_n$ where μ_n is the learning rate of this iteration n.

Based on this framework, we can take a look at the five parameters in the returned function:

```
fun f w g p g' -> ...
```

Here, g and p are gradient and direction vectors from the previous round; g' is the gradient of the current round. f is the function to be optimized itself, with input data w. The CG process can thus be implemented as

```
fun _f _w g p g' ->
  let b = ... in
  Maths.(neg g' + (b * p))
```

In the classic CG method:

$$\beta_n = \frac{g_n^T \left(g_n - g_{n-1} \right)}{-d_{n-1}^T \left(g_n - g_{n-1} \right)}.$$ (4.5)

Here, g_n, d_n, etc. are assumed to be vectors. Note how this parameter and the CG method framework utilize information such as gradient and direction from the previous iteration (g_{n-1} and d_{n-1}). We can implement Eq. 4.5 as

```
let b =
  let y = Maths.(g' - g) in
  Maths.(sum' (g' * y) / (sum' (p * y) + _f 1e-32))
```

It uses the sum' function to perform vector multiplication, and the extra epsilon value 1e-32 is used to make sure the denominator is not zero.

In the nonlinear conjugate method (NonlinearCG) [21]

$$\beta_n = \frac{g_n^T g_n}{g_{n-1}^T g_{n-1}}.$$

It can thus be implemented as

```
let b = Maths.(l2norm_sqr' g' / l2norm_sqr' g)
```

Here, l2norm_sqr' g calculates the square of l2 norm (or Euclidean norm) of all elements in g, which is $g^T g$.

Similarly, in the conjugate gradient method proposed by Dai and Yuan (DaiYuanCG) in [16]

$$\beta_n = -\frac{g_n^T g_n}{d_n \left(g_n - g_{n-1} \right)}.$$

The corresponding code is

```
let b =
  let y = Maths.(g' - g) in
  Maths.(l2norm_sqr' g' / sum' (p * y))
```

Newton's method is another iterative descent method to find optimal values. It follows the update sequence as shown in the following:

$$x_{n+1} = x_n - \alpha \mathbf{H}^{-1} \nabla f(x_n) \tag{4.6}$$

Here, H is the hessian of f, that is, the second-order gradient of f. The code is a direct translation of this equation:

```
fun f w _ _ _ ->
  let g', h' = gradhessian f w in
  Maths.(neg (g' *@ inv h'))
```

Here, the `Algodiff.gradhessian` function returns both gradient and hessian of function f at point w. The `*@` operator is the alias for matrix multiplication, and `inv` is the inverse of a matrix. Rather than moving only in the direction of the gradient, Newton's method combines the gradient with the second-order gradients of a function, starting from a random position and iterating until convergence. Newton's method guarantees quadratic convergence provided that f is strongly convex with Lipschitz Hessian and that the initial point x_0 is close enough to the prima x^*. Note that this method is not to be confused with the Newton method that aims to find the root of a function.

Momentum

The basic gradient descent process can be further enhanced by the *momentum* mechanism. It allows some "inertia" in choosing the optimization search direction, which utilizes previous direction information. It helps to reduce noisy gradient descent that bounces in search direction. The code of the `Momentum` module is listed as follows. Its key component is the `run` function.

```
module Momentum = struct
    type typ =
        | Standard of float
        | Nesterov of float
```

```
    | None

  let run = function
    | Standard m -> fun u u' -> Maths.((_f m * u) + u')
    | Nesterov m -> fun u u' ->
      Maths.((_f m * _f m * u) + ((_f m + _f 1.) * u'))
    | None        -> fun _ u' -> u'

  let default = function
    | Standard _ -> Standard 0.9
    | Nesterov _ -> Nesterov 0.9
    | None        -> None

  let to_string = function
    | Standard m -> Printf.sprintf "standard %g" m
    | Nesterov m -> Printf.sprintf "nesterov %g" m
    | None        -> Printf.sprintf "none"
end
```

Recall in the basic structure of gradient descent, the change of value x at the nth iteration is

$$d_n = -\mu \nabla f(x_n)$$

With momentum, this process is revised to be

$$d_n = -\mu \nabla f(x_n) + m d_{n-1}. \tag{4.7}$$

The float number m is the momentum parameter that indicates the impact of direction information in the previous iteration.

The run function in this module returns a function that takes two inputs: the previous direction u and the current direction u' (calculated using any combination of learning rate and gradient methods). Therefore, the momentum method described earlier can be simply implemented as Maths.((_f m * u) + u'). This is the standard momentum method. If we decide not to use any momentum (None), it simply returns the current direction u'.

This module also supports the Nesterov Accelerated Gradient (Nesterov) method [40]. It employs a simple change on the standard momentum in Eq. 4.7, by first applying the momentum item on the parameter itself and then calculating the gradient ∇f, before adding the momentum item again:

$$d_n = -\mu \nabla f \left(x_n + d_{n-1} m \right) + m d_{n-1}.$$

In this module, we have implemented the solution by Bengio et al.

Batch

There is one more submodule we need to mention: the Batch module. It is about how the input data are divided into chunks and then fed into a training process. From the previous introduction about gradient descent, you might assume the function accepts scalar as input. However, in many applications, we should consider applying optimization on a vector **x**. That means in calculating the gradients, we need to consider using a group of data points instead of only one.

From the perspective of calculation, there is not much difference, and we can still use all the data in calculating the gradients. However, one big application field of such an optimization method is regression or, more broadly, machine learning, where there could be millions of data points just to find the optima. We will talk about regression in Section 4.4. In practice, computing optimization with large quantities of input data can be unavailable due to the limit of hardware factors such as memory size of the computer. Therefore, optimization for such problems is often repeated for several executive rounds, each round called an *epoch*. In each epoch, the given input data are split into batches. Each batch can choose to use a batch strategy, as the run function code shown as follows:

```
module Batch = struct
  type typ =
    | Full
    | Mini        of int
    | Sample      of int
    | Stochastic
```

```
let run typ x y i =
  match typ with
  | Full       -> x, y
  | Mini c     -> Utils.get_chunk x y i c
  | Sample c   -> Utils.draw_samples x y c
  | Stochastic -> Utils.draw_samples x y 1

let batches typ x =
  match typ with
  | Full       -> 1
  | Mini c     -> Utils.sample_num x / c
  | Sample c   -> Utils.sample_num x / c
  | Stochastic -> Utils.sample_num x

let to_string = function
  | Full       -> Printf.sprintf "%s" "full"
  | Mini c     -> Printf.sprintf "mini of %i" c
  | Sample c   -> Printf.sprintf "sample of %i" c
  | Stochastic -> Printf.sprintf "%s" "stochastic"
end
```

The Full strategy uses all the provided data. The Mini c and Sample c strategies both take in c data points each time; the former chooses data sequentially, and the latter does randomly. Finally, the Stochastic method only selects one random data point from existing ones.

Checkpoint

So far, we have introduced how the learning rate, gradients, and momentum modules return functions which utilize information such as the gradient or direction of the previous iteration. But where are they stored? The answer lies in the Checkpoint module. It stores all the information during optimization for later use and saves them as files on the hard disk if necessary. Its code is shown as follows:

```
module Checkpoint = struct
  type state = {
    mutable current_batch : int;
    mutable batches_per_epoch : int;
```

```
    mutable epochs : float;
    mutable batches : int;
    mutable gs : t array array;
    mutable ps : t array array;
    mutable us : t array array;
    mutable ch : t array array array
    mutable stop : bool;
  }

  type typ =
    | Batch  of int (* default checkpoint at every specified batch
      interval *)
    | Epoch  of float (* default  *)
    | Custom of (state -> unit) (* customised checkpoint called at every
      batch *)
    | None

  ....
end
```

The state type includes fields that we have introduced so far. The ch is used in the learning rate module and contains parameters to be updated from the previous iteration. The gs is the gradient of the previous iteration, and ps is the direction of the previous iteration. Both are used in the gradient methods. The us represents the direction update of the previous iteration and is the parameter used in momentum methods. Besides storing this information, there is also the stop boolean value, which indicates optimization stops if set to true. It also contains other information, including the current iteration progress in batch, the number of batches in each epoch, and the total number of epochs to run.

The typ decides at what point the checkpoint should be executed. Batch means to checkpoint at every specified batch interval. Epoch then checkpoints at every specified epoch interval. Besides these two, the user can also build customized functions that take a state type as input to decide when the most proper time is to checkpoint for a specific application.

...

```
let init_state batches_per_epoch epochs =
  let batches = float_of_int batches_per_epoch *. epochs
    |> int_of_float in {
      current_batch = 1
    ; batches_per_epoch
    ; epochs
    ; batches
    ; stop = false
    ; gs = [| [| _f 0. |] |]
    ; ps = [| [| _f 0. |] |]
    ; us = [| [| _f 0. |] |]
    ; ch = [| [| [| _f 0.; _f 0. |] |] |]
    }

let default_checkpoint_fun save_fun =
  let file_name =
    Printf.sprintf "%s/%s.%i" (Sys.getcwd ())
      "model" (Unix.time () |> int_of_float)
  in
  Owl_log.info "checkpoint => %s" file_name;
  save_fun file_name

let to_string = function
  | Batch i  -> Printf.sprintf "per %i batches" i
  | Epoch i  -> Printf.sprintf "per %g epochs" i
  | Custom _ -> Printf.sprintf "customised f"
  | None     -> Printf.sprintf "none"
```

...

The init_state returns initial values for the different fields in a state. The users need to specify the number of epochs in optimization and the input data batches in one epoch. The default_checkpoint_fun executes a function to save certain content in a file. This save function should be defined by users. And similar to previous modules, the to_string method provides a convenient print function to show the configuration information about this module. Finally, the run function decides a suitable checkpoint interval and executes the checkpoint function, either the default one or the customized one provided by the user.

```
let run typ save_fun current_batch current_loss state =
  state.loss.(current_batch) <- primal' current_loss;
  state.stop <- state.current_batch >= state.batches;
  let interval =
    match typ with
    | Batch i  -> i
    | Epoch i  -> i *.
      float_of_int state.batches_per_epoch |> int_of_float
    | Custom _ -> 1
    | None     -> max_int
  in
  if state.current_batch mod interval = 0 &&
    state.current_batch < state.batches then (
      match typ with
      | Custom f -> f state
      | _        -> default_checkpoint_fun save_fun)
end
```

Params

The Params submodules are what brings all the other submodules together. It provides an entry point for users to access various aspects of optimization. The code is shown as follows:

```
module Params = struct
  type typ =
    { mutable epochs : float
    ; mutable batch : Batch.typ
    ; mutable gradient : Gradient.typ
    ; mutable learning_rate : Learning_Rate.typ
    ; mutable momentum : Momentum.typ
```

```
; mutable checkpoint : Checkpoint.typ
; mutable verbosity : bool
}
...
```

The Params type consists of the types of other submodules, such as Gradient.typ. It also includes some other fields such as the number of epochs and a flag verbosity to indicate if the full information of parameters should be printed out during optimization.

```
let default () =
  { epochs = 1.
  ; batch = Batch.Sample 100
  ; gradient = Gradient.GD
  ; learning_rate = Learning_Rate.(default (Const 0.))
  ; momentum = Momentum.None
  ; checkpoint = Checkpoint.None
  ; verbosity = true
  }

let config ?batch ?gradient ?learning_rate
    ?momentum ?checkpoint ?verbosity epochs
  =
  let p = default () in
  (match batch with
  | Some x -> p.batch <- x
  | None    -> ());
  (match gradient with
  | Some x -> p.gradient <- x
  | None    -> ());
  (match learning_rate with
  | Some x -> p.learning_rate <- x
  | None    -> ());
  (match momentum with
  | Some x -> p.momentum <- x
  | None    -> ());
```

```
    (match checkpoint with
    | Some x -> p.checkpoint <- x
    | None    -> ());
    (match verbosity with
    | Some x -> p.verbosity <- x
    | None    -> ());
    p.epochs <- epochs;
    p

  let to_string p =
    Printf.sprintf "--- Training config\n"
    ^ Printf.sprintf "epochs: %g\n" p.epochs
    ^ Printf.sprintf "batch: %s\n" (Batch.to_string p.batch)
    ^ Printf.sprintf "method: %s\n" (Gradient.to_string p.gradient)
    ^ Printf.sprintf
        "learning rate: %s\n"
        (Learning_Rate.to_string p.learning_rate)
    ^ Printf.sprintf "momentum: %s\n" (Momentum.to_string p.momentum)
    ^ Printf.sprintf "checkpoint: %s\n"
      (Checkpoint.to_string p.checkpoint)
    ^ Printf.sprintf
        "verbosity: %s\n"
        (if p.verbosity then "true" else "false")
    ^ "---"
end
```

The other three functions are straightforward. default assigns default values to each parameter, config sets parameter values using the given input, and to_string prints existing values.

4.3 Gradient Descent Implementation

Putting all the aforementioned submodules together, we can now turn to the implementation of a robust gradient descent optimization method. In the Optimise module, we implement the minimise_fun, and we will explain its code as follows:

```
let minimise_fun params f x =
  let open Params in
  let grad_fun = Gradient.run params.gradient in
  let rate_fun = Learning_Rate.run params.learning_rate in
  let momt_fun = Momentum.run params.momentum in
  let upch_fun = Learning_Rate.update_ch params.learning_rate in
  let chkp_fun = Checkpoint.run params.checkpoint in
  let optz_fun = f in
  ...
```

The function accepts three inputs: the function f, the initial input x, and the optimization parameter params. It starts by defining the run function from various submodules.

```
let iterate xi =
  let loss, g = grad' optz_fun xi in
  loss |> primal', g, optz_fun
in
...
```

iterate defines operations in the *i*th iteration. It utilizes the Algodiff module to compute the primal value loss of evaluating optz_fun at point xi and the corresponding gradient g at that point.

```
let state = Checkpoint.init_state 1 params.epochs
let x = ref x in
while Checkpoint.(state.stop = false) do
  ...
done;
state, !x
```

The preceding code shows the outline of the optimization procedure. First, it initializes a new state of the optimization process. Here, we set it to one batch per epoch. Next, the code keeps updating the state during the body of the while loop until the stop status is set to true. The optimization result x and state are finally returned. The state contains various historical information as we have explained. Each iteration of the while loop contains the following steps:

```
let loss', g', optz' = iterate !x in
chkp_fun (fun _ -> ())
  Checkpoint.(state.current_batch) loss' state;
```

First, we execute `iterate` to get gradients. We can define the checkpoint of the current progress; here, we provide an empty save function, which means no need to save the current state into the file.

```
let p' = Checkpoint.(grad_fun optz' !x
  state.gs.(0).(0) state.ps.(0).(0) g') in
Checkpoint.(state.ch.(0).(0)
  <- upch_fun g' state.ch.(0).(0));
```

Next, we calculate the gradient descent direction p' using grad_fun, based on gradient g'. Also, the learning rate parameter ch should be updated.

```
let u' =
  Checkpoint.(Maths.(p' * rate_fun
    state.current_batch g' state.ch.(0).(0)))
  in
let u' = momt_fun Checkpoint.(state.us.(0).(0)) u' in
```

Then, the optimization direction is adjusted, first based on the learning rate and then on momentum.

```
x := Maths.(!x + u') |> primal';
```

The optimal value is then updated according to the direction u'.

```
(if params.momentum <> Momentum.None then
  Checkpoint.(state.us.(0).(0) <- u'));
Checkpoint.(state.gs.(0).(0) <- g');
Checkpoint.(state.ps.(0).(0) <- p');
Checkpoint.(state.current_batch <- state.current_batch + 1);
```

Finally, the values calculated in this iteration, such as the gradients, direction, etc., are saved in the state for future use. That's all for one iteration. Let's look at one example of optimization using gradient descent. Here, we use Himmelblau's function; it is often used as a performance test for optimization problems. The function contains two inputs and is defined as in Eq. 4.8.

$$f(x,y)=\left(x^2+y-11\right)^2+\left(x+y^2-7\right)^2. \qquad (4.8)$$

Its definition can be expressed using Owl code as

```
open Algodiff.D
module N = Dense.Ndarray.D

let himmelblau a =
  let x = Mat.get a 0 0 in
  let y = Mat.get a 0 1 in
  Maths.(x ** (F 2.) + y - (F 11.) ** (F 2.) +
    (x + y ** (F 2.) - (F 7.)) ** (F 2.) |> sum')
```

First, let's look at what the code would look like without using the Optimise module. Let's apply the gradient descent method according to its definition in Section 4.1.

```
let v = N.of_array [|-2.; 0.|] [|1; 2|]
let traj = ref (N.copy v)
let a = ref v
let eta = 0.0001
let n = 2000;;
```

Here, we use an initial starting point [-2., 0.]. The step size eta is set to 0.0001, and the iteration number is 2000. Then we can perform the iterative descent process.

```
let _ =
  for i = 1 to n - 1 do
  let u = grad himmelblau (Arr !a) |> unpack_arr in
  a := N.(sub !a (scalar_mul eta u));
  traj := N.concatenate [|!traj; (N.copy !a)|]
  done;;
```

We apply the grad method in the Algodiff module to the Himmelblau function iteratively, and the updated data a is stored in the traj array. Utilizing the Plot module in Owl, we can visualize this function and the optimization trajectory using the following code:

```
let plot () =
  let a, b = Dense.Matrix.D.meshgrid (-4.) 4. (-4.) 4. 50 50 in
  let c = N.(add
    (sub_scalar (add (pow_scalar a 2.) b) 11.)
    (pow_scalar (sub_scalar (add a (pow_scalar b 2.)) 7.) 2.)
  ) in
  let h = Plot.create ~m:1 ~n:2 "plot_himm.pdf" in
  Plot.subplot h 0 0;
  Plot.(mesh ~h ~spec:[ NoMagColor ] a b c);

  Plot.subplot h 0 1;
  Plot.contour ~h a b c;
  let vx = N.get_slice [[]; [0]] !traj in
  let vy = N.get_slice [[]; [1]] !traj in
  Plot.plot ~h vx vy;
  Plot.output h
```

And the generated figures are shown in Figure 4-1.

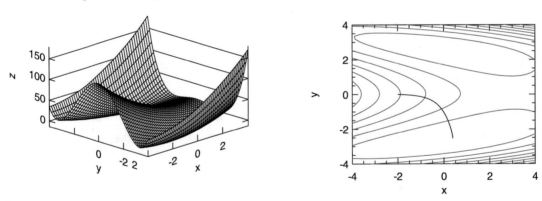

Figure 4-1. *Optimization process of gradient descent on the multimodal Himmelblau function*

To solve the same problem, we can also use the `minimise_fun` function introduced in the previous section. First, we set up the parameters:

```
let p = Owl_optimise.D.Params.default ()
let _ = p.epochs <- 10.
let _ = p.gradient <- Owl_optimise.D.Gradient.GD;;
```

It suffices to simply set the iteration limit epochs to something like 10 or 20 iterations. Then we set the gradient method to be the classic gradient descent and then execute the code, starting from the same initial values:

```
let init_value = N.of_array [|-2.;0.|] [|1;2|] |> pack_arr
let _ = Owl_optimise.D.minimise_fun p himmelblau init_value;;
```

This function outputs execution logs to track the intermediate results, looking in part like the following. It shows how the function value, starting from 2926 at the initial point, is quickly reduced to about 2.5 within only 10 steps using gradient descent. It shows the efficiency of the gradient descent method in finding optima.

```
...
10:46:49.805 INFO : T: 00s | E: 1.0/10 | B: 1/10 | L: 2026.000
10:46:49.806 INFO : T: 00s | E: 2.0/10 | B: 2/10 | L: 476.1010
10:46:49.807 INFO : T: 00s | E: 3.0/10 | B: 3/10 | L: 63.83614
10:46:49.807 INFO : T: 00s | E: 4.0/10 | B: 4/10 | L: 37.77679
10:46:49.808 INFO : T: 00s | E: 5.0/10 | B: 5/10 | L: 21.39686
10:46:49.809 INFO : T: 00s | E: 6.0/10 | B: 6/10 | L: 11.74234
10:46:49.809 INFO : T: 00s | E: 7.0/10 | B: 7/10 | L: 6.567733
10:46:49.809 INFO : T: 00s | E: 8.0/10 | B: 8/10 | L: 4.085909
10:46:49.810 INFO : T: 00s | E: 9.0/10 | B: 9/10 | L: 3.016714
10:46:49.810 INFO : T: 00s | E: 10.0/10 | B: 10/10 | L: 2.5943
...
```

4.4 Regression

In this section, we introduce a broad area that heavily relies on optimization: *regression*. Regression is an important topic in statistical modeling and machine learning. It's about modeling problems which include one or more variables (also called "features" or "predictors") and require us to make predictions of another variable ("output variable") based on previous values of the predictors. Regression analysis includes a wide range of models, from linear regression to isotonic regression, each with different theoretical backgrounds and applications. In this section, we use the most widely used linear regression as an example to demonstrate how optimization plays a key part in solving regression problems.

Linear Regression

Linear regression models the relationship between input features and the output variable with a linear model. It is the most widely used regression model. Without loss of generality, let's look at an example with a single variable in the model. Such a linear regression problem can be informally stated as follows. Suppose we have a series of (x, y) data points:

```
-----------------------------
|x|  5.16 |  7.51 |  6.53 |  ...
-----------------------------
|y|  0.36 |  5.84 |  16.9 |  ...
-----------------------------
```

Given that the relationship between these two quantities is $y \approx h_{\theta(x)}$, where $h_\theta(x) = \theta_0 + \theta_1 x$, can we find out the θ_0 and θ_1 values that can fit the observed data points as closely as possible? This problem can be further formalized later. Denote the list of x's and y's as two vectors $\mathbf{x}$ and $\mathbf{y}$. Suppose we have a function C that measures the distances between $\mathbf{x}$ and $\mathbf{y}$: $C_\theta(\mathbf{x}, \mathbf{y})$. The target is to find suitable parameters θ that minimize the distance. That's where optimization comes to help.

Loss

So the next question is: How to represent this distance mathematically? One good choice is to use the Euclidean distance. That means the target is to minimize function:

$$C_\theta\left(\mathbf{x},\mathbf{y}\right)=\frac{1}{2n}\sum_{i=1}^{n}\left(h_\theta\left(x^{(i)}\right)-y^{(i)}\right)^2 \tag{4.9}$$

Here, $x^{(i)}$ indicates the ith element in the vector $\mathbf{x}$. The factor $\frac{1}{2n}$ is used to normalize the distance. Other forms of distance can also be applied here. Due to its importance, this distance is called the `loss` and abstracted as the `Loss` submodule in the optimization module. Its code is shown as follows:

```
module Loss = struct
  type typ =
    | Hinge
    | L1norm
```

```
  | L2norm
  | Quadratic
  | Cross_entropy
  | Custom          of (t -> t -> t)

let run typ y y' =
  match typ with
  | Hinge          -> Maths.(sum' (max2 (_f 0.) (_f 1. - (y * y'))))
  | L1norm         -> Maths.(l1norm' (y - y'))
  | L2norm         -> Maths.(l2norm' (y - y'))
  | Quadratic      -> Maths.(l2norm_sqr' (y - y'))
  | Cross_entropy  -> Maths.(cross_entropy y y')
  | Custom f       -> f y y'

...
end
```

It contains several methods to calculate the distance, or loss, between two values y and y'. What we have described is the Quadratic method. It also supports the l1 or l2

norm: $\sum_i \left| x^{(i)} - y^{(i)} \right|$ and $\sqrt{\sum_i \left(x^{(i)} - y^{(i)} \right)^2}$. The cross-entropy measures the performance

of a classification model, the output of which is a probability value between 0 and 1. It is

calculated as $-\sum_i x^{(i)} \log\left(y^{(i)} \right)$. The cross-entropy loss is most commonly used in

training neural networks, as we will show in Chapter 5.

Implementation of Linear Regression

In the source code of Owl, the owl_regression_generic.ml file lists all several regression methods, and they are all based on a core linear regression implementation. This function optimizes parameters w and b in a general regression problem: minimize $l_{w,b}(x^T w + b - y)$. Here, each data point x can be a vector of the same length as T, since there can be more parameters than that shown in Eq. 4.9. The code is listed as follows:

```
module Make (Optimise : Owl_optimise_generic_sig.Sig) = struct
  module Optimise = Optimise
  open Optimise
  open Optimise.Algodiff
```

```
let _linear_reg bias params x y =
  let s = A.shape x in
  let l, m = s.(0), s.(1) in
  let n = A.col_num y in
  let o = if bias = true then m + 1 else m in
  let x = if bias = true then A.concatenate
    ~axis:1 [| x; A.ones [| l; 1 |] |] else x in

  let r = 1. /. float_of_int o in
  let p = Arr A.(uniform ~a:(float_to_elt
    (-.r)) ~b:(float_to_elt r) [| o; n |]) in
  ...

end
```

The regression module is a functor that is parameterized by the Optimise module. The _linear_reg function takes in the x and y values and the optimization parameters as input. The argument bias is a boolean flag that indicates if the b parameter should be trained. This bias is the θ_0 parameter we have seen, which does not multiply with x. If we are to include it in the optimization, the shape of parameters should be changed accordingly, as shown in the code. Here, p is a randomly generated initial parameter matrix.

```
let f w x =
  let w = Mat.reshape o n w in
  Maths.(x *@ w) in
```

f is the function to minimize. It represents $xw + b$ using a single matrix multiplication.

```
let w =
  minimise_weight params f (Maths.flatten p) (Arr x) (Arr y)
  |> snd
  |> Mat.reshape o n
  |> unpack_arr
in
match bias with
```

```
  | true  -> A.split ~axis:0 [| m; 1 |] w
  | false -> [| w |]

  ...
end
```

The core step of this regression function is to apply optimization on the function f using the given parameters, with proper shape manipulation. If the bias is included in the optimization target, the returned result is split into two parts, first being *w* and second being *b*.

Note that we have introduced `minimise_fun` for optimization, but here it uses the `minimise_weight`. These two functions are actually very similar in implementation, but with one key difference. In `minimise_fun f x`, it keeps calculating gradients with regard to input x and changes the x accordingly until it reaches a point that minimizes $f(x)$. In `minimise_weight f w x` though, it keeps calculating gradients regarding the function's own parameter w and changes it accordingly until it reaches a point that minimizes $f_w(x)$. The input data x stays the same in each round of optimization.

Based on this function, the linear regression can be implemented by choosing suitable optimization parameters:

```
let ols ?(i = false) x y =
  let params =
    Params.config
      ~batch:Batch.Full
      ~learning_rate:(Learning_Rate.Adagrad 1.)
      ~gradient:Gradient.GD
      ~loss:Loss.Quadratic
      ~verbosity:false
      ~stopping:(Stopping.Const 1e-16)
      100.
  in
  _linear_reg i params x y
```

In linear regression, we utilize all the input data in one iteration or epoch (`Full` batch mode). We use the Adagrad learning method, classic gradient descent, and the Euclidean distance as the loss function. The optimization lasts 100 iterations until the loss value is smaller than `1e-16`. The `Stopping` is a helper module in `optimise` that accepts a threshold, so that the optimization process can exit early.

Other Types of Regression

Even though linear regression is powerful and widely used, the linear model cannot fit all problems. A lot of data follow other patterns than a linear one. For example, sometimes the relationship between the feature x and the output variable can be modeled as an nth degree polynomial with regard to feature x:

$$h_\theta(x) = \theta_0 + \theta_1 x + \theta_2 x^2 + \theta_3 x^3 \dots \tag{4.10}$$

This is called a *polynomial* regression. Owl provides a function `poly` in the `Regression` module to get the model parameter. The first two parameters are still x and y, and the third parameter limits the order of the polynomial model. Its implementation can also be concisely expressed with `_linear_reg`:

```
let poly x y n =
  let z =
    Array.init (n + 1) (fun i -> A.(pow_scalar x
      (float_of_int i |> float_to_elt)))
  in
  let x = A.concatenate ~axis:1 z in
  let params =
    Params.config
      ~batch:Batch.Full
      ~learning_rate:(Learning_Rate.Const 1.)
      ~gradient:Gradient.Newton
      ~loss:Loss.Quadratic
      ~verbosity:false
      ~stopping:(Stopping.Const 1e-16)
      100.
  in
  (_linear_reg false params x y).(0)
```

The key is to first process the data, so that each data point x can be projected to a series of new features z, so that $z_i = x^i$. Eq. 4.10 then becomes a multivariable linear regression:

$$h_\theta(z) = \theta_0 + \theta_1 z_1 + \theta_2 z_2 + \theta_3 z_3 \dots$$

Another important type of regression is *logistic regression*, where the data y contain integers that indicate different classes of data, instead of real numbers. Therefore, it is most suitable for classification tasks, such as "age group," "nationality," etc. Logistic regression replaces its target optimization function to be

$$C_\theta(\mathbf{x},\mathbf{y}) = \frac{1}{m}\sum_{i=1}^{m} g\left(h_\theta\left(x^{(i)}\right), y^{(i)}\right),$$ (4.11)

where m is the total number of data points in input data x and y; the function g is defined as

$$g\left(h_\theta(x), y\right) = \begin{cases} -\log\left(h_\theta(x)\right), & \text{if } y = 1 \\ -\log\left(1 - h_\theta(x)\right), & \text{if } y = 0 \end{cases}$$ (4.12)

The logistic gradient can be implemented by using the cross-entropy loss function:

```
let logistic ?(i = false) x y =
  let params =
    Params.config
      ~batch:Batch.Full
      ~learning_rate:(Learning_Rate.Adagrad 1.)
      ~gradient:Gradient.GD
      ~loss:Loss.Cross_entropy
      ~verbosity:false
      ~stopping:(Stopping.Const 1e-16)
      1000.
  in
  _linear_reg i params x y
```

Regularization

There is one thing we need to understand: regression is more than just optimization after all. Its purpose is to create a model that fits the given data, and all too often, this model should be used to predict the output of future input. Therefore, if a model fits the given data *too well*, it may lose generality for future data. That's where the idea of *regularization* comes in. This technique prevents a model from being tuned too closely to a particular dataset and thus may fail to predict future observations well.

Think about the polynomial regression. The regularization technique favors simple and low-order models. It modifies the optimization target function to penalize high-order parameters, so that the large parameter values lead to higher cost. Therefore, by minimizing the target function, we keep the unwanted parameters relatively small. This can be implemented by adding an extra term at the end of the original target function.

Owl supports multiple types of such regularization terms in the `Regularisation` submodule, which also belongs to the `Optimiser` module. Its core function `run` is shown as follows:

```
let run typ x =
  match typ with
  | L1norm a -> Maths.(_f a * l1norm' x)
  | L2norm a -> Maths.(_f a * l2norm' x)
  | Elastic_net (a, b) ->
    Maths.((_f a * l1norm' x) + (_f b * l2norm' x))
  | None -> _f 0.
```

The `L2norm` regularization function adds the L2 norm of θ as the penalty term: $\lambda \sum \theta^2$. The `L1norm` cost function is similar, adding the L1 norm or absolute value of the parameter as penalty: $\lambda \sum |\theta|$. This difference means that `L1norm` permits coefficients to be zero, very useful for feature selection. Regressions using these two regularization techniques are sometimes called Ridge and Lasso regressions. The `Elastic_net` method combines the penalties of the previous two:

$$\lambda \left(\frac{1-a}{2} \sum \theta^2 + a \sum |\theta| \right),$$

where a is a hyperparameter balancing between the former two. This method aims to make feature selection less dependent on the input data.

We can create a new polynomial regression with regularization by simply changing the optimization parameter to the following values:

```
Params.config
  ~batch:Batch.Full
  ~learning_rate:(Learning_Rate.Const 1.)
  ~gradient:Gradient.Newton
  ~loss:Loss.Quadratic
```

```
~regularisation:(Regularisation.L2norm 0.5)
~verbosity:false
~stopping:(Stopping.Const 1e-16)
100.
```

4.5 Summary

In this chapter, we introduced optimization and its implementation in Owl. Focusing on gradient descent, one of the most widely used optimization methods, we introduced various aspects, such as the gradient method, learning rate, momentum, etc. Together they provide a powerful and robust implementation. As an important example, we further introduced regression, a machine learning technique that heavily relies on optimization. We showed how various regression methods can be built efficiently using the optimization module.

CHAPTER 5

Deep Neural Networks

There are many articles teaching people how to build intelligent applications using different frameworks such as TensorFlow, PyTorch, etc. However, except those very professional research papers, very few articles can give us a comprehensive understanding on how to develop such frameworks. In this chapter, rather than just "casting spells," we focus on explaining how to make the magic work in the first place. We will dissect the deep neural network module in Owl, then demonstrate how to assemble different building blocks to build a working framework. Owl's neural network module is a full-featured DNN framework. You can define a neural network in a very compact and elegant way thanks to OCaml's expressiveness. The DNN applications built on Owl can achieve state-of-the-art performance.

5.1 Module Architecture

To explain in layman's terms, you can imagine a neural network as a communication network where data flow from one node to another node without loops. Nodes are referred to as neurons. Every time data pass a neuron, it will be processed in different ways depending on the type of a neuron. The link between neurons represents nonlinear transformation of the data. Neurons can be wired in various ways to exhibit different architectures which specialize in different tasks. During the training phase, data can be fed into a neural network to let it form the knowledge of certain patterns. During the inference phase, the neural network can apply previously learned knowledge to the input data.

A DNN framework is built to let us define the network structure and orchestrate its learning and inference tasks. The framework is a complicated artifact containing lots of technologies. However, from the high-level system perspective, there is only a limited amount of core functions which a framework must implement. Let us take a look at the key functionalities required by Owl's neural network module:

- The **neuron** module defines the functionality of a specific type of neuron. Even though a deep neural network can be directly and equivalently expressed in a computation graph, the graph is often very complicated. The definition is difficult to manually construct and hard to maintain. Using high-level neurons which are packaged with complicated internal processing logic can significantly simplify the network definition.

- The **network** module allows us to define the graph structure of a neural network and provides a set of functions to manipulate the network and orchestrate the training and inference. This module is often the entry point to the system for the majority of users.

- The **optimization** module is the driver of training a neural network. The module allows us to configure and orchestrate the process of training, as well as control how data should be fed into the system. We have introduced this module in Chapter 4.

- The **algorithmic differentiation** module is the underlying technology for optimization. The module provides powerful machinery to automatically calculate derivatives for any given functions, so that other modules can make use of these derivatives for various optimization purposes. We have introduced this module in detail in Chapter 3.

- The **neural network compiler** module optimizes the performance of a neural network by optimizing its underlying computation graphs. The module relies heavily on Owl's computation graph module, which we will introduce in Chapter 6.

In the rest of this chapter, we will examine internal mechanisms of these modules. The optimization and algorithmic differentiation modules are not DNN specific, we will skip them for now; their implementations have been covered in detail in the previous chapters.

5.2 Neurons

Neurons are implemented as modules. Each type of neuron corresponds to a specific module. These modules share many common functions such as mktag, mkpar, update, etc., but their implementation might slightly differ. Every neuron has its own neuron_typ which specifies the shape of the neuron's input and output.

```
module Linear : sig
  type neuron_typ =
    { mutable w : t
    ; mutable b : t
    ; mutable init_typ : Init.typ
    ; mutable in_shape : int array
    ; mutable out_shape : int array
    }

  val create : ?inputs:int -> int -> Init.typ -> neuron_typ
  val connect : int array -> neuron_typ -> unit
  val init : neuron_typ -> unit
  val reset : neuron_typ -> unit
  val mktag : int -> neuron_typ -> unit
  val mkpar : neuron_typ -> t array
  val mkpri : neuron_typ -> t array
  val mkadj : neuron_typ -> t array
  val update : neuron_typ -> t array -> unit
  val copy : neuron_typ -> neuron_typ
  val run : t -> neuron_typ -> t
  val to_string : neuron_typ -> string
  val to_name : unit -> string
end
```

The neuron_typ also includes all the parameters associated with this neuron. For example, the preceding code presents the signature of the Linear neuron which performs $wx + b$ for input x. As you can see, fields x and b are used for storing the weight and bias of this linear function.

Core Functions

The record type neuron_typ is created by calling the create function when constructing the network.

```
let create ?inputs o init_typ =
  let in_shape =
    match inputs with
    | Some i -> [| i |]
    | None   -> [| 0 |]
  in
  { w = Mat.empty 0 0
  ; b = Mat.empty 0 0
  ; init_typ
  ; in_shape
  ; out_shape = [| o |]
  }
```

The parameters are created, but their values need to be initialized in the init function. The bias parameter is set to zero, while the initialization of weight depends on init_typ.

```
let init l =
  let m = l.in_shape.(0) in
  let n = l.out_shape.(0) in
  l.w <- Init.run l.init_typ [| m; n |] l.w;
  l.b <- Mat.zeros 1 n
```

How the weights are initialized matters a lot in the training. If weights are not initialized properly, it takes much longer to train the network. In the worse case, the training may fail to converge. The Init module provides various ways to initialize weights, specified by different type constructors. Some initialization methods require extra parameters. For example, if we want to randomize the weight with Gaussian distribution, we need to specify the mean and variance. As discussed by X. Glorot in [24], the initialization method has a nontrivial impact on model training performance. Besides those supported here, users can also use Custom to implement their own initialization methods.

```
module Init = struct
  type typ =
    | Uniform        of float * float
    | Gaussian       of float * float
    | Standard
    | Tanh
    | GlorotNormal
    | GlorotUniform
    | LecunNormal
    | Custom         of (int array -> t)
end
```

When a neuron is added to the network, the connect function is called to validate that the input shape is consistent with the output shape.

```
let connect out_shape l =
  assert (Array.(length out_shape = length l.in_shape));
  l.in_shape.(0) <- out_shape.(0)
```

The following functions are used to retrieve the parameters and their corresponding primal and adjoint values. These functions are mainly used in the training phase. When the parameters need to be updated during the training, the optimization engine can call the update function to do the job.

```
let mkpar l = [| l.w; l.b |]
```

```
let mkpri l = [| primal l.w; primal l.b |]
```

```
let mkadj l = [| adjval l.w; adjval l.b |]
```

```
let update l u =
  l.w <- u.(0) |> primal';
  l.b <- u.(1) |> primal'
```

The run function is the most important one in the module. This function defines how the input data should be processed and is called by the network during the evaluation. Let us look at the run function of the linear neuron. The function is so simple and contains only one line of code which calculates exactly $wx + b$.

```
let run x l = Maths.((x *@ l.w) + l.b)
```

Most neurons' run functions are just a one-liner; the simplicity is because Owl has implemented a very comprehensive set of numerical functions.

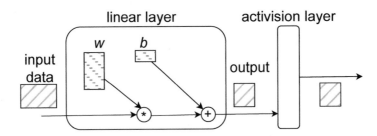

Figure 5-1. *Illustration of a linear layer and an activation layer in a neural network*

Activation Module

One reason we can pile up even just linear neurons to construct a deep neural network is its property of *nonlinearity*, which is introduced by activation neurons. Nonlinearity is a useful property in our models as most real-world data demonstrate nonlinear features. Without nonlinearity, all the linear neurons can be reduced to just one matrix. Activation functions are aggregated in one module called Activation. Similar to other neuron modules, the Activation also has neuron_typ and many similar functions.

```
module Activation = struct
  type typ =
    | Elu (* Exponential linear unit *)
    | Relu (* Rectified linear unit *)
    | Sigmoid (* Element-wise sigmoid *)
    | HardSigmoid (* Linear approximation of sigmoid *)
    | Softmax of int (* Softmax along specified axis *)
    | Softplus (* Element-wise softplus *)
    | Softsign (* Element-wise softsign *)
    | Tanh (* Element-wise tanh *)
    | Relu6 (* Element-wise relu6 *)
    | LeakyRelu of float (* Leaky version of a Rectified Linear Unit *)
    | TRelu of float (* Thresholded Rectified Linear Unit *)
    | Custom of (t -> t) (* Element-wise customised activation *)
    | None
```

```
type neuron_typ =
  { mutable activation : typ
  ; mutable in_shape : int array
  ; mutable out_shape : int array
  }
  ...
end
```

Currently, there are 12 activation functions implemented in the module. We need to choose a proper activation function for the output layers based on the type of prediction problem that is to be solved. For example, ReLU is the most commonly used for hidden layers. To visualize what we have introduced so far, Figure 5-1 illustrates a linear layer and an activation layer, one common combination in many neural network architectures.

5.3 Networks

Essentially, a neural network is a computation graph. Nodes represent neurons which aggregate more complicated data processing logic than nodes in a vanilla computation graph. The following code presents the type definition of the node. A node can have a name for reference. The prev and next fields are used for linking to ancestors and descendants, respectively. The output field is used to store the output of the computation.

The node per se does not contain any data processing logic. Rather, the node refers to the neuron which implements actual numerical operations on the data. The motivation of this design is to separate the mechanism of a network and the logic of neurons. The network field refers to the network that the current node belongs to. Note that the network structure is not necessarily the same in training and inference phases. Some nodes may be dropped during the inference phase, such as dropout. The train field is used for specifying whether a node is only for training purposes.

```
type node =
  { mutable name : string
  ; mutable prev : node array
  ; mutable next : node array
  ; mutable neuron : neuron
```

```
; mutable output : t option
; mutable network : network
; mutable train : bool
}
```

A network can be constructed by wiring up nodes. Looking at the type definition, we can see that a neural network can be identified by a unique id nnid. The size field is used to track the number of nodes in a network. The roots field refers to the data inputs, while the outputs refers to the outputs of a network. The topo is a list of all nodes sorted in topological order; it can be used for iterating nodes when evaluating the network.

```
and network =
  { mutable nnid : string
  ; mutable size : int
  ; mutable roots : node array
  ; mutable outputs : node array
  ; mutable topo : node array
  }
```

As we can see, these type definitions are similar to computation graphs. Even though they contain some specific neural network–related fields, the type definitions are not more complicated than a general-purpose computation graph.

To build up networks, most of the time we use functions that build a node and connect it to an existing node stack. For example:

```
let conv2d ?name ?(padding = SAME) ?(init_typ = Init.Tanh)
      ?act_typ kernel stride input_node =
    let neuron = Conv2D (Conv2D.create padding kernel stride init_typ) in
    let nn = get_network input_node in
    let n = make_node ?name [|||] [|||] neuron None nn in
    add_node ?act_typ nn [| input_node |] n
```

This function first creates a Conv2D neuron with various parameters and wraps it into a node using the make_node function. Then we connect n to its parent nodes using the add_node function. This step uses the connect function of the neuron and also updates the child's input and output shape during connection. With the network graph APIs, we can write concise code to build up a network, such as

```
open Owl
open Neural.S
open Neural.S.Graph

let make_network input_shape =
  input input_shape
  |> conv2d [|1;1;1;6|] [|1;1|] ~act_typ:Activation.Relu
  |> max_pool2d [|2;2|] [|2;2|]
  |> conv2d [|5;5;6;16|] [|1;1|] ~act_typ:Activation.Relu
  |> max_pool2d [|2;2|] [|2;2|]
  |> fully_connected 120 ~act_typ:Activation.Relu
  |> linear 84  ~act_typ:Activation.Relu
  |> linear 10 ~act_typ:Activation.(Softmax 1)
  |> get_network
```

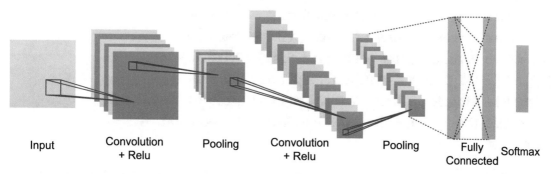

Figure 5-2. *Structure of a basic neural network*

The network definition always starts with an input layer and ends with the get_ network function which finalizes and returns the constructed network. We can also see the shape of the data, and the parameters will be inferred later as long as the input_ shape is determined. We only need to provide the data shape in the input node, and the network can automatically infer the shape in the other nodes.

We have already covered most elements to build up a neural network. For example, Figure 5-2 shows the structure of a basic LeNet-like neural network, combining the convolution layer, pooling layer, linear layer, activation layer, etc. This network is simple yet powerful, perfectly capable of performing the handwritten digit recognition task accurately. But to do that, the network should first be *trained.*

5.4 Training

Training is a complicated, time-consuming, and computation-intensive process. There are many parameters to configure different components in a neural network framework to control the process. The following functor definition can give us a good understanding about what needs to be configured. Fortunately, the Optimise module does all the heavy-lifting job; it implements several engines for different optimization tasks.

```
module Flatten (Graph : Owl_neural_graph_sig.Sig) = struct
  module Graph = Graph

  ...

  module Params = Graph.Neuron.Optimise.Params
  module Batch = Graph.Neuron.Optimise.Batch
  module Learning_Rate = Graph.Neuron.Optimise.Learning_Rate
  module Loss = Graph.Neuron.Optimise.Loss
  module Gradient = Graph.Neuron.Optimise.Gradient
  module Momentum = Graph.Neuron.Optimise.Momentum
  module Regularisation = Graph.Neuron.Optimise.Regularisation
  module Clipping = Graph.Neuron.Optimise.Clipping
  module Stopping = Graph.Neuron.Optimise.Stopping
  module Checkpoint = Graph.Neuron.Optimise.Checkpoint
end
```

We have already introduced these optimization modules in Chapter 4. The main logic of training is encoded in the train_generic function. In addition to the network to be trained nn, inputs x, and labeled data y, the function also accepts optional parameters like state if we want to resume previous training.

```
let train_generic ?state ?params ?(init_model = true) nn x y =
  if init_model = true then init nn;
  let f = forward nn in
  let b = backward nn in
  let u = update nn in
  let s = save nn in
```

```
let p =
  match params with
  | Some p -> p
  | None    -> Optimise.Params.default ()
in
Optimise.minimise_network ?state p f b u s x y
```

We need to specify four important functions: the function for forward evaluation, the function for backward propagation, the function for updating the weights, and the function for saving the network. These four functions are passed as parameters to the `minimise_network` function which is the engine specifically for optimizing neural networks as a function. We have introduced `minimise_fun` in Chapter 4 and used it to find an optimal x^* to minimize $f(x)$. The `minimise_network` function works similarly and is also implemented similarly, with the exception of one subtle difference. Instead of input x, this function aims to find optimal θ^* to minimize $f_\theta(x)$ for a given input x. In the case of optimizing a neural network, θ indicates the weight parameters.

Forward and Backward Pass

Evaluating a neural network can be done in two directions. The direction from inputs to outputs is referred to as *forward pass*, while the opposite direction from outputs to inputs is *backward pass*. The inference only requires a forward pass, but the training requires both a forward and a backward pass in many iterations. The `forward` function has only two steps. The first call to `mktag` is a necessary step required by the algorithmic differentiation, so that we can use AD to calculate derivatives in the following backward pass. For inference, this step is not necessary. The `run` function pushes the data x into network nn and iterates through all the neurons' calculations. `mkpar nn` returns all the parameters of the network, for example, weights.

```
let forward nn x =
  mktag (tag ()) nn;
  run x nn, mkpar nn
```

The core logic of the `run` function is iterating all the neurons in a topological order. For each neuron, the inputs are collected from its ancestors' outputs first, then the neuron's activation function is triggered to process the inputs. The neuron's output is saved in its hosting node. Finally, the output of the whole network is collected and returned.

```
let run x nn =
  Array.iter
    (fun n ->
      (* collect the inputs from parents' output *)
      let input =
        match n.neuron with
        | Input _ -> [| x |]
        | _       -> collect_output n.prev
      in
      (* process the current neuron, save output *)
      let output = run input n.neuron in
      n.output <- Some output)
    nn.topo;
  (* collect the final output from the tail *)
  let sink = [| nn.topo.(Array.length nn.topo - 1) |] in
  (collect_output sink).(0)
```

A backward pass is much more complicated than a forward pass, even though the code in the backward function looks as simple as the forward. The actual complexity is hidden in the reverse_prop which is the core function in the AD module. The purpose of the backward pass is to propagate the errors backward from the output to inputs. By doing so, the neurons along the path can utilize this error information to adjust their parameters and hopefully minimize the future errors as well.

Derivatives can also be calculated in the forward pass, for example, using dual numbers, why do we use backward propagation in the implementation? The reason is that a typical neural network has much more input parameters than output parameters. Backward propagation requires much less computation in this scenario.

```
let backward nn y =
  reverse_prop (_f 1.) y;
  mkpri nn, mkadj nn
```

Here, mkpri and mkadj return the primal and adjoint values of all the parameters.

5.5 Neural Network Compiler

If we consider a neural network as a complicated function, then training this neural network is an iterative process of optimizing the function. In every iteration, the optimization engine first runs the forward pass of the function, then calls an algorithmic differentiation module to obtain the derivative function, and finally runs the backward pass to update the weight. As we can see, there are two computation graphs created dynamically in each iteration, one for the forward pass and the other for the backward pass. In fact, given a fixed neural network, the structure of both computation graphs is identical. This observation serves as the basis of further optimizing the training process. The optimization consists of three parts:

- We dry run the neural network to derive the computation graphs for both forward and backward pass. We reuse these computation graphs in the following iterative process rather than regenerating them.

- We optimize the graph structure to optimize both computation performance and memory usage.

- We replace eager evaluation with lazy evaluation when evaluating a computation graph, which can further optimize the performance.

The `Owl_neural_compiler` functor is designed to automate these steps. Compared to directly using an optimization engine, the neural network compiled by `Owl_neural_compiler` can be trained much faster with much less memory footprint. Let us create a VGG-like convolution neural network to illustrate. The VGG neural network is for image classification tasks, for example, using the CIFAR10 dataset. The network structure is defined by the following code:

```
let make_network input_shape =
  input input_shape
  |> normalisation ~decay:0.9
  |> conv2d [|3;3;3;32|] [|1;1|] ~act_typ:Activation.Relu
  |> conv2d [|3;3;32;32|] [|1;1|] ~act_typ:Activation.Relu ~padding:VALID
  |> max_pool2d [|2;2|] [|2;2|] ~padding:VALID
  |> dropout 0.1
  |> conv2d [|3;3;32;64|] [|1;1|] ~act_typ:Activation.Relu
  |> conv2d [|3;3;64;64|] [|1;1|] ~act_typ:Activation.Relu ~padding:VALID
  |> max_pool2d [|2;2|] [|2;2|] ~padding:VALID
```

```
|> dropout 0.1
|> fully_connected 512 ~act_typ:Activation.Relu
|> linear 10 ~act_typ:Activation.(Softmax 1)
|> get_network
```

The following function first creates the network, then configures the training process, and finally trains the network by calling Graph.train. In fact, the Graph.train function calls the train_generic function we just introduced in the previous section. The train_generic directly passes the neural network along with the configurations to the optimization engine to kick off the optimizing process.

```
let train () =
  let x, _, y = Dataset.load_cifar_train_data 1 in
  let network = make_network [|32;32;3|] in
  Graph.print network;
  let params = Params.config
    ~batch:(Batch.Mini 100) ~learning_rate:(Learning_Rate.Adagrad 0.005)
    ~checkpoint:(Checkpoint.Epoch 1.) ~stopping:(Stopping.Const 1e-6) 10.
  in
  Graph.train ~params network x y
```

However, from a programmer's perspective, if we use the neural compiler, the only thing that needs to be changed is the train function. The network definition remains exactly the same.

```
let train network =
  let x, _, y = Dataset.load_cifar_train_data 1 in
  let x = CGCompiler.Engine.pack_arr x |> Algodiff.pack_arr in
  let y = CGCompiler.Engine.pack_arr y |> Algodiff.pack_arr in
  let params = Params.config
    ~batch:(Batch.Mini 100) ~learning_rate:(Learning_Rate.Adagrad
    0.005) 10.
  in
  CGCompiler.train ~params network x y
```

Except for the mundane packing and unpacking parameters, the most noticeable change is that we are now using CGCompiler.train to train a network. CGCompiler. train is implemented in the neural compiler function. So what is contained in this function? Let us have a look at its implementation.

```
let train ?state ?params network x y =
  let params =
    match params with
    | Some p -> p
    | None    -> Params.default ()
  in
  let network_name = Graph.get_network_name network in
  Owl_log.info "compile network %s into static graph ..." network_name;

  (* compile network into static graph *)
  let x_size = (unpack_arr x |> Engine.shape).(0) in
  let loss, xt, yt, cgraph = compile_deep params network x_size in
  let eval = make_eval_fun loss xt yt cgraph in
  let update = make_update_fun cgraph in
  let save _fname = () in

  (* Optimise graph structure *)
  Engine.save_graph cgraph (network_name ^ "_raw.cgd");
  Engine.optimise cgraph;
  Engine.save_graph cgraph (network_name ^ "_opt.cgd");

  Owl_log.info "start training %s ..." network_name;
  Optimise.minimise_compiled_network ?state params eval update save x y
```

Compared to the train_generic function, CGCompiler.train seems more complicated, but the logic is straightforward. The implementation consists of three steps. First, the function retrieves the training parameters and creates default values if they are not provided. Second, the neural network is compiled into a static graph. Two higher-order functions, that is, eval and update, are created to evaluate computation graphs and update the network weights. Third, the graph structure is optimized by using the functions defined in the computation graph module. Fourth, the optimization engine starts the iterative process to minimize the loss function.

The core of `CGCompiler.train` is the `compile_deep`, which is where the magic happens. However, `compile _deep` is a rather lengthy and complicated function. Instead of studying `compile_deep` as a whole function, let us divide it into many smaller parts and examine them separately:

```
let loss_fun = Loss.run params.loss in
let grad_fun = Gradient.run params.gradient in
let rate_fun = Learning_Rate.run params.learning_rate in
let regl_fun = Regularisation.run params.regularisation in
let momt_fun = Momentum.run params.momentum in
let upch_fun = Learning_Rate.update_ch params.learning_rate in
let clip_fun = Clipping.run params.clipping in
...
```

The first part is simply creating some higher-order functions from the network configuration. The purpose is to simplify the following code:

```
let batch =
  match params.batch with
  | Full       -> full_size
  | Mini n     -> n
  | Sample n   -> n
  | Stochastic -> 1
in
let network_shape = Graph.input_shape network in
let input_shape = Array.append [| batch |] network_shape in
...
```

Because `compile_simple` needs to dry run the network, it needs to know the shape of the input. The input shape depends on how the training is configured. For a small dataset, we can input the whole dataset in each iteration, so the shape will be full size. For a larger dataset, we might want to use different logic to select a batch of data as input, even just one sample per iteration. We can calculate the size from the `params.batch` parameter.

```
(* initialise the network weight *)
Graph.init network;
Graph.mkpar network
```

```
|> Owl_utils.aarr_map (fun v ->
    let v = Algodiff.unpack_arr v in
    Engine.eval_arr [| v |];
    let u = Engine.var_arr "" ~shape:(Engine.shape v) in
    Engine.(assign_arr u (unpack_arr v));
    Algodiff.pack_arr u)
|> Graph.update network;
...
```

Then the neural network is initialized, and the weights are updated. After this step, all the preparation work for a dry run is done.

```
(* derive the computation graph in forward mode *)
let x = Engine.var_arr "x" ~shape:input_shape |> pack_arr in
let y' = Graph.forward network x |> fst in
let output_shape = unpack_arr y' |> Engine.shape in
let y = Engine.var_arr "y" ~shape:output_shape |> pack_arr in
let loss = loss_fun y y' in
let loss = Maths.(loss / _f (Mat.row_num y |> float_of_int)) in
...
```

The most critical step is to derive the computation graph of the backward pass. Before we can do that, we need to first run the forward pass. The outcome of the forward pass y and ground truth y' is fed into the loss function loss_fun which contains the computation graph of the forward pass.

```
let ws = Owl_utils_array.flatten (Graph.mkpri network) in
let reg =
  match params.regularisation <> Regularisation.None with
  | true  -> Array.fold_left
    (fun a w -> Maths.(a + regl_fun w)) (_f 0.) ws
  | false -> _f 0.
in
let loss = Maths.(loss + reg) in
(* assign loss variable name *)
Owl_graph.set_name (unpack_elt loss |> Engine.elt_to_node) "loss";
...
```

Then we further adjust the loss value by adding the regularization term if necessary and assign it with a proper name.

```
(* derive the computation graph in reverse mode *)
let z = Graph.(backward network loss) in
let ws = Owl_utils_array.flatten (fst z) in
let gs' = Owl_utils_array.flatten (snd z) in
...
```

The Graph.backward function created the computation graph of the backward pass, contained in z. The computation graph is also the derivative of the loss function of the network. We also separate out both weights ws and their adjacent value gs' from z. After this step, there is a very lengthy code to further calculate and adjust the gradient with clipping, momentum, etc.

```
(* construct a computation graph with inputs and outputs *)
let network_name = Graph.get_network_name network in
...
let output = Array.append param_o
  [| unpack_elt loss |> Engine.elt_to_node |] in
let cgraph = Engine.make_graph
  ~input:param_i ~output network_name in
...
loss, x, y, cgraph
```

The final computation graph is returned along with the loss function, input, and output.

5.6 Case Study: Object Detection

As a case study to demonstrate how we apply the Neural module in Owl in real-world applications, in this final section we show how to perform instance segmentation using the Mask R-CNN network. It provides both a complex network structure and an interesting application. Object detection is one of the most common DNN tasks, which takes an image of a certain object as input and infers what object this is. However, a neural network can easily get confused if it is applied on an image with multiple objects. For that purpose, *object detection* is another classical computer vision task. Given an image that contains multiple objects, it seeks to classify individual objects and localizes each one using a bounding box. Similarly, the *semantic segmentation* task requires classifying the pixels in an image into different categories. Each segment is recognized by a "mask" that covers the whole object. All possible objects are shown using different masks, but it does not categorize what those objects are. The *Mask R-CNN* (Mask Region-based Convolutional Neural Network) architecture was proposed in 2017 to address all the previous problems. With sufficient training, it can solve these problems at once: detecting objects in an image, labeling each of them, and providing a binary mask for the image to determine which pixels belong to which objects. This task is called *instance segmentation.*

Figure 5-3. *Example of image segmentation: Oxford street view*

As a preliminary example and for visual motivation, Figure 5-3 shows what this network generates. In this example, a normal street view picture is processed by the pretrained Mask R-CNN (MRCNN) network, and the objects (people, sheep, bag, car, bus, etc.) are segmented from the input figure and recognized with probability represented by a number between zero and one. Image segmentation has many important applications, including medical imaging (locating tumors, detecting cancer cells, etc.), traffic control systems, locating objects in satellite images, etc. In the rest of this section, we will explain how this complex network can be built in OCaml using the Neural module. The full code is provided in the GitHub repository.

Object Detection Network Architectures

To present some background knowledge, before explaining the details of Mask R-CNN, we briefly introduce how deep network architectures for object detection and instance segmentation are developed.

R-CNN Architecture

The idea of using a CNN to enhance the object detection task was first proposed in [23]. This paper proposes a "Regions with CNN features" (R-CNN) object detection system. It is divided into several phases. The first phase is to localize possible objects of interest in an input image. Instead of using a sliding window, R-CNN uses a different approach called "regions": for each input image, it first generates a number of (e.g., 2000) *region proposals* that are independent of the object categories used. They are rectangle regions of the image, of different aspects and sizes. The content in each region is then checked to see if it contains any object of interest. Each region proposal is then processed by a CNN to get a 4096-dimension feature vector. This CNN takes an input of fixed size 227×227, and thus each region, regardless of its shape, is morphed into this fixed size before being processed by CNN. As to the output feature vector, it is processed by a trained SVM model to be classified into the accepted results.

Fast R-CNN Architecture

Compared to the previous state of the art, R-CNN improves the mean average precision by more than 30%. However, it has several problems. For one, the R-CNN pipeline consists of several parts, and so training takes multiple stages, including the training of the CNN, the SVM models, etc. Moreover, training is expensive in both space and time. Besides, since the CNN inference pass needs to be performed on all region proposals, the whole object detection process is slow.

To mitigate these challenges, the *Fast R-CNN* approach was proposed by Girshick et al. Similar to R-CNN, the region proposals are first generated based on the input images. But to reduce training costs, the Fast R-CNN consists of one CNN network that can be trained in a single stage. Furthermore, it does not need to perform a forward pass on each region proposal. Instead, it first computes a convolutional feature map for the whole input image and then projects the region of interest (RoI) from the input image to this feature map, deciding which part of it should be extracted. Such a region on the feature map is pooled by a "RoI pooling" layer into a smaller feature map of fixed size, which is then turned into a feature vector by several fully connected layers.

Next, the feature vectors are fed into a branch. One output of this branch contains the classification, and the confidence of that classification, of the object in that region. The other specifies the rectangle location of the object, encoded by four real-valued numbers. The output on this branch contains such four-number tuple for all of the object categories in this task. Compared to R-CNN, this method does not require a lot of space for feature caching, and it proves to be about 9 times faster in training and 213 times faster in inference.

Faster R-CNN Architecture

However, the Fast R-CNN is also not perfect. Region proposals are first generated based on the input image, and object detection is performed using both the convolutional feature map and the region proposal. Note that the feature map, which abstractly represents features in the input image, may already contain sufficient information to perform not just object detection but also to find regions where the objects may be. That important observation leads to the development of the *Faster R-CNN* method.

This approach is developed based on the Fast R-CNN network. It introduces a new network structure: the *Region Proposal Network* (RPN). This extra network operates on the feature maps that are generated by the CNN in Fast R-CNN, generating region proposals that are passed to the RoI pooling step for successive detections. The RPN uses a sliding window over the feature map. At each sliding window location, nine different proposals that are centered around this location are checked to see their coordinates (represented by four real-valued numbers) and the probability that an object exists in the given region. Each such proposal is called an *anchor*. In Faster R-CNN, the authors trained the RPN and used the generated proposals to train Fast R-CNN; the trained network is then used to initialize RPN, so on and so forth. Thus, these two parts are trained iteratively, and so there is no need to use external methods to produce region proposals. Everything is performed in a unified network for the object detection task.

Mask R-CNN Architecture

Based on this existing work, the Mask R-CNN was proposed to perform the task of both object detection and semantic segmentation. It keeps the architecture of Faster R-CNN, adding only one extra branch in the final stage of the RoI feature layer. Where previously outputs included object classification and location, now a third branch contains information about the mask of the detected object in the RoI. Therefore, the Mask R-CNN can retrieve the rectangle bound, classification results, classification possibility, and the mask of that object, for any RoI, in a single pass. In the next section, we will introduce the Mask R-CNN architecture in detail.

Implementation of Mask R-CNN

This section outlines the main parts of the architecture of Mask R-CNN, explaining how it differs from its predecessors. For a more detailed explanation, please refer to the original paper [27]. The OCaml implementation of the inference model is available in the code repository.[1]

Building Mask R-CNN

After a quick introduction to the MRCNN and its development, let's look at the code to understand how it is constructed:

```
open Owl

module N = Dense.Ndarray.S

open CGraph
open Graph
open AD

module RPN = RegionProposalNetwork
module PL = ProposalLayer
module FPN = FeaturePyramidNetwork
module DL = DetectionLayer
module C = Configuration

let image_shape = C.get_image_shape () in
let inps = inputs
    ~names:[|"input_image"; "input_image_meta"; "input_anchors"|]
    [|image_shape; [|C.image_meta_size|]; [|num_anchors; 4|]|] in
```

---

[1] https://github.com/pvdhove/owl-mask-rcnn. Work in this chapter was conducted by Pierre Vandenhove during his internship in the OCaml Labs group at the University of Cambridge Computer Laboratory. The code was ported from the Keras/TensorFlow implementation.

```
let input_image = inps.(0)
and input_image_meta = inps.(1)
and input_anchors = inps.(2) i
```

The network accepts three inputs, each representing images, metadata, and the number of anchors (the rectangular regions). The Configuration module contains a list of constants that will be used in building the network.

Feature Extractor

The picture is first fed to a convolutional neural network to extract features of the image. The first few layers detect low-level features of an image, such as edges and basic shapes. As you go deeper into the network, these simply features are assembled into higher-level features such as "people" and "cars." Five of these layers (called "feature maps") of various sizes, both high and low levels, are then passed on to the next parts. This implementation uses Microsoft's ResNet101 network as a feature extractor.

```
let tdps = C.top_down_pyramid_size in
let str = [|1; 1|] in
let p5 = conv2d [|1; 1; 2048; tdps|] str
  ~padding:VALID ~name:"fpn_c5p5" c5 in

let p4 =
add ~name:"fpn_p4add"
  [|upsampling2d [|2; 2|] ~name:"fpn_p5upsampled" p5;
    conv2d [|1; 1; 1024; tdps|]
      str ~padding:VALID ~name:"fpn_c4p4" c4|] in
let p3 =
add ~name:"fpn_p3add"
  [|upsampling2d [|2; 2|] ~name:"fpn_p4upsampled" p4;
    conv2d [|1; 1; 512; tdps|]
      str ~padding:VALID ~name:"fpn_c3p3" c3|] in
let p2 =
add ~name:"fpn_p2add"
  [|upsampling2d [|2; 2|] ~name:"fpn_p3upsampled" p3;
    conv2d [|1; 1; 256; tdps|]
      str ~padding:VALID ~name:"fpn_c2p2" c2|] in
```

```
let conv_args = [|3; 3; tdps; tdps|] in
let p2= conv2d conv_args str ~padding:SAME ~name:"fpn_p2" p2 in
let p3= conv2d conv_args str ~padding:SAME ~name:"fpn_p3" p3 in
let p4= conv2d conv_args str ~padding:SAME ~name:"fpn_p4" p4 in
let p5= conv2d conv_args str ~padding:SAME ~name:"fpn_p5" p5 in
let p6= max_pool2d [|1; 1|] [|2; 2|]
  ~padding:VALID ~name:"fpn_p6" p5 in

let rpn_feature_maps = [|p2; p3; p4; p5; p6|] in
let mrcnn_feature_maps = [|p2; p3; p4; p5|]
```

The features are extracted by combining both ResNet101 and the Feature Pyramid Network. ResNet extracts features of the image (early layers extract low-level features; later layers extract high-level features). The Feature Pyramid Network creates a second pyramid of feature maps from top to bottom so that every map has access to high- and low-level features. This combination achieves excellent gains in both accuracy and speed.

Proposal Generation

To try to locate the objects, about 250,000 overlapping rectangular regions or anchors are generated.

```
let nb_ratios = Array.length C.rpn_anchor_ratios in
let rpns = Array.init 5 (fun i ->
  RPN.rpn_graph rpn_feature_maps. (i)
  nb_ratios C.rpn_anchor_stride
  ("_p" ^ string_of_int (i + 2))) in
let rpn_class = concatenate 1 ~name:"rpn_class"
               (Array.init 5 (fun i -> rpns. (i).(0))) in
let rpn_bbox = concatenate 1 ~name:"rpn_bbox"
               (Array.init 5 (fun i -> rpns. (i).(1)))
```

Single RPN graphs are applied on different features in rpn_features_maps, and the results from these networks are concatenated. For each bounding box on the image, the RPN returns the likelihood that it contains an object, called its *objectness*, and a refinement for the anchor; both are represented by rank 3 ndarrays.

Next, in the proposal layer, the 1000 best anchors are selected according to their objectness. Anchors that overlap too much with each other are eliminated, to avoid detecting the same object multiple times. Each selected anchor is also refined in case it was not perfectly centered around the object.

```
let rpn_rois =
    let prop_f = PL.proposal_layer
      C.post_nms_rois C.rpn_nms_threshold in
    MrcnnUtil.delay_lambda_array [|C.post_nms_rois; 4|]
      prop_f ~name:"ROI"
      [|rpn_class; rpn_bbox; input_anchors|] in
```

In rpn_rois, the proposal layer picks the top anchors from the RPN output, based on nonmaximum suppression and anchor scores.

Classification

All anchor proposals from the previous layer are resized to a given fixed size and fed into a ten-layer neural network. The network assigns each of them the probability that it belongs to each class. The network is pretrained on fixed classes; changing the set of classes requires retraining the whole network. Note that this step does not take as much time for each anchor as a full-fledged image classifier such as Inception, since it reuses the precomputed feature maps from the Feature Pyramid Network. Therefore, there is no need to go back to the original picture. The class with the highest probability is chosen for each proposal, and thanks to the class predictions, the anchor proposals are even more refined. Proposals classified in the background class are deleted. Eventually, only the proposals with an objectness over some threshold are kept, and we have our final detections, each with a bounding box and a label. This process can be described by the following code:

```
let mrcnn_class, mrcnn_bbox =
FPN.fpn_classifier_graph rpn_rois
  mrcnn_feature_maps input_image_meta
  C.pool_size C.num_classes C.fpn_classif_fc_layers_size in

let detections = MrcnnUtil.delay_lambda_array
  [|C.detection_max_instances; 6|]
  (DL.detection_layer ()) ~name:"mrcnn_detection"
  [|rpn_rois; mrcnn_class; mrcnn_bbox; input_image_meta|] in
```

```
let detection_boxes = lambda_array
  [|C.detection_max_instances; 4|]
  (fun t -> Maths.get_slice [[]; []; [0;3]] t.(0))
  [|detections|]
```

A Feature Pyramid Network classifier associates a class to each proposal and further refines the bounding box for that class. The only thing left to do then is to generate a binary mask for each object. This is handled by a small convolutional neural network which produces a small square of values between 0 and 1 for each detected bounding box. This square is resized to the original size of the bounding box with bilinear interpolation, and pixels with a value over 0.5 are tagged as being part of the object.

```
let mrcnn_mask = FPN.build_fpn_mask_graph
  detection_boxes mrcnn_feature_maps
  input_image_meta C.mask_pool_size C.num_classes
```

Finally, the output contains detection results and masks from the previous steps.

```
outputs ~name:C.name [|detections; mrcnn_mask|]
```

After getting to know the internals of the MRCNN architecture, we can now run the code to see it work. The core code is listed as follows:

```
open Mrcnn

let src = "image.png" in
let fun_detect = Model.detect () in
let Model.({rois; class_ids; scores; masks}) = fun_detect src in
let img_arr = Image.img_to_ndarray src in
let filename = Filename.basename src in
let format = Images.guess_format src in
let out_loc = out ^ filename in
Visualise.display_masks img_arr rois masks class_ids;
let camlimg = Image.img_of_ndarray img_arr in
Visualise.display_labels camlimg rois class_ids scores;
Image.save out_loc format camlimg;
Visualise.print_results class_ids rois scores
```

A key step is to apply the `Model.detect` function on the input images, returning the regions of interest, the classification result ID of the object in each region, the classification certainty scores, and a mask that shows the outline of that object in the region. With this information, the `Visualise` module runs for three passes on the original image: the first for adding bounding boxes and object masks, the second for adding the numbers close to the bounding box, and finally for printing out the resulting images from the previous two steps. In this example, the pretrained weights on 80 classes of common objects are provided, which have been converted from the TensorFlow implementation mentioned earlier. As to the execution speed, processing one image with a size of 1024×1024 pixels takes between 10 and 15 seconds on a moderate laptop.

5.7 Summary

In this chapter, we provided an insight into the neural network module in Owl. Benefiting from solid implementation of algorithmic differentiation and optimization, the `Neural` module is concise and expressive. We explained the neurons and network components in this module and then showed how network training is done in Owl. This chapter also covered how we implement a neural network compiler to automatically optimize the network structure and memory usage. Finally, we introduced in detail a DNN application, instance segmentation, that drives the development of the computation graph module in Owl.

CHAPTER 6

Computation Graph

A computation graph is a basic theoretical tool that underlies modern deep learning libraries. It is also an important component in Owl. This chapter first gives a bird's-eye view on the computation graph in Owl and its importance in computing. We then demonstrate how to use it in Owl with some examples. Then we will continue to cover the design and implementation details of the computation graph module and how it is fitted into Owl's functor stack.

6.1 The Definition of Computation Graph

As a functional programmer, it is basic knowledge that a function takes an input and then produces an output. The input of a function can be the output of another function which then creates dependency. If we view a function as one node in a graph, and its input and output as incoming and outgoing links to other functions, respectively, as the computation continues, these functions are chained together to form a *directed acyclic graph* (DAG). Such a DAG is often referred to as a computation graph.

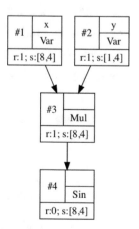

Figure 6-1. *Computation graph of a simple function: sin(x*y)*

© Liang Wang, Jianxin Zhao 2023
L. Wang and J. Zhao, *Architecture of Advanced Numerical Analysis Systems,*
https://doi.org/10.1007/978-1-4842-8853-5_6

Figure 6-1 shows an example graph for calculating function sin (x * y).[1] The computation graph contains several pieces of information which are essential for debugging the applications. These information include the node index, operation type, reference counter, shapes of data, etc. For example, in Figure 6-1 the row vector y of shape [1; 4] is broadcast on the matrix x of shape [8; 4] in the Mul operation.

Dynamic Graph and Static Graph

The computation graph can be either implicitly constructed or explicitly declared in the code. Implicit graph construction is often achieved by operator overloading and a graph is constructed during the runtime, while explicit declaration may use *domain-specific languages* (DSL) to construct a graph during the compilation phase with a fix structure. The two methods lead to two different kinds of computation graphs: *dynamic graph* and *static graph*; each has its own pros and cons.

A dynamic graph is constructed during the runtime. Due to *operator overloading*, its construction can be naturally blended with a language's native constructs such as if ... else ... and for loops. This renders greatest flexibility and expressiveness. By using a dynamic computation graph, users are even free to construct a different network for each training sample. On the other hand, a static graph needs to be declared using a specific DSL, which tends to have a steeper learning curve. It is defined only once in training. Because the structure of a graph is already known during the compilation phase, there is a great space for optimization. However, it is sometimes very difficult to use static graphs to express conditions and loops when using with native code together.

The flexibility of a dynamic graph comes at the price of lower performance. Facebook's PyTorch and Google's TensorFlow are the typical examples of dynamic and static graphs, respectively. Many programmers need to make a choice between these two different types. A common practice is "using PyTorch at home and using TensorFlow in the company." In other words, PyTorch is preferred for prototyping, and TensorFlow is an ideal option for production use.[2]

Owl does something slightly different from these two in order to get the best parts of both worlds. Owl achieves this by converting a dynamic graph into a static one during

---

[1] This figure is generated with the tool provided by the CGraph module in Owl, which we will discuss in detail in this chapter.

[2] In Sep. 2019, TensorFlow rolled out version 2.0. Starting from this version, TensorFlow uses eager execution by default, which aims to be easier for users to get started with.

the runtime. The motivation is based on an observation: in many cases, a computation graph is continuously reevaluated after its construction. This is especially true for those iterative optimization algorithms. Thus, we only update some inputs of the graph in each iteration.

If we know that the graph structure remains the same in every iteration, rather than reconstructing it all the time, we can convert it into a static graph before the iterative evaluation. This is exactly what Owl does. By doing so, the programmer can enjoy the flexibility offered by the dynamic graph construction with operator overloading and, at the same time, still achieve the best performance from a static graph.

Compared to TensorFlow, the time overhead for the graph conversion and optimization is deferred to the runtime in Owl. Owl uses the *just-in-time compilation* (JIT) that is performed during the execution of a program. Since the graph compilation takes place in runtime, the JIT compiler can utilize dynamic runtime information and enable better optimization. You may worry about the performance and wonder if it is going to slow down your fancy DNN application. The fact is, even for large and complex graphs, this JIT compilation and optimization are often quite fast.

For example, in an LSTM network constructed using Owl,[3] there are 15,105 nodes and 21,335 edges. Owl is able to compile the graph within 230ms and then optimize its structure within 210ms. The optimized graph contains only 8224 nodes and 14,444 edges and runs much faster. Note that you only need to do it once before training. For smaller networks, it often just takes several milliseconds. The CGraph module has implemented various graph optimization techniques to achieve this, which will be discussed in Section 6.3.

Technically, JIT is very straightforward to implement in Owl's architecture. Given a deep neural network, Owl first runs both forward pass and backward pass. Because of the computation graph, the calculation becomes symbolic, and we can obtain the complete computation graph to calculate the loss and gradients of a neural network. It then passes this static graph to the optimization engine.

---

[3] Code example: Constructing an LSTM network using Owl. URL: `https://github.com/owlbarn/owl/blob/master/examples/lazy_lstm.ml`

Significance in Computing

Now that you know the basic ideas of a computation graph, you may ask why it matters. Actually, a computation graph plays a core role in any machine learning framework. Both TensorFlow [1] and PyTorch [42], the most popular deep learning libraries, use a computation graph as the central data structure. A computation graph makes many things a lot easier. Here is an incomplete list of its potential benefits:

- Simulating lazy evaluation in a language with eager evaluation

- Incremental computation (a.k.a. self-adjusting computation)

- Reducing computation complexity by optimizing the structure of a graph

- Reducing memory management overhead by preallocating space

- Reducing memory footprint by reusing allocated memory space

- Natural support for parallel and distributed computing

- Natural support for heterogeneous computing

- Natural support for symbolic maths

Some of the benefits are very obvious. Memory usage can certainly be optimized if the graph structure is fixed and the input shapes are known beforehand. One optimization is reusing previously allocated memory, which is especially useful for those applications involving large ndarray calculations. In fact, this optimization can also be performed by a compiler by tracking the reference number of allocated memory, a technique referred to as *linear types* [50]. Some may appear less obvious at first glance. For example, we can decompose a computation graph into multiple independent *subgraphs*, and each can be evaluated in parallel on different cores or even computers. Maintaining the graph structure also improves fault tolerance, by providing natural support for rollback mechanisms.

The computation graph provides a way to abstract the flow of computations; therefore, it is able to bridge the high-level applications and low-level machinery of various hardware devices. This is why it has natural support for heterogeneous computing.

The computation graph has more profound implications on the scalability and security of scientific computing systems. Because the memory allocated for each node is mutable, the algorithmic differentiation becomes more scalable when evaluating large and complex graphs. At the same time, mutable transformation is handled by Owl internally, so programmers can still write safe functional code.

6.2 Applications Inside the Computing System

Before diving into the details of the design of the computation graph module, in this section let's first show some examples of using the CGraph module and how a computation can be transformed into lazy evaluation.

Basic Numerical Operations

Let's start with a simple operation that adds up one ndarray and one scalar. Normally, with the Ndarray module, what we do is

```
module N = Dense.Ndarray.D

let x = N.ones [|2;2|];;
let y = 2.;;
let g = N.add_scalar x y;;
```

Now, let's make this function into a computation graph which can be lazy evaluated by CGraph.

```
module N = Owl_computation_cpu_engine.Make
  (Owl_algodiff_primal_ops.D)
```

The Make function here is actually a *functor*. For those who are not familiar with the idea of functor, it is a powerful tool in OCaml to build generic code and structure large-scale systems. To put into plain words, a functor is a function that creates modules from modules. As we will explain in Section 6.3, the computation graph is designed as a *functor stack*. Different aspects of the computation graph, such as memory management and graph optimization, are added into the CGraph by creating a new module based on an existing one, layer by layer. So far, it suffices to know that the functor creates a module N, which provides exactly the same ndarray operations, except that all the operations are conducted on *symbols* which represent ndarray instead of real objects allocated in memory.

```
let x = N.var_arr ~shape:[|2;2|] "x";;
let y = N.var_elt "y";;
let g = N.add_scalar x y;;
```

Next, we define two variables. The first x is an ndarray (arr), and y is a scalar (elt). At this point, we only define these two as placeholders with no real data. That is to say, we do not care about what specific ndarray or scalar these two variables are. Then we use the add_scalar function to get another lazy evaluated ndarray g. That finishes that lazy calculation. So far, we only know that g is calculated by adding x and y, but have no idea what their values are. To get the value of the lazy expression g, we need to first assign values to x and y:

```
let x_val = Dense.Ndarray.D.ones [|2;2|];;
let y_val = 2.;;
let _ = N.assign_arr x x_val;;
let _ = N.assign_elt y y_val;;
```

Here, x is assigned a double-precision ndarray of 1s, and y is float number 2. Note the two different assignment methods for ndarray and scalar. Finally, we can evaluate the ndarray g:

```
# N.eval_arr [|g|]
- : unit = ()

# N.unpack_arr g
- : Owl_algodiff_primal_ops.D.arr =
C0 C1
R0  3  3
R1  3  3
```

The eval_arr evaluates the whole graph but does not return the result. To extract the calculation result, we need to use the unpack_arr or unpack_elt function. The result is a 2x2 ndarray, the values of which are all 3s, just as expected. So where does the calculation happen? Remember that the CGraph module N is built based on the double-precision type `Owl_algodiff_primal_ops` module. As we have explained in Chapter 3, this module is actually an `Ndarray.D` module, with some extra matrix and linear algebra operations. Therefore, in this example, g is calculated using C-based ndarray calculation. If we switch the base module from `Ndarray` to `Owl_base_ndarray`, the calculation is then performed using native OCaml.

Algorithmic Differentiation with CGraph

In real applications, we often need to deal with CGraphs that are constructed in the algorithmic differentiation process. Here is an example of using the dense ndarray module to compute the gradients of a function:

```
include Owl_algodiff_generic.Make
  (Owl_algodiff_primal_ops.D)
```

```
let f x y = Maths.((x * sin (x + x) + ((pack_flt 1.) * sqrt x)
  / (pack_flt 7.)) * (relu y) |> sum')
```

```
let x = Dense.Ndarray.D.ones [|2;2|] |> pack_arr
let y = pack_elt 2.
let z = (grad (f x)) y |> unpack_elt
```

Based on the chain rule, the `Algodiff` module automatically constructs a graph that computes the gradient of input function f. The result is contained in scalar z. However, the graph is constructed internally, but sometimes we need to have access to this graph and apply optimizations. Obviously, it is extremely difficult for the users to manually construct the computation graph that computes the gradient of the function f. Note that the `Algodiff` module is also built using functors. Its base module follows the Ndarray interface. By changing it from the `Ndarray` to `CGraph` module, we can make z to be a computation graph instead of a scalar value, as the following code snippet shows:

```
module G = Owl_computation_cpu_engine.Make
  (Owl_algodiff_primal_ops.D)
include Owl_algodiff_generic.Make (G)
```

```
let f x y =
    Maths.((x * sin (x + x) + ((pack_flt 1.) *
    sqrt x) / (pack_flt 7.)) * (relu y) |> sum')
```

```
let x = G.var_arr ~shape:[|2;2|] "x" |> pack_arr
let y = G.var_elt "y" |> pack_elt
let z = (grad (f x)) y
```

Most of the code stay unchanged. Notice how the CGraph module is treated as an alternative to the Ndarray module in building the AD module, since they follow the same set of interfaces required by the Algodiff module of its base module. They decide if the AD module uses normal or lazy evaluation. By executing this piece of code, the result z contains a computation graph constructed by the backward propagation pass in performing algorithmic differentiation.

The next thing we need to do is to assign values to inputs and evaluate z. That requires building a graph based on the input and output, as shown by the following code:

```
let inputs  = [|
unpack_arr x |> G.arr_to_node;
unpack_elt y |> G.elt_to_node
|]
let outputs = [| unpack_elt z |> G.elt_to_node |]
let g = G.make_graph inputs outputs "graph"
```

To build a graph, we need to specify the input and output *nodes*. It might be a bit confusing, since there are two layers of packing and unpacking: the first from the AD node to the CGraph element and the second from the CGraph element to ndarray or scalar. We need AD.unpack_arr and AD.unpack_elt to unwrap AD type data (ndarray and scalar) into CGraph ndarray and scalar values. And then, to build the explicit computation graph, we need to use the G.arr_to_node and G.elt_to_node functions to make them into graph nodes first. Finally, an explicit computation graph can be built with the make_graph function.

After constructing the graph g, we can then assign real data values to the computation graph. Note that we need to first unpack the Algodiff values to CGraph values before assignment:

```
let x_val = Dense.Ndarray.D.ones [|2;2|];;
let y_val = 2.;;
let _ = G.assign_arr (unpack_arr x) x_val;;
let _ = G.assign_elt (unpack_elt y) y_val;;
```

Finally, we can evaluate the whole graph by simply calling

```
G.eval_graph g;;
```

Since the whole graph is evaluated, the output ndarray z is also evaluated. We can first unpack it from the Algodiff value into normal CGraph ndarray and then get its value by another layer of unpacking:

```
# unpack_elt z |> G.unpack_elt
- : float = 4.20861827873129801
```

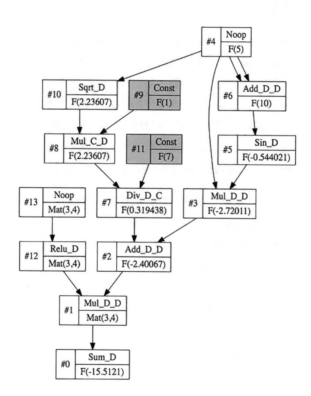

Figure 6-2. *Computation graph of a simple math function*

You might be wondering why bother to build the graph through all these layers of packing and unpacking when we can directly evaluate the value z. One main reason is to enable various optimizations on the graph before executing it, as we will explain in the following sections. Another reason is that evaluation is not always the target. For example, we often need to visualize the generated computation graph. The computation graph is very helpful in both debugging and understanding the characteristics of your numerical computations. Owl provides the graph_to_dot function to facilitate you in generating computation graphs. It converts the computation graph into a dot format string. The dot file can be visualized with tools such as Graphviz. For example, the following code generates a dot file for the graph we have constructed in this example, and this graph is shown in Figure 6-2.

```
let s = G.graph_to_dot g
let _ = Owl_io.write_file "cgraph.dot" s
```

Deep Neural Network

Since the optimization and neural network modules are built on the algorithmic differentiation module, they can also benefit from the power of the computation graph. Suppose we have a network built from CGraph-based neural network nn, we can then use the forward and backward functions to get the forward inference and backward propagation computation graphs from the neural network graph module, with the CGraph ndarray variable. Actually, for ease of access, Owl has provided another functor to build the neural network module based on the CGraph module:

```
module CPU_Engine = Owl_computation_cpu_engine.Make
  (Owl_algodiff_primal_ops.S)
module CGCompiler = Owl_neural_compiler.Make (CPU_Engine)

open CGCompiler.Neural
open CGCompiler.Neural.Graph
open CGCompiler.Neural.Algodiff

let make_network input_shape =
  input input_shape
  |> lambda (fun x -> Maths.(x / pack_flt 256.))
  |> conv2d [|5;5;1;32|] [|1;1|] ~act_typ:Activation.Relu
  |> max_pool2d [|2;2|] [|2;2|]
  |> dropout 0.1
  |> fully_connected 1024 ~act_typ:Activation.Relu
  |> linear 10 ~act_typ:Activation.(Softmax 1)
  |> get_network ~name:"mnist"
```

The CGraph-built neural network module does not require any change of code in building the CNN except for the headers. To build a normal neural network, we use the Neural module, and now we only need to change that to the CGCompiler. Neural module. Here, the owl_neural_compiler functor compiles a DNN definition and training configuration into a device-dependent static graph. As its output, the CGCompiler is a computation graph–powered neural network compiler module. CGCompiler also provides training functions. Note that the data requires proper packing around original ndarray.

```
let pack x = CGCompiler.Engine.pack_arr x
  |> Algodiff.pack_arr

let train network =
  let x, _, y = Dataset.load_mnist_train_data_arr () in
  let x = pack x in
  let y = pack y in
  CGCompiler.train network x y
```

Similarly, the inference can be done with the CGCompiler.model function. To make the existing DNN program into a lazy evaluation version, all we need to do is to update the header and use packing/unpacking properly for the data.

One of the key performance improvements CGraph has on the neural network lies in its ability of graph and memory optimization. To motivate you to understand more about the design and optimization of the CGraph module, here is an example. Let's train a LeNet-like DNN based on the MNIST dataset, using the normal version mnist_cnn. ml and the CGraph-powered version lazy_mnist.ml.[4] Similar to the preceding example code, both scripts train the same convolution neural network in 60 iterations. In one of our evaluations on a normal laptop, mnist_cnn.ml takes 30s to finish and approximately consumes 4GB memory, while lazy_mnist.ml only takes 5s and consumes about 0.75GB. This performance improvement is astounding. If these numbers make you interested in knowing how the magic happens, please keep reading the next section. We will unveil the underlying mechanism of Owl's computation graph.

---

[4] Both code snippets are available from the source code of Owl.

6.3 Design of Computation Graph Module

Owl implements the computation graph in a very unique and interesting way. Let's first see several principles we followed in designing and developing this module:

- Nonintrusive, the original functor stack should work as it was

- Transparent to the programmers as much as possible

- Support both eager and lazy evaluations

- Flexible enough for future extension on other devices

The computation graph is implemented in a self-contained stack. We have devised a way to "inject" it into Owl's original functor stack. If it sounds too abstract, please have a look at the final product in Figure 6-3.

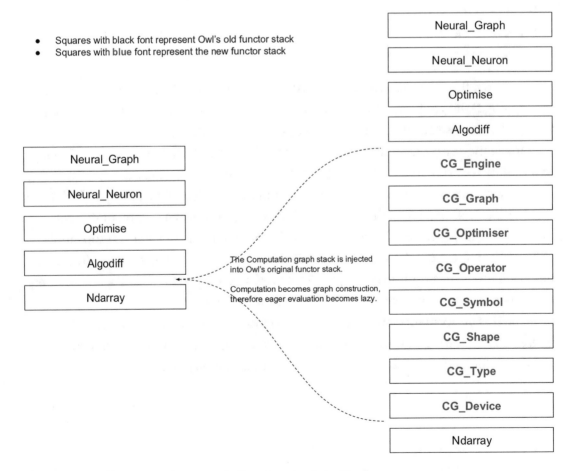

Figure 6-3. *Computation graph functor stack in Owl*

The left figure shows part of Owl's original functor stack, and the right one shows how the current one looks like after injection. In the very initial design, Ndarray implements a set of fundamental n-dimensional array operations, then Algodiff defines abstract mathematical operations for differentiation, finally the Optimise engine glues low-level maths with high-level deep neural network applications. The whole stack is parameterized by the number type abstraction in Ndarray:

- Ndarray: Provides number type abstraction and implements the fundamental numerical operations

- Algodiff: Implements algorithmic differentiation

- Optimise: Uses the derivative information to build an optimization engine

- Neural_Neuron: Implements various kinds of neuron functions which can be optimized

- Neural_Graph: Connects neurons together to form a network so that we can train a useful model

Based on this architecture, the whole functor stack of the computation graph can be inserted between the Ndarray and Algodiff modules. The design principle is that *the functor stack of a numerical system should be parameterized by both number type and device type*. The number type provides data representation (real or complex, single or double, row-based or column-based layout, etc.) which decides how a math construct should be built and operated. The device type provides hardware representation (CPU, GPU, FPGA, etc.) which decides how the computation should be performed on a specific device.

The following list summarizes the functionality of each functor in the CGraph stack. The order and naming of these functors can give you a rough understanding about how it is designed, as follows:

- Device: Device abstraction contains device-dependent types and functions.

- Type: Type definition of various (mathematical) operations.

- Shape: Provides the *shape inference* function in the graph.

- Symbol: Provides various general functions to manipulate symbols.

- `Operator`: Implements math operators (+, -, *, /, etc.) which decide how the symbols should be connected to form a graph.

- `Optimiser`: Optimizes the structure of a given graph by searching and optimizing various patterns.

- `Graph`: Manipulates computation graphs at a high level, for example, visualization, connecting inputs and outputs.

- `Engine`: Evaluates a computation graph on a specific device.

Simply put, the injected computation graph stack provides an abstraction layer similar to symbolic maths. Without injecting the computation graph, the OCaml returns 2 if you calculate 1+1; now it returns a graph of several nodes. Thus, the original eager evaluation becomes symbolic operation and pure graph manipulation, and the graph can be lazily evaluated.

The shape inference functionality is able to infer the data shape of every node in a graph from its input. This allows Owl to calculate how much memory is required to evaluate the graph and preallocate this space. Owl can further track the reference number of each function node and reuse the allocated memory as much as possible, which reduces both memory footprint and garbage collector (GC) overhead, significantly improving the computation speed.

The engine functor sits on top of the stack. This is where a computation graph finally gets executed. The engine functor contains two submodules, one for initializing the graph and the other for evaluating the graph. We can try the following snippet in an OCaml REPL such as `utop`. Both snippets generate a module for DNN applications; the difference is that the first one uses the old stack, whereas the second one uses the new stack with the computation graph.

```
module M =
  Owl_neural_generic.Flatten (
    Owl_neural_graph.Make (
      Owl_neural_neuron.Make (
        Owl_optimise_generic.Make (
          Owl_algodiff_generic.Make (
            Dense.Ndarray.S)))));;
```

As to the new stack that contains computation graph functors, we can see it is indeed much deeper.

```
module M =
  Owl_neural_generic.Flatten (
    Owl_neural_graph.Make (
      Owl_neural_neuron.Make (
        Owl_optimise_generic.Make (
          Owl_algodiff_generic.Make (
            Owl_computation_engine.Flatten (
              Owl_computation_cpu_engine.Make_Nested (
                Owl_computation_graph.Make (
                  Owl_computation_optimiser.Make (
                    Owl_computation_operator.Make (
                      Owl_computation_symbol.Make (
                        Owl_computation_shape.Make (
                          Owl_computation_type.Make (
                            Owl_computation_cpu_device.Make (
                              Dense.Ndarray.S)))))))))))))));;
```

We have introduced the different components of the computation graph module. Next, we will dive deep into the implementation of core functionalities of this module: the construction of a graph, the optimization of the graph structure, the evaluation, the memory optimization in execution, etc.

Computing Device

A computation graph is an abstract construct to express the logic of a function. To calculate the outcome of a function, computation graphs need to be evaluated on a physical device. The device can be anything as long as it has the capability to perform numerical operations, such as the CPU, GPU, etc. To extend Owl on a new device, we only need to create a new device module and define how the basic operations can be performed on this device. Because a majority of the CGraph module is device independent, the device layer becomes very lightweight, which further makes Owl very easy to extend.

The following functor defines a CPU device. The functor's input is the type of data which will be manipulated on the device. In our case, they are either ndarray or scalar values. This makes perfect sense if you are familiar with computer architecture. The data are often stored and processed differently on devices of different architectures. Making a new device is simply creating an abstract record type in OCaml. The other two functions are for packing and unpacking data into the types which a device can process.

```ocaml
module Make (A : Ndarray_Mutable) = struct
  module A = A

  type device =
    { device_type : device_type
    ; initialised : bool
    }

  type value =
    | ArrVal of A.arr
    | EltVal of A.elt

  let make_device () = { device_type = CPU; initialised = false }

  let arr_to_value x = ArrVal x

  let value_to_arr = function
    | ArrVal x -> x
    | _           -> failwith "Owl_computation_device: value_to_arr"

  ...

end
```

For example, OpenCL is a framework for developing cross-platform programs; these programs can execute on heterogeneous platforms consisting of the CPU, GPU, DSP, FPGA, and other processors or hardware accelerators. The following code defines an OpenCL-compatible device. Compared to the CPU device, the most noticeable difference on the OpenCL device is that the values are represented very differently. The data can be stored either on the memory attached to the CPU or the memory attached to the GPU. Quite often, the data has to be transferred between the two disjoint memory systems for performance considerations. Moreover, the computation performed on a

GPU is defined by kernels which are written in C-like DSL. Different computing units communicate through events.

```
module Make (A : Ndarray_Mutable) = struct
  module A = A

  type device =
    { device_type : device_type
    ; initialised : bool
    }

  type cpu_mem = A.arr

  type value =
    { mutable cpu_mem : cpu_mem array
    ; mutable gpu_mem : cl_mem array
    ; mutable kernel : cl_kernel array
    ; mutable events : cl_event array
    }

  let make_device () = { device_type = OpenCL; initialised = false }

  let arr_to_value x =
    let cpu_mem = [| x |] in
    let gpu_mem = [||] in
    let kernel = [||] in
    let events = [||] in
    { cpu_mem; gpu_mem; kernel; events }

  let value_to_arr x =
    if Array.length x.cpu_mem > 0
    then x.cpu_mem.(0)
    else failwith "value_to_arr: not evaluated yet"

  ...

end
```

There are four attributes associated with a value regarding its storage, computation, and communication on an OpenCL device, that is, CPU memory and GPU memory for storage, kernel for computation, and event for communication between computing units.

Types of Operation

The `Owl_computation_type` functor takes a device module as its input, then specifies all the possible operations on the given device. Whenever we want to extend the set of operations, we need to add the corresponding constructor of the new operation to the sum type op. The current set of operations covers a wide range of unary and binary numerical functions, such as Abs, Neg, Add, as well as functions for neural networks such as MaxPool3d.

```
module Make (Device : Owl_types_computation_device.Sig) = struct
  module Device = Device
  open Device

  type state =
    | Valid
    | Invalid

  type t = attr Owl_graph.node

  and block =
    { size : int
    ; block_id : int
    ; mutable active : t option
    ; mutable memory : value
    ; mutable nodes : t list
    }

  and attr =
    { mutable op : op
    ; mutable freeze : bool
    ; mutable reuse : bool
    ; mutable state : state
```

```
    ; mutable shape : int array option array
    ; mutable value : value array
    ; mutable block : block array option
    }
  and arr = Arr of t
  and elt = Elt of t

  and op =
    | Noop
    | Var
    | Const
    | Abs
    | Neg
    ...

end
```

Here, `attr` is a record type containing the properties of an operation. These properties will be utilized to initialize a graph and optimize its memory usage and evaluation performance. For example, the `reuse` field specifies whether the memory associated with an operation can be shared with other operations. The `block` type stores the memory and all the operations which are sharing this memory.

Shape Inference

The shape of data might change while traveling through different nodes in a computation graph. The shape information is very valuable for debugging and optimization purposes. When all the inputs of a given function are known, the shape of the outcome can be decided; hence, the shape information of a computation graph becomes available. The `Owl_computation_shape` functor is created for automating shape inference. The core function of this functor is `infer_shape` which calls the corresponding shape inference function of an operator using pattern matching.

```
module Make (Type : Owl_computation_type_sig.Sig) = struct
  module Type = Type

  let infer_shape operator args =
```

```
let input_shapes = Array.map (fun a -> (Owl_graph.attr
a).shape) args in
match operator with
| Noop -> _infer_shape_01 input_shapes
| Create shape -> [| Some shape |]
...
| Scalar_Add -> _infer_shape_00 input_shapes
| Scalar_Sub -> _infer_shape_00 input_shapes
...
| Abs -> _infer_shape_01 input_shapes
| Neg -> _infer_shape_01 input_shapes
...
| Add -> _infer_shape_03 input_shapes
| Sub -> _infer_shape_03 input_shapes
...
| Conv1d (padding, stride) -> _infer_shape_11 input_shapes
  padding stride
| Conv2d (padding, stride) -> _infer_shape_12 input_shapes
  padding stride
| Conv3d (padding, stride) -> _infer_shape_13 input_shapes
  padding stride
...
```

end

There are over 30 shape inference functions defined. We can take a closer look at those frequently used ones. For example, scalar operators such as Scalar_Add do not require shape information, so its inference function only returns an empty array. The reason for using an array of arrays as the returned type is because an operator might produce multiple ndarrays as outputs.

```
let _infer_shape_00 _input_shapes = [| Some [||] |]
```

The _infer_shape_01 pattern is defined for a *unary operator* with a single input and a single output such as Abs. These operators do not change the shape of the data; the input and output have exactly the same shape. Thus, the inference function simply returns the shape of the input as the shape of the output.

```
let _infer_shape_01 input_shapes =
  match input_shapes.(0).(0) with
  | Some s -> [| Some Array.(copy s) |]
  | None   -> [| None |]
```

If the inputs have the same shape, *binary operators* like Add will produce an output of the same shape. However, if the shapes of inputs are different, broadcasting must be taken into account to correctly calculate the output shape. Luckily, the broadcasting rules can be codified easily from that used in the Ndarray module for shape inference purposes.

```
let _infer_shape_03 input_shapes =
  let s0 = input_shapes.(0).(0) in
  let s1 = input_shapes.(1).(0) in
  match s0, s1 with
  | Some s0, Some s1 -> [| Some Owl_utils_infer_shape.(broadcast1 s0 s1) |]
  | _, _             -> [| None |]
```

We do not cover all the shape inference patterns here. If you are interested, the readers are encouraged to read the source code of Owl to learn more about them. When the shape of a graph is known, we can exploit this information to calculate the total memory consumption, discover optimization opportunities, validate the consistency of inputs and outputs, identify potential bugs, etc.

Creating and Linking Nodes

Now we come to a higher level of abstraction: the graph itself. For inputs, outputs, and operators in a computation graph, we need to create their corresponding nodes. Because numerical operations are composable, the output of a function can become the inputs of other functions. We also need to link the nodes according to their input and output dependencies. The Owl_computation_symbol and Owl_computation_operator functors are developed for this purpose. The input of Owl_computation_symbol is a shape module, so the functor can infer the shape automatically while constructing a graph. The most basic functions like arr_to_node and node_to_arr pack and unpack ndarrays to and from a CGraph node.

```
module Make (Shape : Owl_computation_shape_sig.Sig) = struct
  module Shape = Shape

  let node_to_arr x = Arr x

  let arr_to_node = function
    | Arr x -> x

  let node_to_elt x = Elt x

  let elt_to_node = function
    | Elt x -> x

  ...
end
```

The general function for creating a node is make_node. The function utilizes the node type defined in the Owl_graph module which provides a comprehensive set of functions to manipulate a graph.

```
let make_node ?name ?value ?shape ?freeze ?reuse ?state op =
  let shape =
    match shape with
    | Some s -> s
    | None    -> [| None |]
  in
  let state =
    match state with
    | Some s -> s
    | None    -> Invalid
  in
  let reuse =
    match reuse with
    | Some s -> s
    | None    -> true
  in
```

```
let freeze =
  match freeze with
  | Some s -> s
  | None   -> false
in
let value =
  match value with
  | Some v -> v
  | None   -> [|||]
in
let attr = { op; freeze; reuse; state; shape; value; block = None } in
let node = Owl_graph.node ?name attr in
if value <> [|||] then make_value_block value.(0) node;
node
```

Because the Owl_graph module is designed for general-purpose graph manipulation such as construction, iteration, search, pruning, etc., the node properties are kept minimal and can be extended. The node type has a type parameter as you can see in its definition; therefore, we can attach related attributes of an operation to the node.

```
type 'a node =
  { mutable id : int
  ; mutable name : string
  ; mutable prev : 'a node array
  ; mutable next : 'a node array
  ; mutable attr : 'a
  }
```

Inputs need to connect to an operator to produce an output. If the output becomes the input of another operator, the computations are chained together. make_node only creates nodes, while make_then_connect does the linking job. The make_then_connect function internally calls make_node first to create a child node and then connects the outputs of the parent nodes to the inputs of the child node. Special attention is required if there are duplication in parent nodes, for example, in the $y = x + x$ case.

```
let make_then_connect ?shape op parents =
  let shape =
    match shape with
    | Some s -> s
    | None    -> infer_shape op parents
  in
  let child = make_node ~shape op in
  connect_ancestors parents [| child |];
  let uniq_parents = Owl_utils_array.unique parents in
  Array.iter
    (fun parent ->
      if (attr parent).freeze = false
      then connect_descendants [| parent |] [| child |])
    uniq_parents;
  child
```

For simple creation functions of ndarray, such as empty, zeros, etc., make_node is sufficient because these functions do not require any parents to provide inputs except its own shape information.

```
module Make (Symbol : Owl_computation_symbol_sig.Sig) = struct
  module Symbol = Symbol

  let empty shape = make_node ~shape:[| Some shape |] (Empty shape)
                    |> node_to_arr

  let zeros shape = make_node ~shape:[| Some shape |] (Zeros shape)
                    |> node_to_arr

  ...
end
```

For unary operators which do require the output of a parent node, make_then_connect is called to connect the parent's output to the operator's input. The outputs of parent nodes are unpacked from the arr type, while the outputs of a child are packed back into the arr type.

```
let abs x = make_then_connect Abs [| arr_to_node x |] |> node_to_arr

let neg x = make_then_connect Neg [| arr_to_node x |] |> node_to_arr
```

Binary operators work in a similar way. The only difference is that the inputs are from two parents rather than one comparing to unary operators.

```
let add x y = make_then_connect Add [| arr_to_node x; arr_to_node y |]
              |> node_to_arr

let sub x y = make_then_connect Sub [| arr_to_node x; arr_to_node y |]
              |> node_to_arr

let mul x y = make_then_connect Mul [| arr_to_node x; arr_to_node y |]
              |> node_to_arr

let div x y = make_then_connect Div [| arr_to_node x; arr_to_node y |]
              |> node_to_arr
```

With these basic functions, we can construct very complicated computation graphs. Quite often, the underlying computation graph may appear more complicated than the actual function defined in code; neural network applications are good examples.

Optimization of Graph Structure

The Optimiser functor is in charge of graph structure manipulation. It searches for various *structural patterns* in a graph and then performs various optimizations, such as removing unnecessary computations, fusing computation nodes, etc. All the patterns are defined in the Owl_computation_optimiser functor.

Let us first look at the heart of this functor, _optimise_term function, as follows. This function traverses backward from leaves to their ancestors recursively, looking for certain patterns to optimize. The patterns which the functor can recognize are coded in various pattern_* functions which call each other recursively. The source code is organized so that it is very straightforward to plug in more patterns to extend the optimizer's capability.

```
module Make (Operator : Owl_computation_operator_sig.Sig) = struct
  module Operator = Operator

  let rec _optimise_term x =
    Owl_log.debug "optimise %s ..." (node_to_str x);
    if is_valid x = false
```

```
then (
  (match get_operator x with
  | Noop -> pattern_003 x
  | Empty _shape -> pattern_000 x
  | Zeros _shape -> pattern_000 x
  ...
  | Add -> pattern_001 x
  | Sub -> pattern_000 x
  | Mul -> pattern_019 x
  | Div -> pattern_007 x
  ...
  | Scalar_Add -> pattern_010 x
  | Scalar_Sub -> pattern_010 x m
  ...
  | Dot (_transa, _transb, _alpha, _beta) -> pattern_005 x
  | Fused_Adagrad (_rate, _eps) -> pattern_000 x
  | _ -> failwith "Owl_computation_optimiser:_optimise_term");
  validate x)
end
```

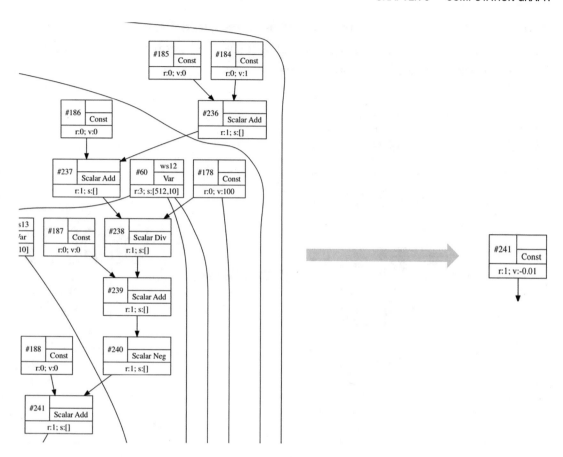

Figure 6-4. *Optimization techniques in a computation graph: constant folding*

In this part, we will explain three most commonly used graph optimization patterns: constant folding, operations fusing, and removing zeros. *Constant folding* is a very basic pattern to reduce graph size. In a computation graph, it is common to see that a lot of constants are involved. As a result, some subgraphs can be precalculated. Figure 6-4 shows such an example. In this subgraph, the nodes #241 depends on are either constants or operations on constants. Therefore, the value of node #241 is already decided. We can thus fold this subgraph into one single node before evaluating the whole graph.

From the definition of the _optimise_term function, we can see the Scalar_Add operator triggers the pattern_010 function. This function first tries to optimize the parent nodes, and then it checks whether both parents are constants. If so, the function evaluates the expression based on the current operator, creates a new constant node for the result, and removes the current node and its parents. By doing so, all the expressions which can be evaluated during this phase will be folded into a constant, which can save a lot of time during the graph evaluation phase.

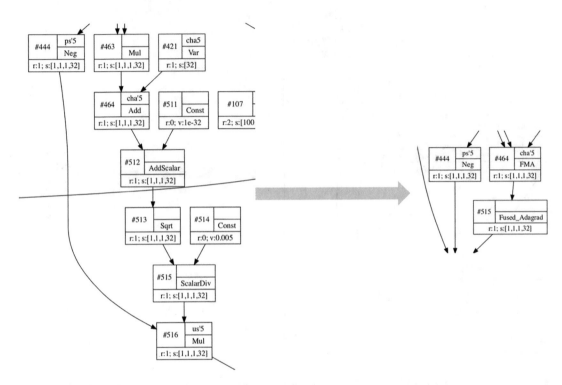

Figure 6-5. *Optimization techniques in a computation graph: fusing operations*

```
and pattern_010 x =
  let parents = parents x in
  let a = parents.(0) in
  let b = parents.(1) in
  _optimise_term a;
  _optimise_term b;
  match get_operator a, get_operator b with
  | Const, Const ->
      let a_val = node_to_elt a |> elt_to_float in
      let b_val = node_to_elt b |> elt_to_float in
      let c_val = pattern_011 (get_operator x) a_val b_val in
      set_parents x [||];
```

```
    set_reuse x false;
    set_operator x Const;
    freeze x;
    set_value x [| float_to_elt c_val |> unpack_elt |> elt_to_value |]
  | _                -> ()
```

The next pattern, *fusing operations*, combines multiple operations into one, if applicable. For example, in Figure 6-5, nodes #421, #463, and #464 are fused into one fma node (i.e., *fused-multiply-add operation*). Owl also recognizes complicated patterns, for example, a pattern formed by nodes #511–#515 appears a lot in DNN training that uses the Adagrad (adaptive subgradient) training method. Fusing all these operations into one single operation can improve computing efficiency as well as numerical accuracy. Besides, this optimization also effectively reduces the round trips to the memory, which saves a lot of time when operating on large ndarrays.

In the source code, fusing FMA operation depends on the pattern_004 function. The function first checks if the current operator is Add, then checks if one of the inputs is from the multiplication operator. If both conditions are satisfied, the pattern is identified. The refnum is a counter tracking how many times the output of an operator has been referred to by other expressions. If refnum is greater than one, we cannot fuse the operator because its output is used by another operator as input.

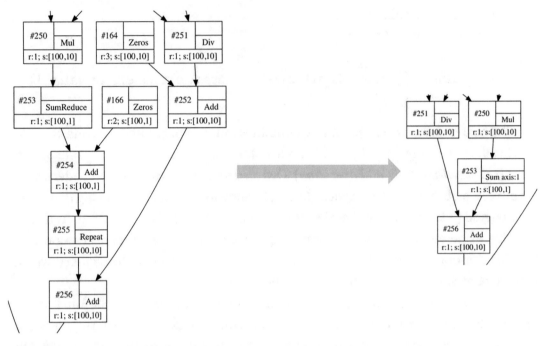

Figure 6-6. *Optimization techniques in a computation graph: adding zero*

```
and pattern_004 x =
  if get_operator x = Add
  then (
    let x_parents = parents x in
    let a = x_parents.(0) in
    let b = x_parents.(1) in
    if get_operator a = Mul && refnum a = 1
    then (
      let new_parents = Owl_utils_array.(parents a @ [| b |]) in
      set_parents x new_parents;
      replace_child a x;
      set_operator x FMA;
      remove_node a)
    else if get_operator b = Mul && refnum b = 1
    then (
      let new_parents = Owl_utils_array.(parents b @ [| a |]) in
      set_parents x new_parents;
```

```
    replace_child b x;
    set_operator x FMA;
    remove_node b))
```

Next, the *adding zero* pattern is trivial to see in the graph. If one node adds another zeros node, then the zeros node can be safely removed. In the example shown in Figure 6-6, nodes #164 and #166 are removed, and the others are folded. Moreover, node #255 for the repeat operation is also removed because the add operation already supports the broadcasting operation. Removing #255 can save some runtime memory in the evaluation.

The pattern_002 function detects both $x + 0$ and $0 + x$ patterns. The implementation is intuitive. After an Add operator is identified, the function checks whether one of the inputs is zero. If so, the Zero node is removed, and the current Add operator is replaced with the Noop operator.

```
and pattern_002 x =
  let x_parents = parents x in
  let a = x_parents.(0) in
  let b = x_parents.(1) in
  if get_operator x = Add
  then (
    match get_operator a, get_operator b with
    | Zeros _, _ ->
      set_operator x Noop;
      remove_edge a x;
      _optimise_term x
    | _, Zeros _ ->
      set_operator x Noop;
      remove_edge b x;
      _optimise_term x
    | _, _          -> ())
```

There are also other patterns that focus on specific calculations, such as multiplication, division, repeat, sum-reduce, etc. Please refer to the source code if you are interested in them. To show how effectively the Optimiser works, we again use the aforementioned LeNet-like CNN that is trained on the MNIST dataset. The original network has 201 nodes and 239 edges; after applying the graph optimization in Optimiser, the whole computation graph consists of only 103 nodes and 140 edges.

Optimizing a graph structure to improve evaluation performance is an advanced topic. But as you can see in the previous step-by-step illustration, advanced functionalities can be decomposed into a set of simple functions identifying specific patterns and optimizing locally using a typical divide-and-conquer approach. The graph optimization in TensorFlow follows a somewhat similar path. The computation graph in TensorFlow is first constructed using the Python frontend, and via a layer of the C API, this graph is converted to a format that the C++ backend can recognize. After that, the graph is optimized using various techniques, including common subexpression elimination, constant folding, removing identity nodes, removing dead nodes, etc. If you look at the source code of TensorFlow, this part of functionalities is taken care of by the common runtime module of its core engine.

Computation Engine

Finally, we have reached the top of the CGraph functor stack: the *computation engine*. Because a computation graph has to be evaluated on the hardware, each type of device must implement its own computing engine. The following code shows the engine for CPU devices. The core function eval_gen consists of two steps. The first step is to initialize the graph by calling _init_terms. The second step is to evaluate the graph by calling _eval_terms.

```
module Make_Nested (Graph : Owl_computation_graph_sig.Sig) = struct
  module Graph = Graph
  module CG_Init = Owl_computation_cpu_init.Make (Graph)
  module CG_Eval = Owl_computation_cpu_eval.Make (Graph)

  let eval_gen nodes =
    CG_Init._init_terms nodes;
    CG_Eval._eval_terms nodes

  let eval_elt xs = Array.map elt_to_node xs |> eval_gen

  let eval_arr xs = Array.map arr_to_node xs |> eval_gen
```

```
  let eval_graph graph =
    Graph.invalidate_rvs graph;
    Graph.get_outputs graph |> eval_gen
end
```

For comparison, let us also create a loop at the computing engine for OpenCL devices. The functor structure of the OpenCL computing engine is almost the same except the eval_gen function.. The function has a bit more code because the procedure of setting up a computing environment is much more complicated on an *OpenCL-compatible device* than on a CPU device. The procedure consists of many steps including specifying context, accelerator, *command queue, kernel programs*, etc. The evaluation outputs also need to be explicitly copied from *GPU memory* to *CPU memory* for further processing.

```
let eval_gen dev_id nodes =
  let ctx = Owl_opencl_context.(get_opencl_ctx default) in
  let dev = Owl_opencl_context.(get_dev default dev_id) in
  let cmdq = Owl_opencl_context.(get_cmdq default dev) in
  let prog = Owl_opencl_context.(get_program default) in
  let param = ctx, cmdq, prog in

  CG_Init.init_nodes nodes param;
  Array.iter
    (fun y ->
      CG_Eval._eval_term y param;
      let y_val = (get_value y).(0) in
      CG_Eval.gpu_to_cpu_copy param y_val |> ignore)
    nodes;
  Owl_opencl_base.CommandQueue.finish cmdq
```

The _eval_terms function consists of many _eval_map_* functions to perform actual computation. Let us look at a simple one _eval_map_00 for CPU devices. This function is for operators with a single input and a single output. The _eval_map_00 simply applies the operator's function f to its input x, then returns the result.

```
and _eval_map_01 x f =
  _eval_terms (parents x);
  let inputs = Array.map (fun parent ->
    value_to_arr (get_value parent).(0)) (parents x) in
  let out = value_to_arr (get_value x).(0) in
  f ~out inputs
```

On the other hand, the similar function for OpenCL devices is more complicated. Because the computation takes place on an accelerator, we need to set up the command queue for communication and *event queue* for synchronizing computing units. We also need to specify the suitable kernels. for computing logic. These kernels are compiled dynamically during the runtime and then copied to the computing units of an accelerator. When the output is finally ready, we must explicitly dispatch the event to notify the dependent.

```
and _eval_map_01 x param =
  Array.iter (fun parent -> _eval_term parent param) (parents x);
  let _, cmdq, _ = param in
  let kernel = (get_value x).(0).kernel.(0) in
  let items = [ node_numel x ] in
  let wait_for = aggregate_events (parents x) |> Array.to_list in
  let event = Owl_opencl_base.Kernel.enqueue_ndrange ~wait_for cmdq kernel
  1 items in
  Device.append_events (get_value x).(0) [| event |]
```

Programming a GPU is very much like programming a computer cluster. The gain of parallel computing comes with inevitable synchronization and communication overhead. Therefore, GPU computing only makes sense when the computation complexity is high enough to dwarf other overheads.

When offloading the computation to a GPU, we should avoid transmitting data back and forth between the host and the device memory, so eager evaluation is not ideal in this context because the performance will be throttled by copying. This is the gap between CPU computing and a language with eager evaluation. The computation graph essentially fills the gap between Owl and GPU computing simply because the laziness can be simulated now.

From an implementation perspective, we only need to write a new engine functor for GPU devices to evaluate a graph; all the others remain the same. Comparing to the CPU engine, the OpenCL engine maintains the memory allocated on both the host and the device for each node, copying only happens whenever it is necessary, and the allocated memory on the device is reused as much as possible.

6.4 Optimizing Memory Usage in Computation Graph

In the previous sections, we have introduced the CGraph stack. Before concluding this chapter, we would like to show optimizations we have made to reduce memory usage in the CGraph module. One principle we have been following during developing Owl is to always get driven by real-world applications. Besides the image recognition example, we have built an image segmentation application, a challenging and interesting use case for Owl. Seeking to push the performance of this application, we manage to further optimize the design of the CGraph module. We will present this deep neural network, Mask R-CNN, in Chapter 5. This section is mainly based on the work done by Pierre Vandenhove on Owl during his internship in the OCaml Labs [49].

The first issue after constructing the network, called *Mask R-CNN*, or MRCNN, in Owl was that its memory usage. in inference mode was huge. The network has over 400 layers. A reasonable input image size for this network is a 1024-pixel-wide square. To avoid reinitializing the network for every picture, it is a good practice to keep its input size fixed and to resize instead all the images to that size. Unfortunately, obtaining detections for one picture with such size required over 11GB of RAM, which was too much for a normal laptop. There is surely a big room for improvement.

We first try to apply the graph structure optimization we have mentioned in the previous section. The number of nodes of the Mask R-CNN network drops from 4095 to 3765, but its effect in memory reduction is limited. To this end, we need to add in the CGraph functor stack another important layer: memory management. Specifically, we need the ability to preallocate a memory space to each node, to decrease the overall memory consumption and reduce the garbage collector overhead. The key is to find the allocated memory block in the graph that is no longer required and assign it to other nodes that are in need.

The memory manipulation functionalities are implemented in the `Engine` functor in the stack. The key data structure is the `block` type we mentioned in Section 6.3. The `block` type is a record which maintains a list of nodes sharing the same memory. The initial strategy to allocate memory to a node u in Owl's computation graph module was simply to reuse the memory of a direct predecessor with the same output shape as u when that is possible. For example, if we add two ndarrays of the same shape, the output ndarray can reuse the memory block of one of them. This optimization decreases the memory consumption of Mask R-CNN from 11GB to 7GB. This 36% reduction looks quite impressive, but can we do even better?

To describe the process of allocating memory in a computation graph, it is interesting to first look at the *pebble game*, which was introduced in 1973 to explain register allocation [45]. The pebble game is played on a directed acyclic graph. Each node can store at most one pebble. The game begins with no pebble on any node. At each step, the player can do one of the following moves:

1. If a vertex v has no predecessor, the player can place a pebble on v.

2. If all predecessors of a vertex v are pebbled, the player can place a pebble on v or `slide` a pebble from one of its predecessors to v.

3. The player can remove any pebble from a vertex (and reuse that pebble later).

The goal of the game is to place a pebble at least once on some fixed output vertices of the graph. Figure 6-7 shows an example of an optimal pebbling strategy using the previous computation graph (gray nodes are pebbled), using moves 1-> 2 -> 3 -> 1 -> 2-> 2. We assume that the goal is to pebble node 5.

This game relates to the memory allocation of the computation graph if we see pebbles as memory blocks used to store the output value of a node. We assume that the values of the inputs are known (move 1). We can only compute the value of a vertex if all its predecessors are simultaneously stored in memory (move 2). The *sliding* move means that the memory of a node can be overwritten by its successor during its computation (*inplace reuse*). We can always reuse a memory block from any other node (move 3). Given a graph, the idea is thus to find a strategy to pebble it using the minimum number of pebbles, in other words, using as little memory as possible.

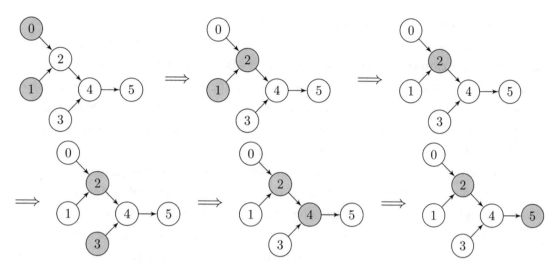

Figure 6-7. *Modeling a computation graph memory optimization problem as a pebble game*

We also want to avoid pebbling any node twice in order to keep the execution time as low as possible, because that would mean that we compute the same node twice. Given these constraints, finding a strategy using the least amount of pebbles is unfortunately NP complete [45]. Since computation graphs can have a few thousand nodes, we implement a fast heuristic instead of an exact algorithm.

Now we can apply the pebble game process in our memory allocation process. We propose to share memory between nodes that (1) are not necessarily a parent/child pair and (2) that do not have the same output size (by allocating a large block of memory once, without necessarily using all of it all the time). To do this efficiently, we first have to fix an evaluation order (in practice, any topological order). Given this order, we can pinpoint the moment when the memory of a node becomes useless by keeping a counter of how many times it has been used. When it has been used by all its children, we can recycle its memory. Then to allocate memory to a node, we simply check which blocks are available, and we select the one with the closest size (in order not to waste too much memory). If no block is available, we allocate a new one. This can be executed in $O(n^* \log(n))$ time, which is negligible compared to the actual cost of evaluating the graph.

Note that some operations cannot overwrite their inputs while they are being computed (the *sliding* move from the pebble game is forbidden) and that some nodes cannot be overwritten for practical purposes, typically constant nodes or neural network weights. When evaluated in the right order, the computation graph needs much smaller blocks of memory than the non-optimized version. As an example, part of an optimized computation graph is shown in Figure 6-8. Each color corresponds to a memory block, and white nodes always need to be kept in memory.

The code in add_node_to_block illustrates the steps of introducing a new node. If the memory block of the parent is reusable, the function checks whether the memory is large enough for accommodating the output of the current operator. If so, the node includes the current operator to the list of nodes sharing the same memory block. Moreover, the memory is reshaped according to the shape of the output.

```
let add_node_to_block x block =
  let dst_shp = node_shape x in
  let dst_numel = node_numel x in
  let src_val = value_to_arr (_get_value_block block) in
  let dst_val = arr_to_value
    (A.reshape (A.sub_left src_val 0 dst_numel) dst_shp) in
  block.nodes <- x :: block.nodes;
  _set_block x [| block |];
  (attr x).value <- [| dst_val |]
```

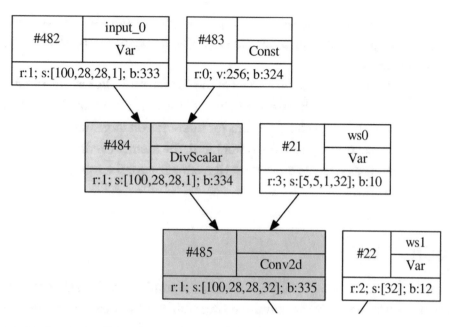

Figure 6-8. *Optimized memory allocation*

Table 6-1. *Evaluation of the Effect of CGraph Memory Optimization Using Different DNN Architectures*

Architecture	Time	Time with CG (Building	Memory	Memory with
	Without CG (s)	+ Evaluating) (s)	Without CG (MB)	CG (MB)
InceptionV3	0.565	0.107 + 0.228 = 0.335	625.76	230.10
ResNet50	0.793	0.140 + 0.609 = 0.749	1309.9	397.07
MNIST (Training)	20.422	0.144 + 10.920 = 11.064	3685.3	895.32
Mask R-CNN	11.538	0.363 + 8.379 = 8.742	6483.4	870.48

Implementing this effectively further reduced the memory consumption of Mask R-CNN from 7GB to 1GB for a 1024x1024 picture. Table 6-1 shows some more statistics illustrating what the computation graph with this new algorithm achieves. These experiments run on a laptop with an Intel i5-6300HQ and 8GB of RAM. In this evaluation, the InceptionV3 and ResNet50 networks are tested with a 299x299 image, and Mask R-CNN is tested with a 768x768 image. The MNIST line refers to the small LeNet-like neural network we used in Section 6.2. The final result is calculated as an average over 30 evaluations, without reusing precomputed nodes when a computation graph is used. The graph building phase includes graph construction, optimization, and memory initialization.

This evaluation result shows the impact of the CGraph module. On one hand, with graph structure optimization, the execution time of the neural network is significantly reduced. This decrease is especially obvious for inference on large networks such as Mask R-CNN or model training. On the other hand, the memory reduction is also impressive, achieving as large as more than 10x reduction for the inference with the Mask R-CNN network.

6.5 Summary

In this chapter, we introduced the core computation graph module in Owl. We started with a general introduction of the computation graph in numerical computing and why we build that in Owl. Then we used several examples to demonstrate how the computation graph module is used in Owl. This was followed by the internal design of this module, most importantly the CGraph stack and its position in the Owl architecture. The computation graph creates a large optimization space, and in this chapter, we presented two of them in detail. The first is the graph structure optimization, and the second is to optimize the memory allocation in the computation graph. A computation graph is an important research topic, and we believe there is still much potential in this module for performance improvement.

CHAPTER 7

Performance Accelerators

7.1 Hardware Accelerators

The Graphics Processing Unit (GPU) has become one of the most important types of hardware accelerators. It is designed to render 3D graphics and videos and still is core to the gaming industry. Besides creating stunning visual effects, programmers also take advantage of the GPU's advantage in parallel processing in many fields to perform computing-heavy tasks, such as in health data analytics, physical simulation, artificial intelligence, etc.

Recall from Chapter 2 the architecture of a typical CPU. The architecture of a GPU core is somewhat similar. Figure 7-1 shows one core of an Nvidia GTX 1080, which contains 20 such cores. Compared with a CPU core, it contains much more multithreading units, including more single-instruction-multiple-data (SIMD) function units, and more cores in a GPU. Another character of the GPU is its small cache. This GPU contains only two levels of caches (this figure only shows the level 1 cache; the level 2 cache is shared by all 20 cores), each smaller than a typical CPU's. Besides, the GPU also focuses on throughput, and thus its bandwidth between cores and memory is much larger than that of a CPU.

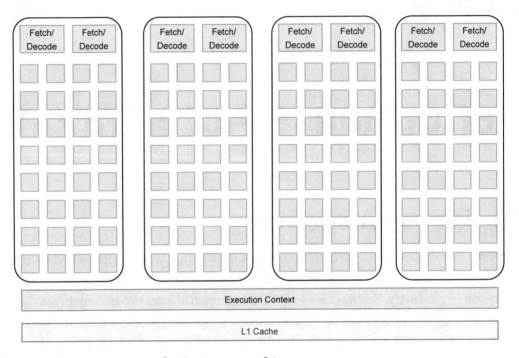

Figure 7-1. *Illustration of a GPU core architecture*

Another type of accelerator that has gain much attention in recent years is the Tensor Processing Unit (TPU). In 2016, Google has announced TPU, its application-specific integrated circuit, and introduced that TPU has been deployed in Google's data centers to accelerate neural network computation.

The design of TPU is based on the fact that matrix multiplication plays a dominant role in neural network–related computing and uses this operation as a primitive operation. In the CPU, the basic calculation unit is scalar, so that we can, for example, add two integers using one single instruction within a cycle. The GPU, on the other hand, widely utilizes multithreading, and thus the user can add two vectors in a cycle. The TPU further proposes to finish a matrix operation in one cycle.

A TPU v2 core consists of a Matrix Multiply Unit (MXU) and a Vector Processing Unit (VPU). The former specializes in matrix multiplication, and the latter takes care of all other types of tasks, such as activations. The MXU utilizes a *systolic array* architecture to enable the single-clock matrix operation. As a result, it can execute up to 128K operations in one cycle. Google reports that the TPU delivered 15–30X higher performance and 30–80X higher performance per watt than contemporary CPUs and GPUs. Besides, due to neural networks' tolerance to errors, TPU also performs quantization to compress calculation by converting continuous float numbers to discrete ones.

Utilizing Accelerators

There is no doubt that numerical computing heavily relies on hardware accelerators: TensorFlow, PyTorch, Julia, MATLAB, etc. They all support multiple types of devices, including at least the CPU and GPU. In general, there are two methods to do that.

The first, and most widely used, is direct support of the hardware. Take the GPU as an example. When programming a GPU, Nvidia CUDA is a widely used choice. CUDA is a parallel computing platform and programming model for computing on Nvidia GPUs. In TensorFlow, a computation graph is first expressed in Python on the frontend and is then accordingly built up using the C++ backend. This graph is further optimized and partitioned onto multiple devices, which can be CPU, GPU, or TPU devices. Each device invokes the corresponding executor to run the assigned computation on its subgraph. For TPU device execution, TensorFlow incorporates a compiler and software stack that translates API calls from TensorFlow computation graphs into TPU instructions. In Julia, support for Nvidia GPUs is provided by its CUDA.jl package. Built on the CUDA toolkit, it enables both interfacing with the CUDA API directly and writing CUDA kernels. NumPy does not support GPUs, but in the vast Python world, there are a lot of GPU-friendly alternatives, such as Numba, CuPy, etc.

Compared with CUDA, the Open Computing Language (OpenCL) serves as an open source standard for cross-platform parallel programming and is not limited to Nvidia GPUs. Therefore, some numerical libraries and software also support it to work on non-Nvidia GPUs. The StreamExecutor that TensorFlow utilizes to process computation tasks on a GPU device is actually a unified wrapper around the CUDA and OpenCL runtimes.

Recently, given a growing number of deep learning frameworks and equally growing number of hardware accelerator platforms, a new approach is to utilize intermediate representations. For example, the *deep learning compiler* has gained rapid growth. A DL compiler takes the model definition described in a deep learning framework and generates efficient implementation specific to certain target hardware. TVM [10] is one popular DL compiler that works with a wide range of frameworks and hardware devices. A closely related idea is an open neural network standard that can be converted to and from various frameworks and can also be compiled and executed on various hardware. One such example is the Open Neural Network Exchange (ONNX) format. In summary, it is a growing trend that the definition of computation can be separated out and the low-level compilers to deal with optimization, code generation, etc. to pursue best computation performance. We can think of DL compilers and open standards as the neck of an hourglass that bridges the gap between two types of ecosystems. In the rest of this chapter, based on the latter approach, we propose `owl_symbolic`, which converts Owl computation to that of ONNX and can further be executed on various hardware accelerators.

7.2 Design

Except for the requirement to be executed on accelerators, the development of the `owl_symbolic` library is motivated by several other factors. For one thing, scientific computation can be considered as consisting of two broad categories: numerical computation and symbolic computation. Owl has achieved a solid foundation in the former, but as yet to support the latter one, which is heavily utilized in a lot of fields.

Besides, tasks such as visualizing a computation also require some form of intermediate representation (IR). Owl has already provided a computation graph layer to separate the definition and execution of computation to improve the performance, as introduced in Chapter 6, but it's not an IR layer to perform these different tasks as mentioned before. Toward this end, we begin to develop an intermediate symbolic representation of computations and facilitate various tasks based on this symbol representation.

One thing to note is that do not mistake our symbolic representation as the classic symbolic computation (or computer algebra system) that manipulates mathematical expressions in a symbolic way, which is similar to the traditional manual computations. It is indeed one of our core motivations to pursue the symbolic computation with Owl. Currently, we provide a symbolic representation layer as the first step toward that target. More discussion will be added in future versions of the development with the support of symbolic math in Owl.

The `owl_symbolic` library is divided into two parts: the core symbolic representation that constructs a symbolic graph and various engines that perform different tasks based on the graph. The architecture design of this system is shown in Figure 7-2.

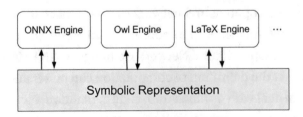

Figure 7-2. *Architecture of the symbolic system*

The core abstraction is an independent symbolic representation layer. Based on this layer, we have built various engines that can be translated to and from this symbolic representation. Currently, we support three engines: the ONNX binary format, the computation graph in Owl, and the LaTeX string. The CAS engine is currently still an ongoing research project, and we envision that, once finished, this engine can be used to preprocess a symbolic representation so that it has a simplified canonical form before being processed by other engines.

Core Abstraction

The core part is designed to be minimal and contains only necessary information. Currently, it has already covered many common computation types, such as math operations, tensor manipulations, neural network–specific operations such as convolution, pooling, etc. Each symbol in the symbolic graph performs a certain operation. Input to a symbolic graph can be constants such as integer, float number, complex number, and tensor. The input can also be variables with certain shapes. An empty shape indicates a scalar value. The users can then provide values to the variable after the symbolic graph is constructed.

Symbol

The symbolic representation is defined mainly as an array of symbol. Each symbol is a graph node that has an attribution of type Owl_symbolic_symbol.t. It means that we can traverse through the whole graph by starting with one symbol. Besides symbols, the name field is the graph name, and node_names contains all the nodes' names contained in this graph.

```
type symbol = Owl_symbolic_symbol.t Owl_graph.node

type t =
  { mutable sym_nodes : symbol array
  ; mutable name : string
  ; mutable node_names : string array
  }
```

Let's look at Owl_symbolic_symbol.t. It defines all the operations contained in the symbolic representation:

```
type t =
  | NOOP
  | Int              of Int.t
  | Complex          of Complex.t
  | Float            of Float.t
  | Tensor           of Tensor.t
  | Variable         of Variable.t
  | RandomUniform    of RandomUniform.t
  | Sin              of Sin.t
  | Cos              of Cos.t
  | Exp              of Exp.t
  | ReduceSum        of ReduceSum.t
  | Reshape          of Reshape.t
  | Conv             of Conv.t
  ....
```

There are totally about 150 operations included in our symbolic representation. Each operation is implemented as a module. These modules share common attributes such as names, input operation names, and output shapes, and then each module contains zero or more attributes of itself. For example, the Sin operation module is implemented as

```
module Sin = struct
  type t =
    { mutable name : string
    ; mutable input : string array
    ; mutable out_shape : int array option array
    }

  let op_type = "Sin"

  let create ?name x_name =
    let input = [| x_name |] in
    let name = Owl_symbolic_utils.node_name ?name op_type in
    { name; input; out_shape = [| None |] }
end
```

The module provides properties such as op_type and functions such as `create` that returns objects of type `Sin.t`. The `name`, `input`, and `out_shape` are common attributes in the operation modules.

In implementing the supported operations, we follow the categorization used in ONNX. These operations can be generally divided into different groups as follows:

- Generators: Operations that generate data, taking no input. For example, the `Int`, `Float`, `Tensor`, `Variable`, etc.

- Logical: Logical operations such as `Xor`.

- Math: Mathematical operations. This group of operations makes a large part of the total operations supported.

- Neural network: Neural network–related operations such as convolution and pooling.

- Object detection: Also used in neural networks, but the operations that are closely related with object detection applications, including `RoiAlign` and `NonMaxSuppression`.

- Reduction: Reduction (or folding) math operations such as sum reduce.

- RNN: Recurrent neural network–related operations such as LTSM.

- Tensor: Normal tensor operations, like the ones that are included in the Ndarray module, such as `concat`, `reshape`, etc.

- Sequence: Take multiple tensors as one single object called `sequence`, and there are different corresponding functions on the sequence type data, such as `SequenceInsert`, `SequenceLength`, etc.

Based on these operation modules, we provide several functions on the `Owl_symbolic_symbol.t` type:

- `name`: Get the name of the operation

- `op_type`: Get the operation type string

- `input`: Get the input node name of an operation

- `set_input`: Update the input node name

- output: Get the output node name

- set_output: Update the output node name

There are also some functions that only apply to certain types of operations. The generator type of operations all need to specify the type of data it supports. Therefore, we use the dtype function to check their data types. Another example is the output property. For most of the operation, it has only one output, and therefore its name is its output name. However, for operations such as MaxPool that contains multiple outputs, we need another function: output.

Type Checking

The type supported by owl_symbolic is listed as follows:

```
type number_type =
  | SNT_Noop
  | SNT_Float
  | SNT_Double
  | SNT_Complex32
  | SNT_Complex64
  | SNT_Bool
  | SNT_String
  | SNT_Int8
  | SNT_Int16
  | SNT_Int32
  | SNT_Int64
  | SNT_Uint8
  | SNT_Uint16
  | SNT_Uint32
  | SNT_Uint64
  | SNT_Float16
  | SNT_SEQ of number_type
```

This list of types covers most number and non-number types. Besides, the SNT_SEQ type is used to compose with these basic types to indicate a list of float number, boolean value, string, etc.

Operators

All these operations are invisible to users. What the users really use are the *operators*. To build a graph, we first need to build the required attributes into an operation and then put it into a graph node. This is what an operator does. Take the `sin` operator as an example:

```
let sin ?name x =
  let xn = Owl_symbolic_graph.name x in
  let s = Owl_symbolic_ops_math.Sin.create ?name xn in
  make_node (Owl_symbolic_symbol.Sin s) [| x |]
```

Here, the `sin` operator takes its parent node x as an input, get its name as an input property, and create a symbol node with the function make_node. This function takes an operation and an array of parent symbols and then creates one symbol as a return. What it does is mainly creating a child node using the given operation as node attribution, updating the child's input and output shapes, and then connecting the child with parents before returning the child node. The connection is on both directions:

```
connect_ancestors parents [| child |];
let uniq_parents = Owl_utils_array.unique parents in
Array.iter (fun parent -> connect_descendants [| parent |] [| child |])
uniq_parents
```

Therefore, the users can use the operators to build a graph representation. Here is an example:

```
open Owl_symbolic
open Op
open Infix

let x = variable "x_0"
let y = exp ((sin x ** float 2.) + (cos x ** float 2.))
    + (float 10. * (x ** float 2.))
    + exp (pi () * complex 0. 1.)
```

Here, we start with the `variable` operator, which creates a placeholder for incoming data later. You can specify the shape of the variable with the ~shape parameter. If not specified, then it defaults to a scalar. You can also choose to initialize this variable with a *tensor* so that even if you don't feed any data to the variable, the default tensor value will be used. A tensor in `owl-symbolic` is defined as

```
type tensor =
  { mutable dtype : number_type
  ; mutable shape : int array
  ; mutable str_val : string array option
  ; mutable flt_val : float array option
  ; mutable int_val : int array option
  ; mutable raw_val : bytes option
  }
```

A tensor is of a specific type of data, and then it contains the value: string array, float array, integer array, or bytes. Only one of these fields can be used. If initialized with a tensor, a variable takes the same data type and shape as that of the tensor.

Naming

Currently, we adopt a global naming scheme, which is to add an incremental index number after each node's type. For example, if we have an Add symbol, a Div symbol, and then another Add symbol in a graph, then each node will be named add_0, div_1, and add_1. One exception is the variable, where a user has to explicitly name when creating a variable. Of course, users can also optionally name any node in the graph, but the system will check to make sure the name of each node is unique. The symbolic graph contains the node_names field that includes all the nodes' names in the graph.

Shape Inferencing

One task the symbolic core needs to perform is shape checking and shape inferencing. Shape inference is performed in the make_node function and therefore happens every time a user uses an operation to construct a symbolic node and connect it with previous nodes. It is assumed that the parents of the current node are already known.

```
let (in_shapes : int array option array array)=
  Array.map (fun sym_node ->
    Owl_graph.attr sym_node |> Owl_symbolic_symbol.out_shape
  ) parents
  in
let (shape : int array option array) =
  Owl_symbolic_shape.infer_shape in_shapes sym
...
```

As the code shows, for each node, we first find the output shapes of its parents. The in_shape is of type int array option array array. You can understand it this way: int array is a shape array; int array option means this shape could be None. Then int array option array is one whole input from the previous parent, since one parent may contain multiple outputs. Finally, int array option array array includes output from all parents. The main function Owl_symbolic_shape.infer_shape then infers the output shape of the current node and saves it to the out_shape property of that symbol.

The infer_shape function itself checks the symbol type and then match with specific implementation. For example, a large number of operations actually take one parent and keep its output shape:

```
let infer_shape input_shapes sym =
  | Sin _ -> infer_shape_01 input_shapes
  | Exp _ -> infer_shape_01 input_shapes
  | Log _ -> infer_shape_01 input_shapes
....

let infer_shape_01 input_shapes =
  match input_shapes.(0).(0) with
  | Some s -> [| Some Array.(copy s) |]
  | None   -> [| None |]
```

This pattern infer_shape_01 covers these operations. It simply takes the input shape and returns the same shape.

There are two possible reasons for the input shape to be None. At first, each node will be initialized with a None output shape. During shape inference, in certain cases, the output shape depends on the runtime content of input nodes, not just the shapes of input nodes and attributions of the current node. In that case, the output shape is set to None. Once the input shapes contain None, the shape inference results hereafter will all be None, which means the output shapes cannot be decided at compile time.

Multiple Outputs

Most of the operators are straightforward to implement, but some of them return multiple symbols. In that case, an operation returns not a node, but a tuple or, when output numbers are uncertain, an array of nodes. For example, the MaxPool operation returns two outputs: one is the normal maxpooling result, and the other is the corresponding tensor that contains indices of the selected values during pooling. Or we have the Split operation that splits a tensor into a list of tensors, along the specified axis. It returns an array of symbols.

Engines

Based on this simple core abstraction, we use different *engines* to provide functionalities: converting to and from other computation expression formats, print out to human-readable format, graph optimization, etc. As we have said, the core part is kept minimal. If the engines require information other than what the core provides, each symbol has an `attr` property as an extension point. All engines must follow the following signature:

```
type t

val of_symbolic : Owl_symbolic_graph.t -> t
val to_symbolic : t -> Owl_symbolic_graph.t
val save : t -> string -> unit
val load : string -> t
```

It means that each engine has its own core type `t`, be it a string or another format of graph, and it needs to convert `t` to and from the core symbolic graph type or save/load a type `t` data structure to a file. An engine can also contain extra functions besides these four. Now that we have explained the design of `owl_symbolic`, let's look at the details of some engines in the next few sections.

7.3 ONNX Engine

The ONNX engine is the current focus of development in `owl_symbolic`. ONNX is a widely adopted Open Neural Network Exchange format. A neural network model defined in ONNX can be, via suitable converters, run on different frameworks and thus hardware accelerators. The main target of ONNX is to promote the interchangeability of neural network and machine learning models, but it is worth noting that the standard covers a lot of basic operations in scientific computation, such as power, logarithms, trigonometric functions, etc. Therefore, the ONNX engine serves as a good starting point for its coverage of operations.

Taking a symbolic graph as input, how would then the ONNX engine produce the ONNX model? We use the ocaml-protoc, a protobuf compiler for OCaml, as the tool. The ONNX specification is defined in an onnx.proto file, and the `ocaml-protoc` can compile this protobuf files into OCaml types along with serialization functions for a variety of encodings. For example, the top-level message type in onnx.proto is ModelProto, defined as follows:

```
message ModelProto {
  optional int64 ir_version = 1;
  repeated OperatorSetIdProto opset_import = 8;
  optional string producer_name = 2;
  optional string producer_version = 3;
  optional string domain = 4;
  optional int64 model_version = 5;
  optional string doc_string = 6;
  optional GraphProto graph = 7;
  repeated StringStringEntryProto metadata_props = 14;
};
```

And the generated OCaml types and serialization function are

```
open Owl_symbolic_specs.PT

type model_proto =
  { ir_version : int64 option
  ; opset_import : operator_set_id_proto list
  ; producer_name : string option
  ; producer_version : string option
  ; domain : string option
  ; model_version : int64 option
  ; doc_string : string option
  ; graph : graph_proto option
  ; metadata_props : string_string_entry_proto list
  }

val encode_model_proto : Onnx_types.model_proto -> Pbrt.Encoder.t -> unit
```

Besides the meta-information such as model version, IR version, etc., a model is mainly a graph, which includes input/output information and an array of nodes. A node specifies the operator type, input and output node names, and its own attributions, such as the axis attribution in reduction operations.

Therefore, all we need is to build up a `model_proto` data structure gradually from attributions to nodes, graph, and model. It can then be serialized using `encode_model_proto` to generate a protobuf format file, and that is the ONNX model we want.

Besides building up the model, one other task to be performed in the engine is type checking and type inferencing. For example, the sine function can only accept an input of float or double number types and generate the same type of input as that of the input. Each type of operator has its own rules of type checking and inferencing. Starting from input nodes, which must contain specific type information, this chain if inferencing can thus verify the whole computation meets the type constraints for each node and then yield the final output types of the whole graph. The reason that type checking is performed at the engine side instead of the core is that each engine may have different type constraints and type inferencing rules for the operators.

Example 1: Basic Operations

Let's look at several examples of using the ONNX engine, starting with a simple one:

```
open Owl_symbolic
open Op
open Infix

let x = variable "X"
let y = variable "Y"
let z = exp ((sin x ** float 2.)
             + (cos x ** float 2.))
             + (float 10. * (y ** float 2.))
let g = SymGraph.make_graph [| z |] "sym_graph"
let m = ONNX_Engine.of_symbolic g
let _ = ONNX_Engine.save m "test.onnx"
```

After including necessary library components, the first three lines of code create a symbolic representation z using the symbolic operators such as `sin`, `pow`, and `float`. The x and y are variables that accept user inputs. It is then used to create a symbolic graph. This step mainly checks if there is any duplication of node names. Then the `of_symbolic` function in the ONNX engine takes the symbolic graph as input and generates a `model_proto` data structure, which can be further saved as a model named `test.onnx`.

To use this ONNX model, we could use any framework that supports ONNX. Here, we use the Python-based ONNX Runtime as an example. We prepare a simple Python script as follows:

```
import numpy as np
import math
import onnxruntime as rt

sess = rt.InferenceSession("test.onnx")
input_name_x = sess.get_inputs()[0].name
input_name_y = sess.get_inputs()[1].name
x = np.asarray(math.pi, dtype="float32")
y = np.asarray(3., dtype="float32")

pred_onx = sess.run(None, {input_name_x: x, input_name_y: y})[0]
print(pred_onx)
```

This script is very simple: it loads the ONNX model we have just created and then gets the two input variables and assigns two values to them in the `sess.run` command. All the user needs to know in advance is that there are two input variables in this ONNX model. Note that we could define not only scalar type inputs but also tensor type variables in `owl_symbolic` and then assign a NumPy array to them when evaluating.

Example 2: Variable Initialization

We can initialize the variables with tensor values so that these default values are used even if no data are passed in. Here is one example:

```
open Owl_symbolic
open Op

let _ =
  let flt_val = [| 1.; 2.; 3.; 4.; 5.; 6. |] in
  let t = Type.make_tensor ~flt_val [| 2; 3 |] in
  let x = variable ~init:t "X" in
  let y = sin x in
  let g = SymGraph.make_graph [| y |] "sym_graph" in
  let z = ONNX_Engine.of_symbolic g in
  ONNX_Engine.save z "test.onnx"
```

This computation simply takes an input variable x and then applies the sin operation. Let's look at the Python side:

```
import numpy as np
import onnxruntime as rt

sess = rt.InferenceSession("test.onnx")
pred_onx = sess.run(None, input_feed={})
print(pred_onx[0])
```

The expected output is

```
[[ 0.84147096  0.9092974   0.14112   ]
 [-0.7568025  -0.9589243  -0.2794155 ]]
```

Note how the initializer works without users providing any input in the input feed dictionary. Of course, the users can still provide their own data to this computation, but the mechanism may be a bit different. For example, in onnx_runtime, using sess. get_inputs() gives an empty set this time. Instead, you should use get_overridable_ initializers():

```
input_x = sess.get_overridable_initializers()[0]
input_name_x = input_x.name
input_shape_x = input_x.shape
x = np.ones(input_shape_x, dtype="float32")
pred_onx = sess.run(None, {input_name_x: x})
```

Example 3: Neural Network

The main purpose of the ONNX standard is to express neural network models, and we have already covered most of the common operations that are required to construct neural networks. However, to construct a neural network model directly from existing owl_symbolic operations requires a lot of details such as input shapes or creating extra nodes. For example, if we want to build a neural network with operators directly, we need to write something like

```
let dnn =
  let x = variable ~shape:[| 100; 3; 32; 32 |] "X" in
  let t_conv0 = conv ~padding:Type.SAME_UPPER x
```

```
     (random_uniform ~low:(-0.138) ~high:0.138 [| 32; 3; 3; 3 |]) in
let t_zero0 =
  let flt_val = Array.make 32 0. in
  let t = Type.make_tensor ~flt_val [| 32 |] in
  tensor t
in
let t_relu0 = relu (t_conv0 + t_zero0) in
let t_maxpool0, _ = maxpool t_relu0
                          ~padding:VALID
                          ~strides:[| 2; 2 |]
                          [| 2; 2 |] in
let t_reshape0 = reshape [| 100; 8192 |] t_maxpool0 in
let t_rand0 = random_uniform ~low:(-0.0011) ~high:0.0011 [| 8192;
512 |] in
....
```

Apparently, that's too much information for the users to handle. To make things easier for the users, we create a neural network layer based on existing symbolic operations. This lightweight layer takes only 180 LoC, and yet it provides an Owl-like clean syntax for the users to construct neural networks. For example, we can construct an MNIST-DNN model:

```
open Owl_symbolic_neural_graph
let nn =
  input [| 100; 3; 32; 32 |]
  |> normalisation
  |> conv2d [| 32; 3; 3; 3 |] [| 1; 1 |]
  |> activation Relu
  |> max_pool2d [| 2; 2 |] [| 2; 2 |] ~padding:VALID
  |> fully_connected 512
  |> activation Relu
  |> fully_connected 10
  |> activation (Softmax 1)
  |> get_network
```

```
let _ =
  let onnx_graph = Owl_symbolic_engine_onnx.of_symbolic nn in
  Owl_symbolic_engine_onnx.save onnx_graph "test.onnx"
```

Besides this simple DNN, we have also created the complex architectures such as ResNet, InceptionV3, SqueezeNet, etc. They are all adapted from existing Owl DNN models with only a minor change. The execution of the generated ONNX model is similar:

```
import numpy as np
import onnxruntime as rt

sess = rt.InferenceSession("test.onnx")
input_name_x = sess.get_inputs()[0].name
input_name_shape = sess.get_inputs()[0].shape
input_x = np.ones(input_name_shape , dtype="float32")
pred_onx = sess.run(None, {input_name_x: input_x})[0]
```

For simplicity, we generate a dummy input for the execution/inference phase of this model. Of course, currently, in our model the weight data is not trained. Training of a model should be completed on a framework such as TensorFlow. Combining trained weight data into the ONNX model remains to be a future work.

Furthermore, by using tools such as js_of_ocaml, we can convert both examples into JavaScript; executing them can create the ONNX models, which in turn can be executed on the browser using ONNX.js that utilizes WebGL. In summary, using ONNX as the intermediate format for exchange computation across platforms enables numerous promising directions.

7.4 LaTeX Engine

The LaTeX engine takes a symbolic representation as input and produces LaTeX strings which can then be visualized using different tools. Its design is simple, mainly about matching symbol type and projecting it to correct implementation. Again, let's look at an example that builds up a symbolic representation of a calculation $\exp\left(\sin\left(x_0\right)^2 + \cos\left(x_0\right)^2\right) + 10 \times x_0^2 + \exp\left(\pi\, i\right)$:

```
open Owl_symbolic
open Op
open Infix

let make_expr0 () =
  let x = variable "x_0" in
  let y =
    exp ((sin x ** float 2.) + (cos x ** float 2.))
    + (float 10. * (x ** float 2.))
    + exp (pi () * complex 0. 1.)
  in
  SymGraph.make_graph [| y |] "sym_graph"
```

This expression can be converted into a corresponding LaTeX string:

```
# let () = make_expr0 ()
    |> LaTeX_Engine.of_symbolic
    |> print_endline
\exp(\sin(x_0) ^ 2 + \cos(x_0) ^ 2) + 10 \times x_0 ^ 2 + \exp(\pi \
times 1.00i)
```

Simply putting it in the raw string form is not very helpful for visualization. We have built a web UI in this engine that utilizes KaTeX, which renders LaTeX string directly on a browser. In the following, we use the html function provided by the engine to show this string on our web UI using the functionality the engine provides:

```
# let () =
    let exprs = [ make_expr0 () ] in
    LaTeX_Engine.html ~dot:true ~exprs "example.html"
```

The generated "example.html" web page is a stand-alone page that contains all the required scripts. Once opened in a browser, it looks like Figure 7-3.

For each expression, the web UI contains its rendered LaTeX form and corresponding computation graph.

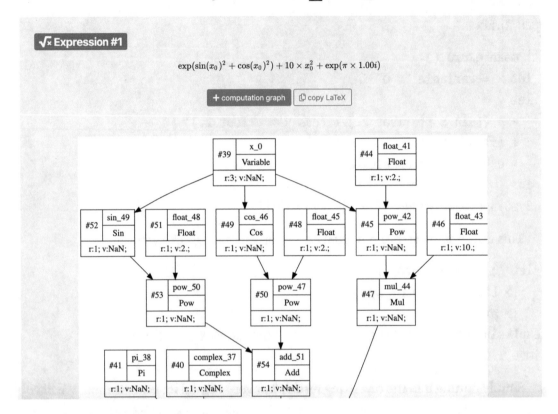

Figure 7-3. *UI of the LaTeX engine*

7.5 Owl Engine

An Owl engine enables converting an Owl computation graph to or from a symbolic representation. A symbolic graph can thus benefit from the concise syntax and powerful features such as algorithmic differentiation in Owl.

The conversion between Owl CGraph and the symbolic representation is straightforward, since both are graph structures. We only need to focus on making the operation projection between these two systems correct.

```
let cnode_attr = Owl_graph.attr node in
match cnode_attr.op with
| Sin -> Owl_symbolic_operator.sin ~name sym_inputs.(0)
| Sub -> Owl_symbolic_operator.sub ~name sym_inputs.(0) sym_inputs.(1)
```

```
| SubScalar -> Owl_symbolic_operator.sub ~name sym_inputs.(0) sym_
inputs.(1)
| Conv2d (padding, strides) ->
    let pad =
      if padding = SAME then
        Owl_symbolic_types.SAME_UPPER
      else
        Owl_symbolic_types.VALID
    in
    Owl_symbolic_operator.conv ~name
                              ~padding:pad
                              ~strides
                              sym_inputs.(0)
                              sym_inputs.(1)
```

The basic idea is simple: find the type of symbol and its input node in CGraph, and then do the projection to symbolic representation. For most of the math operators such as sin, the projection is one to one, but that's not all the cases. For some operations such as subtraction, we have Sub, SubScalar, ScalarSub, etc. depending on the type of input, but they can all be projected to the sub operator in symbolic representation. Or for the convolution operation, we need to first convert the parameters in a suitable way before the projection.

Let's look at an example of using the Owl engine:

```
open Owl_symbolic
module G = Owl_computation_cpu_engine.Make (Owl_algodiff_primal_ops.S)
module AD = Owl_algodiff_generic.Make (G)
module OWL_Engine = Owl_symbolic_engine_owl.Make (G)

let make_graph () =
  let x = G.ones [| 2; 3 |] |> AD.pack_arr in
  let y = G.var_elt "y" |> AD.pack_elt in
  let z = AD.Maths.(sin x + y) in
  let input = [| AD.unpack_elt y |> G.elt_to_node |] in
  let output = [| AD.unpack_arr z |> G.arr_to_node |] in
  G.make_graph ~input ~output "graph"

let g = make_graph () |> OWL_Engine.to_symbolic
```

Here, we build a simple computation graph with the algorithmic differentiation module in Owl. Then we perform the conversion by calling `OWL_Engine.to_symbolic`.

We can also chain multiple engines together. For example, we can use the Owl engine to converge the computation defined in Owl to a symbolic graph, which can then be converted to an ONNX model and get executed on multiple frameworks. Here is such an example. A simple computation graph created by `make_graph ()` is processed by two chained engines and generates an ONNX model.

```
let _ =
  let k = make_graph ()
          |> OWL_Engine.to_symbolic
          |> ONNX_Engine.of_symbolic
  in
  ONNX_Engine.save k "test.onnx"
```

And this `test.onnx` file can further be processed with Python code as introduced in the previous section.

7.6 Summary

In this chapter, we briefly discussed the topic of supporting hardware accelerators in Owl. To improve the performance of computation, it is necessary to utilize the power of hardware accelerators, such as GPU, TPU, etc. It is a growing trend that the definition and execution of computation can be separated out. To this end, we built a symbolic representation based on Owl to facilitate exporting computations to other frameworks that support multiple hardware accelerators. This representation can be executed by multiple backend engines. Currently, it supports the ONNX, LaTeX, and Owl itself as engines. This chapter introduced the design of this symbolic representation and used several examples to demonstrate how the computation in Owl can be executed on other frameworks or visualized.

## CHAPTER 8

Compiler Backends

For a numerical library, it is always beneficial and challenging to extend to multiple execution backends. We have seen how we support accelerators such as the GPU by utilizing a symbolic representation and computation graph standard such as ONNX. In this chapter, we introduce how Owl can be used on more edge-oriented backends, including JavaScript and unikernel.

8.1 Base Library

Before we start, we need to understand how Owl enables compiling to multiple backends by providing different implementations. Owl, as well as many of its external libraries, is actually divided into two parts: a *base* library and a *core* library. The base library is implemented with pure OCaml. For some backends such as JavaScript, we can only use the functions implemented in OCaml.

You may wonder how much we will be limited by the base library. Fortunately, the most advanced modules in Owl are often implemented in pure OCaml, and they live in the base, which includes the modules we have introduced in the previous chapters: algorithmic differentiation, optimization, even neural networks, and many others. Figure 8-1 shows the structure of the core functor stack in Owl.

As we have introduced in Chapter 2, the Ndarray module is the core building block in Owl. The base library aims to implement all the necessary functions as the core library Ndarray module. The stack is implemented in such a way that the user can switch between these two different implementations without the modules of higher layer. In the Owl functor stack, Ndarray is used to support the computation graph module to provide lazy evaluation functionality. Here, we use the Owl_base_algodiff_primal_ops module, which is simply a wrapper around the base Ndarray module. It also includes a small number of matrix and linear algebra functions. By providing this wrapper instead of

© Liang Wang, Jianxin Zhao 2023
L. Wang and J. Zhao, *Architecture of Advanced Numerical Analysis Systems*,
https://doi.org/10.1007/978-1-4842-8853-5_8

using the Ndarray module directly, we can avoid mixing all the functions in the Ndarray module and make it a large Goliath.

Next, the algorithmic differentiation can build up its computation module based on normal ndarray or its lazy version. For example, you can have an AD that relies on the normal single-precision base ndarray module:

```
module AD = Owl_algodiff_generic.Make
  (Owl_base_algodiff_primal_ops.S)
```

Or it can be built on a double-precision lazy evaluated core Ndarray module:

```
module CPU_Engine = Owl_computation_cpu_engine.Make
  (Owl_algodiff_primal_ops.D)
module AD = Owl_algodiff_generic.Make (CPU_Engine)
```

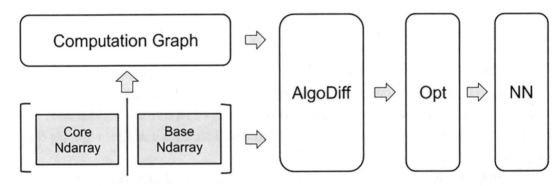

Figure 8-1. *Core functor stack in Owl*

Going up even further on the stack, we have the more advanced optimization and neural network modules. They are both based on the AD module. For example, the following code shows how we can build a neural graph module by layers of functors from the base Ndarray:

```
module G = Owl_neural_graph.Make
            (Owl_neural_neuron.Make
              (Owl_optimise_generic.Make
                (Owl_algodiff_generic.Make
                  (Owl_base_algodiff_primal_ops.S))))
```

Normally, the users do not have to care about how these modules are constructed layer by layer, but understanding the functor stack and typing is nevertheless beneficial, especially when you are creating new module that relies on the base ndarray module.

These examples show that once we have built an application with the core `Ndarray` module, we can then seamlessly switch it to base `Ndarray` without changing anything else. That means that all the code and examples we have seen so far can be used directly on different backends that require pure implementation.

The base library is still an ongoing work, and there is still a lot to do. Though the `Ndarray` module is a large part in the base library, there are other modules that also need to be reimplemented in OCaml, such as the linear algebra module. We need to add more functions such as SVD factorization. Even for the `Ndarray` itself, we still have not totally covered all the functions yet.

Our strategy is to add the base Ndarray functions gradually. We put most of the signature files in the base library, and the core library signature file includes its corresponding signature file from the base library, plus functions that are currently unique to the core library. The target is to total coverage so that the core and base libraries provide exactly the same functions.

As can be expected, the pure OCaml implementation normally performs worse than the C code implemented version. For example, for the convolution operation, without the help of optimized routines from OpenBLAS, etc., we can only provide the naive implementation that includes multiple for-loops. Its performance is orders of magnitude slower than the core library version. Currently, our priority is to implement the functions themselves instead of caring about function optimization, nor do we intend to outperform C code with pure OCaml implementation.

8.2 Backend: JavaScript

At first glance, JavaScript has very little to do with high-performance scientific computing. One important reason we aim to include that in Owl is that the web browser is arguably the most widely deployed technology on various edge devices, for example, mobile phones, tablets, laptops, etc. More and more functionalities are being pushed from data centers to edge for reduced latency, better privacy, and security. And JavaScript applications running in a browser are getting more complicated and powerful. Moreover, JavaScript interpreters are being increasingly optimized, and even relatively complicated computational tasks can run with reasonable performance.

This chapter uses two simple examples to demonstrate how to compile Owl applications into JavaScript code so that you can deploy the analytical code into browsers, using both native OCaml code and Facebook Reason. It additionally requires the use of dune, a build system designed for OCaml/Reason projects. As you will see, this will make the compilation to JavaScript effortless.

Native OCaml

We rely on the tool js_of_ocaml to convert native OCaml code into JavaScript. Js_of_ocaml is a compiler from OCaml bytecode programs to JavaScript. The process can thus be divided into two phases: first, compile the OCaml source code into bytecode executables, and then apply the js_of_ocaml command to it. It supports the core Bigarray module among most of the OCaml standard libraries. However, since the Sys module is not fully supported, we are careful to not use functions from this module in the base library.

We have described how algorithmic differentiation plays a core role in the ecosystem of Owl, so now we use an example of AD to demonstrate how we convert a numerical program into JavaScript code and then get executed. The example is about optimizing the mathematical function sin. The first step is writing down our application in OCaml as follows, then save it into a file demo.ml.

```
module AlgodiffD = Owl_algodiff_generic.Make
    (Owl_base_algodiff_primal_ops.D)
open AlgodiffD

let rec desc ?(eta=F 0.01) ?(eps=1e-6) f x =
    let g = (diff f) x in
    if (unpack_flt g) < eps then x
    else desc ~eta ~eps f Maths.(x - eta * g)

let _ =
    let f = Maths.sin in
    let y = desc f (F 0.1) in
    Owl_log.info "argmin f(x) = %g" (unpack_flt y)
```

The code is very simple: the desc defines a gradient descent algorithm, and then we use desc to calculate the minimum value of the Maths.sin function. In the end, we print out the result using the Owl_log module's info function. Note that we pass in the base Ndarray module to the AD functor to create a corresponding AD module.

In the second step, we need to create a dune file as follows. This file will instruct how the OCaml code will be first compiled into bytecode and then converted into JavaScript by calling js_of_ocaml.

```
(executable
  (name demo)
  (modes byte js)
  (libraries owl-base))
```

With these two files in the same folder, we can then run the following command in the terminal:

```
dune build demo.bc && js_of_ocaml _build/default/demo.bc
```

Or even better, since js_of_ocaml is natively supported by dune, we can simply execute:

```
dune build
```

The command builds the application and generates a demo.bc.js in the _build/ default/ folder. Finally, we can run the JavaScript using Node.js (or loading into a browser using an appropriate HTML page).

```
node _build/default/demo.bc.js
```

As a result, we should be able to see the output result showing a value that minimizes the sin function and should be similar to

```
argmin f(x) = -1.5708
```

Even though we present a simple example here, the base library can be used to produce more complex and interactive browser applications.

Facebook Reason

Facebook Reason leverages OCaml as a backend to provide type-safe JavaScript. It is gaining its momentum and becoming a popular choice of developing web applications. It actually uses another tool, BuckleScript, to convert the Reason/OCaml code to JavaScript. Since Reason is basically a syntax layer built on top of OCaml, it is very straightforward to use Owl in Reason to develop advanced numerical applications.

In this example, we use reason code to manipulate multidimensional arrays, the core data structure in Owl. First, we save the following code into a reason file called demo.re. Note the suffix is *.re* now. It includes several basic math and Ndarray operations in Owl.

```
open! Owl_base;

/* calculate math functions */
let x = Owl_base_maths.sin(5.);
Owl_log.info("Result is %f", x);

/* create random ndarray then print */
let y = Owl_base_dense_ndarray.D.uniform([|3,4,5|]);
Owl_base_dense_ndarray.D.set(y,[|1,1,1|],1.);
Owl_base_dense_ndarray.D.print(y);

/* take a slice */
let z = Owl_base_dense_ndarray.D.get_slice([[],[],[0,3]],y);
Owl_base_dense_ndarray.D.print(z);
```

The preceding code is simple. It creates a random ndarray, takes a slice, and then prints them out. The Owl library can be seamlessly used in Reason. Next, instead of using Reason's own translation of this frontend syntax with bucklescript, we still turn to js_of_ocaml for help. Let's look at the dune file, which turns out to be the same as that in the previous example:

```
(executable
 (name demo)
 (modes js)
 (libraries owl-base))
```

As in the previous example, you can then compile and run the code with the following commands:

```
dune build
node _build/default/demo.bc.js
```

As you can see, except that the code is written in different languages, the rest of the steps are identical in both example thanks to js_of_ocaml and dune.

8.3 Backend: MirageOS

Besides JavaScript, another choice of backend we aim to support is the MirageOS. It is an approach to build *unikernels*. A unikernel is a specialized, single address space machine image constructed with library operating systems. Unlike a normal virtual machine, it only contains a minimal set of libraries required for one application. It can run directly on a hypervisor or hardware without relying on operating systems such as Linux and Windows. The unikernel is thus concise and secure, and extremely efficient for distribution and execution on either cloud or edge devices.

MirageOS is one solution to building unikernels. It utilizes the high-level language OCaml and a runtime to provide an API for operating system functionalities. In using MirageOS, the users can think of the Xen hypervisor as a stable hardware platform, without worrying about the hardware details such as devices. Furthermore, since the Xen hypervisor is widely used in platforms such as Amazon EC2 and Rackspace Cloud, MirageOS-built unikernel can be readily deployed on these platforms. Besides, benefiting from its efficiency and security, MirageOS also aims to form a core piece of the Nymote/MISO tool stack to power the Internet of Things.

Example: Gradient Descent

Since MirageOS is based around the OCaml language, we can safely integrate the Owl library with it. To demonstrate how we use MirageOS as a backend, we again use the previous algorithmic differentiation–based optimization example. Before we start, please make sure to follow the installation instruction of the MirageOS. Let's look at the code:

```
module A = Owl_algodiff_generic.Make
  (Owl_algodiff_primal_ops.S)
open A

let rec desc ?(eta=F 0.01) ?(eps=1e-6) f x =
  let g = (diff f) x in
  if (unpack_flt (Maths.abs g)) < eps then x
  else desc ~eta ~eps f Maths.(x - eta * g)

let main () =
  let f x = Maths.(pow x (F 3.) - (F 2.) *
    pow x (F 2.) + (F 2.)) in
  let init = Stats.uniform_rvs ~a:0. ~b:10. in
  let y = desc f (F init) in
  Owl_log.info "argmin f(x) = %g" (unpack_flt y)
```

This part of the code is mostly the same as before. By applying the diff function of the algorithmic differentiation module, we use the gradient descent method to find the value that minimizes the function $x^3 - 2x^2 + 2$. Then we need to add something different:

```
module GD = struct
  let start = main (); Lwt.return_unit
end
```

Here, the start is an entry point to the unikernel. It performs the normal OCaml function main and then returns an Lwt thread that will be evaluated to unit. Lwt is a concurrent programming library in OCaml. It provides the "promise" data type that can be determined in the future.

All the preceding code is written to a file called gd_owl.ml. To build a unikernel, next we need to define its configuration. In the same directory, we create a file called configure.ml:

```
open Mirage

let main =
  foreign
    ~packages:[package "owl"]
    "Gd_owl.GD" job
```

```
let () =
  register "gd_owl" [main]
```

It's not complex. First, we need to open the `Mirage` module. Then we declare a value `main` (or you can name it any other name). It calls the `foreign` function to specify the configuration. First, in the `package` parameter, we declare that this unikernel requires the Owl library. The next string parameter "Gd_owl.GD" specifies the name of the implementation file and in that file the module GD that contains the `start` entry point. The third parameter `job` declares the type of devices required by a unikernel, such as network interfaces, network stacks, file systems, etc. Since here we only do the calculation, there is no extra device required, so the third parameter is a `job`. Finally, we register the unikernel entry file gd_owl with the `main` configuration value.

That's all it takes for coding. Now we can take a look at the compiling part. MirageOS itself supports multiple backends. The crucial choice therefore is to decide which one to use at the beginning by using `mirage configure`. In the directory that holds the previous two files, you run `mirage configure -t unix`, and it configures to build the unikernel into a Unix ELF binary that can be directly executed. Or you can use `mirage configure -t xen`, and then the resulting unikernel will use the hypervisor backend like Xen or KVM. Either way, the unikernel runs as a virtual machine after starting up. In this example, we choose to use Unix as backends. So we run

```
mirage configure -t unix
```

This command generates a `Makefile` based on the configuration information. It includes all the building rules. Next, to make sure all the dependencies are installed, we need to run

```
make depend
```

Finally, we can build the unikernels by simply running

```
make
```

and it calls the `mirage build` command. As a result, now the current directory contains the _build/gd_owl.native executable, which is the unikernel we want. Executing it yields a similar result as before:

```
argmin f(x) = 1.33333
```

Example: Neural Network

As a more complex example, we have also built a simple neural network to perform the MNIST handwritten digit recognition task with MirageOS:

```
module N  = Owl_base_algodiff_primal_ops.S
module NN = Owl_neural_generic.Make (N)
open NN
open NN.Graph
open NN.Algodiff

let make_network input_shape =
  input input_shape
  |> lambda (fun x -> Maths.(x / F 256.))
  |> fully_connected 25 ~act_typ:Activation.Relu
  |> linear 10 ~act_typ:Activation.(Softmax 1)
  |> get_network
```

This neural network has two hidden layers, has a small weight size (146KB), and works well in testing (92% accuracy). We can write the weight into a text file. This file is named simple_mnist.ml, and similar to the previous example, we can add a unikernel entry point function in the file:

```
module Main = struct
  let start = infer (); Lwt.return_unit
end
```

Here, the infer function creates a neural network, loads the weight, and then performs inference on an input image. We also need a configuration file. Again, it's mostly the same:

```
open Mirage

let main =
  foreign
    ~packages:[package "owl-base"]
    "Simple_mnist.Main" job

let () =
  register "Simple_mnist" [main]
```

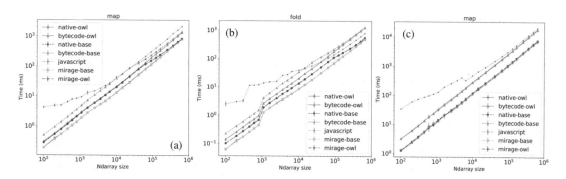

Figure 8-2. *Performance of map and fold operations on ndarray on a laptop and Raspberry Pi*

Once compiled to MirageOS unikernel with Unix backends, the generated binary is 10MB. You can also try compiling this application to JavaScript.

By these examples, we show that the Owl library can be readily deployed into unikernels via MirageOS. The numerical functionality can then greatly enhance the express ability of possible OCaml-MirageOS applications. Of course, here we cannot cover all the important topics about MirageOS; please refer to the documentation of MirageOS and Xen Hypervisor for more information.

8.4 Evaluation

In this section, we mainly compare the performance of different backends. Specifically, we observe three representative groups of operations: (1) map and fold operations on ndarray; (2) using gradient descent, a common numerical computing subroutine, to get *argmin* of a certain function; (3) conducting inference on complex DNNs, including SqueezeNet and a VGG-like convolution network. The evaluations are conducted on a ThinkPad T460S laptop with an Ubuntu 16.04 operating system. It has an Intel Core i5-6200U CPU and 12GB RAM.

The OCaml compiler can produce two kinds of executables: bytecode and native. Native executables are compiled for specific architectures and are generally faster, while bytecode executables have the advantage of being portable.

For JavaScript, we use the js_of_ocaml approach as described in the previous sections. Note that for convenience we refer to the pure implementation of OCaml and the mix implementation of OCaml and C as base-lib and owl-lib separately, but they are in fact all included in the Owl library. For Mirage compilation, we use both libraries.

Figure 8-2 shows the performance of map and fold operations on ndarray. We use simple functions such as plus and multiplication on 1-d (size <1, 000) and 2-d arrays. The log-log relationship between the total size of ndarray and the time each operation takes keeps linear. For both operations, owl-lib is faster than base-lib, and native executables outperform bytecode ones. The performance of Mirage executives is close to that of native code. Generally, JavaScript runs the slowest, but note how the performance gap between JavaScript and the others converges when the ndarray size grows. For the fold operation, JavaScript even runs faster than bytecode when size is sufficiently large.

Note that for the fold operation, there is an obvious increase in time used at around input size of 10^3 for fold operations, while there is no such change for the map operation. That is because I change the input from one-dimensional ndarray to two-dimensional starting that size. This change does not affect the map operation, since it treats an input of any dimension as a one-dimensional vector. On the other hand, the fold operation considers the factor of dimension, and thus its performance is affected by this change.

In Figure 8-3, we want to investigate if the preceding observations still hold in more complex numerical computation. We choose to use a gradient descent algorithm to find the value that locally minimizes a function. We choose the initial value randomly between [0, 10]. For both $sin(x)$ and $x^3 - 2x^2 + 2$, we can see that JavaScript runs the slowest, but this time the base-lib slightly outperforms owl-lib.

We further compare the performance of DNN, which requires large amount of computation. We compare SqueezeNet and a VGG-like convolution network. They have different sizes of weight and network structure complexities.

Table 8-1 shows that though the performance difference between owl-lib and base-lib is not obvious, the former is much better. So is the difference between native and bytecode for base-lib. JavaScript is still the slowest. The core computation required for DNN inference is the convolution operation. Its implementation efficiency is the key to these differences. Currently, we are working on improving its implementation in base-lib.

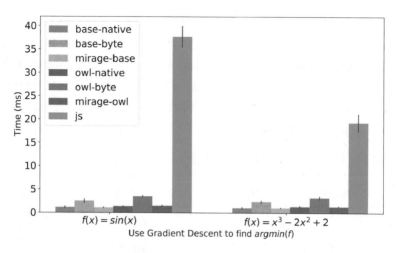

Figure 8-3. *Performance of gradient descent on function f*

Table 8-1. *Inference Speed of Deep Neural Networks*

Time (ms)	VGG	SqueezeNet
owl-native	7.96 (± 0.93)	196.26(± 1.12)
owl-byte	9.87 (± 0.74)	218.99(± 9.05)
base-native	792.56(± 19.95)	14470.97 (± 368.03)
base-byte	2783.33(± 76.08)	50294.93 (± 1315.28)
mirage-owl	8.09(± 0.08)	190.26(± 0.89)
mirage-base	743.18 (± 13.29)	13478.53 (± 13.29)
JavaScript	4325.50(± 447.22)	65545.75 (± 629.10)

We have also conducted the same evaluation experiments on Raspberry Pi 3 Model B. Figure 8-2c shows the performance of the fold operation on ndarray. Besides the fact that all backends run about one order of magnitude slower than that on the laptop, previous observations still hold. This figure also implies that, on resource-limited devices such as Raspberry Pi, the key difference is between native code and bytecode, instead of owl-lib and base-lib for this operation.

Finally, we also briefly compare the size of executables generated by different backends. We take the SqueezeNet, for example, and the results are shown in Table 8-2. It can be seen that `owl-lib` executives have larger size compared to `base-lib` ones, and JavaScript code has the smallest file size. There does not exist a dominant method of deployment for all these backends. It is thus imperative to choose a suitable backend according to the deployment environment.

Table 8-2. *Size of Executables Generated by Backends*

Size (KB)	Native	Bytecode	Mirage	JavaScript
Base	2437	4298	4602	739
Native	14,875	13,102	16,987	-

8.5 Summary

The base library in Owl was separated from the core module mainly to accommodate multiple possible execution backends. This chapter introduced how the base module works. Then we showed two possible backends: the JavaScript and the unikernel virtual machine. Both backends are helpful to extend the application of Owl to more devices. Finally, we used several examples to demonstrate how these backends are used and their performances.

CHAPTER 9

Composition and Deployment

In this chapter, we first present Zoo, a script subsystem we have originally developed for OCaml file sharing. We will introduce how it is used and its design. Based on this system, we discuss the problem of computation composition and deployment in a numerical library.

9.1 Script Sharing with Zoo

The core functionality of the Zoo is simple: sharing OCaml scripts. It is known that we can use OCaml as a scripting language as Python (at certain performance cost because the code is compiled into bytecode). Even though compiling into native code for production use is recommended, scripting is still useful and convenient, especially for light deployment and fast prototyping. In fact, the performance penalty in most Owl scripts is almost unnoticeable because the heaviest numerical computation part is still offloaded to Owl which runs native code.

While designing Owl, our goal is always to make the whole ecosystem open, flexible, and extensible. Programmers can make their own "small" scripts and share them with others conveniently, so they do not have to wait for such functions to be implemented in Owl's master branch or submit something "heavy" to OPAM.

Example

To illustrate how to use Zoo, let's start with a simple synthetic scenario. Alice is a data analyst and uses Owl in her daily job. One day, she realized that the functions she needed had not been implemented yet in Owl. Therefore, she spent an hour in her

© Liang Wang, Jianxin Zhao 2023
L. Wang and J. Zhao, *Architecture of Advanced Numerical Analysis Systems*,
https://doi.org/10.1007/978-1-4842-8853-5_9

computer and implemented these functions by herself. She thought these functions might be useful to others, for example, her colleague Bob; she decided to share these functions using the Zoo system. Now let's see how Alice manages to do so in the following, step by step.

First, Alice needs to create a folder (e.g., `myscript` folder) for her shared script. What to put in the folder then? She needs at least two files in this folder. The first one is of course the file (i.e., `coolmodule.ml`) implementing the function as follows. The function `sqr_magic` returns the square of a magic matrix; it is quite useless in reality but serves as an example here.

```
#!/usr/bin/env owl
```

```
open Owl
let sqr_magic n = Mat.(magic n |> sqr)
```

The second file she needs is a `#readme.md` which provides a brief description of the shared script. Note that the first line of the `#readme.md` will be used as a short description for the shared scripts. This short description will be displayed when you use the `owl -list` command to list all the available Zoo code snippets on your computer.

```
Square of Magic Matrix
```

```
`Coolmodule` implements a function to generate the square of magic
matrices.
```

Second, Alice needs to distribute the files in the `myscript` folder. The distribution is done via Gist, so you must have gist installed on your computer. For example, if you use Mac, you can install `gist` with `brew install gist`. Owl provides a simple command-line tool to upload the Zoo code snippets. Note that you need to log in to your GitHub account for `gist` and `git`.

```
owl -upload myscript
```

The `owl -upload` command simply uploads all the files in `myscript` as a bundle to your Gist page. The command also prints out the URL after a successful upload. The bundle Alice uploaded before is assigned a unique id, that is, 9f0892ab2b96f81baacd7322d73a4b08. In order to use the `sqr_magic` function, Bob only needs to use the `#zoo` directive in his script, for example, `bob.ml`, in order to import the function.

```
#!/usr/bin/env owl
#zoo "9f0892ab2b96f81baacd7322d73a4b08"

let _ = Coolmodule.sqr_magic 4 |> Owl.Mat.print
```

Bob's script is very simple, but there are a couple of things worth pointing out:

- The Zoo system will automatically download the bundle of a given id if it is not cached locally.

- All the ml files in the bundle will be imported as modules, so you need to use `Coolmodule.sqr_magic` to access the function.

- You may also want to use `chmod +x bob.ml` to make the script executable. This is obvious if you are a heavy terminal user.

Note that to use the `#zoo` directive in REPL such as `utop`, you need to manually load the `owl-zoo` library with `#require "owl-zoo";;`. Alternatively, you can also load `owl-top` using `#require "owl-top";;` which is an OCaml top-level wrapper of Owl. If you want to make `utop`, load the library automatically by adding this line to `~/.ocamlinit`.

Version Control

Alice has modified and uploaded her scripts several times. Each version of her code is assigned a unique version id. Different versions of code may work differently, so how could Bob specify which version to use? The good news is that he barely needs to change his code.

```
#!/usr/bin/env owl
#zoo "9f0892ab2b96f81baacd7322d73a4b08?
    vid=71261b317cd730a4dbfb0ffeded02b10fcaa5948"

let _ = Coolmodule.sqr_magic 4 |> Owl.Mat.print
```

The only thing he needs to add is a version id using the parameter vid. The naming scheme of Zoo is designed to be similar with the field-value pair in a RESTful query. The version id can be obtained from a gist's revisions page.

Besides specifying a version, it is also quite possible that Bob prefers to use the newest version Alice provides, whatever its id may be. The problem here is that, how often does Bob need to contact the Gist server to retreat the version information? Every time he runs his code? Well, that may not be a good idea in many cases considering the communication overhead and response time. Zoo caches gists locally and tends to use the cached code and data rather than downloading them all the time.

To solve this problem, Zoo provides another parameter in the naming scheme: tol. It is the threshold of a gist's tolerance of the time it exists on the local cache. Any gist that exists on a user's local cache for longer than tol seconds is deemed outdated and thus requires updating the latest vid information from the Gist server before being used. For example:

```
#!/usr/bin/env owl
#zoo "9f0892ab2b96f81baacd7322d73a4b08?tol=300"

let _ = Coolmodule.sqr_magic 4 |> Owl.Mat.print
```

By setting the tol parameter to 300, Bob indicates that if Zoo has already fetched the version information of this gist from the remote server within the past 300 seconds, then keep using its local cache; otherwise, contact the Gist server to check if a newer version is pushed. If so, the newest version is downloaded to local cache before being used. In the case where Bob doesn't want to miss every single update of Alice's gist code, he can simply set tol to 0, which means fetching the version information every time he executes his code. The vid and tol parameters enable users to have fine-grained version control of Zoo gists. Of course, these two parameters should not be used together. When vid is set in a name, the tol parameter will be ignored. If both are not set, as shown in the previous code snippet, Zoo will use the latest locally cached version if it exists.

A user can either choose a specific version id or use the latest version, which means the newest version on local cache. Obviously, using latest introduces cache inconsistency. The latest version on one machine might not be the same on the other. To get the up-to-date version from a Gist server, the download time of the latest version on a local machine will be saved as metadata. The newest version on the server will be pulled to the local cache after a certain period of time, if the latest flag is set in the Gist name. Ideally, every published service should contain a specific version id, and latest should only be used during development.

9.2 Service Deployment and Composition

Based on the Zoo system, in the rest of this chapter, we discuss the computation service deployment and composition problem. First, let's briefly present some background. Recently, computation on edge and mobile devices has gained rapid growth in both the industry and academia, such as personal data analytics in the home, DNN application on a tiny stick, semantic search and recommendation on a web browser [53], etc. HUAWEI has identified speed and responsiveness of native AI processing on mobile devices as the key to a new era in smartphone innovation. Many challenges arise when moving machine learning (ML) analytics from cloud to edge devices.

One problem is not yet well defined and investigated: model composition. Training a model often requires large datasets and rich computing resources, which are often not available to normal users. That is one of the reasons that they are bound to the models and services provided by large companies. To this end, we propose the idea of *composable service*. Its basic idea is that many services can be constructed from basic ones such as image recognition, speech-to-text, and recommendation to meet new application requirements. Modularity and composition will be the key to increasing usage of ML-based data analytics.

Composing components into a more complex entity is not uncommon to see in the computer science. One such example is the composition of web services. A web service is a software application that is identified by a URI and supports machine-to-machine interaction over a network. Messages in formats such as XML and JSON are transferred among web services according to their prescribed interfaces. The potential of the web service application architecture lies in that the developers can compose multiple services and build a larger application via the network. In web service composition, one problem is to select proper participant services so that they can work together properly. A lot of research effort has been made on composition methods that consider information such as interfaces, message types, and dynamic message sequences exchanged.

A similar paradigm is the microservices architecture. With this architecture, a large monolithic software application should be decomposed into small components, each with distinct functionalities. These components can communicate with each other via predefined APIs. This approach provides multifolds of benefits, such as module reusability, service scalability, fault isolation, etc. Many companies, such as Netflix, have successfully adopted this approach. In the composition of different microservices, the application API plays a key role.[1] Another field that advocates the composition approach is the serverless computing, where the stateless functions can be composed into more complex ones. Based on the observation that existing serverless systems spend a large portion of time on booting function containers and interaction between functions, the SAND system investigates the combination of different functions. By proposing application-level sandboxing and a hierarchical message bus, this system reduces latency and improves resource utility.

In this chapter, as a contribution, the Zoo system provides a small domain-specific language (DSL) to enable the composition of advanced data analytics services. Benefiting from OCaml's powerful type system, the Zoo provides type checking for the composition. Besides, the Zoo DSL supports fine-grained version control in composing different services provided by different developers, since the code of these services may be in constant change.

Another challenge in conducting ML-based data analytics on edge devices is the deployment of data analytics services. Most existing machine learning frameworks, such as TensorFlow and Caffe, focus mainly on the training of analytics models. On the other hand, end users, many of whom are not ML professionals, mainly use trained models to perform inference. This gap between the current ML systems and users' requirements is growing.

The deployment of service is close to the idea of model serving. The Clipper [13] serving system is used for ML model–based prediction, and it features choosing the model that has the lowest latency from models on multiple ML frameworks. It enables users to access models based on multiple machine learning frameworks. These models are implemented in the form of containers. Compared with Clipper, the TensorFlow Serving focuses on using TensorFlow itself as a model execution framework. The models are in the form of `SavedModel`, and they can be deployed as a container that contains TensorFlow to serve prediction requests. Another field that employs the idea of service deployment is in the serverless computing. In serverless platforms such as Amazon Lambda and OpenLambda, utilizing the powerful ecosystem of existing cloud providers, the stateless functions provided by users can be deployed on different types of devices to get access to resources such as database and cloud files. For this aspect, as a contribution, the Zoo DSL also involves deploying composed services to multiple backends: not only containers but also unikernels and JavaScripts. We have discussed them in Chapter 8.

---

[1] Engineering Trade-Offs and The Netflix API Re-Architecture. The Netflix Tech Blog. `https://bit.ly/3evFz9g`

9.3 System Design

Based on these basic functionalities, we extend the Zoo system to address the composition and deployment challenges. Specifically, we design a small DSL to enable script sharing, type-checked composition of different data analytics services with version control, and deployment of services to multiple backends. First, we would like to briefly introduce the workflow of Zoo as shown in Figure 9-1. The workflow consists of two parts: *development* on the left side and *deployment* on the right.

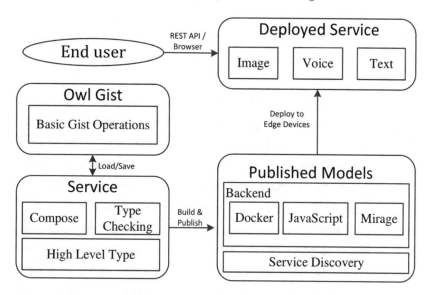

Figure 9-1. *Zoo system architecture*

Development concerns the design of interaction workflow and the computational functions of different services. One basic component is the Gist. By using Zoo, a normal Gist script will be loaded as a module in OCaml. To compose functionalities from different Gists only requires a developer to add one configuration file to each Gist. This file is in JSON format. It consists of one or more name-value pairs. Each pair is a signature for a function the script developer wants to expose as a service. These Gists can be imported and composed to make new services. When a user is satisfied with the result, they can save the new service as another Zoo Gist.

Deployment takes a Gist and creates models in different backends. These models can be published and deployed to edge devices. It is separated from the logic of development. Basic services and composed ones are treated equally. Besides, users can move services from being local to remote and vice versa, without changing the structure of the constructed service. Deployment is not limited to edge devices, but can also be on cloud servers, or a hybrid of both cases, to minimize the data revealed to the cloud and the associated communication costs. Thus, by this design, a data analytics service can easily be distributed to multiple devices. In the rest of this section, we will elaborate on the design and give details of different parts of this workflow.

Service

Gist is a core abstraction in Zoo. It is the center of code sharing. However, to compose multiple analytics snippets, Gist alone is insufficient. For example, it cannot express the structure of how different pieces of code are composed together. Therefore, we introduce another abstraction: `service`.

A service consists of three parts: *Gists, types,* and the *dependency graph.* A *Gist* is the list of Gist ids this service requires. *Types* are the parameter types of this service. Any service has zero or more input parameters and one output. This design follows that of an OCaml function. A *dependency graph* is a graph structure that contains information about how the service is composed. Each node in it represents a function from a Gist and contains the Gist's name, id, and a number of parameters of this function.

Zoo provides three core operations about a service: create, compose, and publish. The *create_service* creates a dictionary of services given a Gist id. This operation reads the service configuration file from that Gist and creates a service for each function specified in the configuration file. The *compose_service* provides a series of operations to combine multiple services into a new service. A compose operation does type checking by comparing the "types" field of two services. An error will be raised if incompatible services are composed. A composed service can be saved to a new Gist or be used for further composition. The *publish_service* makes a service's code into such forms that can be readily used by end users. Zoo is designed to support multiple backends for these publication forms. Currently, it targets the Docker container, JavaScript, and MirageOS [37] as backends.

Type Checking

As mentioned in Section 9.3, one of the most important tasks of service composition is to make sure the type matches. For example, suppose there is an image analytics service that takes a PNG format image, and if we connect to it another one that produces a JPEG image, the resulting service will only generate meaningless output for data type mismatch. OCaml provides primary types such as integer, float, string, and Boolean. The core data structure of Owl is ndarray. However, all these types are insufficient for high-level service type checking as mentioned. That motivates us to derive richer high-level types.

To support this, we use generalized algebraic data types (GADTs) in OCaml. There already exist several model collections on different platforms, for example, Caffe and MXNet. I observe that most current popular deep learning models can generally be categorized into three fundamental types: `image`, `text`, and `voice`. Based on them, we define subtypes for each: PNG and JPEG images, French and English text, and voice, that is, `png img`, `jpeg img`, `fr text`, `en text`, `fr voice`, and `en voice` types. More can be further added easily in Zoo. Therefore, type checking in OCaml ensures type-safe and meaningful composition of high-level deep learning services.

DSL

Zoo provides a minimal DSL for service composition and deployment.

Composition: To acquire services from a Gist of id *gid*, we use $gid to create a dictionary, which maps from service name strings to services. I implement the dictionary data structure using `Hashtbl` in OCaml. The # operator is overloaded to represent the "get item" operation. Therefore

$$\$gid\#sname$$

can be used to get a service that is named "sname." Now suppose we have n services: f_1, f_2, ..., f_n. Their outputs are of type t_{f1}, t_{f2}, ..., t_{fn}. Each service s accepts m_s input parameters, which have type t_s^1, t_s^2, ..., $t_s^{m_s}$. Also, there is a service g that takes n inputs, each of

them has type t_g^1, t_g^2, ..., t_g^n. Its output type is t_o. Here, Zoo provides the $> operator to compose a list of services with another:

$$\left[f_1, f_2, \ldots, f_n\right]\$ > g$$

This operation returns a new service that has $\sum_{s=1}^{n} m_s$ inputs and is of output type t_o.

This operation does type checking to make sure that $t_{fi} = t_g^i, \forall i \in 1, 2, \ldots, n$.

Deployment: Taking a service s, be it a basic or composed one, it can be deployed using the following syntax:

$$s\$@ \text{ backend}$$

The $@ operator publishes services to a certain backend. It returns a string of URI of the resources to be deployed.

Note that the $> operator leads to a tree structure, which is in most cases sufficient for our real-world service deployment. However, a more general operation is to support a graph structure. This will be my next-step work.

Service Discovery

The services require a service discovery mechanism. For simplicity's sake, each newly published service is added to a public record hosted on a server. The record is a list of items, and each item contains the following: a Gist id that the service is based on; a one-line description of this service; a string representing the input and output types of this service, such as "image → int → string → text,"; a service URI. For the container deployment, the URI is a Docker Hub link, and for the JavaScript backend, the URI is a URL link to the JavaScript file itself. The service discovery mechanism is implemented using an off-the-shelf database.

9.4 Use Case

To illustrate the preceding workflow, let us consider a synthetic scenario. Alice is a French data analyst. She knows how to use ML and DL models on existing platforms, but is not an expert. Her recent work is about testing the performance of different image classification neural networks. To do that, she needs to first modify the image using the DNN-based Neural Style Transfer (NST) algorithm. NST takes two images and outputs to a new image, which is similar to the first image in content and the second in style. This new image should be passed to an image classification DNN for inference. Finally, the classification result should be translated to French. She does not want to put academic-related information on Google's server, but she cannot find any single pretrained model that performs this series of tasks.

Here comes the Zoo system to help. Alice finds Gists that can do image recognition, NST, and translation separately. Even better, she can perform image segmentation to greatly improve the performance of NST using another Gist. All she has to provide is some simple code to generate the style images she needs to use. She can then assemble these parts together easily using Zoo.

```
open Zoo
(* Image classification *)
let s_img = $ "aa36e" # "infer";;
(* Image segmentation *)
let s_seg = $ "d79e9" # "seg";;
(* Neural style transfer *)
let s_nst = $ "6f28d" # "run";;
(* Translation from English to French *)
let s_trans = $ "7f32a" # "trans";;
(* Alice's own style image generation service *)
let s_style = $ alice_Gist_id # "image_gen";;

(* Compose services *)
let s = [s_seg; s_style] $> s_nst
  $> n_img $> n_trans;;
(* Publish to a new Docker Image *)
let pub = (List.hd s) $@
  (CONTAINER "alice/image_service:latest");;
```

Note that the Gist id used in the code is shortened from 32 digits to 5 due to column length limit. Once Alice creates the new service and publishes it as a container, she can then run it locally, send a request with image data to the deployed machine, and get image classification results back in French.

9.5 Discussion

One thing to note is that, in service composition, type checking is a nice property to have, but not the only one. From web services to microservices, the industry and researchers have studied the composition issue for years. Besides checking the static information such as message types, interfaces, etc., sometimes the dynamic behavior between services should also be checked. It is the same in our data analytics services composition scenario.

For example, the Generative Adversarial Network (GAN) is a huge family of networks. A GAN consists of two parts: generator and discriminator. The generator tries its best to synthesize images based on existing parameters. The discriminator takes the images produced by the generator and tries its best to separate the generated data from true data, using a Boolean or percentage value. This mutual deception process is iterated until the discriminator can no longer tell the difference between the generated data and the true data. Using Zoo, the users may want to compose a generator with different discriminators to see which combination produces the most trustworthy fake images. To do this, only matching the types of these two services is not enough. The users also need to specify the dynamic information such as the order and number and messages exchanged in between.

To solve this problem, some kind of formalisms may need to be introduced in as theoretical foundation to structure interaction and reason over communicating processes between services. One such option is the session types [31]. Session types are a type discipline for communication-centric programming. It is based on the π-calculi, and its basic idea is that the communication protocol can be described as a type, which can be checked at runtime or statically. The session types have gained much attention recently and are already implemented in multiple languages, including OCaml. This approach can effectively enhance the type checking in Zoo and is a promising future direction to pursue in my next step on this work.

9.6 Summary

In this chapter, we first introduced Zoo, a scripting sharing tool in Owl, including its usage and design. Based on it, we explored two topics: service composition and deployment. Zoo provides a small DSL to enable type-checked composition of different data analytics services with version control and deployment of services to multiple backends. It benefits from OCaml's powerful type system. A use case was presented to demonstrate the expressiveness of this DSL in composing advanced ML services such as image recognition, text translation, etc. The Zoo DSL also enables deploying composed services to multiple backends: containers, unikernels, and JavaScripts; service deployment often requires choosing a suitable one.

CHAPTER 10

Distributed Computing

Distributed computing has been playing a significant role in current smart applications in various fields. In this chapter, we first briefly give a bird's-eye view of this topic, introducing various programming paradigms. Next, we introduce Actor, an OCaml-based distributed computing engine, and how it works together with Owl. We then focus on one key element in distributed computing: the synchronization. We introduce four different types of synchronization methods or "barriers" that are commonly used in current systems. Next, we elaborate how these barriers are designed and provide illustrations from the theoretical perspective. Finally, we use evaluations to show the performance trade-offs in using different barriers.

10.1 Distributed Machine Learning

Machine learning has achieved phenomenal breakthroughs in various fields, such as image recognition, language processing, gaming industry, product management, healthcare, etc. The power of machine learning lies in utilizing the growing size of training data as well as models so as to achieve high accuracy. As a large amount of data is increasingly generated from mobile and edge devices (smart homes, mobile phones, wearable devices, etc.), it becomes essential for many applications to train machine learning models in parallel across many nodes. In distributed learning, a model is trained via the collaboration of multiple workers. One of the most commonly used training methods is the stochastic gradient descent (SGD), which iteratively optimizes the given objective function until it converges by following the gradient direction of the objective. In each iteration of SGD, typically a descent gradient is calculated using a batch of training data, and then the model parameters are updated by changing along the direction of the gradient at a certain step. There are mainly three types of paradigms to perform distributed machine learning: parameter servers (PS), All-Reduce, and decentralized approaches (or peer-to-peer).

© Liang Wang, Jianxin Zhao 2023
L. Wang and J. Zhao, *Architecture of Advanced Numerical Analysis Systems*,
https://doi.org/10.1007/978-1-4842-8853-5_10

Parameter server [34] (PS) is a frequently used distributed training architecture. The server keeps the model parameters; the workers *pull* the parameters, compute the gradients, and *push* them back to the server for aggregation. It is commonly implemented as a key-value store. Another paradigm is All-Reduce. In this paradigm, each computing node expects each participating process to provide an equally sized tensor, collectively applies a given arithmetic operation to input tensors from all processes, and returns the same result tensor to each participant. A naive implementation could simply let every process broadcast its input tensor to all peers and then apply the arithmetic operation independently. The Ring All-Reduce architecture organizes workers as a ring structure to utilize the bandwidth effectively. The Horovod framework provides a high-performance implementation of the All-Reduce.

Besides these two, the decentralized architecture has drawn more attention. It allows point-to-point communication between nodes according to a communication graph. The peer-to-peer approach can effectively solve problems such as communication bottlenecks, unfairness caused by information concentration, etc., and provides more opportunities for optimization. One of the most commonly used algorithms in the P2P training paradigm is the decentralized parallel SGD (D-PSGD) [36], where each node has its own set of parameters and only synchronizes with its neighbors in the graph. In time, the local information during training propagates across the whole graph gradually. A lot of challenges remain to be addressed to train a model with good performance in a decentralized system.

These training paradigms are (perhaps partly) supported by various popular learning frameworks, such as TensorFlow, PyTorch, etc. Normally, they rely on high-performance computing backends to provide efficient communication in these paradigms. For example, NCCL is a stand-alone library of standard communication routines for GPUs, and it implements various communication patterns. It has been optimized to achieve high bandwidth. Another communication backend is the Intel MPI Library, a multifabric message-passing library that implements the open source MPICH specification. It aims to create, maintain, and test advanced, complex applications that perform better on high-performance computing clusters.

One of the emerging distributed training paradigms is the *Federated Learning* [6]. Federated Learning allows machine learning tasks to take place without requiring data to be centralized. There are a variety of motivations behind, for example, maintaining privacy by preventing individuals from revealing their personal data to others or latency by allowing data processing to take place closer to where and when the data is generated.

Due to these reasons, it has been gaining increasing popularity in various research and application fields. Federated Learning emphasizes the training data are not always IID. That is, a device's local data cannot be simply regarded as samples drawn from the overall distribution. The data distribution has an enormous impact on model training. Some research work provide theoretical analysis distributed training with non-IID data. Some works are proposed to address the imbalanced data problem. Besides data enhancement, its strategies include a combination of sequential update and BSP in updating, given how biased the data is.

10.2 The Actor Distributed Engine

Actor is an OCaml language–based distributed data processing system. It is developed to support the aforementioned distributed computing paradigms in Owl. It has implemented core APIs in both map-reduce and parameter server engines. Both map-reduce and parameter server engines need a (logical) centralized entity to coordinate all the nodes' progress. We also extended the parameter server engine to the peer-to-peer (p2p) engine. The p2p engine can be used to implement both data and model parallel applications; both data and model parameters can be, although not necessarily, divided into multiple parts and then distributed over different nodes. Orthogonal to these paradigms, Actor also implements all four types of synchronization barriers.

Each engine has its own set of APIs. For example, the map-reduce engine includes map, reduce, join, collect, etc., while the peer-to-peer engine provides four major APIs: push, pull, schedule, and barrier. It is worth noting there is one function shared by all the engines, that is, the barrier function which implements various barrier control mechanisms. Next, we will introduce these three different kinds of engines of Actor.

Map-Reduce Engine

Following the *MapReduce* programming model, nodes can be divided by tasks: either map or reduce. A map function processes a key/value pair to generate a set of intermediate key/value pairs, and a reduce function aggregates all the intermediate key/value pairs with the same key. Execution of this model can automatically be paralleled. Mappers compute in parallel while reducers receive the output from all mappers and combine to produce the accumulated result. This parameter update is then broadcast to all nodes. Details such as distributed scheduling, data divide, and communication in the cluster are mostly transparent to the programmers so that they can focus on the logic of mappers and reducers in solving a problem within a large distributed system. This simple functional style can be applied to a surprisingly wide range of applications. For example, the following code shows an example of using the map-reduce engine to implement the classic wordcount task:

```
module Ctx = Actor.Mapre

let print_result x = List.iter (fun (k,v) ->
    Printf.printf "%s : %i\n" k v) x
let stop_words = ["a";"are";"is";"in";"it";"that";
    "this";"and";"to";"of";"so"; "will";"can";"which";
    "for";"on";"in";"an";"with";"the";"-"]

let wordcount () =
  Ctx.init Sys.argv.(1) "tcp://localhost:5555";
  Ctx.load "unix://data/wordcount.data"
  |> Ctx.flatmap Str.(split (regexp "[ \t\n]"))
  |> Ctx.map String.lowercase_ascii
  |> Ctx.filter (fun x -> (String.length x) > 0)
  |> Ctx.filter (fun x -> not (List.mem x stop_words))
  |> Ctx.map (fun k -> (k,1))
  |> Ctx.reduce_by_key (+)
  |> Ctx.collect
  |> List.flatten |> print_result;
  Ctx.terminate ()

let _ = wordcount ()
```

Parameter Server Engine

The parameter server module is similar. Nodes are divided into servers, holding the shared global view of the up-to-date model parameters, and workers, each holding its own view of the model and executing training. The workers and servers communicate in the format of key-value pairs. It mainly consists of four APIs for the users:

- schedule: Decide what model parameters should be computed to update in this step. It can be either a local decision or a central decision.

- pull: Retrieve the updates of model parameters from somewhere and then apply them to the local model. Furthermore, the local updates will be computed based on the scheduled model parameter.

- push: Send the updates to the model plane. The updates can be sent to either a central server or to individual nodes depending on which engine is used (e.g., map-reduce, parameter server, or peer-to-peer).

- barrier: Decide whether to advance the local step. Various synchronization methods can be implemented. Besides the classic BSP, SSP, and ASP, we also implement the proposed PSP within this interface.

The following code shows the interfaces of the parameter server engine:

```
open Actor_types

type barrier =
   | ASP      (* Asynchronous Parallel *)
   | BSP      (* Bulk Synchronous Parallel *)
   | SSP      (* Stale Synchronous Parallel *)
   | PSP      (* Probabilistic Synchronous Parallel *)

(** core interfaces to parameter server *)

val register_barrier : ps_barrier_typ -> unit
val register_schedule : ('a, 'b, 'c) ps_schedule_typ -> unit
val register_pull : ('a, 'b, 'c) ps_pull_typ -> unit
val register_push : ('a, 'b, 'c) ps_push_typ -> unit
val register_stop : ps_stop_typ -> unit

val get : 'a -> 'b * int
val set : 'a -> 'b -> unit
val keys : unit -> 'a list

val start : ?barrier:barrier -> string -> string -> unit
val worker_num : unit -> int
```

The interface is intuitive. It implements the key-value mechanism of parameter servers in the get, set, and keys functions. The user can define a barrier function, scheduler, pull function executed at master, and push function executed at worker in the register_* functions. This design provides a flexible distributed computing framework.

Based on these interfaces, here is a simple example using the parameter server engine to assign random numbers as tasks to participating workers in the system:

```
module PS = Actor_param

let schedule workers =
  let tasks = List.map (fun x ->
    let k, v = Random.int 100, Random.int 1000 in (x, [(k,v)])
  ) workers in tasks

let push id vars =
  let updates = List.map (fun (k,v) ->
    Owl_log.info "working on %i" v;
    (k,v) ) vars in
  updates

let test_context () =
  PS.register_schedule schedule;
  PS.register_push push;
  PS.start Sys.argv.(1) Actor_config.manager_addr;
  Owl_log.info "do some work at master node"

let _ = test_context ()
```

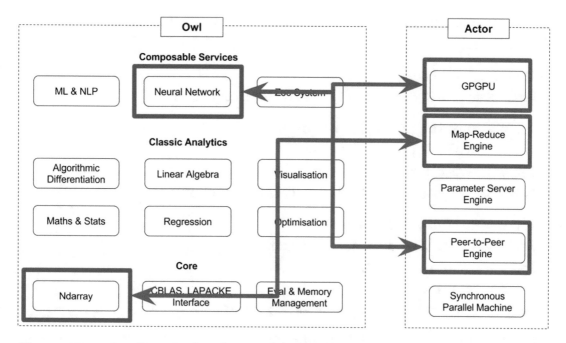

Figure 10-1. *Combine Owl and Actor frameworks*

Compose Actor with Owl

One of the most notable advantages of Actor lies in that it can compose with Owl. Parallel and distributed computing in Owl is achieved by composing the different data structures in Owl's core library with specific engines in the Actor system.

As shown in Figure 10-1, all the three distributed engines can be used to compose with the Ndarray module in Owl. And the composition is quite straightforward:

```
module M = Owl.Parallel.Make (Dense.Ndarray.S) (Actor.Mapre)
```

That's all it takes. By using a functor provided in Owl, it builds up a distributed version of the n-dimensional array module. In this functor, we choose to use the single-precision dense Ndarray module and the MapReduce engine as parameters. Using this distributed Ndarray module is also easy. The following code shows an example. You can see that the composed Ndarray module provides all the normal ndarray operations, including initialization, map, fold, sum, slicing, adding, etc. And these computations perform on a distributed cluster.

```
module M1 = Owl_parallel.Make_Distributed (Owl.Dense.Ndarray.D)
(Actor.Mapre)

let test_owl_distributed () =
  Actor.Mapre.init Sys.argv.(1) "tcp://localhost:5555";

  let y = M1.init [|2;3;4|] float_of_int in
  let _ = M1.set y [|1;2;3|] 0. in
  let y = M1.add x y in
  Owl.Dense.Ndarray.D.print (M1.to_ndarray y); flush_all ();

  let x = M1.ones [|200;300;400|] in
  let x = M1.map (fun a -> a +. 1.) x in
  let a = M1.fold (+.) x 0. in
  let b = M1.sum x in
  Owl_log.info "fold vs. sum ===> %g, %g" a b;

  Owl_log.info "start retrieving big x";
  let x = M1.to_ndarray x in
  Owl_log.info "finsh retrieving big x";
  Owl_log.info "sum x = %g" (Owl.Arr.sum' x)
```

Similarly, this composition also applies to more advanced and complicated data structures such as neural networks. Remember that Ndarray is the core data structure in Owl, which the neural network module relies on. Therefore, we can create a distributed version neural network module using the same functor:

```
module M = Owl.Parallel.Make (Owl.Neural.S.Graph) (Actor.Param)
```

Here, we use the single-precision neural network graph module and the parameter server distributed engine to parameterize the new module. It enables parallel training on a computer cluster. The following code shows an example. Most of the code stays unchanged. All it requires is to use the M2.train function instead of the original one to train a network.

```
module M2 = Owl_neural_parallel.Make (Owl.Neural.S.Graph) (Actor.Param)

let test_neural_parallel () =
  let open Owl.Neural.S in
  let open Graph in
```

```
let nn =
  input [|32;32;3|]
  |> normalisation ~decay:0.9
  |> conv2d [|3;3;3;32|] [|1;1|] ~act_typ:Activation.Relu
  |> conv2d [|3;3;32;32|] [|1;1|] ~act_typ:Activation.Relu ~padding:VALID
  |> max_pool2d [|2;2|] [|2;2|] ~padding:VALID
  |> dropout 0.1
  |> conv2d [|3;3;32;64|] [|1;1|] ~act_typ:Activation.Relu
  |> conv2d [|3;3;64;64|] [|1;1|] ~act_typ:Activation.Relu ~padding:VALID
  |> max_pool2d [|2;2|] [|2;2|] ~padding:VALID
  |> dropout 0.1
  |> fully_connected 512 ~act_typ:Activation.Relu
  |> linear 10 ~act_typ:Activation.(Softmax 1)
  |> get_network
in

let x, _, y = Owl.Dataset.load_cifar_train_data 1 in
let chkpt state =
  if Checkpoint.(state.current_batch mod 1 = 0) then (
    Checkpoint.(state.stop <- true);
  )
in

let params = Params.config
  ~batch:(Batch.Sample 100)
  ~learning_rate:(Learning_Rate.Adagrad 0.001)
  ~checkpoint:(Checkpoint.Custom chkpt)
  ~stopping:(Stopping.Const 1e-6) 10.
in
let url = Actor_config.manager_addr in
let jid = Sys.argv.(1) in
M2.train ~params nn x y jid url
```

10.3 Synchronization: Barrier Control Methods

One critical component of distributed and federated machine learning systems is barrier synchronization: the mechanism by which participating nodes coordinate in the iterative distributed computation. As noted earlier, the statistical and iterative nature of machine learning means that errors are incrementally removed from the system. To be perfectly consistent, where every node proceeds to the next iteration together risks reducing throughput. Relaxing consistency can improve system performance without ultimately sacrificing accuracy. This trade-off is embodied in the *barrier control* mechanism. In the rest of this chapter, we will focus on this aspect in distributed computing.

In parallel computing, a barrier is used for synchronization. If in the source code a barrier is applied on a group of threads or processes, at this point a thread or process cannot proceed until all others have finished their workload before the barrier. With this, it is guaranteed that certain calculations are finished. For example, the following code shows the `barrier` pragma in OpenMP, an application programming interface that supports shared memory multiprocessing programming. Here, the calculation is distributed among multiple threads and executed in parallel, but the computation of y cannot proceed until the other threads have computed their own values of x. Execution past the barrier point continues in parallel.

```
#pragma omp parallel
{
  x = some_calculation();
#pragma omp barrier
  y = x + 1
}
```

The preceding example shows a strict version of barrier methods. In distributed training, there exist multiple forms of barrier control methods for synchronization. Current barrier control mechanisms can be divided into four types, discussed in detail later. These barrier methods provide different trade-offs between system performance and model accuracy. They can be applied in different distributed machine learning systems we have discussed in the previous section, including parameter servers, peer-to-peer, etc. In the rest of this section, we will introduce them.

The **Bulk Synchronous Parallel (BSP)** is the most strict, which requires all workers to proceed in lockstep moving to the next iteration only when all the workers are ready. **Bulk Synchronous Parallel (BSP)** is a deterministic scheme where workers perform a computation phase followed by a synchronization/communication phase to exchange updates, under control of a central server [54]. BSP programs are often serializable, that is, they are equivalent to sequential computations, if the data and model of a distributed algorithm have been suitably scheduled, making BSP the strongest barrier control method [30]. Numerous variations of BSP exist, for example, allowing a worker to execute more than one iteration in a cycle [14]. Federated Learning also uses BSP for its distributed computation [6]. Moreover, BSP requires centralized coordination.

The **Asynchronous Parallel (ASP)** [41] is the least strict barrier control, since it allows each worker to proceed at its own pace without waiting for the others. **Asynchronous Parallel (ASP)** takes the opposite approach to BSP, allowing computations to execute as fast as possible by running all workers completely asynchronously [41]. ASP can result in fast convergence because it permits the highest possible rate of iteration [54]. However, the lack of any coordination means that updates are calculated based on old model state, resulting in reduced accuracy. There are no theoretical guarantees as to whether algorithms converge. The Hogwild scheme proposed in [41] has many limits, for example, it requires a convex function and sparse update. Many work have tried to extend these limits in application and theoretical analysis [35]. These studies often lead to carefully tuned step size in training. [59] proposes a delay-compensated SGD that mitigates delayed updates in ASP by compensating the gradients received at the parameter server. [32] introduces another variant of ASP specifically for wide area networks: as communication is a dominant factor, it advocates allowing insignificant updates to be delayed indefinitely in WAN.

Table 10-1. *Classification of Synchronization Methods Used by Different Systems*

System	Synchronization Constraint	Barrier Method
MapReduce [17]	Requires a map to complete before reducing	BSP
Hogwild! [41]	ASP but system-level bounds on delays	ASP, SSP
Parameter servers [34]	Swappable synchronization method	BSP, ASP, SSP
Hadoop [46], Spark [57]	Aggregate updates after task completion	BSP
Yahoo! LDA [2]	Checkpoints	SSP, ASP
SSP [30]	Updates delayed by up to $N-1$ steps	SSP
Gaia [32]	Accumulate weight locally	BSP, SSP
Astraea [19]	Combination with sequential update	BSP
Owl+Actor[51]	Swappable synchronization method	BSP, ASP, SSP, PSP

The third one is the **Stale Synchronous Parallel (SSP)** [30], which relaxes BSP by allowing workers to proceed to the next iteration once all workers' iterations are within a certain limit with each other. **Stale Synchronous Parallel (SSP)** is a bounded asynchronous model that balances between BSP and ASP. Rather than requiring all workers to proceed to the next iteration together, it requires only that the iteration of any two workers in the system differs by at most s, a predefined *staleness* bound. The staleness parameter limits error and allows SSP to provide deterministic convergence guarantees [30, 15, 54]. Built on SSP, [58] investigates the *n-softsync*, the synchronization method that makes the parameter server updating its weight after collecting certain number of updates from any workers. [9] proposes to remove a small amount of "longtail" workers or add a small amount of backup nodes to mitigate this effect while avoiding asynchronous noise.

The final one is called **Probabilistic Synchronous Parallel (PSP)**. Its basic idea is to introduce a *sampling* primitive in the system and to use a sampled subset of participating workers to estimate progress of the entire system. PSP introduces a second dimension to this trade-off: from how many nodes must we receive updates before proceeding to the next iteration. By composing our *sampling* primitive with traditional barrier controls, it obtains a family of barrier controls better suited for supporting iterative learning in the heterogeneous networks.

The core idea behind PSP is simple yet powerful: we require that only some proportion, not all, of the working nodes be synchronized in progress. By "progress" we mean the number of updates pushed to the server at the client's side and the total number of updates collected at the server's side. In a centralized training framework, the server builds this subset of the training nodes based on system information, such as their current local progress. This subset can be sampled by various approaches. One common and intuitive way is to sample randomly among all the workers.

The parameter in PSP, the sampling size, therefore controls how precise this estimation is. Assuming this random subset is not biased with respect to nodes' performance, the server can use the resulting distribution to derive an estimate of the percentage of nodes which have passed a given progress. This estimation depends on the specific method used within the subset, as will be discussed in Section 10.4. Accordingly, the server can decide whether to allow the trainers to pass the barrier and advance their local progress.

Figure 10-2 illustrates the difference among these four types of barriers. Here, the computing progress is measured by super steps, or iterations. Communication may happen at the barrier to ensure consistency through the global state. A central server may also be required in order to maintain the global state, denoted by the clock symbol.

Table 10-1 summarizes the barrier synchronization methods used by different machine learning systems. You can see that, regardless if it is a classic system or a new one, the barrier synchronization has been an important component in the system.

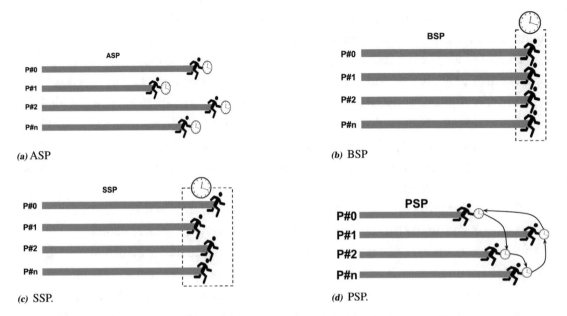

Figure 10-2. *Illustration of various barrier control methods*

10.4 System Design Space and Parameters

In the previous section, we have introduced the existing barrier control methods. In this section, we will further explain how they are designed and their relationship with each other.

In a distributed training system that utilizes an iterative learning algorithm, the main target is to achieve faster convergence, a state in which loss keeps to be within an error range around the final value of training. The convergence of training is positively correlated with two factors: *consistency* and *iteration rate*. Consistency is the agreement between multiple nodes in a distributed training system to achieve convergence. It can be indicated by the difference of training iterations of the nodes. Weak consistency can be detrimental to the update quality of the model in each iteration. On the other hand, the iteration rate is how fast the training processes. This relationship can be captured by Eq. 10.1.

$$\text{Convergence } \alpha \text{ consistency} \times \text{iteration rate} \tag{10.1}$$

BSP and ASP are good examples to illustrate these two factors. In BSP, workers must wait for others to finish in a training round, and all the workers are of the same progress. Therefore, of all barrier methods the BSP can offer the best consistency and highest accuracy in each update. BSP is a deterministic algorithm. As a price, if there are *stragglers* in the training nodes, the system progress will be bottlenecked by the slowest node. On the other hand, ASP allows nodes to execute as fast as possible, with no need to consider the progress of other nodes. As a result, ASP leads to the highest possible rate of iteration. However, the lack of any coordination means that updates are calculated based on out-of-date model state, resulting in reduced consistency.

The design of SSP clearly shows a good trade-off between these two extremes. As shown in Figure 10-3, SSP attempts to exploit this trade-off by bounding the difference in iterations between participating nodes. On one hand, it does not require all the nodes to have exactly the same progress as in BSP and thus improves its iteration rate. On the other hand, its stale bound provides a more strict consistency bound on nodes than ASP. As a result, it achieves a balance between these two ends, hence leading to a higher rate of convergence. The parameter staleness covers the spectrum on this one-dimensional tuning space.

But is that all about the design space of a barrier control method? Let's look deep into the current model again. We start by visualizing the iterative update process, as shown in Figure 10-4.

The model is simple. A sequence of updates is applied to an initial global state x_0. Here, u(p,t) denotes update(node id, timestamp), that is, the updates are generated for all the nodes on all its clock ticks. In this example, there are three nodes. Ideally, in clock tick t_i we expect to have three updates: $u(0, t_i)$, $u(1, t_i)$, and $u(2, t_i)$. However, due to the noisy environment, these updates are divided into two sets. The deterministic ones are those we expect if everything goes well as stated earlier. The probabilistic ones are those out-of-order updates due to packet loss, network delay, node failure, etc. Although it is simple, this model can represent most iterative learning algorithms.

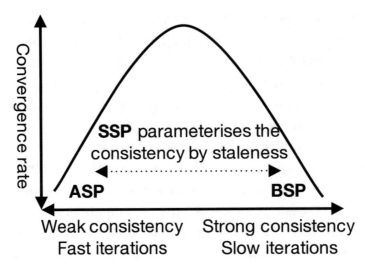

Figure 10-3. *The trade-off among ASP, SSP, and BSP*

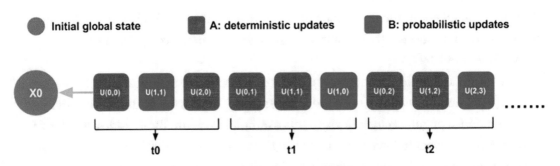

Figure 10-4. *Analytical model of the iterative update process in distributed learning*

Then we use the analytical model to express each barrier method as in Figure 10-5. The left part deals with the consistency. The += operator is the server logic about how to incorporate updates submitted to the central server into the global state. The right part deals with synchronization; computers either communicate to each other or contact the central server to coordinate their progress. As discussed earlier, the right side can be divided into two types of updates: deterministic and probabilistic.

The formulation reveals some very interesting structures from a system design perspective. For BSP and SSP, the central server *couples* the control logic of both consistency and synchronization. That is to say, if you choose tight consistency, you must also choose global synchronization control by a logic central server. For both BSP and SSP, one logical server is assigned to update model parameters and coordinate the progress of all nodes in an iterative learning algorithm. In a distributed system, this is often the bottleneck and single point of failure. ASP avoids such coupling by giving up synchronization and consistency completely.

The PSP, however, decouples consistency and synchronization. It achieves so by finding out that there exists another dimension in the design space of barrier methods: the *completeness*. Note that, for the previous three barriers, the degree of consistency is enforced upon the whole population. All the participating nodes are equally consistent.

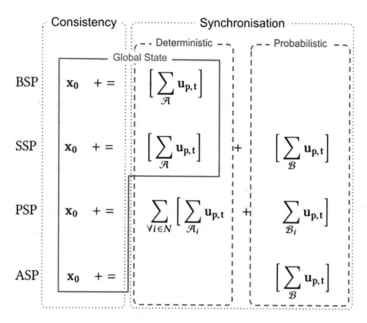

Figure 10-5. *Decoupling consistency and synchronization*

PSP exploits this dimension of the degree of completeness in a sample, which renders a distribution of degree of consistency. In PSP, each computer synchronizes with a small group of others, and the consistency is only enforced within the group. The completeness presents the level of coordination among the nodes. By changing the sample size, this dimension goes from fully complete (all working nodes are considered in synchronization) to not complete (each single node is considered separately).

The sampling strategy of PSP has a profound implication on the design of barrier control methods. By adding in this extra dimension, the convergence is now impacted by three factors, and Eq. 10.1 now becomes

Convergence α consistency of sample $\times$ completeness of sample $\times$ iteration rate   (10.2)

In Eq. 10.2, the consistency is thus further decomposed into the consistency degree in a sample and the completeness of this sample.

Thus, PSP shows a tuning space that incorporates all the other barriers. As shown in Figures 10-6 and 10-7, in the refined design space, the ASP is placed at the bottom left, since it shows the weakest consistency (no control on the progress of other nodes) and completeness (each node only considers itself). On the other hand, BSP and SSP show full completeness, since they require a central server to synchronize the progress of all nodes. Similar to Figure 10-3, they show different levels of consistency.

Compatibility

As a more general framework, one noteworthy advantage of PSP lies in that it is straightforwardly compatible with existing synchronization methods, which provides the tuning dimension of consistency. In classic BSP and SSP, their barrier control mechanisms are invoked by a central server to test the synchronization condition with the given inputs. For BSP and SSP to use the *sampling* primitive, they simply need to use the sampled states rather than the global states when evaluating the barrier control condition. Within each sampled subset, these traditional mechanisms can then be applied. Users can thus easily derive probabilistic versions of BSP and SSP, namely, *pBSP* and *pSSP*. For example, Figure 10-8 shows that PSP can be applied to other synchronous machines as a higher-order function to derive probabilistic versions.

Formally, at the barrier control point, a worker samples β out of P workers without replacement. If one lags more than s updates behind the current worker, then the worker waits. This process is pBSP (based on BSP) if the staleness parameter $s = 0$ and pSSP (based on SSP) if $s > 0$. If $s = \infty$, PSP reduces to ASP.

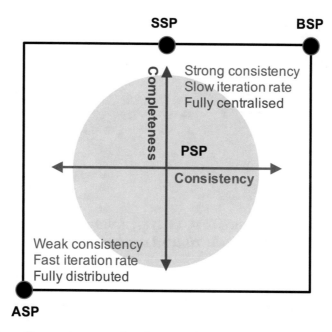

Figure 10-6. *Two dimensions in the design of barrier control methods*

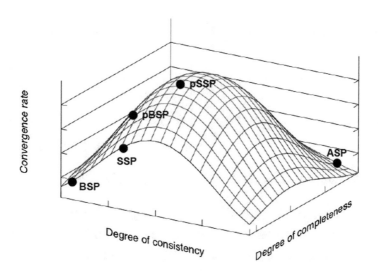

Figure 10-7. *The new dimension allows us to explore a larger design space, which further makes it possible to find a better trade-off to achieve better convergence rate*

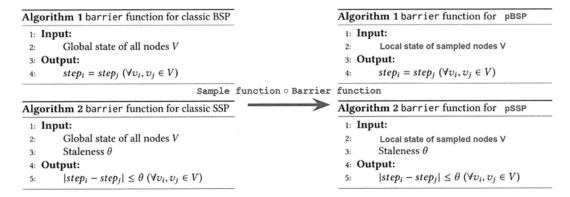

Algorithm 1 barrier function for classic BSP	**Algorithm 1** barrier function for pBSP
1: **Input:**	1: **Input:**
2: Global state of all nodes V	2: Local state of sampled nodes V
3: **Output:**	3: **Output:**
4: $step_i = step_j \ (\forall v_i, v_j \in V)$	4: $step_i = step_j \ (\forall v_i, v_j \in V)$

Sample function ∘ Barrier function

Algorithm 2 barrier function for classic SSP	**Algorithm 2** barrier function for pSSP
1: **Input:**	1: **Input:**
2: Global state of all nodes V	2: Local state of sampled nodes V
3: Staleness θ	3: Staleness θ
4: **Output:**	4: **Output:**
5: $|step_i - step_j| \le \theta \ (\forall v_i, v_j \in V)$	5: $|step_i - step_j| \le \theta \ (\forall v_i, v_j \in V)$

Figure 10-8. *PSP can be applied to other synchronous machines as a higher-order function to further derive a fully distributed version*

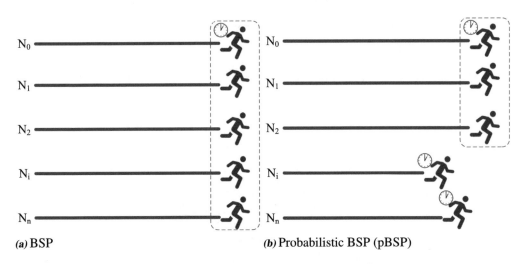

(a) BSP   (b) Probabilistic BSP (pBSP)

Figure 10-9. *Compose PSP with Bulk Synchronous Parallel*

As an illustration, Figure 10-9 depicts how to compose BSP with PSP, namely, a subset of the population of nodes is chosen, and then the BSP is applied within the subset (pBSP). The composition of PSP and SSP (pSSP) follows the same idea.

Besides existing barrier control methods, PSP is also compatible with both centralized and decentralized training approaches. As described earlier, the extra completeness dimension decouples consistency and synchronization. The other full complete synchronization control methods require a centralized node to hold the global state. By using a sampling primitive, they can be transformed into fully distributed solutions. In a decentralized setting, based on the information it gathers from its neighboring nodes, a trainer node may either decide to pass the barrier control by advancing its local progress or wait until the threshold is met.

The benefits of exploring this two-dimensional design space are thus multitude. First, it enables constructing fully distributed barrier control mechanisms that are more scalable. As illustrated in Figure 10-2d, each node depends only on several other nodes to decide its own barrier, not on all other nodes. Second, it allows exploring barriers that can achieve better convergence. To ignore the status of the other workers with impunity, it relies on the fact that, in practice, many iterative learning algorithms can tolerate a certain degree of error as they converge to their final answers [12]. By controlling the sampling method and size, PSP reduces the impact of lagging nodes while also limiting the error introduced by nodes returning updates based on stale information. Third, in an unreliable environment, using the sampling primitive can minimize the impact of outliers and stragglers by probabilistically choosing a subset of the total workers as estimation. In summary, by tuning the sampling size and staleness parameters carefully, the generated barrier control methods can be robust against the effect of stragglers while also ensuring a degree of consistency between iterations as the algorithm progresses. In Section 10.6, we will investigate the performance in more detail.

Table 10-2. *Notation Table*

Notation	Explanation
$f(r)$	Probabilities of a node lagging r steps
$F(r)$	Cumulative distribution function of $f(r)$
$R[X]$	Difference between optimal and noisy state
a	$F(r)^\beta$, where β is the sample size
γ_t	Sequence inconsistency at length t
T	Total length of update sequence
L	Lipschitz constant
σ	Initial learning rate, constant
N	Total number of workers, constant

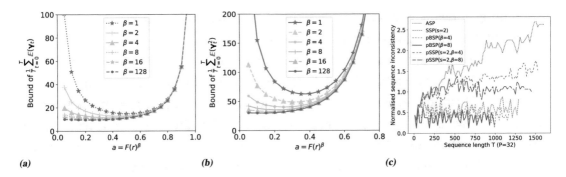

Figure 10-10. *(a–b) Bounds on mean and variance of sampling distribution as a function of F(r)ᵝ. The staleness r is set to 4 with T equal to 10000. (c) Sequence inconsistency observed in empirical training*

10.5 Convergence Analysis

In this section, we present a theoretical analysis of PSP and show how it affects the convergence of ML algorithms (SGD used in the analysis). The analysis mainly shows that (1) under PSP, the algorithm only has a small probability not to converge, and the upper limit of this probability decreases with the training iterations; (2) instead of choosing large sampling size, it is proved that a small number is already sufficient to provide a good performance. The notations used in the following analysis are presented in Table 10-2.

The analysis is based on the model shown in Figure 10-4. In a distributed machine learning process, these N workers keep generating updates, and a shared model is updated with them continuously. We count these updates by first looping over all workers at one iteration and then across all the iterations. In this process, each one is incrementally indexed by integer t. The total length of this update sequence is T. We apply an analysis framework similar to that of [15]. At each barrier control point, every worker A samples β out of N workers without replacement. If one of these sampled workers lags more than s steps behind worker A, it waits. The probabilities of a node lagging r steps are drawn from a distribution with a probability mass function $f(r)$ and cumulative distribution function (CDF) $F(r)$. Without loss of generality, we set both staleness r and sample size β parameters to be constants.

Ideally, in a fully deterministic barrier control system such as BSP, the ordering of updates in this sequence should be deterministic. We call it a *true sequence*. However, in reality, what we get is often a *noisy sequence*, where updates are reordered irregularly due to sporadic and random network and system delays. These two sequences share the same length. We define *sequence inconsistency* as the number of index difference between these two sequences and denote it by γ_t. It shows how much a series of updates deviate from an ideal case. If the sequence inconsistency is bounded, it means that what a true sequence achieves, in time, a noisy sequence can also achieve, regardless of the order of updates. This metric is thus a key instrument in theoretically proving the convergence property of an asynchronous barrier method.

Let $R[X]=\sum_{t}^{T}f_t(\tilde{x}_t)-f_t(x^*)$. This is the sum of the differences between the optimal value of the function and the current value given a noisy state. To put it plainly, it shows the difference between "the computation result we get if all the parameter updates we receive are in perfect ideal order" and "the computation result we get in the real world when using, for example, PSP barrier." Now we show the noisy system state, $\tilde{x}_t$, converges in expectation toward the optimal, x^*, in probability. Specifically, since $R[X]$ is accumulated over time, to get a time-independent metric, we need to show the value $\dfrac{R[X]}{T}$ is bounded.

Theorem: SGD under PSP, convergence in probability Let $f(x)=\sum_{t=1}^{T}f_t(x)$ be a convex function where each $f_t \in R$ is also convex. Let $x^* \in R^d$ be the minimizer of this function. Assume that f_t are L-Lipschitz and that the distance between two points x and x' is bounded: $D(x\|x')=\dfrac{1}{2}\|x-x'\|_2^2 \leq F^2$, where F is constant. Let an update be given by $u_t=-\eta_t\nabla f_t(\tilde{x}_t)$ and the learning rate by $\eta_t=\dfrac{\sigma}{\sqrt{t}}$. We have bound:

$$P\left(\frac{R[X]}{T}-\frac{1}{\sqrt{T}}\left(\sigma L^2-\frac{2F^2}{\sigma}\right)-q\geq\delta\right)\leq e^{-\frac{T\delta^2}{c+\frac{b\delta}{3}}},\qquad(10.3)$$

where δ is a constant and $b \leq 4NTL\sigma$. The b term here is the upper bound on the random variables which are drawn from the lag distribution $f(r)$. The q and c are two values that are related to the mean and variance of γ_t. If we assume that $0 < a < 1$, then it can be proved that both q and c are bounded. Furthermore, if we assume with probability Φ that $\forall t. \ 4NL\sigma\gamma_t < O(T)$, then $b < O(T)$. That means $\dfrac{R[X]}{T}$ converges to $O(T^{-1/2})$, in probability Φ with an exponential tail bound that decreases as time increases.

In other words, this theorem claims that as long as the difference between the noisy update sequence and the ideal sequence is bounded, and that the nodes in the system do not lag behind too far, PSP guarantees that (with certain probability) the difference between the result we get and the optimal result diminishes as more updates are generated and appended in the sequence. A formal proof of this theorem can be seen in [52].

How Effective Is Sampling

One key step in proving the preceding theorem is to prove the sequence inconsistency γ_t is bounded. We have proved that the mean and variance of vector γ_t are both bounded. Specifically, the average inconsistency (normalized by sequence length T) is bounded by

$$\frac{1}{T}\sum_{t=0}^{T}\mathbf{E}(\gamma_t) \leq S\left(\frac{r(r+1)}{2} + \frac{a(r+2)}{(1-a)^2}\right), \tag{10.4}$$

and the variance has a similar bound:

$$\frac{1}{T}\sum_{t=0}^{T}\mathbf{E}(\gamma_t^2) < S\left(\frac{r(r+1)(2r+1)}{6} + \frac{a(r^2+4)}{(1-a)^3}\right), \tag{10.5}$$

where

$$S = \frac{1-a}{F(r)(1-a)+a-a^{T-r+1}}. \tag{10.6}$$

As intimidating as these bounds may seem, they can both be treated as constants for fixed a, T, r, and β values. They provide a means to quantify the impact of the PSP *sampling* primitive and provide stronger convergence guarantees than ASP, shown in Figure 10-11. They do not depend upon the entire lag distribution.

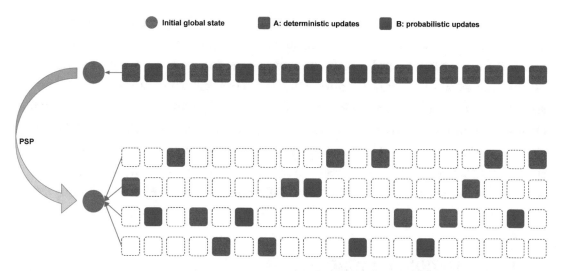

Figure 10-11. *Sampling primitive decomposes the original sequence into multiple sampling processes (assuming no replacement for simplicity), and each has a partial view of the original one. Smaller sample size results in more sampling processes; each has even less complete view of the original one (i.e., less completeness), further reducing the synchronization level*

The intuition provided in Eq. 10.4 and Eq. 10.5 is that, when applying PSP, the update sequence we get is not too different from the true sequence, regarding both mean and variance of the difference. To demonstrate the impact of the *sampling* primitive on bounds quantitatively, Figures 10-10a and 10-10b show how increasing the sampling count, β (from 1 to 128, marked with different line colors on the right), yields tighter bounds. *Notably, only a small number of nodes need to be sampled to yield bounds close to the optimal. This result has an important implication to justify using the sampling primitive in large distributed learning systems due to its effectiveness.* This will be further verified in the evaluation section.

The discontinuities at $a = 0$ and $a = 1$ reflect edge cases of the behavior of the barrier method control. Specifically, with $a = 0$, no probability mass is in the initial r steps, so no progress can be achieved if the system requires $\beta > 0$ workers to be within r steps of the fastest worker. If $a = 1$ and $\beta = 0$, then the system is operating in ASP mode, so the bounds are expected to be large. However, these are overly generous. Better bounds are $O(T)$ for the mean and $O(T^2)$ for the variance, which we give in our proof. When $a = 1$ and $\beta \neq 0$, the system should never wait and workers could slip as far as they like as long as they returned to be within r steps before the next sampling point.

Besides theoretical analysis, an intuitive visualization of sequence inconsistency γ_t is shown in Figure 10-10c. We run a distributed training experiment with various barrier methods for 100 seconds and measure the number of difference between true and noisy sequence at a fixed interval during the whole process. The result shows that the sequence inconsistency using ASP keeps growing linearly, while in SSP it increases and decreases within a certain bound, which is decided by the staleness parameter. Applying sampling to SSP relaxes that bound, but unlike ASP, inconsistencies using pSSP grow sublinearly with sequence length. BSP is omitted in the figure, since its true and noisy sequence is always the same. pBSP shows a tight bound (about 0.5) even with only 5% sampling.

Implementation Technique

As shown in Table 10-1, barrier control methods are widely used in existing systems, such as parameter servers, Hadoop, etc. Indeed, PSP is not yet widely available in many systems, which means the completeness dimension in synchronization method design cannot be readily utilized. The good news is that bringing the extra design dimension requires minimal effort. To implement PSP atop of current data analytics frameworks, developers only need to add a new primitive: sampling. As shown in Section 10.4, it is straightforward to compose existing barrier methods in a distributed system.

By default, we choose the trainers randomly. There are various ways to guarantee the random sampling, for example, organizing the nodes into a structural overlay such as the Distributed Hash Table (DHT). The random sampling is based on the fact that node identifiers are uniformly distributed in a namespace. Nodes can estimate the population size based on the allocated ID density in the namespace.

The choice of samples has a great impact on the performance of PSP. The sampling of PSP provides an estimate of the total distribution of the progress of all the workers. In a worst-case scenario where the sampled subset happens to be all stragglers, this subset cannot provide a very efficient estimation of all the workers. Different sampling strategies can be used in certain scenarios.

For example, we can change how frequently the sample changes during distributed computing. Or, we can choose the workers according to their previous computation time. Specifically, at each round, all the workers are categorized into two groups according to their historical computing time per iteration, one slow and one fast, and then choose equal numbers of workers from both groups to form the target subset. We can use clustering algorithms such as K-Means.

10.6 Evaluation

In this section, we investigate the performance of various barrier control methods in experiments and the trade-off they make. We focus on two common metrics in evaluating barrier strategies: the accuracy and system progress. Using these metrics, we explore various barrier controls with regard to the impact of sample settings and stragglers in the Federated Learning system. Besides, we also use a new metric called *progress inconsistency* as a metric of training accuracy, but without the impact of specific application hyperparameters.

Experiment Setup

We perform extensive experiments on the real-world dataset FEMNIST, which is part of LEAF, a modular benchmarking framework for learning in federated settings, and includes a suite of open source federated datasets [8]. Similar to MNIST, the FEMNIST dataset is for image classification tasks. But it contains 62 different classes (10 digits, 26 lowercases, and 26 uppercases). Each image is of size 28 by 28 pixels. The dataset contains 805,263 samples in total. The number of samples is distributed evenly across different classes.

To better study the performance of the proposed method with non-IID data distribution in Federated Learning, we follow the data partition setting in [7]. We first sort the data by class labels, divide them into $2n$ shards, and assign each of n workers 2 shards. This pathological non-IID partition makes the training data on different workers overlap as little as possible. The validation set is 10% of the total data. Besides, we preprocess it so that the validation set is roughly balanced in each class. As for training hyperparameters, we use a batch size of 128, and we use the Adam optimizer, with learning rate of 0.001 and coefficient of (0.9, 0.999).

We conduct our experiment on a server that has 56 Intel(R) Xeon(R) CPU E5-2680 v4 and a memory of 256G. In the rest of this section, if not otherwise mentioned, we use 16 workers by default. Besides, one extra worker is used for model validation to compute its accuracy. In the rest of this section, we aim to show the wide range of tuning space enabled by the sampling parameter and how existing barrier methods can be incorporated into PSP.

Accuracy

We execute the training process using each method on the non-IID FEMNIST dataset for about eight epochs. The results are shown in Figure 10-12. The subfigure uses time as the x axis. It shows the change of trained model accuracy in about 10,000 seconds. It compares the ASP, BSP, and pBSP (composing PSP with BSP) where the sampling size equals 4.

The first thing to note here is, though the performance of ASP looks optimal at the beginning due to its quick accumulation of updates from different workers, it quickly deteriorates and fails to converge. Compared to the unstable performance of ASP, BSP steadily converges. Then the pBSP clearly outperforms these two regarding model accuracy, especially in the later part of training. Due to its probabilistic nature, the pBSP line shows larger jitters than BSP, but also follows the general trend of BSP toward convergence steadily.

The strength of PSP lies in that it combines the advantages of existing methods. In the lower subfigure of Figure 10-12, we use the accumulated total number of updates the parameter server has received as the x axis to compare the "efficiency" of the updates in ASP, SSP, and pSSP. The staleness parameter of SSP and pSSP is set to 4 here. We can see that as updates are accumulating, despite using sampling, the accuracy increase of pSSP is similar to that of SSP.

Meanwhile, pSSP is much faster than SSP with regard to the update progress or the rate at which the updates accumulate at the parameter server. Figure 10-13 shows the number of updates at the server with regard to time (here, we show only results from the beginning of evaluations). As can be seen, at any given time, both pBSP and pSSP progress faster than BSP and SSP correspondingly. Of course, ASP progresses the fastest since it does not require any synchronization among workers, but its nonconverged updates make this advantage obsolete.

The difference of the number of updates can be directly interpreted as the communication cost, since each update means the transmission of weight and gradient between the server and clients. For example, **at about 600s, the pSSP incurs 35% more traffic than SSP; and pBSP even doubles the traffic in BSP**. In our experiments, the PSP can reduce communication overhead without sacrificing the final model accuracy.

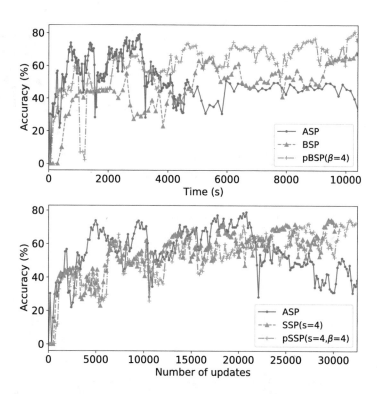

Figure 10-12. *Performance comparison between different synchronization methods*

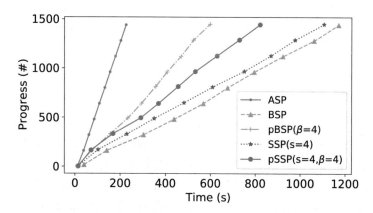

Figure 10-13. *Number of updates accumulated at the parameter server for different barrier methods*

PSP combines the best of two worlds. On one hand, it has similar update efficiency as SSP and BSP; on the other hand, it achieves faster update progress that is similar to ASP. As a result, it outperforms the existing barrier control methods.

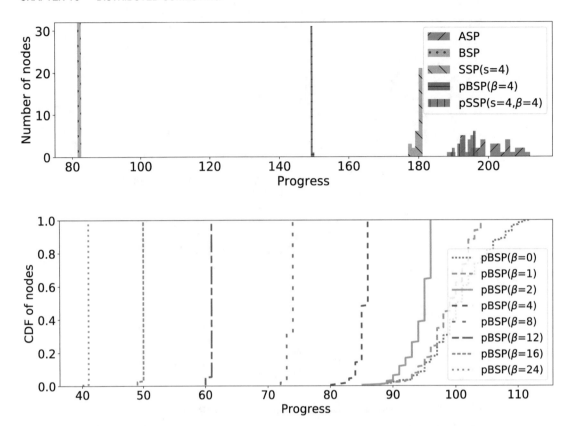

Figure 10-14. *(a) System progress distribution; (b) pBSP parameterized by different sample sizes, from 0 to 24. Increasing the sample size makes the curves shift from right to left with decreasing spread, covering the whole spectrum from the most lenient ASP to the most strict BSP*

System Progress

In this section, we use 32 workers and run the evaluation for 400 seconds. Figure 10-14a shows the distribution of all nodes' progress when evaluation is finished.

As expected, the most strict BSP leads to a tightly bounded progress distribution, but at the same time, using BSP makes all the nodes progress slowly. At the end of the experiment, all the nodes only proceed to about the 80th update. As a comparison, using ASP leads to a much faster progress of around 200 updates. But the cost is a much loosely spread distribution, which shows no synchronization at all among nodes. SSP allows certain staleness (4 in our experiment) and sits between BSP and ASP.

PSP shows another dimension of performance tuning. We set sample size β to 4, that is, a sampling ratio of only 12.5%. The result shows that pBSP is almost as tightly bound as BSP and also much faster than BSP itself. The same is also true when comparing pSSP and SSP. In both cases, PSP improves the iteration efficiency while limiting dispersion.

To further investigate the impact of the sample size, we focus on BSP and choose different sample sizes. In Figure 10-14b, we vary the sample size from 0 to 24. As we increase the sample size, the curves start shifting from right to left with tighter and tighter spread, indicating less variance in nodes' progress. With sample size 0, the pBSP exhibits exactly the same behavior as that of ASP; with increased sample size, pBSP starts becoming more similar to SSP and BSP with tighter requirements on synchronization.

Another important observation worth mentioning is, with a very small sample size of one or two (i.e., very small communication cost on each individual node), pBSP can already effectively synchronize most of the nodes compared to ASP. The tail caused by stragglers can be further trimmed by using a larger sample size. This observation confirms our theoretical analysis in Section 10.5, which explicitly shows that a small sample size can effectively push the probabilistic convergence guarantee to its optimum even for a large system size, which further indicates the superior scalability of the proposed solution.

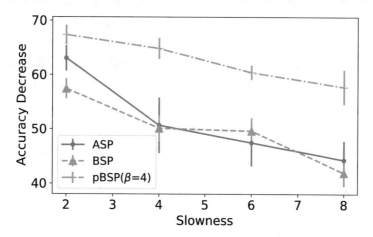

Figure 10-15. *Stragglers impact both system performance and accuracy of model updates. Probabilistic synchronization control by a sampling primitive is able to mitigate such impacts*

When composed with BSP, PSP can increase the system progress of BSP by about 85% while retaining the almost the same tight bound on progress distribution. Besides, by tuning the sample size, the evaluation result shows that a small size such as 2 or 4 in a system of 32 workers can effectively provide a tight convergence guarantee.

Robustness to Straggler

Stragglers are not uncommon in traditional distributed training and are pervasive in the workers of Federated Learning. In this section, we show the impact of stragglers on system performance and accuracy of model updates and how probabilistic synchronization control by a sampling primitive can be used to mitigate such impacts.

As explained before, we model the system stragglers by increasing the training time of each slow trainer to n-fold, namely, on average they spend n times as much time as normal nodes to finish one iteration. The parameter n here is the "slowness" of the system. In the experiment shown in Figure 10-15, we keep the portion of slow nodes fixed and increase the slowness from 2 to 8. Then we measure the accuracy of using a certain barrier control method at the end of training. To be more precise, we choose a period of results before the ending and use their mean value and standard for each observation point.

Figure 10-15 plots the decreasing model accuracy due to stragglers as a function of the straggler slowness. As we can see, both ASP and BSP are sensitive to stragglers, both dropping about 20% accuracy by increasing slowness from 2x to 8x, while that of pBSP only drops by less than 10%. For BSP, this is mainly because the stragglers severely reduce the training update progress; for ASP, this can be explained as the result of its asynchronous nature, where updates from slow workers are delayed. This problem is exacerbated by the non-IID data, where the data overlap between different workers is limited, if not none at all. Once again, PSP takes the best of both worlds. As we have shown before, its probabilistic sampling mitigates the effect of data distribution and is also less prone to the progress reduction caused by stragglers.

PSP is less prone to the stragglers in the system. When the slowness increases from 2x to 8x, both ASP and BSP are sensitive to stragglers, both dropping about 20% accuracy, while that of pBSP only decreases by less than 10%.

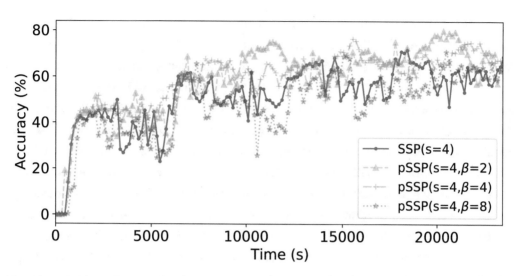

Figure 10-16. *Varying sample sizes in pSSP*

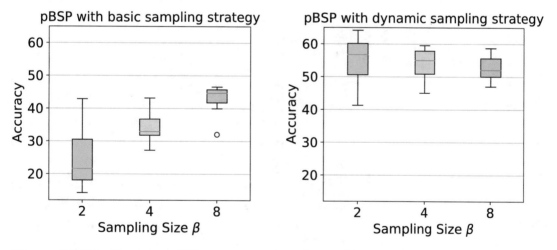

Figure 10-17. *Compare different strategies of sampling in PSP*

Sampling Settings

In Section 10.6, we investigate how the choice of sampling size affects the progress in PSP. One question is then: How to choose the suitable sample size? As pointed out in Section 10.5, one important observation that can be derived from our theory proof is that a small number of sampling can achieve similar performance as that using large sample numbers.

To demonstrate this point in evaluation, we choose different numbers of sampling size, from 2 to 8, in a 16-worker training, and compare them to SSP. The training lasts for a fixed time for all the used methods. In Figure 10-16, we can see that, **even though the number of samples changes, the performance of pSSP is still close to that of SSP**. In this scenario, choosing a smaller number of sampling leads to better performance than the others, due to its fast progress of updates. However, it is not a rule of thumb to always use a small sample size. Choosing suitable parameters in a great tuning space enabled by PSP is a nontrivial task, and we are working to illustrate this challenging problem in our future work.

In Section 10.4, we discuss three different sampling strategies. First is the basic strategy that chooses a certain number of workers as a subset and uses them to estimate training progress of all the workers. The second one, the *dynamic sampling* strategy, rechooses this subset dynamically instead of keeping it fixed. The third is a grouping strategy that precluster workers into two groups according to their execution speed and then chooses T samples equally from both groups.

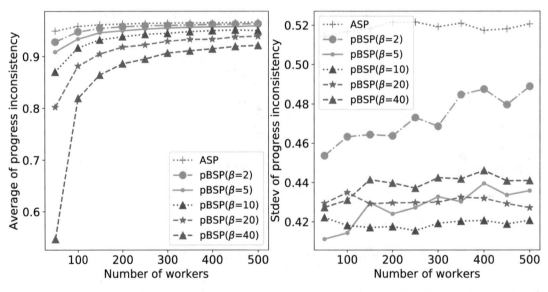

Figure 10-18. *Average and variance of normalized progress inconsistency in PSP with regard to sample size (100 nodes in total)*

To compare these strategies, we use 24 workers and set 6 of them to be stragglers (1x slower in computing backpropagation). We use pBSP and increase its sampling size from 2 to 8. Both training use the same number of epochs. The results are shown in Figure 10-17. Each box shows the distribution of model accuracy numbers near the end of each training; the last ten results are used in this experiment.

The result shows that, compared to the basic strategy, the dynamic one can effectively increase the efficiency of PSP. The increase ranges from about 25% to twofold for different sampling sizes. The low accuracy of the basic strategy shows that it tends to result in a more asynchronous training, which is more similar to ASP than BSP.

The grouping strategy achieves similar results as the dynamic one, but shows smaller deviation of box, which means a smoother curve in training (result figure omitted due to space limit). Besides, in dynamic strategy, the sampling size does not visibly affect the model accuracy, which means that the smaller sample size can be used to increase system progress without sacrificing model accuracy. Also note that in both cases, the larger sampling size leads to smaller deviation. This also agrees with the design and analysis of PSP shown in previous sections.

We learned two things in this section. First, by varying the setting of the sampling size from 2 to 8 in pSSP by using a worker size of 16, it can be seen that a small sampling size can still achieve that of a large one, regarding model accuracy. Second, the dynamic and grouping sampling strategies can both effectively improve the performance. Compared to the basic strategy, both can effectively increase the efficiency of PSP. The increase ranges from about 25% to twofold for different sampling sizes.

Progress Inconsistency

In the previous section, we have evaluated the impact of barrier control methods on the accuracy of three different models. However, the training accuracy is affected not only by the barrier method, which controls training inconsistency, but also hyperparameters such as learning rate. The tolerance of error in training for different applications also varies greatly. To better understand the impact of barriers on model consistency during training without considering the influence of these factors, we use progress inconsistency as a metric to compare barriers.

In distributed training, for a worker, between the time it pulls a model from a server and updates its own local model, the server likely has already received several updates from other workers. These updates are the source of training inconsistency. We define progress inconsistency as the number of these updates between a worker's corresponding read and update operations. In this experiment, we collect the progress inconsistency value of each node at its every step during training.

We investigate the relationship between the number of nodes and inconsistency of pBSP. All executions run for 100 seconds, and we increase workers from 50 to 500. We measure the average and variance of progress inconsistency, both normalized with the number of workers, as shown in Figure 10-18. The average inconsistency of ASP is mostly unaffected by size. With a smaller sample size, that of pBSP becomes close to ASP, but note that only the initial increase of network size has a considerable impact. With sample size fixed and network size growing, the average inconsistency grows sublinearly, which is an ideal property. As to the standard deviation values of pBSP, they mostly keep stable regardless of network size.

According to these observations, we can see that for PSP, both the average training inconsistency (denoted by mean) and the noise (denoted by variance) grow sublinearly toward a certain limit for different sample sizes, limited by that of ASP and BSP/SSP.

10.7 Summary

In this chapter, we explored the topic of distributed computing in Owl, with a focus on the topic of synchronization barriers. We showed Actor, an OCaml-based distributed computing engine, which has implemented three different computing paradigms, namely, map-reduce, parameter server, and peer-to-peer. Orthogonal to that, it also has implemented four different types of barrier control methods.

We proposed the Probabilistic Synchronous Parallel, which is suitable for data analytic applications deployed in large and unreliable distributed systems. It strikes a good trade-off between the efficiency and accuracy of iterative learning algorithms by probabilistically controlling how data is sampled from distributed workers. In Actor, we implemented PSP with a core system primitive of "*sampling*." We showed that the *sampling* primitive can be combined with existing barrier control methods to derive fully distributed solutions. We then evaluated the performance of various barrier control methods. The effectiveness of PSP in different application scenarios depends on the suitable parameter, that is, the sample size. Similar to the performance tuning in numerical computation, we suggest resorting to prior knowledge and empirical measurement for its parameter tuning and regard this as the challenge for the future exploration.

CHAPTER 11

Testing Framework

Every proper software requires testing, and so is Owl. All too often, we have found that testing can help us discover potential errors we failed to notice during development. In this chapter, we briefly introduce the philosophy of testing in Owl, the tool we use for conducting the unit test, and examples to demonstrate how to write unit tests. Issues such as using functors in tests and other things to notice in writing test code for Owl, etc. are also discussed in this chapter.

11.1 Unit Test

There are multiple ways to perform test on your code. One common way is to use assertion or catching/raising errors in the code. These kinds of tests are useful, but the testing code is mixed with the function code itself, while we need separate test modules that check the implementation of functions against expected behaviors.

In Owl, we apply a *unit test* to ensure the correctness of numerical routines as much as possible. A unit test is a software test method that checks the behavior of individual units in the code. In our case, the "unit" often means a single numerical function.

There is an approach of software development that is called *test-driven development*, where you write test code even before you implement the function to be tested itself. Though we don't enforce such approach, there are certain testing principles we follow during the development of Owl. For example, we generally don't trust code that is not tested, so in a GitHub pull request, it is always a good practice to accompany your implementation with a unit test in the test/ directory in the source code. Besides, try to keep the function short and simple, so that a test case can focus on a certain aspect.

We use the alcotest framework for testing in Owl. It is a lightweight test framework with simple interfaces. It exposes a simple TESTABLE module type, a check function to assert test predicates, and a run function to perform a list of unit -> unit test callbacks.

© Liang Wang, Jianxin Zhao 2023
L. Wang and J. Zhao, *Architecture of Advanced Numerical Analysis Systems,*
https://doi.org/10.1007/978-1-4842-8853-5_11

11.2 Example

Let's look at an example of using `alcotest` in Owl. Suppose you have implemented some functions in the linear algebra module, including the functions such as rank, determinant, inversion, etc., and try to test them before making a pull request. The testing code can be included in one test unit, and each unit consists of four major sections.

In the first section, we define some utility function and common constants which will be used in the unit. For this example, we specify the required precision and some predefined input data. Here, we use `1e-6` as the precision threshold. Two ndarrays are deemed the same if the sum of their difference is less than `1e-6`, as shown in `mpow`. The predefined input data can also be defined in each test case, as in `is_triu_1`.

```
open Owl
open Alcotest

module M = Owl.Linalg.D

(* Section #1 *)

let approx_equal a b =
  let eps = 1e-6 in
  Stdlib.(abs_float (a -. b) < eps)

let x0 = Mat.sequential ~a:1. 1 6
```

The second section is the core. It contains the actual testing logic, for example, whether the det function can correctly calculate the determinant of a given matrix. Every testing function defined in the To_test module has self-contained logic to validate the implementation of the target function.

```
(* Section #2 *)

module To_test = struct
  let rank () =
    let x = Mat.sequential 4 4 in
    M.rank x = 2

  let det () =
    let x = Mat.hadamard 4 in
```

```
  M.det x = 16.

let vecnorm_01 () =
  let a = M.vecnorm ~p:1. x0 in
  approx_equal a 21.

let vecnorm_02 () =
  let a = M.vecnorm ~p:2. x0 in
  approx_equal a 9.539392014169456

let is_triu_1 () =
  let x = Mat.of_array [| 1.; 2.; 3.; 0.;
    5.; 6.; 0.; 0.; 9. |] 3 3 in
  M.is_triu x = true

let mpow () =
  let x = Mat.uniform 4 4 in
  let y = M.mpow x 3. in
  let z = Mat.(dot x (dot x x)) in
  approx_equal Mat.(y - z |> sum') 0.
end
```

The most common test function used in Owl has the type `unit -> bool`. The idea is that each test function compares a certain aspect of a function with expected results. If there are multiple test cases for the same function, such as the case in `vecnorm`, we tend to build different test cases instead of using one large test function to include all the cases. The common pattern of these functions can be summarized as

```
let test_func () =
    let expected = expected_value in
    let result = func args in
    assert (expected = result)
```

It is important to understand that the equal sign does not necessarily mean the two values have to be the same; in fact, if the floating-point number is involved, which is quite often the case, we only need the two values to be approximately equal within an error range. If that's the case, you need to pay attention to which precision you are using:

double or float. The same threshold might be enough for a single-precision float number, but could still be a large error for double-precision computation.

The third section contains mostly boilerplate code which notifies the testing framework two important pieces of information. The first one is the name of the testing function, so the testing framework can store in its log for post-analysis. The second one is the anticipated result which will be used by the testing framework to check against the outcome of the testing function. If the outcome does not match the expected result, the testing fails and the failure will be logged.

Here, we expect all the test functions to return `true`, though `alcotest` does support testing returning a lot of other types such as string, int, etc. Please refer to its source file for more details.

```
(* Section #3 *)

let rank () =
  Alcotest.(check bool) "rank" true (To_test.rank ())

let det () =
  Alcotest.(check bool) "det" true (To_test.det ())

let vecnorm_01 () =
  Alcotest.(check bool) "vecnorm_01" true (To_test.vecnorm_01 ())

let vecnorm_02 () =
  Alcotest.(check bool) "vecnorm_02" true (To_test.vecnorm_02 ())

let is_triu_1 () =
  Alcotest.(check bool) "is_triu_1" true (To_test.is_triu_1 ())

let mpow () =
  Alcotest.(check bool) "mpow" true (To_test.mpow ())
```

Now let us look at the last section of a test unit.

```
(* Section #4 *)

let test_set =
  [ "rank", `Slow, rank
  ; "det", `Slow, det
```

```
; "vecnorm_01", `Slow, vecnorm_01
; "vecnorm_02", `Slow, vecnorm_02
; "is_triu_1", `Slow, is_triu_1
; "mpow", `Slow, mpow ]
```

In the final section, we take functions from section 3 and put them into a list of test set. The test set specifies the name and mode of the test. The test mode is either Quick or Slow. Quick tests run on any invocations of the test suite. Slow tests are for stress tests that run only on occasion, typically before a release or after a major change. We can further specify the execution order of these testing functions.

After this step, the whole file is named unit_linalg.ml and put under the test/ directory, as with all other unit test files. Now the only thing left is to add it in the test_runner.ml:

```
let () =
  Alcotest.run
    "Owl"
    [ "stats_rvs", Unit_stats_rvs.test_set
    ; "maths", Unit_maths.test_set
    ; "linear algebra", Unit_linalg.test_set
    ...
    ; "conv3d_mec", Unit_conv_mec_naive.Conv3D_MEC.test_set
    ; "conv2d_naive", Unit_conv_mec_naive.Conv2D_NAIVE.test_set
    ; "conv3d_naive", Unit_conv_mec_naive.Conv3D_NAIVE.test_set
    ; "dilated_conv2d", Unit_dilated_conv2d.test_set
    ; "dilated_conv3d", Unit_dilated_conv3d.test_set
    ; "base: algodiff diff", Unit_base_algodiff_diff.test_set
    ; "base: algodiff grad", Unit_base_algodiff_grad.test_set
    ; "base: slicing basic", Unit_base_slicing_basic.test_set
    ; "base: pooling2d", Unit_base_pool2d.test_set
    ; "base: pooling3d", Unit_base_pool3d.test_set
    ... ]
```

That's all. Now you can try make test and check if the functions are implemented well. The compilation result is shown in Figure 11-1. It shows that all tests are successful.

```
dune external-lib-deps --missing @install @runtest
dune runtest -j 1 --no-buffer -p owl
Done: 1683/1685 (jobs: 1)Testing Owl.
This run has ID `A77EF9E1-8D18-4772-96BD-559DA37AA1E3`.
[OK]                linear algebra        0   rank.
[OK]                linear algebra        1   det.
[OK]                linear algebra        2   vecnorm_01.
[OK]                linear algebra        3   vecnorm_02.
[OK]                linear algebra        4   is_triu_1.
[OK]                linear algebra        5   mpow.
The full test results are available in `/Users/stark/Code/owl/_build/defaul
t/test/_build/_tests/A77EF9E1-8D18-4772-96BD-559DA37AA1E3`.
Test Successful in 0.004s. 6 tests_run.
```

Figure 11-1. *All tests passed*

What if one of the test functions does not pass? Let's intentionally make a failing test, such as asserting the matrix in the rank test equals 1 instead of the correct answer 2, and run the test again.

As we can see in Figure 11-2, the failure was detected and logged directly onto the standard output.

```
dune external-lib-deps --missing @install @runtest
dune runtest -j 1 --no-buffer -p owl
Done: 1683/1685 (jobs: 1)Testing Owl.
This run has ID `2A19E5B0-A8EF-4578-B394-EE1A3158CAC8`.
[ERROR]             linear algebra        0   rank.
[OK]                linear algebra        1   det.
[OK]                linear algebra        2   vecnorm_01.
[OK]                linear algebra        3   vecnorm_02.
[OK]                linear algebra        4   is_triu_1.
[OK]                linear algebra        5   mpow.
-- linear algebra.000 [rank.] Failed --
in /Users/stark/Code/owl/_build/default/test/_build/_tests/2A19E5B0-A8EF-45
78-B394-EE1A3158CAC8/linear algebra.000.output:

------------------------------------------------------------------------
ASSERT rank
------------------------------------------------------------------------

[failure] Error rank: expecting
true, got
false.

The full test results are available in `/Users/stark/Code/owl/_build/defaul
t/test/_build/_tests/2A19E5B0-A8EF-4578-B394-EE1A3158CAC8`.
1 error! in 0.005s. 6 tests run.
```

Figure 11-2. *Error in tests*

11.3 What Could Go Wrong

"Who's watching the watchers?" Beware that the test code itself is still code and thus can also be wrong. We need to be careful in implementing the testing code. There are certain cases that you may want to check.

Corner Cases

Corner cases involve situations that occur outside of normal operating parameters. That is obvious in the testing of convolution operations. As the core operation in deep neural networks, convolution is complex: it contains input, kernel, strides, padding, etc. as parameters. Therefore, special cases such as 1x1 kernel, strides of different height and width, etc. are tested in various combinations, sometimes with different input data.

```
module To_test_conv2d_back_input = struct
   (* conv2D, 1x1 kernel *)
   let fun00 () =
     let expected =
       [| 30.0; 36.0; 42.0; 66.0; 81.0; 96.0; 102.0
        ; 126.0; 150.0; 138.0; 171.0; 204.0
        ; 174.0; 216.0; 258.0; 210.0; 261.0; 312.0 |]
     in
     verify_value test_conv2d
       [| 1; 2; 3; 3 |] [| 1; 1; 3; 3 |] [| 1; 1 |]
       VALID expected

   (* conv2D, 1x2 kernel, stride 3. width 5 *)
   let fun01 () =
     let expected =
       [| 2271.0; 2367.0; 2463.0
        ; 2901.0; 3033.0; 3165.0 |]
     in
     verify_value test_conv2d
       [| 1; 2; 3; 3 |] [| 2; 2; 3; 3 |] [| 1; 1 |]
       VALID expected
```

```
(* conv2D, 1x2 kernel, stride 3, width 6 *)
let fun02 () = ...

(* conv2D, 1x2 kernel, stride 3, width 7 *)
let fun03 () = ...

(* conv2D, 2x2 kernel, padding: Same *)
let fun04 () = ...

...


(* conv2D, 2x2 kernel, stride 2, padding: Same *)
let fun09 () = ...
```

Test Coverage

Another issue is test coverage. It means the percentage of code for which an associated test has existed. Though we don't seek a strict 100% coverage for now, wider test coverage is always a good idea. For example, in our implementation of the repeat operation, depending on whether the given axes contain one or multiple integers, the implementation changes. Therefore, in the test functions, it is crucial to cover both cases.

11.4 Use Functor

Note that we can still benefit from all the powerful features in OCaml such as the functor. For example, in testing the convolution operations, we would like to test the implementation of both that in the core library (which is implemented in C) and that in the base library (in pure OCaml). Apparently, there is no need to write the same unit test code twice for these two sets of implementation. To solve that problem, we have a test file unit_conv2d_genericl.ml that has a large module that contains all the previous four sections:

```
module Make (N : Ndarray_Algodiff with type elt = float) = struct
    (* Section #1 - #4 *)
    ...
end
```

And in the specific testing file for core implementation unit_conv2d.ml, it simply contains one line of code:

```
include Unit_conv2d_generic.Make (Owl_algodiff_primal_ops.S)
```

Or in the test file for the base library unit_base_conv2d.ml:

```
include Unit_conv2d_generic.Make (Owl_base_algodiff_primal_ops.S)
```

11.5 Performance Tests

For a numerical library, being able to calculate correct results is not enough. How fast a function can calculate also matters; actually, it matters a lot in modern real-time data analysis, which has wide applications in many fields such finance, robotics, flight control, etc. In addition to correctness, a performance test is also included in the Owl testing framework. The following simple generic function runs a target function for certain amount of times, then calculates the average speed:

```
(* test one operation c times, output the mean time *)
let test_op s c op =
  let ttime = ref 0. in
  for i = 1 to c do
    Gc.compact ();
    let t0 = Unix.gettimeofday () in
    let _ = op () in
    let t1 = Unix.gettimeofday () in
    ttime := !ttime +. (t1 -. t0)
  done;
  ttime := !ttime /. (float_of_int c);
  Printf.printf "| %s :\t %.8fs \n" s !ttime;
  flush stdout
```

This function for testing each operation is similar but prints out the traces more eagerly in every iteration:

```
(* test one operation c time, output the used time in each evaluation *)
let test_op_each c op =
  Printf.printf "| test some fun %i times\n" c;
```

```
let ttime = ref 0. in
for i = 1 to c do
  Gc.compact ();
  let t0 = Unix.gettimeofday () in
  let _ = op () in
  let t1 = Unix.gettimeofday () in
  Printf.printf "| #%0i\t:\t %.8fs \n" i (t1 -. t0);
  flush stdout;
  ttime := !ttime +. (t1 -. t0)
done;
ttime := !ttime /. (float_of_int c);
Printf.printf "| avg.\t:\t %.8fs \n" !ttime
```

With these two generic functions, we can write up a list of tests very quickly. An example that tests the execution time of various matrix operations is shown as follows:

```
let _ =
  Random.self_init ();
  let m, n = 5000, 20000 and c = 1 in
  print_endline (String.make 60 '+');
  Printf.printf "| test matrix size: %i x %i    exps: %i\n" m n c;
  print_endline (String.make 60 '-');
  let x, y = (M.uniform Float64 m n), (M.uniform Float64 m n) in
  test_op "empty           " c (fun () -> M.empty Float64 m n);
  test_op "zeros           " c (fun () -> M.zeros Float64 m n);
  test_op "col             " c (fun () -> M.col x (n-1));
  test_op "row             " c (fun () -> M.row x (m-1));
  test_op "cols            " c (fun () -> M.cols x [|1;2|]);
  test_op "rows            " c (fun () -> M.rows x [|1;2|]);
  test_op "map             " c (fun () -> M.map (fun y -> 0.) x);
  ...
```

11.6 Summary

In this chapter, we briefly introduced how the unit tests are performed with the `alcotest` framework in the existing Owl codebase. We used one example piece of test code for the linear algebra module in Owl to demonstrate the general structure of the Owl test code. We then discussed some tips we find helpful in writing tests, such as considering corner cases, test coverage, and using functors to simplify the test code. In practice, we find the unit tests come really handy in development, and we just cannot have too much of them.

APPENDIX A

Basic Analytics Examples

Owl supports a variety of classical numerical analytics methods, including mathematical functions, linear algebra, statistics, ordinary differential equations, signal processing, etc. In this appendix, we introduce some of the classic analytics supported in Owl and architecture design.

A.1 Mathematical Functions

As the first step in classic analytics, Owl provides various sorts of mathematical operations, from the basic ones such as addition or subtraction to complex ones such as trigonometry functions to even more complex special functions such as the Beta functions. They are included in the `Maths` module. These functions are fundamental to any scientific computation applications in different fields including mathematical analysis, physics, and so on.

To ensure performance, these functions are implemented in C. Many rely on the standard math library in C such as those included in the `math.h`, and many special functions are interfaced to the Cephes Mathematical Functions Library [39], a C language library that provides implementation of such functions of interest to scientists and engineers. It provides good cross-platform consistency and accurate long double computation.

A.2 Linear Algebra

Linear algebra is an important area of mathematics. It is widely used in all scientific domains. As a result, optimized linear algebra routines have been well studied. The core implementation of linear algebra follows the Basic Linear Algebra Subprograms (BLAS) and Linear Algebra Package (LAPACK) interfaces. There are well-established libraries to implement these interfaces, such as OpenBLAS and Intel MKL.

Owl has implemented the full linear algebra interface to CBLAS and LAPACKE. You might notice the extra C in CBLAS and E in LAPACKE because they are the corresponding C interface of FORTRAN implementations. To this end, Owl has implemented several internal modules. The Owl_cblas module provides the raw interface to CBLAS functions, from levels 1 to 3. The interfaced functions have the same names as those in CBLAS. The Owl_lapacke_generated module provides the raw interface to LAPACKE functions (over 1000), which also have the same names defined in lapacke.h. The Owl_lapacke module is a very thin layer of interface between the Owl_lapacke_generated module and Linalg module. The purpose is to provide a unified function to make generic functions over different number types.

The functions in Owl_cblas and Owl_lapacke_generated are very low level, for example, you need to deal with calculating parameters, allocating workspace, postprocessing results, and many other tedious details. End users do not really need to use them directly unless they have enough background in numerical analysis and chase after the performance. So, for example, the LU factorization is performed using the sgetrf or dgetrf function in the Owl_lapacke_generated module, the signature of which looks like this:

```
val sgetrf : layout:int -> m:int -> n:int -> a:float ptr ->
             lda:int -> ipiv:int32 ptr -> int
```

Instead of exposing all these parameters, the getrf function in the Owl_lapacke module provides interfaces that are more straightforward:

```
val getrf : a:(`a, `b) t -> (`a, `b) t * (int32, int32_elt) t
```

These low-level functions provide more general access for users. If this still looks a bit unfamiliar to you, in the Linalg module we have

```
val lu : (`a, `b) t -> (`a, `b) t * (`a, `b) t * (int32, int32_elt) t
```

Here, the function lu x -> (l, u, ipiv) calculates the LU decomposition of input matrix x and returns the L, U matrix together with the pivoting index. In practice, a user should always use the Linalg module which gives you a high-level wrapper for frequently used functions.

Following these CBLAS and LAPACKE implementations, Owl can be used to facilitate the full scope of linear algebra topics, such as eigenvector and eigenvalue (Linalg.S/D.eig), singular value decomposition (Linalg.S/D.svd), etc.

A.3 Statistical Distributions

Statistical distributions are one of the most fundamental analytic tools in mathematics, but are also prevalent in modern applications. For example, in both softmax activation layers in a neural network and logistic regression, their outputs can be interpreted as posterior distribution. To facilitate statistical functions, Owl provides the Stats module. It contains many frequently used distributions, both discrete and continuous, such as Gaussian, exponential, logistic, Laplace, Poisson, Rayleigh, etc. For each distribution, there is a set of related functions having the distribution's name as a common prefix. For example, the module provides the following functions for the Gaussian distribution:

- gaussian_rvs, random number generator
- gaussian_pdf, probability density function
- gaussian_cdf, cumulative distribution function
- gaussian_ppf, percent point function (inverse of CDF)
- gaussian_sf, survival function (1 – CDF)
- gaussian_isf, inverse survival function (inverse of SF)
- gaussian_logpdf, logarithmic probability density function
- gaussian_logcdf, logarithmic cumulative distribution function
- gaussian_logsf, logarithmic survival function

Of these functions, the random number generator, probability density function, and cumulative distribution function are the key functions for a given distribution. We can use a simple binomial probability distribution as an example to demonstrate their usages, as the following code shows. These routines provide intuitive interfaces.

```
# let x = [|0; 1; 2; 3|]
# let p = Array.map (Stats.binomial_pdf ~p:0.3 ~n:3) x
val p : float array =
  [|0.342999999999999916; 0.440999999999999837;
    0.188999999999999918; 0.0269999999999999823|]
```

As in Ndarray, these functions are implemented in C code and interfaced to OCaml. For example, the Cauchy random variable is implemented simply according to its definition:

```
double cauchy_rvs(double loc, double scale) {
  double std_cauchy_rvs = std_gaussian_rvs() / std_gaussian_rvs();
  return loc + scale * std_cauchy_rvs;
}
```

Some of the implementations, though, require low-level *pseudo-random number generator* functions to work. Random number generators are widely applied in fields where unpredictable results are desirable, such as gambling, computer simulation, cryptography, etc. Advanced analytics such as neural networks also rely on random generators, for example, for weight initialization. Therefore, its performance is of crucial importance. Owl utilizes the C-based SIMD-oriented Fast Mersenne Twister (SFMT) generator that generates a 128-bit pseudorandom integer at one step, with good performance on modern CPUs.

Table A-1. *Functions in the FFT Module*

Functions	Description
fft ~axis x	One-dimensional discrete Fourier transform
ifft ~axis x	One-dimensional inverse discrete Fourier transform
rfft ~axis otyp x	One-dimensional discrete Fourier transform for real input
irfft ~axis ~n otyp x	One-dimensional inverse discrete Fourier transform for real input

A.4 Signal Processing

We rely on signals such as sound and images to convey information. Signal processing is then the field concerned with analyzing, generating, and transforming signals. Its applications can be found in a wide range of fields: audio processing, speech recognition, image processing, communication system, data science, etc. The most important functionality in signal processing is no doubt the fast Fourier transform (FFT). Owl provides a series of FFT functions.

The core functions in the FFT module are the `fft` function and its reverse `rfft`. This module provides these basic FFT functions as listed in Table A-1. The inputs to these functions are ndarrays. As with `Ndarray`, the FFT module also provides four number types: float (S), double precision (D), single-precision complex (C), and double-precision complex (Z). The `axis` specifies along which axis of the input ndarray a function is performed. It is set to the highest dimension if not specified. The parameter `n` specifies the size of output.

Here, we use a one-dimensional Fourier transform example to demonstrate the usages of these functions, especially the most basic `fft` and its inverse transform function `ifft`. We plot the FFT of the sum of two sine waves showing the power of FFT to separate signals of different frequencies. This example uses 600 sampling points, and the sample spacing is $\dfrac{1}{800}$.

```
# module G = Dense.Ndarray.Generic
# let n = 600.
# let t = 1. /. 800.
# let x = Arr.linspace 0. (n *. t) (int_of_float n)
# let y1 = Arr.((50. *. 2. *. Owl_const.pi) $* x |> sin)
# let y2 = Arr.(0.5 $* ((80. *. 2. *. Owl_const.pi)
                $* x |> sin))
```

In the preceding code, we create two sine signals of different frequencies: $y_1(x)=\sin(100\pi x)$, $y_2(x)=\dfrac{1}{2}\sin(160\pi x)$, shown in Figure A-1a. We then mix them together:

```
# let y = Arr.(y1 + y2) |> G.cast_d2z
```

The combined signal in Figure A-1b shows an irregular shape. Next, we apply FFT on this mixed signal:

```
# let yf = Owl_fft.D.fft y
```

In the result `yf`, each tuple can be seen as a frequency vector in the complex space. We can plot the length of these vectors, represented by `z` in the following code. Again, we use only half of the elements that have positive frequencies in array `yf`. The plot is shown in Figure A-1c.

```
# let z = Dense.Ndarray.Z.(abs yf |> re)
```

Finally, we plot the result using the following code:

```
# let h = Plot.create "plot.png" in
  let xa = Arr.linspace 1. 600. 600 in
  Plot.plot ~h xa z;
  Plot.output h;;
```

The performance of FFT is an important and well-investigated issue. As a result, there exist a lot of libraries that provide high-performance FFT routines, such as FFTW and Intel MKL, which provides superb performance on a lot of modern Intel platforms. The implementation of the FFT module in the Owl library interfaces to the FFTPACK C language implementation. FFTPACK is an open source package of subprograms for the fast Fourier transform of periodic and other symmetric sequences. It includes complex, real, sine, cosine, and quarter-wave transforms.

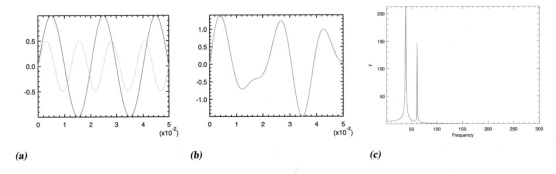

(a)   (b)   (c)

Figure A-1. *(a) Two sine signals of different frequencies, (b) combined signal, (c) using FFT to separate two sine signals from their mixed signal*

A.5 Ordinary Differential Equation

A *differential equation* is an equation that contains a function and one or more of its derivatives. They have been studied ever since the invention of calculus, driven by applications in fields including mechanics, astronomy, geometry, biology, engineering, economics, and many more [56]. If the function and its derivatives in a differential equation concern only one variable, we call it an *ordinary differential equation* (ODE), and it can model a one-dimensional dynamical system. Owl provides the functionalities to solve ODEs. In general, an ODE can be expressed as

$$F\left(x, y', y'', \ldots, y^{(n)}\right) = 0. \tag{A.1}$$

That is, as a function of derivatives with boundary conditions. They can be used to model dynamical systems. The initial state of the system is called its *initial values*, and these values are often known and can be represented as

$$y\big|_{x=x_0}=y_0\,,y'\big|_{x=x_1}=y_1\,,\ldots,\tag{A.2}$$

where the y_0, y_1, etc. are known. The highest order of derivatives occurring in Eq. A.1 is the *order* of the differential equation. A first-order differential equation can be generally expressed as $\dfrac{dy}{dx}=f(x,y)$, where f is any function that contains x and y. Solving Eq. A.1 and fitting to the given initial values as in Eq. A.2 is called the *initial value problem*. Solving such problems is the main target of many numerical ODE solvers.

A real-world system often contains multiple interdependent components, each described by a function that evolves over time. For example, the Lorenz attractor system has three components that change with time: the rate of convection in the atmospheric flow and the horizontal and vertical temperature variations. Such system is an example of *first-order linear systems of ODE* or just *linear systems of ODE*. Generally, if we have

$$\mathbf{y}(t)=\begin{bmatrix}y_1(t)\\ \vdots\\ y_n(t)\end{bmatrix},\mathbf{A}(t)=\begin{bmatrix}a_{11}(t) & \cdots & a_{1n}(t)\\ \vdots & \cdots & \vdots\\ a_{n1}(t) & \cdots & a_{nn}(t)\end{bmatrix},\text{and }\mathbf{g}(t)=\begin{bmatrix}g_1(t)\\ \vdots\\ g_n(t)\end{bmatrix},$$

then a linear system can be expressed as

$$\mathbf{y}'(t)=\mathbf{A}(t)\mathbf{y}(t)+\mathbf{g}(t).\tag{A.3}$$

This linear system contains n time-dependent components: $y_1(t)$, $y_2(t)$, ..., $y_n(t)$. As we will soon show, first-order linear systems are especially amenable to numerical solution. Therefore, transforming a high-order single-component ODE into a linear system is sometimes necessary as we will see in the two-body problem example. But let's get back to the start and examine the basics of solving ODEs numerically.

Built on the computational functionality and ndarray data structures already introduced, the package owl_ode performs the tasks of solving the initial value problems. We will use a classical linear oscillator system example to demonstrate how to use the owl-ode package to solve ODE problems. Consider the following time-independent linear dynamic system of two states:

$$\frac{dy}{dt} = Ay, \text{where } A = \begin{bmatrix} 1 & -1 \\ 2 & -3 \end{bmatrix}.$$

This equation represents an oscillator system where y is the state of the system, t is time, and the initial state at $t = 0$ is $y_0 = [-1, 1]^T$. We wish to know the system state at $t = 2$. The *function* can be expressed in Owl using the matrix module.

```
let f y t =
  let a = [|[|1.; -1.|];[|2.; -3.|]|]|> Mat.of_arrays in
  Mat.(a *@ y)
```

Next, we want to specify the *timespan* of this problem: from 0 to 2 using a step of 0.001.

```
let tspec = Owl_ode.Types.
            (T1 {t0 = 0.; duration = 2.; dt=1E-3})
```

The last requirement for solving the problem is to have the initial values:

```
let x0 = Mat.of_array [|-1.; 1.|] 2 1
```

Finally, we input these parameters to the rk4 solver in Owl_ode to obtain

```
# let ts, ys = Owl_ode.Ode.odeint
                Owl_ode.Native.D.rk4 f x0 tspec ()
```

This is the rk4 solver, short for "fourth-order Runge-Kutta method," that we have introduced before. The result shows both the steps *ts* and the system values at each step *ys*.

The owl-ode library abstracts the initial value problems as four different parts:

- A function f to show how the system evolves in equation $y'(t) = f(y, t)$

- A specification of the timespan

- The system's initial values

- And most importantly, a solver

Indeed, the signature of a solver clearly indicates these four parts. Building on this uniform abstraction, you can choose a suitable solver and use it to solve many complex and practical ODE problems. Note that due to the difference of solvers, the requirements of different solvers vary, for example, some require the state to be two matrices, while others process data in a more general ndarray format.

The owl-ode library provides a wide range of solvers. It implements native solvers based on the basic step-by-step update idea discussed earlier. There are also many mature off-the-shelf tools for solving ODEs, and we interface to two of them: sundials[1] and ODEPACK.[2] Both are well implemented and widely used in practical use. For example, the SciPy provides a Python wrap of the sundials, and NASA also uses its CVODE/CVODES solvers for spacecraft trajectory simulations. The sundials is a SUite of Nonlinear and DIfferential/ALgebraic equation Solvers. It contains six solvers, and we interface to its CVODE solver for solving initial value problems. ODEPACK is a collection of FORTRAN solvers for the initial value problem for ordinary differential equation systems. We interface to its LSODA solver which is for solving the explicit form ODE.

---

[1] https://computing.llnl.gov/projects/sundials
[2] https://computing.llnl.gov/casc/odepack/

APPENDIX B

System Conventions

All software systems have their own rules and conventions with which developers must comply, and Owl is no exception. In this appendix, we cover function naming and various other conventions in the Owl library.

B.1 Pure vs. Impure

The Ndarray module contains functions to manipulate and perform mathematical operations over ndarrays. The **pure** (or immutable) functions are those that do not modify the provided variables but instead return a new one as a result. In contrast, **impure** (or mutable) functions are those which modify the passed-in variables in place.

Functional programming in general promotes the use of immutable data structures as impure functions make it more difficult to reason about the correctness of code. On the other hand, generating a fresh 1000×1000 matrix every time you modify a single element does not seem very practical. The introduction of impure functions into Owl is thus only done under careful, practical consideration. In-place modification avoids expensive memory allocation and deallocation which can significantly improve runtime performance of a numerical application, especially when large ndarrays and matrices are involved. Thus, many pure functions in the Ndarray module have corresponding impure versions indicated by an underscore "_" added at the end of the function name. For example, the following pure functions in the Arr module, Arr.sin and Arr.add, have corresponding impure functions, Arr.sin_ and Arr.add_.

For unary operators such as Arr.sin_ x, the situation is rather straightforward when x will be modified in place. However, binary operators are more complex. For example, in Arr.add_scalar x a, x will be modified in place to store the final result – relatively straightforward as a is a scalar. In Arr.add_ x y, the question is where to store the final result when both inputs are ndarrays. Let's look at the type of Arr.add_ function:

```
val Arr.add_ : ?out:Arr.arr -> Arr.arr -> Arr.arr -> unit
```

© Liang Wang, Jianxin Zhao 2023
L. Wang and J. Zhao, *Architecture of Advanced Numerical Analysis Systems*,
https://doi.org/10.1007/978-1-4842-8853-5

As we can see from the type signature, the output is specified in the optional out parameter. If out is not provided, the first operand (x) will be attempted to store the final result – as binary operators support broadcasting operations by default, when using impure functions every dimension of the first argument x must not be smaller than that of the second argument y. In other words, impure functions only allow broadcasting smaller y onto an x that is big enough to accommodate the result.

Most binary math functions have an associated shorthand operator, such as +, -, *, and /. The impure versions also have associated operators, for example, rather than Arr. (x + y) which returns the result in a new ndarray, you can write Arr.(x += y) which adds x and y and saves the result into x. These operators are listed in Table B-1.

Table B-1. *Alias of Pure and Impure Binary Math Functions*

Function Name	Pure	Impure
add	+	+=
sub	-	-=
mul	*	*=
div	/	/=
add_scalar	+$	+$=
sub_scalar	-$	-$=
mul_scalar	*$	*$=
div_scalar	/$	/$=

B.2 Ndarray vs. Scalar

There are three general ndarray operators: *map, scan,* and *reduce.* Many Ndarray functions can be categorized as reduce operations, such as Arr.sum, Arr.prod, Arr.min, Arr.mean, and Arr.std. For example, we can sum all the elements in an ndarray using sum function.

```
let x = Arr.sequential [|3;3;3|];;
let a = Arr.sum x;;
```

The result is a one-element ndarray, so to treat it as a scalar, you must retrieve the single value by calling the get function.

```
let b = Arr.get a [|0|] in
b +. 10.;;
```

This becomes inconvenient in OCaml if we must always extract the scalar value from the return of reduce operations. In languages like Python and Julia, the return type is dynamically determined, but OCaml's strong typing requires that we either use a unified type or implement another set of functions. In the end, Owl picked the latter in its design, so every reduce operation has two versions:

- One allowing you to reduce along the specified axis or to reduce all the elements, but always returning an ndarray

- One that reduces all the elements, always returning a scalar value

The difference between the two is indicated by naming those returning a scalar with an extra " ' " character in their names. For example, those functions returning an ndarray are named Arr.sum, Arr.prod, mean, etc., while those returning a scalar are named Arr.sum', Arr.prod', mean', etc.

B.3 Module Structures

Owl's Dense module contains modules supporting dense data structures such as Dense.Matrix supporting operations on dense matrices and the Sparse module with modules supporting sparse data structures. We have four basic modules: dense ndarray, dense matrix, sparse ndarray, and sparse matrix. In this book, we mostly use Dense modules, and, indeed, the matrix modules are a special case that's built upon the corresponding ndarray modules.

With Dense.Ndarray, we can create a dense n-dimensional array of no more than 16 dimensions. This constraint originates from the underlying Bigarray.Genarray module in OCaml. In practice, this constraint makes sense since the space requirement will explode as the dimension increases. If you need anything higher than 16 dimensions, you need to use Sparse.Ndarray to create a sparse data structure. All four modules consist of five submodules to handle different types of numbers:

- The S module supports single-precision float numbers float32.

- The D module supports double-precision float numbers float64.

- The C module supports single-precision complex numbers complex32.

- The Z module supports double-precision complex numbers complex64.

- The Generic module supports all aforementioned number types via a GADT.

Technically, S, D, C, and Z are wrappers of the Generic module with explicit type information provided. Therefore, you can save the type constructor which was passed into the Generic module if you use these submodules directly. In short, the Generic module can do everything that submodules can, but for some functions (e.g., creation), you must explicitly pass in the type information.

In practice, we often work with double-precision numbers, so Owl provides shortcuts to the data structures of double-precision floating-point numbers. Arr is equivalent to double-precision real Dense.Ndarray.D, and, similarly, Mat is equivalent to double-precision real Dense.Matrix.D. These two modules are frequently used in this book. You can cast one value from one type to another one by using the cast_* functions in the Generic module. For example, Generic.cast_s2d casts from float32 to float64, and Generic.cast_c2z casts from complex32 to complex64.

Many functions in the Generic module can handle the aforementioned four different number types. This polymorphism is achieved by pattern matching and general abstract data type in OCaml. In the following code, we use the sum function in the Dense.Matrix.Generic module as an example:

```
open Owl;;

let x = Dense.Matrix.S.eye 5 in
Dense.Matrix.Generic.sum x;;

let x = Dense.Matrix.D.eye 5 in
Dense.Matrix.Generic.sum x;;

let x = Dense.Matrix.C.eye 5 in
Dense.Matrix.Generic.sum x;;

let x = Dense.Matrix.Z.eye 5 in
Dense.Matrix.Generic.sum x;;
```

As we can see, no matter what kind of numbers are held in an identity matrix, we can always pass it to the `Dense. Matrix.Generic.sum` function. Similarly, we can do the same thing for other modules (`Dense.Ndarray`, `Sparse. Matrix`, etc.) and other functions (`add`, `mul`, `neg`, etc.).

B.4 Infix Operators

In each `Ndarray` and `Matrix` module, some frequently used functions have the corresponding infix operators as convenient aliases. Table B-2 summarizes the operators. In the table, both x and y represent either a matrix or an ndarray, while a represents a scalar value.

Several things in this table should be noted:

- +$ has its corresponding operator $+ if we flip the order of parameters. However, it is important to be very careful about operator precedence in these cases: *OCaml determines precedence based on the first character of the infix operator.* +$ preserves the precedence, whereas $+ does not. We thus recommend using $+ with great care and always using parentheses to explicitly specify precedence. The same applies to $-, $*, and $/.

- For comparison operators, for example, both = and =. compare all the elements in two variables x and y. The difference is that = returns a boolean value, whereas =. returns a matrix or ndarray of the same shape and type as x and y. In the returned result, the value in a given position is 1 if the values of the corresponding position in x and y satisfy the predicate; otherwise, it is 0.

- The comparison operators ending with $ are used to compare a matrix/ndarray to a scalar value.

Table B-2. *Infix Operators in Ndarray and Matrix Modules*

Operator	Example	Operation	Dense/Sparse	Ndarray/Matrix
+	x + y	Element-wise add	Both	Both
-	x - y	Element-wise sub	Both	Both
*	x * y	Element-wise mul	Both	Both
/	x / y	Element-wise div	Both	Both
+$	x +$ a	Add scalar	Both	Both
-$	x -$ a	Sub scalar	Both	Both
*$	x *$ a	Mul scalar	Both	Both
/$	x /$ a	Div scalar	Both	Both
$+	a $+ x	Scalar add	Both	Both
$-	a $- x	Scalar sub	Both	Both
$*	a $* x	Scalar mul	Both	Both
$/	a $/ x	Scalar div	Both	Both
=	x = y	Comparison	Both	Both
!=	x != y	Comparison	Both	Both
	x <> y	Same as !=	Both	Both
>	x > y	Comparison	Both	Both
<	x < y	Comparison	Both	Both
>=	x >= y	Comparison	Both	Both
<=	x <= y	Comparison	Both	Both
=.	x =. y	Element-wise cmp	Dense	Both
!=.	x !=. y	Element-wise cmp	Dense	Both
.	x <>. y	Same as !=.	Dense	Both
>.	x >. y	Element-wise cmp	Dense	Both
<.	x <. y	Element-wise cmp	Dense	Both
=$	x =$ y	Comp to scalar	Dense	Both

(continued)

Table B-2. (*continued*)

Operator	Example	Operation	Dense/Sparse	Ndarray/Matrix
!=$	x !=$ y	Comp to scalar	Dense	Both
$	x <>$ y	Same as !=	Dense	Both
>$	x >$ y	Compare to scalar	Dense	Both
<$	x <$ y	Compare to scalar	Dense	Both
>=$	x >=$ y	Compare to scalar	Dense	Both
<=$	x <=$ y	Compare to scalar	Dense	Both
=.$	x =.$ y	Element-wise cmp	Dense	Both
!=.$	x !=.$ y	Element-wise cmp	Dense	Both
.$	x <>.$ y	Same as !=.$	Dense	Both
>.$	x >.$ y	Element-wise cmp	Dense	Both
<.$	x <.$ y	Element-wise cmp	Dense	Both
>=.$	x >=.$ y	Element-wise cmp	Dense	Both
<=.$	x <=.$ y	Element-wise cmp	Dense	Both
=~`	x =~ y	Approx =	Dense	Both
=~$	x =~$ y	Approx =$	Dense	Both
=~.	x =~. y	Approx =.	Dense	Both
=~.$	x =~.$ y	Approx =.$	Dense	Both
%	x % y	Mod divide	Dense	Both
%$	x %$ a	Mod divide scalar	Dense	Both
**	x ** y	Power function	Dense	Both
*@	x *@ y	Matrix multiply	Both	Matrix
/@	x /@ y	Solve linear system	Both	Matrix
**@	x **@ a	Matrix power	Both	Matrix
@=	x @= y	Concatenate vertically	Dense	Both
@——	x @— y —	Concatenate horizontally	Dense	Both

APPENDIX C

Metric Systems and Constants

In many scientific computing problems, numbers are not abstract but reflect the realistic meanings. In other words, these numbers only make sense on top of a well-defined metric system. For example, when we talk about the distance between two objects, we write down a number 30, but what does 30 mean in reality? Is it meters, kilometers, miles, or lightyears? Another example, what is the speed of light? Well, this really depends on what metrics you are using, for example, *km/s*, *m/s*, *mile/h*, etc. Things can get really messy in computation if we do not unify the metric system in a numerical library. The translation between different metrics is often important in a real-world application; therefore, a full-featured numerical library is obliged to provide sufficient support for managing different metric systems. In this appendix, we briefly introduce the metric system and constants provided in the Owl library to support scientific computing.

C.1 Four Metric Systems

There are four metrics adopted in Owl, and all of them are wrapped in the `Owl. Const` module:

- `Const.SI`: International System of Units

- `Const.MKS`: MKS System of Units

- `Const.CGS`: Centimeter-Gram-Second System of Units

- `Const.CGSM`: Electromagnetic System of Units

© Liang Wang, Jianxin Zhao 2023
L. Wang and J. Zhao, *Architecture of Advanced Numerical Analysis Systems*,
https://doi.org/10.1007/978-1-4842-8853-5

All the metrics defined in these four systems can be found in the interface file `owl_const.mli`. In general, SI is much newer and recommended to use. The International System of Units (French: Système international d'unités, SI) is historically also called the MKSA system of units for meter-kilogram-second-ampere. The SI system of units extends the MKS system and has seven base units, by expressing any measurement of physical quantities using fundamental units of length, mass, time, electric current, thermodynamic temperature, amount of substance, and luminous intensity, which are meter, kilogram, second, ampere, kelvin, mole, and candela, respectively.

With a well-defined metric system, we can safely talk about the distance between two objects, light of speed, and a lot of other real-world stuff with a well-defined metric system in Owl. See the following examples:

```
Const.SI.light_year;;      (* light year in SI system *)
Const.MKS.light_year;;     (* light year in MKS system *)
Const.CGS.light_year;;     (* light year in CGS system *)
Const.CGSM.light_year;;    (* light year in CGSM system *)
```

How about Planck's constant?

```
Const.SI.plancks_constant_h;;      (* in SI system *)
Const.MKS.plancks_constant_h;;     (* in MKS system *)
Const.CGS.plancks_constant_h;;     (* in CGS system *)
Const.CGSM.plancks_constant_h;;    (* in CGSM system *)
```

Table C-1 shows some physical constants that the SI module includes.

As a computer scientist, you must be familiar with prefixes such as *kilo, mega,* and *giga.* The SI system includes the definition of these prefixes as well. But be careful (especially for computer science guys), the base is 10 instead of 2. These prefixes are defined in the `Const.Prefix` module.

Table C-1. *Physical Constants*

Constant Name	Explanation
speed_of_light	Speed of light in vacuum
gravitational_constant	Newtonian constant of gravitation
plancks_constant_h	Planck constant
plancks_constant_hbar	Reduced Planck constant
astronomical_unit	One astronomical unit in meters
light_year	One light year in meters
parsec	One light year in meters
grav_accel	Standard acceleration of gravity
electron_volt	Electron volt
mass_electron	Electron mass
mass_muon	Muon mass
mass_proton	Proton mass
mass_neutron	Neutron mass
rydberg	Rydberg constant
boltzmann	Boltzmann constant
molar_gas	Molar gas constant
standard_gas_volume	Molar volume of ideal gas (273.15 K, 100 kPa)
bohr_radius	Bohr radius
stefan_boltzmann_constant	Stefan-Boltzmann constant
thomson_cross_section	Thomson cross section in square meter
bohr_magneton	Bohr magneton in Joules per Tesla
nuclear_magneton	Nuclear magneton in Joules per Tesla
electron_magnetic_moment	Electron magnetic moment in Joules per Tesla
proton_magnetic_moment	Proton magnetic moment in Joules per Tesla
faraday	Faraday constant

(continued)

Table C-1. (*continued*)

Constant Name	Explanation
electron_charge	Electron volt in Joules
vacuum_permittivity	Vacuum electric permittivity
vacuum_permeability	Vacuum magnetic permeability
debye	One debye in coulomb meter
gauss	One gauss in maxwell per square meter

```
module Prefix = struct
  let fine_structure = 7.297352533e-3
  let avogadro      = 6.02214199e23
  let yotta         = 1e24
  let zetta         = 1e21
  let exa           = 1e18
  let peta          = 1e15
  let tera          = 1e12
  let giga          = 1e9
  let mega          = 1e6
  let kilo          = 1e3
  let hecto         = 1e2
  let deca          = 1e1
  let deci          = 1e-1
  let centi         = 1e-2
  let milli         = 1e-3
  let micro         = 1e-6
  let nano          = 1e-9
  let pico          = 1e-12
  let femto         = 1e-15
  let atto          = 1e-18
  let zepto         = 1e-21
  let yocto         = 1e-24
end
```

Some basic mathematical constants are also provided in Owl, though some constants in advanced mathematics are not yet included such as the golden ratio or Euler-Mascheroni constant. They are shown in Table C-2.

Table C-2. *Math Constants*

Constant Name	Explanation
pi	Pi
e	Natural constant
euler	Euler constant

Besides these constants, we also provide some frequently used computations based on them, including

- *log2e* is defined as ($\log_2 e$).

- *log10e* is defined as ($\log_{10} e$).

- *loge2* is defined as ($\log_e 2$).

- *loge10* is defined as ($\log_e 10$).

- *logepi* is defined as ($\log_e \pi$).

- *pi2* is defined as (2π).

- *pi4* is defined as (4π).

- *pi_2* is defined as ($\pi/2$).

- *pi_4* is defined as ($\pi/4$).

- *sqrt1_2* is defined as ($\sqrt{\dfrac{1}{2}}$).

- *sqrt2* is defined as ($\sqrt{2}$).

- *sqrt3* is defined as ($\sqrt{3}$).

- *sqrtpi* is defined as ($\sqrt{\pi}$).

C.2 International System of Units

Now that you know how to use constants, we will use the International System of Units (SI) module as an example to show the constants we include in Owl. The source code is included as follows from where you can check the real values defined for all constants:

```
module SI = struct
  let speed_of_light = 2.99792458e8
  let gravitational_constant = 6.673e-11
  let plancks_constant_h = 6.62606896e-34
  let plancks_constant_hbar = 1.05457162825e-34
  let astronomical_unit = 1.49597870691e11
  let light_year = 9.46053620707e15
  let parsec = 3.08567758135e16
  let grav_accel = 9.80665e0
  let electron_volt = 1.602176487e-19
  let mass_electron = 9.10938188e-31
  let mass_muon = 1.88353109e-28
  let mass_proton = 1.67262158e-27
  let mass_neutron = 1.67492716e-27
  let rydberg = 2.17987196968e-18
  let boltzmann = 1.3806504e-23
  let molar_gas = 8.314472e0
  let standard_gas_volume = 2.2710981e-2
  let minute = 6e1
  let hour = 3.6e3
  let day = 8.64e4
  let week = 6.048e5
  let inch = 2.54e-2
  let foot = 3.048e-1
  let yard = 9.144e-1
  let mile = 1.609344e3
  let nautical_mile = 1.852e3
  let fathom = 1.8288e0
  let mil = 2.54e-5
  let point = 3.52777777778e-4
  let texpoint = 3.51459803515e-4
```

```
let micron = 1e-6
let angstrom = 1e-10
let hectare = 1e4
let acre = 4.04685642241e3
let barn = 1e-28
let liter = 1e-3
let us_gallon = 3.78541178402e-3
let quart = 9.46352946004e-4
let pint = 4.73176473002e-4
let cup = 2.36588236501e-4
let fluid_ounce = 2.95735295626e-5
let tablespoon = 1.47867647813e-5
let teaspoon = 4.92892159375e-6
let canadian_gallon = 4.54609e-3
let uk_gallon = 4.546092e-3
let miles_per_hour = 4.4704e-1
let kilometers_per_hour = 2.77777777778e-1
let knot = 5.14444444444e-1
let pound_mass = 4.5359237e-1
let ounce_mass = 2.8349523125e-2
let ton = 9.0718474e2
let metric_ton = 1e3
let uk_ton = 1.0160469088e3
let troy_ounce = 3.1103475e-2
let carat = 2e-4
let unified_atomic_mass = 1.660538782e-27
let gram_force = 9.80665e-3
let pound_force = 4.44822161526e0
let kilopound_force = 4.44822161526e3
let poundal = 1.38255e-1
let calorie = 4.1868e0
let btu = 1.05505585262e3
let therm = 1.05506e8
let horsepower = 7.457e2
let bar = 1e5
let std_atmosphere = 1.01325e5
```

```
  let torr = 1.33322368421e2
  let meter_of_mercury = 1.33322368421e5
  let inch_of_mercury = 3.38638815789e3
  let inch_of_water = 2.490889e2
  let psi = 6.89475729317e3
  let poise = 1e-1
  let stokes = 1e-4
  let stilb = 1e4
  let lumen = 1e0
  let lux = 1e0
  let phot = 1e4
  let footcandle = 1.076e1
  let lambert = 1e4
  let footlambert = 1.07639104e1
  let curie = 3.7e10
  let roentgen = 2.58e-4
  let rad = 1e-2
  let solar_mass = 1.98892e30
  let bohr_radius = 5.291772083e-11
  let newton = 1e0
  let dyne = 1e-5
  let joule = 1e0
  let erg = 1e-7
  let stefan_boltzmann_constant = 5.67040047374e-8
  let thomson_cross_section = 6.65245893699e-29
  let bohr_magneton = 9.27400899e-24
  let nuclear_magneton = 5.05078317e-27
  let electron_magnetic_moment = 9.28476362e-24
  let proton_magnetic_moment = 1.410606633e-26
  let faraday = 9.64853429775e4
  let electron_charge = 1.602176487e-19
  let vacuum_permittivity = 8.854187817e-12
  let vacuum_permeability = 1.25663706144e-6
  let debye = 3.33564095198e-30
  let gauss = 1e-4
end
```

These units are all derived from the seven basic units we have mentioned and can be categorized according to different application fields.

Time: The time units are shown in Table C-3. The base SI unit for time measurement is second.

Table C-3. *Time Units*

Constant Name	Explanation
Minute	One minute in seconds
Hour	One hour in seconds
Day	One day in seconds
week	One week in seconds

Length: The length units are shown in Table C-4. The base SI unit for length measurement is meter.

Table C-4. *Length Units*

Constant Name	Explanation
inch	One inch in meters
foot	One foot in meters
yard	One yard in meters
mile	One mile in meters
mil	One mil in meters
fathom	One fathom in meters
point	One point in meters
micron	One micron in meters
angstrom	One angstrom in meters
nautical_mile	One nautical_mile in meters

Area: The area units are shown in Table C-5. Measuring area and volume still relies on the SI base unit meter.

Table C-5. *Area Units*

Constant Name	Explanation
hectare	One hectare in square meters
acre	One acre in square meters
barn	One barn in square meters

Volume: The volume units are shown in Table C-6. The base SI unit for volume measurement is cubic meter.

Table C-6. *Volume Units*

Constant Name	Explanation
liter	One liter in cubic meters
us_gallon	One gallon (US) in cubic meters
uk_gallon	One gallon (UK) in cubic meters
canadian_gallon	One Canadian gallon in cubic meters
quart	One quart in cubic meters
cup	One cup in cubic meters
pint	One pint in cubic meters
fluid_ounce	One fluid ounce (US) in cubic meters
tablespoon	One tablespoon in cubic meters

Speed: The speed units are shown in Table C-7. The base units for speed are that of time and length.

Table C-7. *Speed Units*

Constant Name	Explanation
miles_per_hour	Miles per hour in meters per second
kilometers_per_hour	Kilometers per hour in meters per second
knot	One knot in meters per second

Mass: The mass units are shown in Table C-8. The base unit for presenting mass is kilogram (kg).

Table C-8. *Mass Units*

Constant Name	Explanation
pound_mass	One pound (avoirdupois) in kg
ounce_mass	One ounce in kg
metric_ton	1000 kg
ton	One short ton in kg
uk_ton	One long ton in kg
troy_ounce	One Troy ounce in kg
carat	One carat in kg
unified_atomic_mass	Atomic mass constant
solar_mass	One solar mass in kg

Force: The force units are shown in Table C-9. Measuring force relies on the SI derived unit, newton, and one newton is equal to one kilogram meter per squared second.

Table C-9. *Force Units*

Constant Name	Explanation
newton	SI derived unit ($kg \cdot m \cdot s^{-2}$)
gram_force	One gram force in newtons
kilogram_force	One kilogram force in newtons
pound_force	One pound force in newtons
poundal	One poundal in newtons
dyne	One dyne in newtons

Energy: The energy units are shown in Table C-10. The unit of measuring the energy level is joule, which is equal to one kilogram square meter per square second.

Table C-10. *Energy Units*

Constant Name	Explanation
joule	SI base unit
calorie	One calorie (thermochemical) in Joules
btu	One British thermal unit (International Steam Table) in Joules
therm	One therm (US) in Joules
erg	One erg in Joules

Power: The energy units are shown in Table C-11. The unit of power is watts, an SI derived unit. One watt is equal to one kilogram square meter per cubic second, or one Joule per second.

Table C-11. *Power Units*

Constant Name	Explanation
horsepower	One horsepower in watts

Pressure: The pressure units are shown in Table C-12. To measure pressure, we often use pascal as a standard unit. One pascal is equal to a kilogram per meter per square second, or a newton per square meter.

Table C-12. *Pressure Units*

Constant Name	Explanation
bar	One bar in pascals
std_atmosphere	Standard atmosphere in pascals
torr	One torr (mmHg) in pascals
meter_of_mercury	One meter of mercury in pascals
inch_of_mercury	One inch of mercury in pascals
inch_of_water	One inch of water in pascals
psi	One psi in pascals

Viscosity: The viscosity units are shown in Table C-13. The poise is a unit in dynamic viscosity, and the "stokes" is for kinematic viscosity. They are actually included in the CGS-based system for electrostatic units.

Table C-13. *Viscosity Units*

Constant Name	Explanation
poise	Base unit
stokes	Base unit

Luminance: The luminance units are shown in Table C-14. Candela is the base unit for luminance, and both lumen and lux are derived units.

Table C-14. *Luminance Units*

Constant Name	Explanation
stilb	Candela per square meter
lumen	Luminous flux, Candela square radian, SI derived unit
phot	Base unit
lux	One lux in phots, SI derived unit
footcandle	One footcandle in phots
lambert	Base unit
footlambert	One footlambert in lambert

Radioactivity: The radioactivity units are shown in Table C-15. The SI unit of radioactivity is becquerel, named in honor of the scientist Henri Becquerel, defined as one transformation (or decay or disintegration) per second. The other base units such as ampere, second, and kilogram are also used.

Table C-15. *Radioactivity Units*

Constant Name	Explanation
curie	One curie in becquerel
roentgen	One ampere second per kilogram
rad	Erg per gram

APPENDIX D

Algodiff Module

In the rest of appendixes, we provide some important pieces of source code of several Owl modules. It complements existing materials we have discussed in this book, so that the readers can have a deeper understanding of how they work.

In this appendix, we provide the full source code of several components in the algorithmic differentiation module. It consists of three parts. First are the templates to generate operators (`owl_algodiff_ops_builder.ml`) and examples that generate operators using these templates (`owl_algodiff_ops.ml`). Learning these code is instrumental in understanding how AD works. Second are the core functionalities provided in `owl_algodiff_core.ml` and `owl_algodiff_generic.ml`. These functionalities look simple enough, but they make the backbone of the whole module. Third is the graph traversal module that can convert the AD graph into multiple formats. It comes handy when debugging and better understanding the details of an AD graph.

D.1 Operator Building

The builder templates:

```
(** owl_algodiff_ops_builder.ml *)

module Make (Core : Owl_algodiff_core_sig.Sig) = struct
  open Core

  let cmp_tag ai bi = if ai > bi then 1 else if ai < bi then -1 else 0

  module type Siso = sig
    val label : string
    val ff_f : A.elt -> t
    val ff_arr : A.arr -> t
```

© Liang Wang, Jianxin Zhao 2023
L. Wang and J. Zhao, *Architecture of Advanced Numerical Analysis Systems*,
https://doi.org/10.1007/978-1-4842-8853-5

```
  val df : t -> t -> t -> t
  val dr : t -> t -> t ref -> t
end

let build_siso =
  (* single input single output operation *)
  let op_siso ~ff ~fd ~df ~r a =
    match a with
    | DF (ap, at, ai)          ->
      let cp = fd ap in
      DF (cp, df cp ap at, ai)
    | DR (ap, _, _, _, ai, _) ->
      let cp = fd ap in
      DR (cp, ref (zero cp), r a, ref 0, ai, ref 0)
    | ap                       -> ff ap
  in
  fun (module S : Siso) ->
    let rec f a =
      let open S in
      let ff = function
        | F a   -> S.ff_f a
        | Arr a -> S.ff_arr a
        | _       -> error_uniop label a
      in
      let fd a = f a in
      let r a =
        let adjoint cp ca t = (S.dr (primal a) cp ca, a) :: t in
        let register t = a :: t in
        let label = S.label, [ a ] in
        adjoint, register, label
      in
      op_siso ~ff ~fd ~df:S.df ~r a
    in
    f
```

```
module type Sipo = sig
  val label : string

  val ff_f : A.elt -> t * t

  val ff_arr : A.arr -> t * t

  val df : t -> t -> t -> t

  val dr : t -> t -> t ref * t ref -> t ref * t ref -> t
end

let build_sipo =
  (* single input pair outputs operation *)
  let op_sipo ~ff ~fd ~df ~r a =
    match a with
    | DF (ap, at, ai)          ->
      let cp1, cp2 = fd ap in
      DF (cp1, df cp1 ap at, ai), DF (cp2, df cp2 ap at, ai)
    | DR (ap, _, _, _, ai, _) ->
      let cp1, cp2 = fd ap in
      let ca1_ref = ref (zero cp1) in
      let ca2_ref = ref (zero cp2) in
      let cp1_ref = ref cp1 in
      let cp2_ref = ref cp2 in
      let tracker = ref 0 in
      (* tracker: int reference In reverse_reset, i keeps track of the
         number of times
         cp1 and cp2 has been called such that in reverse_push, we do not
         update the
         adjoint of ap before we've fully updated both ca1 and ca2 *)
      ( DR
          ( cp1
          , ca1_ref
          , r (a, (cp1_ref, cp2_ref), (ca1_ref, ca2_ref))
          , ref 0
          , ai
          , tracker )
```

```
        , DR
            ( cp2
            , ca2_ref
            , r (a, (cp1_ref, cp2_ref), (ca1_ref, ca2_ref))
            , ref 0
            , ai
            , tracker ) )
      | ap                           -> ff ap
  in
  fun (module S : Sipo) ->
    let rec f a =
      let open S in
      let ff = function
        | F a    -> S.ff_f a
        | Arr a -> S.ff_arr a
        | _       -> error_uniop label a
      in
      let fd = f in
      let r (a, cp_ref, ca_ref) =
        let adjoint cp _ca t = (S.dr (primal a) cp cp_ref ca_ref,
        a) :: t in
        let register t = a :: t in
        let label = S.label, [ a ] in
        adjoint, register, label
      in
      op_sipo ~ff ~fd ~df ~r a
    in
    f

module type Sito = sig
  val label : string

  val ff_f : A.elt -> t * t * t

  val ff_arr : A.arr -> t * t * t

  val df : t -> t -> t -> t
```

328

```
  val dr : t -> t -> t ref * t ref * t ref -> t ref * t ref * t ref -> t
end

let build_sito =
  (* single input three outputs operation *)
  let op_sito ~ff ~fd ~df ~r a =
    match a with
    | DF (ap, at, ai)           ->
      let cp1, cp2, cp3 = fd ap in
      DF (cp1, df cp1 ap at, ai), DF (cp2, df cp2 ap at, ai), DF (cp3, df
      cp3 ap at, ai)
    | DR (ap, _, _, _, ai, _) ->
      let cp1, cp2, cp3 = fd ap in
      let ca1_ref = ref (zero cp1) in
      let ca2_ref = ref (zero cp2) in
      let ca3_ref = ref (zero cp3) in
      let cp1_ref = ref cp1 in
      let cp2_ref = ref cp2 in
      let cp3_ref = ref cp3 in
      let tracker = ref 0 in
      ( DR
          ( cp1
          , ca1_ref
          , r (a, (cp1_ref, cp2_ref, cp3_ref), (ca1_ref, ca2_ref, ca3_ref))
          , ref 0
          , ai
          , tracker )
      , DR
          ( cp2
          , ca2_ref
          , r (a, (cp1_ref, cp2_ref, cp3_ref), (ca1_ref, ca2_ref,
          ca3_ref))
          , ref 0
          , ai
          , tracker )
```

```
          , DR
              ( cp3
              , ca3_ref
              , r (a, (cp1_ref, cp2_ref, cp3_ref), (ca1_ref, ca2_ref, ca3_ref))
              , ref 0
              , ai
              , tracker ) )
      | ap                          -> ff ap
  in
  fun (module S : Sito) ->
    let rec f a =
      let open S in
      let ff = function
        | F a    -> S.ff_f a
        | Arr a -> S.ff_arr a
        | _        -> error_uniop label a
      in
      let fd = f in
      let r (a, cp_ref, ca_ref) =
        let adjoint cp _ca t = (S.dr (primal a) cp cp_ref ca_ref,
        a) :: t in
        let register t = a :: t in
        let label = S.label, [ a ] in
        adjoint, register, label
      in
      op_sito ~ff ~fd ~df ~r a
    in
    f

module type Siao = sig
  val label : string

  val ff_f : A.elt -> t array

  val ff_arr : A.arr -> t array

  val df : t array -> t -> t -> t array
```

```
  val dr : t -> t -> t ref array -> t ref array -> t
end

let build_siao =
  (* single input array outputs operation *)
  let op_siao ~ff ~fd ~df ~r a =
    match a with
    | DF (ap, at, ai)          ->
      let cp_arr = fd ap in
      let ct_arr = df cp_arr ap at in
      Array.map2 (fun cp ct -> DF (cp, ct, ai)) cp_arr ct_arr
    | DR (ap, _, _, _, ai, _) ->
      let cp_arr = fd ap in
      let cp_arr_ref = Array.map (fun cp -> ref cp) cp_arr in
      let tracker = ref 0 in
      let ca_ref_arr = Array.map (fun cp -> ref (zero cp)) cp_arr in
      Array.map2
        (fun cp ca_ref ->
          DR (cp, ca_ref, r (a, cp_arr_ref, ca_ref_arr), ref 0, ai,
          tracker))
        cp_arr
        ca_ref_arr
    | ap                       -> ff ap
  in
  fun (module S : Siao) ->
    let rec f a =
      let open S in
      let ff = function
        | F a   -> S.ff_f a
        | Arr a -> S.ff_arr a
        | _     -> error_uniop label a
      in
      let fd = f in
      let r (a, cp_arr_ref, ca_arr_ref) =
        let adjoint cp _ca_ref t = (S.dr (primal a) cp cp_arr_ref ca_arr_
        ref, a) :: t in
```

```
            let register t = a :: t in
            let label = S.label, [ a ] in
            adjoint, register, label
        in
        op_siao ~ff ~fd ~df ~r a
    in
    f

module type Piso = sig
  val label : string

  val ff_aa : A.elt -> A.elt -> t

  val ff_ab : A.elt -> A.arr -> t

  val ff_ba : A.arr -> A.elt -> t

  val ff_bb : A.arr -> A.arr -> t

  val df_da : t -> t -> t -> t -> t

  val df_db : t -> t -> t -> t -> t

  val df_dab : t -> t -> t -> t -> t -> t

  val dr_ab : t -> t -> t -> t ref -> t * t

  val dr_a : t -> t -> t -> t ref -> t

  val dr_b : t -> t -> t -> t ref -> t
end

let build_piso =
  (* pair input single output operation *)
  let op_piso ~ff ~fd ~df_da ~df_db ~df_dab ~r_d_d ~r_d_c ~r_c_d a b =
    match a, b with
    | F _ap, DF (bp, bt, bi) ->
      let cp = fd a bp in
      DF (cp, df_db cp a bp bt, bi)
    | DF (ap, at, ai), F _bp ->
      let cp = fd ap b in
```

```
     DF (cp, df_da cp ap at b, ai)
  | Arr _ap, DF (bp, bt, bi) ->
    let cp = fd a bp in
    DF (cp, df_db cp a bp bt, bi)
  | DF (ap, at, ai), Arr _bp ->
    let cp = fd ap b in
    DF (cp, df_da cp ap at b, ai)
  | F _ap, DR (bp, _, _, _, bi, _) ->
    let cp = fd a bp in
    DR (cp, ref (zero cp), r_c_d a b, ref 0, bi, ref 0)
  | DR (ap, _, _, _, ai, _), F _bp ->
    let cp = fd ap b in
    DR (cp, ref (zero cp), r_d_c a b, ref 0, ai, ref 0)
  | Arr _ap, DR (bp, _, _, _, bi, _) ->
    let cp = fd a bp in
    DR (cp, ref (zero cp), r_c_d a b, ref 0, bi, ref 0)
  | DR (ap, _, _, _, ai, _), Arr _bp ->
    let cp = fd ap b in
    DR (cp, ref (zero cp), r_d_c a b, ref 0, ai, ref 0)
  | DF (ap, at, ai), DR (bp, _, _, _, bi, _) ->
    (match cmp_tag ai bi with
    | 1 ->
      let cp = fd ap b in
      DF (cp, df_da cp ap at b, ai)
    | -1 ->
      let cp = fd a bp in
      DR (cp, ref (zero cp), r_c_d a b, ref 0, bi, ref 0)
    | _ -> failwith "error: forward and reverse clash at the
    same level")
  | DR (ap, _, _, _, ai, _), DF (bp, bt, bi) ->
    (match cmp_tag ai bi with
    | -1 ->
      let cp = fd a bp in
      DF (cp, df_db cp a bp bt, bi)
```

```
        | 1 ->
          let cp = fd ap b in
          DR (cp, ref (zero cp), r_d_c a b, ref 0, ai, ref 0)
        | _ -> failwith "error: forward and reverse clash at the
          same level")
      | DF (ap, at, ai), DF (bp, bt, bi) ->
        (match cmp_tag ai bi with
        | 0 ->
          let cp = fd ap bp in
          DF (cp, df_dab cp ap at bp bt, ai)
        | 1 ->
          let cp = fd ap b in
          DF (cp, df_da cp ap at b, ai)
        | _ ->
          let cp = fd a bp in
          DF (cp, df_db cp a bp bt, bi))
      | DR (ap, _, _, _, ai, _), DR (bp, _, _, _, bi, _) ->
        (match cmp_tag ai bi with
        | 0 ->
          let cp = fd ap bp in
          DR (cp, ref (zero cp), r_d_d a b, ref 0, ai, ref 0)
        | 1 ->
          let cp = fd ap b in
          DR (cp, ref (zero cp), r_d_c a b, ref 0, ai, ref 0)
        | _ ->
          let cp = fd a bp in
          DR (cp, ref (zero cp), r_c_d a b, ref 0, bi, ref 0))
      | a, b -> ff a b
    in
  fun (module S : Piso) ->
    let rec f a b =
      let ff a b =
        match a, b with
        | F a, F b     -> S.ff_aa a b
        | F a, Arr b   -> S.ff_ab a b
```

```
  | Arr a, F b    -> S.ff_ba a b
  | Arr a, Arr b -> S.ff_bb a b
  | _               -> error_binop S.label a b
in
let fd = f in
let r_d_d a b =
  let adjoint cp ca_ref t =
    let abar, bbar = S.dr_ab (primal a) (primal b) cp ca_ref in
    (abar, a) :: (bbar, b) :: t
  in
  let register t = a :: b :: t in
  let label = S.label ^ "_d_d", [ a; b ] in
  adjoint, register, label
in
let r_d_c a b =
  let adjoint cp ca_ref t = (S.dr_a (primal a) b cp ca_ref,
  a) :: t in
  let register t = a :: t in
  let label = S.label ^ "_d_c", [ a; b ] in
  adjoint, register, label
in
let r_c_d a b =
  let adjoint cp ca_ref t = (S.dr_b a (primal b) cp ca_ref,
  b) :: t in
  let register t = b :: t in
  let label = S.label ^ "_c_d", [ a; b ] in
  adjoint, register, label
in
op_piso
  ~ff
  ~fd
  ~df_da:S.df_da
  ~df_db:S.df_db
  ~df_dab:S.df_dab
  ~r_d_d
```

```
              ~r_d_c
              ~r_c_d
              a
              b
      in
      f

  module type Aiso = sig
    val label : string

    val ff : t array -> t

    val df : int list -> t -> t array -> t array -> t

    val dr : int list -> t array -> t -> t ref -> t list
  end

  let build_aiso =
    let build_info =
      Array.fold_left
        (fun (i, t, m, idxs) x ->
          match m, x with
          | _, F _ | _, Arr _ -> succ i, t, m, idxs
          | `normal, DR (_, _, _, _, t', _) -> succ i, t', `reverse, [ i ]
          | `forward, DR (_, _, _, _, t', _) ->
            if t' > t
            then succ i, t', `reverse, [ i ]
            else if t' = t
            then failwith "error: forward and reverse clash on the
            same level"
            else succ i, t, `forward, idxs
          | `reverse, DR (_, _, _, _, t', _) ->
            if t' > t
            then succ i, t', `reverse, [ i ]
            else if t' = t
            then succ i, t', `reverse, i :: idxs
            else succ i, t, m, idxs
          | `normal, DF (_, _, t') -> succ i, t', `forward, [ i ]
```

```
      | `forward, DF (_, _, t') ->
        if t' > t
        then succ i, t', `forward, [ i ]
        else if t' = t
        then succ i, t', `forward, i :: idxs
        else succ i, t, `forward, idxs
      | `reverse, DF (_, _, t') ->
        if t' > t
        then succ i, t', `forward, [ i ]
        else if t' = t
        then failwith "error: forward and reverse clash on the
        same level"
        else succ i, t, `reverse, idxs)
    (0, -50000, `normal, [])
  in
  fun (module S : Aiso) ->
    let rec f a =
      let _, max_t, mode, idxs = build_info a in
      let idxs = idxs |> List.rev in
      match mode with
      | `normal  -> S.ff a
      | `forward ->
        let ap =
          Array.map
            (fun x ->
              match x with
              | DF (p, _, t') ->
                if max_t = t'
                then p
                else if t' > max_t
                then failwith "no tags should be higher than max_t"
                else x
              | x              -> x)
            a
        in
```

```
        let cp = f ap in
        let at =
          let at = a |> Array.map zero in
          List.iter (fun k -> at. (k) <- tangent a. (k)) idxs;
          S.df idxs cp ap at
        in
        DF (cp, at, max_t)
      | `reverse ->
        let ap =
          Array.map
            (fun x ->
              match x with
              | DR (p, _, _, _, t', _) ->
                if max_t = t'
                then p
                else if t' > max_t
                then failwith "no tags should be higher than max_t"
                else x
              | x                    -> x)
            a
        in
        let cp = f ap in
        let adjoint cp ca t =
          (* use primal of inputs to calculate adjoint *)
          let ar = S.dr idxs ap cp ca |> Array.of_list in
          List.append List.(mapi (fun i k -> ar. (i), a. (k)) idxs) t
        in
        let register t = List.fold_left (fun t i -> a. (i) :: t)
        t idxs in
        let label = S.label, List.(map (fun i -> a. (i)) idxs) in
        DR (cp, ref (zero cp),
          (adjoint, register, label), ref 0, max_t, ref 0)
    in
    f
end
```

338

(** owl_algodiff_ops.ml *)

```
module Make (Core : Owl_algodiff_core_sig.Sig) = struct
  open Core
  module Builder = Owl_algodiff_ops_builder.Make (Core)
  open Builder

  module Maths = struct
    (* squeeze x so that it has shape s *)
    let rec _squeeze_broadcast x s =
      let shp_x = shape x in
      let dim_x = Array.length shp_x in
      let dim = Array.length s in
      if shp_x = s
      then x
      else if dim_x < dim
      then
        Printf.sprintf
          "_squeeze_broadcast: x must have dimension greater than %i,
          instead has  \
           dimension %i"
          dim
          dim_x
        |> failwith
      else if dim = 0
      then sum' x
      else (
        let s, shp_x = Owl_utils_array.align `Left 1 s shp_x in
        let fold =
          Array.fold_left (fun (k, accu) shp_x ->
              if s. (k) = shp_x
              then succ k, accu
              else if s. (k) = 1
              then succ k, k :: accu
              else
                failwith
```

```
                    Printf.(
                      sprintf
                        "_squeeze_broadcast: there ought to have been a
                        broadcasting error \
                          in the forward pass"))
    in
    let _, axis = fold (0, []) shp_x in
    let idxs = Array.of_list axis in
    sum_reduce ~axis:idxs x)

(* single input single output operations *)
and _neg =
  lazy
    (build_siso
      (module struct
        let label = "neg"

        let ff_f a = F A.Scalar.(neg a)

        let ff_arr a = Arr A.(neg a)

        let df _cp _ap at = neg at

        let dr _a _cp ca = neg !ca
      end : Siso))

and neg a = Lazy.force _neg a

and _tan =
  lazy
    (build_siso
      (module struct
        let label = "tan"

        let ff_f a = F A.Scalar.(tan a)

        let ff_arr a = Arr A.(tan a)

        let df _cp ap at = at / sqr (cos ap)
```

```
          let dr a _cp ca = !ca / sqr (cos a)
        end : Siso))

and tan a = Lazy.force _tan a

and ( / ) a b = div a b

and _div =
  lazy
    (build_piso
      (module struct
        let label = "div"

        let ff_aa a b = F A.Scalar.(div a b)

        let ff_ab a b = Arr A.(scalar_div a b)

        let ff_ba a b = Arr A.(div_scalar a b)

        let ff_bb a b = Arr A.(div a b)

        let df_da _cp _ap at bp = at / bp

        let df_db cp _ap bp bt = neg bt * cp / bp

        let df_dab cp _ap at bp bt = (at - (bt * cp)) / bp

        let dr_ab a b _cp ca =
          ( _squeeze_broadcast (!ca / b) (shape a)
          , _squeeze_broadcast (!ca * (neg a / (b * b))) (shape b) )

        let dr_a a b _cp ca = _squeeze_broadcast (!ca / b) (shape a)

        let dr_b a b _cp ca = _squeeze_broadcast (!ca * (neg a / (b *
        b))) (shape b)
      end : Piso))

and div a = Lazy.force _div a

and _set_slice =
  lazy
    (fun i ->
      build_piso
```

```
      (module struct
        let label = "set_slice"

        let ff_aa a _b = error_uniop label (pack_elt a)

        let ff_ab a _b = error_uniop label (pack_elt a)

        let ff_ba _a b = error_uniop label (pack_elt b)

        let ff_bb a b =
          let a = A.copy a in
          A.(set_slice i a b);
          Arr a

        let df_da _cp _ap at bp = set_slice i at (zero bp)

        let df_db _cp ap _bp bt = set_slice i (zero ap) bt

        let df_dab _cp _ap at _bp bt = set_slice i at bt

        let dr_ab _a b _cp ca = set_slice i !ca (zero b), get_
          slice i !ca

        let dr_a _a b _cp ca = set_slice i !ca (zero b)

        let dr_b _a _b _cp ca = get_slice i !ca
      end : Piso))

  and set_slice i = Lazy.force _set_slice i

  (* single input pair outputs *)
  and _qr =
    let _qr_backward (cp1, cp2) (ca1, ca2) =
      let q = !cp1
      and r = !cp2
      and qbar = !ca1
      and rbar = !ca2 in
      let m = (rbar *@ transpose r) - (transpose q *@ qbar) in
      linsolve r (transpose (qbar + (q *@ copyutl m))) |> transpose
    in
    lazy
```

```
(build_sipo
  (module struct
    let label = "qr"

    let ff_f a = error_uniop "qr" (pack_elt a)

    let ff_arr a =
      let q, r = A.(Linalg.qr a) in
      Arr q, Arr r

    let df _cp _ap _at =
      raise (Owl_exception.NOT_IMPLEMENTED "owl_algodiff_ops.qr")

    let dr _a _cp cp_ref ca_ref = _qr_backward cp_ref ca_ref
  end : Sipo))

and qr a = Lazy.force _qr a

(* single input triple outputs *)
and _svd =
  let _svd_backward (o1, o2, o3) (ca1, ca2, ca3) thin =
    let u, s, vt = !o1, !o2, !o3
    and ubar, sbar, vbart = !ca1, !ca2, !ca3 in
    let ut = transpose u
    and v = transpose vt in
    let ubart = transpose ubar
    and vbar = transpose vbart in
    let eye n = A.(ones [| 1; n |]) |> pack_arr |> diagm in
    let e_m = eye (row_num u) in
    let e_n = eye (row_num v) in
    let k = row_num vt in
    let f =
      let s2 = sqr s in
      pack_arr
        A.(
          init_nd [| k; k |] (fun idx ->
              let i = idx.(0)
              and j = idx.(1) in
```

```
                        if i = j
                        then float_to_elt 0.
                        else (
                          let s2_i = get_item s2 0 i |> unpack_flt in
                          let s2_j = get_item s2 0 j |> unpack_flt in
                          1. /. (s2_j -. s2_i) |> float_to_elt)))
          in
          let inv_s = pack_flt 1. / s in
          if thin
          then
            (u * sbar *@ vt)
            + (((u *@ (f * ((ut *@ ubar) - (ubart *@ u))) * s)
              + ((e_m - (u *@ ut)) *@ ubar * inv_s))
             *@ vt)
            + (u
              *@ ((transpose s * (f * ((vt *@ vbar) - (vbart *@ v))) *@ vt)
                + (transpose inv_s * vbart *@ (e_n - (v *@ vt)))))
          else raise (Owl_exception.NOT_IMPLEMENTED "owl_algodiff_ops.svd")
      in
      lazy
        (fun ~thin ->
          build_sito
            (module struct
              let label = "svd"

              let ff_f a = error_uniop "svd" (pack_elt a)

              let ff_arr a =
                let u, s, vt = A.(Linalg.svd ~thin a) in
                Arr u, Arr s, Arr vt

              let df _cp _ap _at =
                raise (Owl_exception.NOT_IMPLEMENTED "owl_algodiff_ops.svd")

              let dr _a _cp o ca = _svd_backward o ca thin
            end : Sito))

  and svd ?(thin = true) = Lazy.force _svd ~thin
```

```
(* pair outputs single input *)
and _lyapunov =
  let _lyapunov_backward_a a ca cp =
    let s = lyapunov (transpose a) (neg ca) in
    (s *@ transpose cp) + (transpose s *@ cp)
  in
  let _lyapunov_backward_q a ca = neg (lyapunov (transpose a)
  (neg ca)) in
  let _lyapunov_backward_aq a ca cp =
    let s = lyapunov (transpose a) (neg ca) in
    (s *@ transpose cp) + (transpose s *@ cp), neg s
  in
  lazy
    (build_piso
      (module struct
          let label = "lyapunov"

          let ff_aa a _q = error_uniop label (pack_elt a)

          let ff_ab a _q = error_uniop label (pack_elt a)

          let ff_ba _a q = error_uniop label (pack_elt q)

          let ff_bb a q = Arr A.(Linalg.lyapunov a q)

          let df_da cp ap at _qp =
            lyapunov ap (neg ((at *@ cp) + (cp *@ transpose at)))

          let df_db _cp ap _qp qt = lyapunov ap qt

          let df_dab cp ap at _qp qt =
            lyapunov ap (qt - ((at *@ cp) + (cp *@ transpose at)))

          let dr_ab a _b cp ca =
            let abar, qbar = _lyapunov_backward_aq a !ca cp in
            abar, qbar

          let dr_a a _q cp ca = _lyapunov_backward_a a !ca cp

          let dr_b a _q _cp ca = _lyapunov_backward_q a !ca
        end : Piso))
```

```
and lyapunov a = Lazy.force _lyapunov a

and _care =
  lazy
    (let unpack a = a.(0), a.(1), a.(2), a.(3) in
    let care_forward ~diag_r p a b r at bt qt rt =
      let tr_b = transpose b in
      let r = if diag_r then diag r else r in
      let inv_r = if diag_r then pack_flt 1. / r else inv r in
      let k = if diag_r then transpose inv_r * tr_b *@ p else inv_r *@
      tr_b *@ p in
      let acl = a - (b *@ k) in
      let tr_acl = transpose acl in
      let da () =
        let pat = p *@ at in
        neg (transpose pat) - pat
      in
      let dq () = neg qt in
      let dr () = neg (transpose k *@ rt *@ k) in
      let db () =
        let x = p *@ bt *@ k in
        x + transpose x
      in
      tr_acl, [| da; db; dq; dr |]
    in
    let care_backward ~diag_r a b _q r p pbar =
      let tr_b = transpose b in
      let inv_r = if diag_r then pack_flt 1. / diag r else inv r in
      let k = if diag_r then transpose inv_r * tr_b *@ p else inv_r *@
      tr_b *@ p in
      let tr_k = transpose k in
      let acl = a - (b *@ k) in
      let s =
        (* we can symmetrise without loss of generality as p is
        symmetric *)
        let pbar = pack_flt 0.5 * (pbar + transpose pbar) in
```

```
    let s = lyapunov acl (neg pbar) in
    pack_flt 0.5 * (s + transpose s)
  in
  (* the following calculations are not calculated unless needed *)
  let qbar () = s in
  let rbar () = k *@ s *@ tr_k in
  let abar () = pack_flt 2. * p *@ s in
  let bbar () = neg (pack_flt 2.) * p *@ s *@ tr_k in
  [| abar; bbar; qbar; rbar |]
in
fun ~diag_r ->
  build_aiso
    (module struct
      let label = "care"

      let ff a =
        match unpack a with
        | Arr a, Arr b, Arr q, Arr r -> A.Linalg.care ~diag_r a b q r
        |> pack_arr
        | _                          -> error_uniop "care" a.(0)

      let df idxs p inp tangents =
        let a, b, _, r = unpack inp in
        let at, bt, qt, rt = unpack tangents in
        let tr_acl, dp = care_forward ~diag_r p a b r at bt qt rt in
        let dx =
          List.map
            (fun k ->
              (* we can do symmetrise without loss of generality
                 because the output of care is symmetric *)
              let dp = dp. (k) () in
              pack_flt 0.5 * (dp + transpose dp))
            idxs
            |> List.fold_left ( + ) (pack_flt 0.)
        in
        lyapunov tr_acl dx
```

```
            let dr idxs inp p pbar_ref =
              let pbar = !pbar_ref in
              let bars =
                let a, b, q, r = unpack inp in
                care_backward ~diag_r a b q r p pbar
              in
              List.map (fun k -> bars. (k) ()) idxs
            end : Aiso))

  and care ?(diag_r = false) a b q r = Lazy.force _care ~diag_r [| a;
b; q; r |]
end
```

(neural network module: for specialised neural network operations *)*
module NN = struct
  open Maths

(NOTE: these functions are for neural network. There are many
restrictions at the moment. E.g. they do not support higher-order
derivatives, and some do not support forward mode, so use them when you
know what you are doing. *)*

(a:input; b:kernel; s:stride *)*
```
  let _conv2d =
    (* a:input; b:kernel; s:stride; o:output' *)
    let conv2d_backward_input a b s o =
      let a = unpack_arr a in
      let b = unpack_arr b in
      let o = unpack_arr o in
      A.conv2d_backward_input a b s o |> pack_arr
    in
    (* a:input; b:kernel; s:stride; o:output' *)
    let conv2d_backward_kernel a b s o =
      let a = unpack_arr a in
      let b = unpack_arr b in
      let o = unpack_arr o in
      A.conv2d_backward_kernel a b s o |> pack_arr
```

```
    in
    lazy
      (fun ~padding a b s ->
        build_piso
          (module struct
              let label = "conv2d"

              let ff_aa a _b = error_uniop label (pack_elt a)

              let ff_ab a _b = error_uniop label (pack_elt a)

              let ff_ba _a b = error_uniop label (pack_elt b)

              let ff_bb a b = Arr A.(conv2d ?padding a b s)

              let df_da _cp _ap at _bp = at

              let df_db _cp _ap _bp bt = bt

              let df_dab _cp _ap at _bp bt = at + bt

              let dr_ab a b _cp ca =
                conv2d_backward_input a b s !ca, conv2d_backward_kernel
                a b s !ca

              let dr_a a b _cp ca = conv2d_backward_input a b s !ca

              let dr_b a b _cp ca = conv2d_backward_kernel a b s !ca
            end : Piso)
            a
            b)

let conv2d ?padding = Lazy.force _conv2d ~padding

(* v: padded value; p:padding index; a:input *)
let _pad =
  (* TODO: sources required to confirm this backward op *)
  (* o:outut'; p: padding index *)
  let pad_backward o p =
    (* assume p is full legal index for pad operation *)
    let o = unpack_arr o in
```

```
      let os = A.shape o in
      let q = Owl_utils.llss2aarr p in
      Array.iteri (fun i x -> x.(1) <- Stdlib.(os. (i) - 1 - x.(1))) q;
      let q = Owl_utils.aarr2llss q in
      A.(get_slice q o) |> pack_arr
    in
    lazy
      (fun ~v p a ->
        build_siso
          (module struct
            let label = "pad"

            let ff_f a = error_uniop label (pack_elt a)

            let ff_arr a = Arr A.(pad ?v p a)

            let df _cp _ap _at = failwith "pad:df"

            let dr _a _cp ca = pad_backward !ca p
          end : Siso)
          a)

  let pad ?v = Lazy.force _pad ~v
end

module Mat = struct
  let empty m n = A.empty [| m; n |] |> pack_arr

  let zeros m n = A.zeros [| m; n |] |> pack_arr

  let eye n = A.Mat.eye n |> pack_arr

  let ones m n = A.ones [| m; n |] |> pack_arr

  let uniform ?a ?b m n = A.uniform ?a ?b [| m; n |] |> pack_arr

  let gaussian ?mu ?sigma m n = A.gaussian ?mu ?sigma [| m; n |] |>
pack_arr

  let reset x = x |> unpack_arr |> A.reset
```

```
let reshape m n x = Maths.reshape x [| m; n |]

let shape x =
  let s = A.shape (unpack_arr x) in
  s.(0), s.(1)

let row_num x = (unpack_arr x |> A.shape).(0)

let col_num x = (unpack_arr x |> A.shape).(1)

let numel x = numel x

let row x i = Maths.get_row x i

let get x i j = Maths.get_item x i j

let set x i j a = Maths.set_item x i j a

(* unary math operators *)

let mean x = Maths.mean x

(* binary math operators *)

let add x y = Maths.add x y

let sub x y = Maths.sub x y

let mul x y = Maths.mul x y

let div x y = Maths.div x y

let dot x y = Maths.dot x y

let map_by_row f x = x |> Maths.to_rows |> Array.map f |> Maths.of_rows

let print x = A.print (unpack_arr x)

let of_arrays x = A.of_arrays x |> pack_arr

let init_2d n_rows n_cols f =
  Array.init n_rows (fun i -> Array.init n_cols (fun j -> f i j)) |>
Maths.of_arrays
end
```

```
module Arr = struct
    let empty d = A.empty d |> pack_arr

    let zeros d = A.zeros d |> pack_arr

    let ones d = A.ones d |> pack_arr

    let uniform ?a ?b d = A.uniform ?a ?b d |> pack_arr

    let gaussian ?mu ?sigma d = A.gaussian ?mu ?sigma d |> pack_arr

    let reset x = x |> unpack_arr |> A.reset

    let reshape x s = Maths.reshape x s

    let shape x = A.shape (unpack_arr x)

    let numel x = numel x

    (* binary math operators *)

    let add x y = Maths.add x y

    let sub x y = Maths.sub x y

    let mul x y = Maths.mul x y

    let div x y = Maths.div x y

    let dot x y = Maths.dot x y
  end
end
```

D.2 Core Modules

(** Owl_algodiff_core.ml *)

```
module Make (A : Owl_types_ndarray_algodiff.Sig) = struct
  include Owl_algodiff_types.Make (A)
  module A = A

  (* generate global tags *)
  let _global_tag = ref 0
```

```
let tag () =
  _global_tag := !_global_tag + 1;
  !_global_tag

(* helper functions of the core AD component *)

let reset_zero = function
  | F _ -> F A.(float_to_elt 0.)
  | Arr ap ->
    A.reset ap;
    Arr ap
  | _ -> failwith "error: reset_zero"

let primal = function
  | DF (ap, _, _)          -> ap
  | DR (ap, _, _, _, _, _) -> ap
  | ap -> ap

let rec primal' = function
  | DF (ap, _, _)          -> primal' ap
  | DR (ap, _, _, _, _, _) -> primal' ap
  | ap -> ap

let rec zero = function
  | F _                    -> F A.(float_to_elt 0.)
  | Arr ap                 -> Arr A.(zeros (shape ap))
  | DF (ap, _, _)          -> ap |> primal' |> zero
  | DR (ap, _, _, _, _, _) -> ap |> primal' |> zero

let tangent = function
  | DF (_, at, _)  -> at
  | DR _           -> failwith "error: no tangent for DR"
  | ap             -> zero ap

let adjref = function
  | DF _                    -> failwith "error: no adjref for DF"
  | DR (_, at, _, _, _, _)  -> at
  | ap                      -> ref (zero ap)
```

```
let adjval = function
    | DF _                      -> failwith "error: no adjval for DF"
    | DR (_, at, _, _, _, _) -> !at
    | ap                        -> zero ap

  let shape x =
    match primal' x with
    | F _     -> [|||]
    | Arr ap -> A.shape ap
    | _       -> failwith "error: AD.shape"

  let rec is_float x =
    match x with
    | Arr _ -> false
    | F _   -> true
    | DF _ -> is_float (primal' x)
    | DR _ -> is_float (primal' x)

  let rec is_arr x =
    match x with
    | Arr _ -> false
    | F _    -> true
    | DF _   -> is_arr (primal' x)
    | DR _   -> is_arr (primal' x)

  let row_num x = (shape x).(0)

  let col_num x = (shape x).(1)

  let numel x =
    match primal' x with
    | Arr x -> A.numel x
    | _      -> failwith "error: AD.numel"

  let clip_by_value ~amin ~amax x =
    match primal' x with
    | Arr x -> Arr A.(clip_by_value ~amin ~amax x)
    | _      -> failwith "error: AD.clip_by_value"
```

```
let clip_by_l2norm a x =
  match primal' x with
  | Arr x -> Arr A.(clip_by_l2norm a x)
  | _       -> failwith "error: AD.clip_by_l2norm"

let copy_primal' x =
  match primal' x with
  | Arr ap -> Arr A.(copy ap)
  | _        -> failwith "error: AD.copy"

let tile x reps =
  match primal' x with
  | Arr x -> Arr A.(tile x reps)
  | _       -> failwith "error: AD.tile"

let repeat x reps =
  match primal' x with
  | Arr x -> Arr A.(repeat x reps)
  | _       -> failwith "error: AD.repeat"
```

(* packing and unpacking functions *)

```
let pack_elt x = F x

let unpack_elt x =
  match primal x with
  | F x -> x
  | _    -> failwith "error: AD.unpack_elt"

let pack_flt x = F A.(float_to_elt x)

let _f x = F A.(float_to_elt x)
```

(* shorcut for type conversion *)

```
let unpack_flt x =
  match primal x with
  | F x -> A.elt_to_float x
  | _    -> failwith "error: AD.unpack_flt"
```

```ocaml
let pack_arr x = Arr x

let unpack_arr x =
  match primal x with
  | Arr x -> x
  | _     -> failwith "error: AD.unpack_arr"

(* functions to report errors, help in debugging *)

let deep_info x =
  match primal' x with
  | F a    -> Printf.sprintf "F(%g)" A.(elt_to_float a)
  | Arr a ->
    Printf.sprintf "Arr(%s)" (A.shape a |> Owl_utils_array.to_string
    string_of_int)
  | _      -> "you should not have reached here!"

let type_info x =
  match x with
  | F _a                        -> Printf.sprintf "[%s]" (deep_info x)
  | DF (ap, _at, ai)            -> Printf.sprintf "[DF tag:%i ap:%s]"
    ai (deep_info ap)
  | DR (ap, _at, _ao, _af, ai, _) ->
    Printf.sprintf "[DR tag:%i ap:%s]" ai (deep_info ap)
  | _                           -> Printf.sprintf "[%s]" (deep_info x)

let error_binop op a b =
  let s0 = "#0:" ^ type_info a in
  let s1 = "#1:" ^ type_info b in
  failwith (op ^ " : " ^ s0 ^ ", " ^ s1)

let error_uniop op a =
  let s = type_info a in
  failwith (op ^ " : " ^ s)
end
```

```
(** Owl_algodiff_generic.ml *)

module Make (A : Owl_types_ndarray_algodiff.Sig) = struct
  (* include functions in the Core module *)
  module Core = Owl_algodiff_core.Make (A)
  include Core

  (* include graph conversion functions *)
  include Owl_algodiff_graph_convert.Make (Core)

  (* instantiate operations *)
  module Ops = Owl_algodiff_ops.Make (Core)
  include Ops

  (* include core reverse mode functions *)
  module Reverse = Owl_algodiff_reverse.Make (struct
    include Core

    let reverse_add = Maths.add
  end)

  (* convenient wrappers *)

  let make_forward p t i = DF (p, t, i)

  let make_reverse p i =
    let adjoint _cp _ca t = t in
    let register t = t in
    let label = "Noop", [] in
    DR (p, ref (zero p), (adjoint, register, label), ref 0, i, ref 0)

  (* expose reverse prop: propagate gradients *)
  let reverse_prop = Reverse.reverse_prop

  (* derivative of f (scalar -> scalar) at x, forward ad *)
  let diff' f x =
    if not (is_float x) then failwith "input of `diff` must be a scalar";
    let x = make_forward x (pack_flt 1.) (tag ()) in
    let y = f x in
    primal y, tangent y
```

```
(* derivative of f (scalar -> scalar) at x, forward ad *)
let diff f x = diff' f x |> snd

(* gradient of f (vector -> scalar) at x, reverse ad *)
let grad' f x =
  let x = make_reverse x (tag ()) in
  let y = f x in
  if not (is_float y) then failwith "output of `grad` must be a scalar";
  Reverse.reverse_reset y;
  Reverse.reverse_push (pack_flt 1.) y;
  primal y, x |> adjval

(* gradient of f (vector -> scalar) at x, reverse ad *)
let grad f x = grad' f x |> snd
```

D.3 Graph Converter

*(** owl_algodiff_graph_converter.ml *)*

```
odule Make (Core : Owl_algodiff_core_sig.Sig) = struct
  open Core

  (* _traverse_trace and its related functions are used to convert the
     computation graph generated in backward mode into human-readable format.
     You can make your own convert function to generate needed format. *)
  let _traverse_trace x =
    (* init variables for tracking nodes and indices *)
    let nodes = Hashtbl.create 512 in
    let index = ref 0 in
    (* local function to traverse the nodes *)
    let rec push tlist =
      match tlist with
      | [] -> ()
      | hd :: tl ->
        if Hashtbl.mem nodes hd = false
        then (
```

```
      let op, prev =
        match hd with
        | DR (_ap, _aa, (_, _, label), _af, _ai, _) -> label
        | F _a -> Printf.sprintf "Const", []
        | Arr _a -> Printf.sprintf "Const", []
        | DF (_, _, _) -> Printf.sprintf "DF", []
      in
      (* check if the node has been visited before *)
      Hashtbl.add nodes hd (!index, op, prev);
      index := !index + 1;
      push (prev @ tl))
    else push tl
in
(* iterate the graph then return the hash table *)
push x;
nodes

(* convert graph to terminal output *)
let _convert_terminal_output nodes =
Hashtbl.fold
  (fun v (v_id, v_op, v_prev) s0 ->
    let v_ts = type_info v in
    s0
    ^ List.fold_left
        (fun s1 u ->
          let u_id, u_op, _ = Hashtbl.find nodes u in
          let u_ts = type_info u in
          s1
          ^ Printf.sprintf
            "{ i:%i o:%s t:%s } -> { i:%i o:%s t:%s }\n"
            u_id
            u_op
            u_ts
            v_id
            v_op
            v_ts)
```

```
                  ""
              v_prev)
        nodes
          ""


(* convert graph to dot file output *)
let _convert_dot_output nodes =
  let network =
    Hashtbl.fold
      (fun _v (v_id, _v_op, v_prev) s0 ->
        s0
        ^ List.fold_left
            (fun s1 u ->
              let u_id, _u_op, _ = Hashtbl.find nodes u in
              s1 ^ Printf.sprintf "\t%i -> %i;\n" u_id v_id)
            ""
            v_prev)
      nodes
      ""
  in
  let attrs =
    Hashtbl.fold
      (fun v (v_id, v_op, _v_prev) s0 ->
        if v_op = "Const"
        then
          s0
          ^ Printf.sprintf
            "%i [ label=\"#%i | { %s | %s }\" fillcolor=gray,
            style=filled ];\n"
            v_id
            v_id
            v_op
            (deep_info v)
        else
          s0
          ^ Printf.sprintf
```

```
                "%i [ label=\"#%i | { %s | %s }\" ];\n"
                v_id
                v_id
                v_op
                (deep_info v))
          nodes
          ""
    in
    network ^ attrs

let to_trace nodes = _traverse_trace nodes |> _convert_terminal_output

let to_dot nodes =
  _traverse_trace nodes
  |> _convert_dot_output
  |> Printf.sprintf "digraph CG {\nnode [shape=record];\n%s}"

let pp_num formatter x = Format.fprintf formatter "%s" (type_info x)
end
```

APPENDIX E

Neural Network Module

E.1 Graph Module

```
(*
* OWL - OCaml Scientific Computing
* Copyright (c) 2016-2022 Liang Wang <liang@ocaml.xyz>
*)

(** Neural network: Graphical neural network *)

open Owl_types

(* Make functor starts *)

module Make (Neuron : Owl_neural_neuron_sig.Sig) = struct
  module Neuron = Neuron
  open Neuron
  open Neuron.Optimise.Algodiff

  (* graph network and node definition *)

  type node =
    { mutable name : string
    ; (* name of a node *)
      mutable prev : node array
    ; (* parents of a node *)
      mutable next : node array
    ; (* children of a node *)
      mutable neuron : neuron
    ; (* neuron contained in a node *)
      mutable output : t option
```

```
 ; (* output of a node *)
   mutable network : network
 ; (* network a node belongs to *)
   mutable train : bool (* specify if a node is only for training *)
 }

and network =
  { mutable nnid : string
 ; (* name of the graph network *)
   mutable size : int
 ; (* size of the graph network *)
   mutable roots : node array
  ; (* roots of the graph network, i.e. inputs *)
   mutable outputs : node array
 ; (* outputs of the graph network *)
     mutable topo : node array (* nodes sorted in topological order *)
 }

(* functions to manipulate the network *)

let make_network ?nnid size roots topo =
  let nnid =
    match nnid with
    | Some s -> s
    | None -> "Graphical network"
  in
  { nnid; size; roots; topo; outputs = [|||] }

let make_node ?name ?(train = false) prev next neuron output network =
  let name =
    match name with
    | Some s -> s
    | None -> Printf.sprintf "%s_%i" (to_name neuron) network.size
  in
  { name; prev; next; neuron; output; network; train }
```

```
let get_roots nn =
  match nn.roots with
  | [||] -> failwith "Owl_neural_graph:get_roots"
  | x -> x

let get_outputs nn = nn.outputs

let get_node nn name =
  let x = Owl_utils.Array.filter (fun n -> n.name = name) nn.topo in
  if Array.length x = 0 then failwith "Owl_neural_graph:get_node"
  else x.(0)

let get_network ?name n =
  let name =
    match name with
    | Some s -> s
    | None -> Random.int 65535 |> string_of_int
  in
  n.network.nnid <- name;
  (* if run and run_inputs are merged, the next line is necessary. *)
  n.network.outputs <- [| n |];
  n.network

let outputs ?name nodes =
  assert (Array.length nodes > 0);
  let name =
    match name with
    | Some s -> s
    | None -> Random.int 65535 |> string_of_int
  in
  (* assumes that all the outputs are part of the same network *)
  let nn = nodes.(0).network in
  nn.nnid <- name;
  nn.outputs <- nodes;
  nn

let get_network_name n = n.nnid
```

```ocaml
  let set_network_name n name = n.nnid <- name

  let input_shape n = (get_roots n).(0).neuron |> Neuron.get_in_shape

  let input_shapes n = Array.map (fun r -> r.neuron |> Neuron.get_in_shape)
(get_roots n)
  (* collect the outputs of a given set of nodes *)
  let collect_output nodes =
    Array.map
      (fun n ->
        match n.output with
        | Some o -> o
        | None -> failwith "Owl_neural_graph:collect_output")
      Nodes

  let connect_pair prev next =
    if Array.mem prev next.prev = false
    then next.prev <- Array.append next.prev [| prev |];
    if Array.mem next prev.next = false
    then prev.next <- Array.append prev.next [| next |]

  let connect_to_parents parents child =
    (* update the child's input and output shape *)
    if Array.length parents > 0
    then (
      let out_shapes = Array.map (fun n -> n.neuron |> get_out_shape)
      parents in
      connect out_shapes child.neuron);
    (* connect the child to the parents *)
    Array.iter (fun p -> connect_pair p child) parents
  (* add child node to nn and connect to parents *)
  let rec add_node ?act_typ nn parents child =
    nn.size <- nn.size + 1;
    connect_to_parents parents child;
    nn.topo <- Array.append nn.topo [| child |];
    child.network <- nn;
```

```
(* if activation is specified, recursively add_node *)
match act_typ with
| Some act ->
  let neuron = Activation (Activation.create act) in
  let child_of_child = make_node [||] [||] neuron None nn in
  add_node nn [| child |] child_of_child
| None -> child

(* functions to interface to optimisation engine *)

let init nn = Array.iter (fun n -> init n.neuron) nn.topo

let reset nn = Array.iter (fun n -> reset n.neuron) nn.topo

let mktag t nn = Array.iter (fun n -> mktag t n.neuron) nn.topo

let mkpar nn = Array.map (fun n -> mkpar n.neuron) nn.topo

let mkpri nn = Array.map (fun n -> mkpri n.neuron) nn.topo

let mkadj nn = Array.map (fun n -> mkadj n.neuron) nn.topo

let update nn us = Array.iter2 (fun n u -> update n.neuron u) nn.topo us

let run_inputs inputs nn =
  assert (Array.(length inputs = length (get_roots nn)));
  Array.iter
    (fun n ->
      (* collect the inputs from parents' output *)
      let input =
        match n.neuron with
        | Input _ ->
          let index =
            Owl_utils.Array.index_of (Array.map (fun r -> r.name) (get_
            roots nn)) n.name
          in
          [| inputs.(index) |]
        | _ -> collect_output n.prev
      in
```

```
        (* process the current neuron, save output *)
        let output = run input n.neuron in
        n.output <- Some output)
      nn.topo;
    (* collect the final outputs *)
    collect_output nn.outputs

  let run x nn =
    Array.iter
      (fun n ->
         (* collect the inputs from parents' output *)
         let input =
           match n.neuron with
           | Input _ -> [| x |]
           | _ -> collect_output n.prev
         in
         (* process the current neuron, save output *)
         let output = run input n.neuron in
       n.output <- Some output)
    nn.topo;
    (* collect the final output from the tail *)
    let sink = [| nn.topo.(Array.length nn.topo - 1) |] in
    (collect_output sink).(0)

  let forward nn x =
    mktag (tag ()) nn;
    run x nn, mkpar nn

  let forward_inputs nn x =
    mktag (tag ()) nn;
    run_inputs x nn, mkpar nn

  let backward nn y =
    reverse_prop (_f 1.) y;
    mkpri nn, mkadj nn

  let copy nn =
    let nn' = make_network ~nnid:nn.nnid nn.size [||] [||] in
```

```
(* first iteration to copy the neurons *)
nn'.topo
  <- Array.map
        (fun node ->
          let neuron' = copy node.neuron in
          make_node ~name:node.name ~train:node.train [|||] [|||] neuron'
          None nn')
      nn.topo;
(* second iteration to re-construct the structure and infer the
shape *)
Array.iter2
  (fun node node' ->
     node'.prev <- Array.map (fun n -> get_node nn' n.name) node.prev;
     node'.next <- Array.map (fun n -> get_node nn' n.name) node.next;
   connect_to_parents node'.prev node')
  nn.topo
  nn'.topo;
(* set roots and outputs to finalise the structure *)
nn'.roots <- Array.map (fun n -> get_node nn' n.name) (get_roots nn);
nn'.outputs <- Array.map (fun n -> get_node nn' n.name) (get_
outputs nn);
nn'

let _remove_training_nodes nn =
  let topo' =
    Owl_utils.Array.filter
      (fun n ->
         if n.train = true
         then (
           (* remove myself from my parents *)
           Array.iter
             (fun m ->
               let next' = Owl_utils.Array.filter (fun x -> x.name <>
               n.name) m.next in
               m.next <- next')
           n.prev;
```

```
        (* remove myself from my children *)
        Array.iter
          (fun m ->
            let prev' = Owl_utils.Array.filter (fun x -> x.name <>
            n.name) m.prev in
            m.prev <- prev')
         n.next;
        (* connect my parents and my children *)
        Array.iter (connect_to_parents n.prev) n.next);
      not n.train)
    nn.topo
  in
  nn.topo <- topo'

let model nn =
  if Array.length nn.roots > 1
  then failwith "Owl_neural_graph:model Did you mean to use model_
  inputs?";
  let nn = copy nn in
  _remove_training_nodes nn;
  let inference x =
    match run (Arr x) nn with
    | Arr y -> y
    | _ -> failwith "Owl_neural_graph:model"
  in
  inference

let model_inputs nn =
  let nn = copy nn in
  _remove_training_nodes nn;
  let inference inputs =
    let outputs = run_inputs (Array.map (fun x -> Arr x) inputs) nn in
    Array.map unpack_arr outputs
  in
  inference
```

(* functions to create functional nodes *)

```
let input ?name inputs =
  let neuron = Input (Input.create inputs) in
  let nn = make_network 0 [|||] [|||] in
  let n = make_node ?name [|||] [|||] neuron None nn in
  nn.roots <- [| n |];
  add_node nn [|||] n

let inputs ?names input_shapes =
  let names =
    match names with
    | Some x ->
      assert (Array.(length x = length input_shapes));
      Array.map (fun name -> Some name) x
    | None -> Array.(make (length input_shapes) None)
  in
  let neurons = Array.map (fun s -> Input (Input.create s)) input_
  shapes in
  let nn = make_network 0 [|||] [|||] in
  let ns =
    Array.map2
      (fun n name -> make_node ?name [|||] [|||] n None nn |> add_node
      nn [|||])
      neurons
      names
  in
  nn.roots <- ns;
  ns

let activation ?name act_typ input_node =
  let neuron = Activation (Activation.create act_typ) in
  let nn = get_network input_node in
  let n = make_node ?name [|||] [|||] neuron None nn in
  add_node nn [| input_node |] n
```

```
let linear ?name ?(init_typ = Init.Standard) ?act_typ outputs
input_node =
  let neuron = Linear (Linear.create outputs init_typ) in
  let nn = get_network input_node in
  let n = make_node ?name [||] [||] neuron None nn in
  add_node ?act_typ nn [| input_node |] n

let linear_nobias ?name ?(init_typ = Init.Standard) ?act_typ outputs
input_node =
  let neuron = LinearNoBias (LinearNoBias.create outputs init_typ) in
  let nn = get_network input_node in
  let n = make_node ?name [||] [||] neuron None nn in
  add_node ?act_typ nn [| input_node |] n

let embedding ?name ?(init_typ = Init.Standard) ?act_typ in_dim out_dim
input_node =
  let neuron = Embedding (Embedding.create in_dim out_dim init_typ) in
  let nn = get_network input_node in
  let n = make_node ?name [||] [||] neuron None nn in
  add_node ?act_typ nn [| input_node |] n

let recurrent ?name ?(init_typ = Init.Standard) ~act_typ outputs hiddens
input_node =
  let neuron = Recurrent (Recurrent.create hiddens outputs act_typ
  init_typ) in
  let nn = get_network input_node in
  let n = make_node ?name [||] [||] neuron None nn in
  add_node nn [| input_node |] n

let lstm ?name ?(init_typ = Init.Tanh) cells input_node =
  let neuron = LSTM (LSTM.create cells init_typ) in
  let nn = get_network input_node in
  let n = make_node ?name [||] [||] neuron None nn in
  add_node nn [| input_node |] n

let gru ?name ?(init_typ = Init.Tanh) cells input_node =
  let neuron = GRU (GRU.create cells init_typ) in
```

```
  let nn = get_network input_node in
  let n = make_node ?name [|||] [|||] neuron None nn in
  add_node nn [| input_node |] n

let conv1d
    ?name
    ?(padding = SAME)
    ?(init_typ = Init.Tanh)
    ?act_typ
    kernel
    stride
    input_node
  =
  let neuron = Conv1D (Conv1D.create padding kernel stride init_typ) in
  let nn = get_network input_node in
  let n = make_node ?name [|||] [|||] neuron None nn in
  add_node ?act_typ nn [| input_node |] n

let conv2d
    ?name
    ?(padding = SAME)
    ?(init_typ = Init.Tanh)
    ?act_typ
    kernel
    stride
    input_node
  =
  let neuron = Conv2D (Conv2D.create padding kernel stride init_typ) in
  let nn = get_network input_node in
  let n = make_node ?name [|||] [|||] neuron None nn in
  add_node ?act_typ nn [| input_node |] n

let conv3d
    ?name
    ?(padding = SAME)
    ?(init_typ = Init.Tanh)
```

```
    ?act_typ
    kernel
    stride
    input_node
  =
  let neuron = Conv3D (Conv3D.create padding kernel stride init_typ) in
  let nn = get_network input_node in
  let n = make_node ?name [|||] [|||] neuron None nn in
  add_node ?act_typ nn [| input_node |] n

let dilated_conv1d
    ?name
    ?(padding = SAME)
    ?(init_typ = Init.Tanh)
    ?act_typ
     kernel
    stride
    rate
    input_node
  =
  let neuron =
    DilatedConv1D (DilatedConv1D.create padding kernel stride rate
    init_typ)
  in
  let nn = get_network input_node in
  let n = make_node ?name [|||] [|||] neuron None nn in
  add_node ?act_typ nn [| input_node |] n

let dilated_conv2d
    ?name
    ?(padding = SAME)
    ?(init_typ = Init.Tanh)
    ?act_typ
    kernel
    stride
    rate
```

```
    input_node

    =

    let neuron =
      DilatedConv2D (DilatedConv2D.create padding kernel stride rate
        init_typ)
    in
    let nn = get_network input_node in
    let n = make_node ?name [|||] [|||] neuron None nn in
    add_node ?act_typ nn [| input_node |] n

let dilated_conv3d
    ?name
    ?(padding = SAME)
    ?(init_typ = Init.Tanh)
    ?act_typ
    kernel
    stride
    rate
    input_node

    =

    let neuron =
      DilatedConv3D (DilatedConv3D.create padding kernel stride rate
        init_typ)
    in
    let nn = get_network input_node in
    let n = make_node ?name [|||] [|||] neuron None nn in
    add_node ?act_typ nn [| input_node |] n

let transpose_conv1d
    ?name
    ?(padding = SAME)
    ?(init_typ = Init.Tanh)
    ?act_typ
    kernel
    stride
```

```
      input_node
  =
  let neuron =
      TransposeConv1D (TransposeConv1D.create padding kernel stride
      init_typ)
  in
  let nn = get_network input_node in
  let n = make_node ?name [|||] [|||] neuron None nn in
  add_node ?act_typ nn [| input_node |] n

let transpose_conv2d
    ?name
    ?(padding = SAME)
    ?(init_typ = Init.Tanh)
    ?act_typ
    kernel
    stride
    input_node
  =
  let neuron =
      TransposeConv2D (TransposeConv2D.create padding kernel stride
      init_typ)
  in
  let nn = get_network input_node in
  let n = make_node ?name [|||] [|||] neuron None nn in
  add_node ?act_typ nn [| input_node |] n

let transpose_conv3d
    ?name
    ?(padding = SAME)
    ?(init_typ = Init.Tanh)
    ?act_typ
    kernel
    stride
    input_node
  =
```

```
let neuron =
  TransposeConv3D (TransposeConv3D.create padding kernel stride
  init_typ)
in
let nn = get_network input_node in
let n = make_node ?name [||] [|||] neuron None nn in
add_node ?act_typ nn [| input_node |] n

let fully_connected ?name ?(init_typ = Init.Standard) ?act_typ outputs
input_node =
  let neuron = FullyConnected (FullyConnected.create outputs init_typ) in
  let nn = get_network input_node in
  let n = make_node ?name [||] [|||] neuron None nn in
  add_node ?act_typ nn [| input_node |] n

let max_pool1d ?name ?(padding = SAME) ?act_typ kernel stride
input_node =
  let neuron = MaxPool1D (MaxPool1D.create padding kernel stride) in
  let nn = get_network input_node in
  let n = make_node ?name [||] [|||] neuron None nn in
  add_node ?act_typ nn [| input_node |] n

let max_pool2d ?name ?(padding = SAME) ?act_typ kernel stride
input_node =
  let neuron = MaxPool2D (MaxPool2D.create padding kernel stride) in
  let nn = get_network input_node in
  let n = make_node ?name [||] [|||] neuron None nn in
  add_node ?act_typ nn [| input_node |] n

let avg_pool1d ?name ?(padding = SAME) ?act_typ kernel stride
input_node =
  let neuron = AvgPool1D (AvgPool1D.create padding kernel stride) in
  let nn = get_network input_node in
  let n = make_node ?name [||] [|||] neuron None nn in
  add_node ?act_typ nn [| input_node |] n
```

```
let avg_pool2d ?name ?(padding = SAME) ?act_typ kernel stride
input_node =
  let neuron = AvgPool2D (AvgPool2D.create padding kernel stride) in
  let nn = get_network input_node in
  let n = make_node ?name [|||] [|||] neuron None nn in
  add_node ?act_typ nn [| input_node |] n

let global_max_pool1d ?name ?act_typ input_node =
  let neuron = GlobalMaxPool1D (GlobalMaxPool1D.create ()) in
  let nn = get_network input_node in
  let n = make_node ?name [|||] [|||] neuron None nn in
  add_node ?act_typ nn [| input_node |] n

let global_max_pool2d ?name ?act_typ input_node =
  let neuron = GlobalMaxPool2D (GlobalMaxPool2D.create ()) in
  let nn = get_network input_node in
  let n = make_node ?name [|||] [|||] neuron None nn in
  add_node ?act_typ nn [| input_node |] n

let global_avg_pool1d ?name ?act_typ input_node =
  let neuron = GlobalAvgPool1D (GlobalAvgPool1D.create ()) in
  let nn = get_network input_node in
  let n = make_node ?name [|||] [|||] neuron None nn in
  add_node ?act_typ nn [| input_node |] n

let global_avg_pool2d ?name ?act_typ input_node =
  let neuron = GlobalAvgPool2D (GlobalAvgPool2D.create ()) in
  let nn = get_network input_node in
  let n = make_node ?name [|||] [|||] neuron None nn in
  add_node ?act_typ nn [| input_node |] n

let upsampling2d ?name ?act_typ size input_node =
  let neuron = UpSampling2D (UpSampling2D.create size) in
  let nn = get_network input_node in
  let n = make_node ?name [|||] [|||] neuron None nn in
  add_node ?act_typ nn [| input_node |] n
```

```
let padding2d ?name ?act_typ padding input_node =
  let neuron = Padding2D (Padding2D.create padding) in
  let nn = get_network input_node in
  let n = make_node ?name [|||] [|||] neuron None nn in
  add_node ?act_typ nn [| input_node |] n

let dropout ?name rate input_node =
  let neuron = Dropout (Dropout.create rate) in
  let nn = get_network input_node in
  let n = make_node ?name ~train:true [|||] [|||] neuron None nn in
  add_node nn [| input_node |] n

let gaussian_noise ?name sigma input_node =
  let neuron = GaussianNoise (GaussianNoise.create sigma) in
  let nn = get_network input_node in
  let n = make_node ?name ~train:true [|||] [|||] neuron None nn in
  add_node nn [| input_node |] n

let gaussian_dropout ?name rate input_node =
  let neuron = GaussianDropout (GaussianDropout.create rate) in
  let nn = get_network input_node in
  let n = make_node ?name ~train:true [|||] [|||] neuron None nn in
  add_node nn [| input_node |] n

let alpha_dropout ?name rate input_node =
  let neuron = AlphaDropout (AlphaDropout.create rate) in
  let nn = get_network input_node in
  let n = make_node ?name ~train:true [|||] [|||] neuron None nn in
  add_node nn [| input_node |] n

let normalisation ?name ?(axis = -1) ?training ?decay ?mu ?var
input_node =
  let neuron = Normalisation (Normalisation.create ?training ?decay ?mu
  ?var axis) in
  let nn = get_network input_node in
  let n = make_node ?name [|||] [|||] neuron None nn in
  add_node nn [| input_node |] n
```

```
let reshape ?name outputs input_node =
  let neuron = Reshape (Reshape.create outputs) in
  let nn = get_network input_node in
  let n = make_node ?name [|||] [|||] neuron None nn in
  add_node nn [| input_node |] n

let flatten ?name input_node =
  let neuron = Flatten (Flatten.create ()) in
  let nn = get_network input_node in
  let n = make_node ?name [|||] [|||] neuron None nn in
  add_node nn [| input_node |] n

let slice ?name slice input_node =
  let neuron = Slice (Slice.create slice) in
  let nn = get_network input_node in
  let n = make_node ?name [|||] [|||] neuron None nn in
  add_node nn [| input_node |] n

let lambda ?name ?act_typ ?out_shape lambda input_node =
  let neuron = Lambda (Lambda.create ?out_shape lambda) in
  let nn = get_network input_node in
  let n = make_node ?name [|||] [|||] neuron None nn in
  add_node ?act_typ nn [| input_node |] n

let lambda_array ?name ?act_typ out_shape lambda input_node =
  let neuron = LambdaArray (LambdaArray.create out_shape lambda) in
  let nn = get_network input_node.(0) in
  let n = make_node ?name [|||] [|||] neuron None nn in
  add_node ?act_typ nn input_node n

let add ?name ?act_typ input_node =
  let neuron = Add (Add.create ()) in
  let nn = get_network input_node.(0) in
  let n = make_node ?name [|||] [|||] neuron None nn in
  add_node ?act_typ nn input_node n

let mul ?name ?act_typ input_node =
  let neuron = Mul (Mul.create ()) in
  let nn = get_network input_node.(0) in
```

```
  let n = make_node ?name [|||] [|||] neuron None nn in
  add_node ?act_typ nn input_node n

let dot ?name ?act_typ input_node =
  let neuron = Dot (Dot.create ()) in
  let nn = get_network input_node.(0) in
  let n = make_node ?name [|||] [|||] neuron None nn in
  add_node ?act_typ nn input_node n

let max ?name ?act_typ input_node =
  let neuron = Max (Max.create ()) in
  let nn = get_network input_node.(0) in
  let n = make_node ?name [|||] [|||] neuron None nn in
  add_node ?act_typ nn input_node n

let average ?name ?act_typ input_node =
  let neuron = Average (Average.create ()) in
  let nn = get_network input_node.(0) in
  let n = make_node ?name [|||] [|||] neuron None nn in
  add_node ?act_typ nn input_node n

let concatenate ?name ?act_typ axis input_node =
  let neuron = Concatenate (Concatenate.create axis) in
  let nn = get_network input_node.(0) in
  let n = make_node ?name [|||] [|||] neuron None nn in
  add_node ?act_typ nn input_node n

(* I/O functions *)

let to_string nn =
  let s = ref (nn.nnid ^ "\n\n") in
  Array.iter
    (fun n ->
      let prev =
        Array.map (fun n -> n.name) n.prev |> Owl_utils_array.to_string
        (fun s -> s)
      in
      let next =
```

```
            Array.map (fun n -> n.name) n.next |> Owl_utils_array.to_string
            (fun s -> s)
        in
        s
          := !s
              ^ Printf.sprintf "\x1b[31m[ Node %s ]:\x1b[0m\n" n.name
              ^ Printf.sprintf "%s" (to_string n.neuron)
              ^ Printf.sprintf " prev:[%s] next:[%s]\n\n" prev next)
      nn.topo;
    !s

  let pp_network formatter nn =
    Format.open_box 0;
    Format.fprintf formatter "%s" (to_string nn);
    Format.close_box ()

  let print nn = pp_network Format.std_formatter nn

  let save ?(unsafe = false) nn f =
    if unsafe = true
    then (
      Owl_log.warn
      "Unsafely saved network can only be loaded back in exactly the same
      version of \
      OCaml and Owl.";
      Owl_io.marshal_to_file ~flags:[ Marshal.Closures ] (copy nn) f)
    else Owl_io.marshal_to_file (copy nn) f

  let load f : network = Owl_io.marshal_from_file f

  let save_weights nn f =
    let h = Hashtbl.create nn.size in
    Array.iter
      (fun n ->
        let ws = Neuron.save_weights n.neuron in
        Hashtbl.add h n.name ws)
      nn.topo;
    Owl_io.marshal_to_file h f
```

```
let load_weights nn f =
  let h = Owl_io.marshal_from_file f in
  Array.iter
    (fun n ->
      let ws = Hashtbl.find h n.name in
      Neuron.load_weights n.neuron ws)
    nn.topo

let make_subnetwork ?(copy = true) ?(make_inputs = [|||]) nn
output_names =
  let subnn = make_network 0 [|||] [|||] in
  let in_nodes = ref [] in
  (* collect neurons belonging to subnetwork *)
  let rec collect_subnn_nodes n acc =
    if List.exists (fun in_acc -> in_acc.name = n.name) acc
    then acc
    else if Array.mem n.name make_inputs
    then (
      let shape = get_out_shape n.neuron in
      let in_neur = Input (Input.create shape) in
      let new_in = make_node ~name:n.name [|||] [|||] in_neur None subnn in
      in_nodes := new_in :: !in_nodes;
      new_in :: acc)
    else (
      let neur = if copy then Neuron.copy n.neuron else n.neuron in
      let new_node = make_node ~name:n.name ~train:n.train [|||] [|||] neur
      None subnn in
      match neur with
      | Input _ ->
        in_nodes := new_node :: !in_nodes;
        new_node :: acc
      | _ ->
        let acc = new_node :: acc in
        Array.fold_left (fun a prev -> collect_subnn_nodes prev a)
        acc n.prev)
  in
```

```
let new_nodes =
  Array.fold_left
    (fun acc name -> collect_subnn_nodes (get_node nn name) acc)
    []
    output_names
in
(* sorts the new topology *)
let new_topo =
  Array.fold_left
    (fun acc n ->
      match List.find_opt (fun n' -> n'.name = n.name) new_nodes with
      | Some n' -> n' :: acc
      | None -> acc)
    []
    nn.topo
  |> List.rev
  |> Array.of_list
in
subnn.topo <- new_topo;
(* re-construct network structure *)
Array.iter
  (fun node' ->
    let node = get_node nn node'.name in
    if not (List.memq node' !in_nodes)
    then node'.prev <- Array.map (fun n -> get_node subnn n.name)
    node.prev;
    if not (Array.mem node.name output_names)
    then (
      (* only process nodes that are part of the subnetwork *)
      let next =
        Owl_utils_array.filter
          (fun n -> Array.exists (fun n' -> n'.name = n.name)
          subnn.topo)
          node.next
      in
```

```
      (* With custom input nodes, next could contain an input node. *)
        node'.next <- Array.map (fun n -> get_node subnn n.name) next);
      connect_to_parents node'.prev node')
    subnn.topo;
    (* TODO: Warn if not all names in in_names were used? *)
    subnn.roots <- Array.of_list !in_nodes;
    subnn.outputs <- Array.map (fun name -> get_node subnn name)
    output_names;
  subnn

(* training functions *)

(* generic minimisation functions
    forward: function to run the forward pass
    backward: function to run the backward pass
    update: function to update the weights according to the gradient
    save: function to save the model for checkpoint
*)
  let train_generic ?state ?params ?(init_model = true) nn x y =
    if init_model = true then init nn;
    let f = forward nn in
    let b = backward nn in
    let u = update nn in
    let s = save nn in
    let p =
      match params with
      | Some p -> p
      | None -> Optimise.Params.default ()
    in
    Optimise.minimise_network ?state p f b u s x y

  let train ?state ?params ?init_model nn x y =
  train_generic ?state ?params ?init_model nn (Arr x) (Arr y)
end

(* Make functor ends *)
```

E.2 Neuron Modules

Activation Module

```
module Activation = struct
  type typ =
    | Elu (* Exponential linear unit *)
    | Relu (* Rectified linear unit *)
    | Sigmoid (* Element-wise sigmoid *)
    | HardSigmoid (* Linear approximation of sigmoid *)
    | Softmax of int (* Softmax along specified axis *)
    | Softplus (* Element-wise softplus *)
    | Softsign (* Element-wise softsign *)
    | Tanh (* Element-wise tanh *)
    | Relu6 (* Element-wise relu6 *)
    | LeakyRelu of float (* Leaky version of a Rectified Linear Unit *)
    | TRelu of float (* Thresholded Rectified Linear Unit *)
    | Custom of (t -> t) (* Element-wise customised activation *)
    | None

  (* None activation *)

  type neuron_typ =
    { mutable activation : typ
    ; mutable in_shape : int array
    ; mutable out_shape : int array
    }

  let create activation = { activation; in_shape = [||]; out_shape = [||] }

  let connect out_shape l =
    l.in_shape <- Array.copy out_shape;
    l.out_shape <- Array.copy out_shape

  let run_activation x activation =
    match activation with
    | Elu        -> Maths.(relu x + (x |> neg |> relu |> neg |>
      exp) - _f 1.)
    | Relu       -> Maths.relu x
```

```
  | Sigmoid       -> Maths.sigmoid x
  | HardSigmoid -> Maths.(max2 (_f 0.) (min2 (_f 1.) ((_f 0.2 * x) +
    _f 0.5)))
  | Softmax a    -> Maths.softmax ~axis:a x
  | Softplus     -> Maths.softplus x
  | Softsign     -> Maths.softsign x
  | Tanh         -> Maths.tanh x
  | Relu6        -> Maths.(min2 (relu x) (_f 6.))
  | LeakyRelu a  -> Maths.(relu x - (_f a * (x |> neg |> relu)))
  | TRelu a      -> Maths.(relu (x - _f a))
  | Custom f     -> f x
  | None         -> x

let copy l = create l.activation

let run x l = run_activation x l.activation

let activation_to_string = function
  | Elu          -> Printf.sprintf "%s" "elu"
  | Relu         -> Printf.sprintf "%s" "relu"
  | Sigmoid      -> Printf.sprintf "%s" "sigmoid"
  | HardSigmoid -> Printf.sprintf "%s" "hard_sigmoid"
  | Softmax a    -> Printf.sprintf "%s %i" "softmax" a
  | Softplus     -> Printf.sprintf "%s" "softplus"
  | Softsign     -> Printf.sprintf "%s" "softsign"
  | Tanh         -> Printf.sprintf "%s" "tanh"
  | Relu6        -> Printf.sprintf "%s" "relu6"
  | LeakyRelu a -> Printf.sprintf "%s %g" "leaky_relu" a
  | TRelu a      -> Printf.sprintf "%s %g" "threshold_relu" a
  | Custom _     -> Printf.sprintf "%s" "customise"
  | None         -> Printf.sprintf "%s" "none"

let to_string l =
  let in_str = Owl_utils_array.to_string string_of_int l.in_shape in
  let act_str = activation_to_string l.activation in
  Printf.sprintf " Activation : %s in/out:[*,%s]\n" act_str in_str ^ ""

let to_name () = "activation"
end
```

Linear Module

```
module Recurrent = struct
  type neuron_typ =
    { mutable whh : t
    ; mutable wxh : t
    ; mutable why : t
    ; mutable bh : t
    ; mutable by : t
    ; mutable h : t
    ; mutable hiddens : int
    ; mutable act : Activation.typ
    ; mutable init_typ : Init.typ
    ; mutable in_shape : int array
    ; mutable out_shape : int array
    }

  let create ?time_steps ?inputs hiddens o act init_typ =
    let i =
      match inputs with
        | Some i -> i
        | None -> 0
    in
    let t =
      match time_steps with
        | Some i -> i
        | None -> 0
    in
    let h = hiddens in
    { whh = Mat.empty h h
    ; wxh = Mat.empty o h
    ; why = Mat.empty h o
    ; bh = Mat.empty 1 h
    ; by = Mat.empty 1 o
    ; h = Mat.empty o h
    ; hiddens
```

```
  ; act
  ; init_typ
  ; in_shape = [| t; i |]
  ; out_shape = [| o |]
  }

let connect out_shape l =
  assert (Array.(length out_shape = length l.in_shape));
  l.in_shape.(0) <- out_shape.(0);
  l.in_shape.(1) <- out_shape.(1)

let init l =
  let i = l.in_shape.(1) in
  let o = l.out_shape.(0) in
  let h = l.hiddens in
  l.whh <- Init.run l.init_typ [| h; h |] l.whh;
  l.wxh <- Init.run l.init_typ [| i; h |] l.wxh;
  l.why <- Init.run l.init_typ [| h; o |] l.why;
  l.bh <- Mat.zeros 1 h;
  l.by <- Mat.zeros 1 o

let reset l =
  Mat.reset l.whh;
  Mat.reset l.wxh;
  Mat.reset l.why;
  Mat.reset l.bh;
  Mat.reset l.by

let mktag t l =
  l.whh <- make_reverse l.whh t;
  l.wxh <- make_reverse l.wxh t;
  l.why <- make_reverse l.why t;
  l.bh <- make_reverse l.bh t;
  l.by <- make_reverse l.by t

let mkpar l = [| l.whh; l.wxh; l.why; l.bh; l.by |]

let mkpri l = [| primal l.whh; primal l.wxh; primal l.why; primal l.bh;
primal l.by |]
```

```
let mkadj l = [| adjval l.whh; adjval l.wxh; adjval l.why; adjval l.bh;
adjval l.by |]

let update l u =
  l.whh <- u.(0) |> primal';
  l.wxh <- u.(1) |> primal';
  l.why <- u.(2) |> primal';
  l.bh <- u.(3) |> primal';
  l.by <- u.(4) |> primal'

let copy l =
  let l' = create l.hiddens l.out_shape.(0) l.act l.init_typ in
  mkpri l |> Array.map copy_primal' |> update l';
  l'

let run x l =
  let s = shape x in
  l.h <- Mat.zeros s.(0) l.hiddens;
  let act x = Activation.run_activation x l.act in
  for i = 0 to l.in_shape.(0) - 1 do
    let t = Maths.get_slice [ []; [ i ]; [] ] x in
    let t = Maths.reshape t [| s.(0); s.(2) |] in
    (* recurrent logic, calculate the hidden state *)
    l.h <- act Maths.((l.h *@ l.whh) + (t *@ l.wxh) + l.bh)
  done;
  Maths.((l.h *@ l.why) + l.by)

let to_string l =
  let t = l.in_shape.(0) in
  let i = l.in_shape.(1) in
  let o = l.out_shape.(0) in
  let h = l.hiddens in
  Printf.sprintf " Recurrent : matrix in:(*,%i,%i) out:(*,%i) \n" t i o
  ^ Printf.sprintf " init : %s\n" (Init.to_string l.init_typ)
  ^ Printf.sprintf " params : %i\n" ((h * h) + (i * h) + (h * o) + h + o)
  ^ Printf.sprintf " whh : %i x %i\n" h h
  ^ Printf.sprintf " wxh : %i x %i\n" i h
```

```
        ^ Printf.sprintf " why : %i x %i\n" h o
        ^ Printf.sprintf " bh : %i x %i\n" 1 h
        ^ Printf.sprintf " by : %i x %i\n" 1 o
        ^ Printf.sprintf " act : %s\n" (Activation.activation_to_string l.act)

    let to_name () = "recurrent"
end
```

LSTM Module

```
module LSTM = struct
  type neuron_typ =
    { mutable wxi : t
    ; mutable whi : t
    ; mutable wxc : t
    ; mutable whc : t
    ; mutable wxf : t
    ; mutable whf : t
    ; mutable wxo : t
    ; mutable who : t
    ; mutable bi : t
    ; mutable bc : t
    ; mutable bf : t
    ; mutable bo : t
    ; mutable c : t
    ; mutable h : t
    ; mutable init_typ : Init.typ
    ; mutable in_shape : int array
    ; mutable out_shape : int array
    }

  let create ?time_steps ?inputs o init_typ =
    let i =
      match inputs with
        | Some i -> i
        | None -> 0
    in
```

```
let t =
 match time_steps with
 | Some i -> i
 | None -> 0
in
{ wxi = Mat.empty 0 o
; whi = Mat.empty o o
; wxc = Mat.empty 0 o
; whc = Mat.empty o o
; wxf = Mat.empty 0 o
; whf = Mat.empty o o
; wxo = Mat.empty 0 o
; who = Mat.empty o o
; bi = Mat.empty 1 o
; bc = Mat.empty 1 o
; bf = Mat.empty 1 o
; bo = Mat.empty 1 o
; c = Mat.empty 0 o
; h = Mat.empty 0 o
; init_typ
; in_shape = [| t; i |]
; out_shape = [| o |]
}

let connect out_shape l =
  assert (Array.(length out_shape = length l.in_shape));
  l.in_shape.(0) <- out_shape.(0);
  l.in_shape.(1) <- out_shape.(1)

let init l =
  let i = l.in_shape.(1) in
  let o = l.out_shape.(0) in
  l.wxi <- Init.run l.init_typ [| i; o |] l.wxi;
  l.whi <- Init.run l.init_typ [| o; o |] l.whi;
  l.wxc <- Init.run l.init_typ [| i; o |] l.wxc;
  l.whc <- Init.run l.init_typ [| o; o |] l.whc;
```

```
    l.wxf <- Init.run l.init_typ [| i; o |] l.wxf;
    l.whf <- Init.run l.init_typ [| o; o |] l.whf;
    l.wxo <- Init.run l.init_typ [| i; o |] l.wxo;
    l.who <- Init.run l.init_typ [| o; o |] l.who;
    l.bi <- Mat.zeros 1 o;
    l.bc <- Mat.zeros 1 o;
    l.bf <- Mat.zeros 1 o;
    l.bo <- Mat.zeros 1 o

let reset l =
  Mat.reset l.wxi;
  Mat.reset l.whi;
  Mat.reset l.wxc;
  Mat.reset l.whc;
  Mat.reset l.wxf;
  Mat.reset l.whf;
  Mat.reset l.wxo;
  Mat.reset l.who;
  Mat.reset l.bi;
  Mat.reset l.bc;
  Mat.reset l.bf;
  Mat.reset l.bo

let mktag t l =
  l.wxi <- make_reverse l.wxi t;
  l.whi <- make_reverse l.whi t;
  l.wxc <- make_reverse l.wxc t;
  l.whc <- make_reverse l.whc t;
  l.wxf <- make_reverse l.wxf t;
  l.whf <- make_reverse l.whf t;
  l.wxo <- make_reverse l.wxo t;
  l.who <- make_reverse l.who t;
  l.bi <- make_reverse l.bi t;
  l.bc <- make_reverse l.bc t;
  l.bf <- make_reverse l.bf t;
  l.bo <- make_reverse l.bo t
```

```
let mkpar l =
  [| l.wxi; l.whi; l.wxc; l.whc; l.wxf; l.whf; l.wxo; l.who; l.bi; l.bc;
  l.bf; l.bo |]

let mkpri l =
  [| primal l.wxi
  ; primal l.whi
  ; primal l.wxc
  ; primal l.whc
  ; primal l.wxf
  ; primal l.whf
  ; primal l.wxo
  ; primal l.who
  ; primal l.bi
  ; primal l.bc
  ; primal l.bf
  ; primal l.bo
  |]

let mkadj l =
  [| adjval l.wxi
  ; adjval l.whi
  ; adjval l.wxc
  ; adjval l.whc
  ; adjval l.wxf
  ; adjval l.whf
  ; adjval l.wxo
  ; adjval l.who
  ; adjval l.bi
  ; adjval l.bc
  ; adjval l.bf
  ; adjval l.bo
  |]

let update l u =
  l.wxi <- u.(0) |> primal';
  l.whi <- u.(1) |> primal';
```

```
    l.wxc <- u.(2) |> primal';
    l.whc <- u.(3) |> primal';
    l.wxf <- u.(4) |> primal';
    l.whf <- u.(5) |> primal';
    l.wxo <- u.(6) |> primal';
    l.who <- u.(7) |> primal';
    l.bi <- u.(8) |> primal';
    l.bc <- u.(9) |> primal';
    l.bf <- u.(10) |> primal';
    l.bo <- u.(11) |> primal'

let copy l =
    let l' = create l.out_shape.(0) l.init_typ in
    mkpri l |> Array.map copy_primal' |> update l';
    l'

let run x l =
    let s = shape x in
    l.h <- Mat.zeros s.(0) l.out_shape.(0);
    l.c <- Mat.zeros s.(0) l.out_shape.(0);
    for i = 0 to l.in_shape.(0) - 1 do
      let t = Maths.get_slice [ []; [ i ]; [] ] x in
      let t = Maths.reshape t [| s.(0); s.(2) |] in
      (* lstm logic, calculate the output *)
      let i = Maths.((t *@ l.wxi) + (l.h *@ l.whi) + l.bi |> sigmoid) in
      let c' = Maths.((t *@ l.wxc) + (l.h *@ l.whc) + l.bc |> tanh) in
      let f = Maths.((t *@ l.wxf) + (l.h *@ l.whf) + l.bf |> sigmoid) in
      l.c <- Maths.((i * c') + (f * l.c));
      let o = Maths.((t *@ l.wxo) + (l.h *@ l.who) + l.bo |> sigmoid) in
      l.h <- Maths.(o * tanh l.c)
    done;
    l.h

let to_string l =
    let t = l.in_shape.(0) in
    let i = l.in_shape.(1) in
```

```ocaml
  let o = l.out_shape.(0) in
  Printf.sprintf " LSTM : in:(*,%i,%i) out:(*,%i) \n" i t o
  ^ Printf.sprintf " init : %s\n" (Init.to_string l.init_typ)
  ^ Printf.sprintf
      " params : %i\n"
      ((i * o)
      + (o * o)
      + (i * o)
      + (o * o)
      + (i * o)
      + (o * o)
      + (i * o)
      + (o * o)
      + o
      + o
      + o
      + o)
  ^ Printf.sprintf " wxi : %i x %i\n" i o
  ^ Printf.sprintf " whi : %i x %i\n" o o
  ^ Printf.sprintf " wxc : %i x %i\n" i o
  ^ Printf.sprintf " whc : %i x %i\n" o o
  ^ Printf.sprintf " wxf : %i x %i\n" i o
  ^ Printf.sprintf " whf : %i x %i\n" o o
  ^ Printf.sprintf " wxo : %i x %i\n" i o
  ^ Printf.sprintf " who : %i x %i\n" o o
  ^ Printf.sprintf " bi : %i x %i\n" 1 o
  ^ Printf.sprintf " bc : %i x %i\n" 1 o
  ^ Printf.sprintf " bf : %i x %i\n" 1 o
  ^ Printf.sprintf " bo : %i x %i\n" 1 o
  ^ ""

  let to_name () = "lstm"
end
```

Conv2D Module

```
module Conv2D = struct
  type neuron_typ =
    { mutable w : t
    ; mutable b : t
    ; mutable kernel : int array
    ; mutable stride : int array
    ; mutable padding : padding
    ; mutable init_typ : Init.typ
    ; mutable in_shape : int array
    ; mutable out_shape : int array
    }

  let create ?inputs padding kernel stride init_typ =
    let w, h, i, o = kernel.(0), kernel.(1), kernel.(2), kernel.(3) in
    let in_shape =
      match inputs with
      | Some a ->
        assert (i = a.(2));
        a
      | None -> [| 0; 0; i |]
    in
    { w = Arr.empty [| w; h; i; o |]
    ; b = Arr.empty [| o |]
    ; kernel
    ; stride
    ; padding
    ; init_typ
    ; in_shape
    ; out_shape = [| 0; 0; o |]
    }

  let connect out_shape l =
    assert (Array.(length out_shape = length l.in_shape));
    assert (out_shape.(2) = l.in_shape.(2));
    l.in_shape.(0) <- out_shape.(0);
```

```
    l.in_shape.(1) <- out_shape.(1);
    let out_cols, out_rows =
      Owl_utils_infer_shape.calc_conv2d_output_shape
        l.padding
        l.in_shape.(0)
        l.in_shape.(1)
        l.kernel.(0)
        l.kernel.(1)
        l.stride.(0)
        l.stride.(1)
    in
    l.out_shape.(0) <- out_cols;
    l.out_shape.(1) <- out_rows

let init l =
  l.w <- Init.run l.init_typ l.kernel l.w;
  l.b <- Arr.(zeros (shape l.b))

let reset l =
  Arr.reset l.w;
  Arr.reset l.b

let mktag t l =
  l.w <- make_reverse l.w t;
  l.b <- make_reverse l.b t

let mkpar l = [| l.w; l.b |]

let mkpri l = [| primal l.w; primal l.b |]

let mkadj l = [| adjval l.w; adjval l.b |]

let update l u =
  l.w <- u.(0) |> primal';
  l.b <- u.(1) |> primal'

let copy l =
  let l' = create l.padding l.kernel l.stride l.init_typ in
  mkpri l |> Array.map copy_primal' |> update l';
  l'
```

```
let run x l = Maths.(NN.conv2d ~padding:l.padding x l.w l.stride + l.b)

  let to_string l =
    let ws = Arr.shape l.w in
    let bn = Arr.shape l.b in
    let in_str = Owl_utils_array.to_string string_of_int l.in_shape in
    let out_str = Owl_utils_array.to_string string_of_int l.out_shape in
    Printf.sprintf " Conv2D : tensor in:[*;%s] out:[*,%s]\n" in_str out_str
    ^ Printf.sprintf " init : %s\n" (Init.to_string l.init_typ)
    ^ Printf.sprintf " params : %i\n" ((ws.(0) * ws.(1) * ws.(2) * ws.(3))
    + bn.(0))
    ^ Printf.sprintf " kernel : %i x %i x %i x %i\n" ws.(0) ws.(1)
    ws.(2) ws.(3)
    ^ Printf.sprintf " b : %i\n" bn.(0)
    ^ Printf.sprintf " stride : [%i; %i]\n" l.stride.(0) l.stride.(1)
    ^ ""

  let to_name () = "conv2d"
end
```

DilatedConv2D Module

```
module DilatedConv2D = struct
  type neuron_typ =
    { mutable w : t
    ; mutable b : t
    ; mutable kernel : int array
    ; mutable stride : int array
    ; mutable rate : int array
    ; mutable padding : padding
    ; mutable init_typ : Init.typ
    ; mutable in_shape : int array
    ; mutable out_shape : int array
    }

  let create ?inputs padding kernel stride rate init_typ =
    let w, h, i, o = kernel.(0), kernel.(1), kernel.(2), kernel.(3) in
    let in_shape =
```

```
    match inputs with
      | Some a ->
        assert (i = a.(2));
        a
      | None -> [| 0; 0; i |]
  in
  { w = Arr.empty [| w; h; i; o |]
  ; b = Arr.empty [| o |]
  ; kernel
  ; stride
  ; rate
  ; padding
  ; init_typ
  ; in_shape
  ; out_shape = [| 0; 0; o |]
  }

let connect out_shape l =
  assert (Array.(length out_shape = length l.in_shape));
  assert (out_shape.(2) = l.in_shape.(2));
  l.in_shape.(0) <- out_shape.(0);
  l.in_shape.(1) <- out_shape.(1);
  let out_cols, out_rows =
    let col_up = l.kernel.(0) + ((l.kernel.(0) - 1) * (l.rate.
    (0) - 1)) in
    let row_up = l.kernel.(1) + ((l.kernel.(1) - 1) * (l.rate.
    (1) - 1)) in
    Owl_utils_infer_shape.calc_conv2d_output_shape
      l.padding
      l.in_shape.(0)
      l.in_shape.(1)
      col_up
      row_up
      l.stride.(0)
      l.stride.(1)
  in
```

```
  l.out_shape.(0) <- out_cols;
  l.out_shape.(1) <- out_rows

let init l =
  l.w <- Init.run l.init_typ l.kernel l.w;
  l.b <- Arr.(zeros (shape l.b))

let reset l =
  Arr.reset l.w;
  Arr.reset l.b

let mktag t l =
  l.w <- make_reverse l.w t;
  l.b <- make_reverse l.b t

let mkpar l = [| l.w; l.b |]

let mkpri l = [| primal l.w; primal l.b |]

let mkadj l = [| adjval l.w; adjval l.b |]

let update l u =
  l.w <- u.(0) |> primal';
  l.b <- u.(1) |> primal'

let copy l =
  let l' = create l.padding l.kernel l.stride l.rate l.init_typ in
  mkpri l |> Array.map copy_primal' |> update l';
  l'

let run x l = Maths.(NN.dilated_conv2d ~padding:l.padding x l.w l.stride
l.rate + l.b)

let to_string l =
  let ws = Arr.shape l.w in
  let bn = Arr.shape l.b in
  let in_str = Owl_utils_array.to_string string_of_int l.in_shape in
  let out_str = Owl_utils_array.to_string string_of_int l.out_shape in
  Printf.sprintf " DilateConv2D : tensor in:[*;%s] out:[*,%s]\n" in_
  str out_str
```

```
       ^ Printf.sprintf " init : %s\n" (Init.to_string l.init_typ)
       ^ Printf.sprintf " params : %i\n" ((ws.(0) * ws.(1) * ws.(2) * ws.(3))
       + bn.(0))
       ^ Printf.sprintf " kernel : %i x %i x %i x %i\n" ws.(0) ws.(1)
       ws.(2) ws.(3)
       ^ Printf.sprintf " b : %i\n" bn.(0)
       ^ Printf.sprintf " stride : [%i; %i]\n" l.stride.(0) l.stride.(1)
       ^ Printf.sprintf " rate : [%i; %i]\n" l.rate.(0) l.rate.(1)
       ^ ""

  let to_name () = "dilated_conv2d"
end
```

TransposeConv2D Module

```
module TransposeConv2D = struct
  type neuron_typ =
    { mutable w : t
    ; mutable b : t
    ; mutable kernel : int array
    ; mutable stride : int array
    ; mutable padding : padding
    ; mutable init_typ : Init.typ
    ; mutable in_shape : int array
    ; mutable out_shape : int array
    }

  let create ?inputs padding kernel stride init_typ =
    let w, h, i, o = kernel.(0), kernel.(1), kernel.(2), kernel.(3) in
    let in_shape =
      match inputs with
      | Some a ->
        assert (i = a.(2));
        a
      | None -> [| 0; 0; i |]
    in
    { w = Arr.empty [| w; h; i; o |]
```

```
  ; b = Arr.empty [| o |]
  ; kernel
  ; stride
  ; padding
  ; init_typ
  ; in_shape
  ; out_shape = [| 0; 0; o |]
  }

let connect out_shape l =
  assert (Array.(length out_shape = length l.in_shape));
  assert (out_shape.(2) = l.in_shape.(2));
  l.in_shape.(0) <- out_shape.(0);
  l.in_shape.(1) <- out_shape.(1);
  let out_cols, out_rows =
    Owl_utils_infer_shape.calc_transpose_conv2d_output_shape
      l.padding
      l.in_shape.(0)
      l.in_shape.(1)
      l.kernel.(0)
      l.kernel.(1)
      l.stride.(0)
      l.stride.(1)
  in
  l.out_shape.(0) <- out_cols;
  l.out_shape.(1) <- out_rows

let init l =
  l.w <- Init.run l.init_typ l.kernel l.w;
  l.b <- Arr.(zeros (shape l.b))

let reset l =
  Arr.reset l.w;
  Arr.reset l.b

let mktag t l =
  l.w <- make_reverse l.w t;
  l.b <- make_reverse l.b t
```

```
let mkpar l = [| l.w; l.b |]

let mkpri l = [| primal l.w; primal l.b |]

let mkadj l = [| adjval l.w; adjval l.b |]

let update l u =
  l.w <- u.(0) |> primal';
  l.b <- u.(1) |> primal'

let copy l =
  let l' = create l.padding l.kernel l.stride l.init_typ in
  mkpri l |> Array.map copy_primal' |> update l';
  l'

let run x l = Maths.(NN.transpose_conv2d ~padding:l.padding x l.w
l.stride + l.b)

let to_string l =
  let ws = Arr.shape l.w in
  let bn = Arr.shape l.b in
  let in_str = Owl_utils_array.to_string string_of_int l.in_shape in
  let out_str = Owl_utils_array.to_string string_of_int l.out_shape in
  Printf.sprintf " TransposeConv2D : tensor in:[*;%s] out:[*,%s]\n" in_
  str out_str
  ^ Printf.sprintf " init : %s\n" (Init.to_string l.init_typ)
  ^ Printf.sprintf " params : %i\n" ((ws.(0) * ws.(1) * ws.(2) * ws.(3))
  + bn.(0))
  ^ Printf.sprintf " kernel : %i x %i x %i x %i\n" ws.(0) ws.(1)
  ws.(2) ws.(3)
  ^ Printf.sprintf " b : %i\n" bn.(0)
  ^ Printf.sprintf " stride : [%i; %i]\n" l.stride.(0) l.stride.(1)
  ^ ""

let to_name () = "transpose_conv2d"
end
```

FullyConnected Module

```
module FullyConnected = struct
  type neuron_typ =
    { mutable w : t
    ; mutable b : t
    ; mutable init_typ : Init.typ
    ; mutable in_shape : int array
    ; mutable out_shape : int array
    }

  let create ?inputs o init_typ =
    let in_shape =
      match inputs with
      | Some i -> [| i |]
      | None -> [| o |]
    in
    { w = Mat.empty 0 o; b = Mat.empty 1 o; init_typ; in_shape; out_shape =
    [| o |] }

  let connect out_shape l =
    assert (Array.length out_shape > 0);
    l.in_shape <- Array.copy out_shape

  let init l =
    let m = Array.fold_left (fun a b -> a * b) 1 l.in_shape in
    let n = l.out_shape.(0) in
    l.w <- Init.run l.init_typ [| m; n |] l.w;
    l.b <- Mat.zeros 1 n

  let reset l =
    Mat.reset l.w;
    Mat.reset l.b

  let mktag t l =
    l.w <- make_reverse l.w t;
    l.b <- make_reverse l.b t
```

```
  let mkpar l = [| l.w; l.b |]

  let mkpri l = [| primal l.w; primal l.b |]

  let mkadj l = [| adjval l.w; adjval l.b |]

  let update l u =
    l.w <- u.(0) |> primal';
    l.b <- u.(1) |> primal'

  let copy l =
    let l' = create l.out_shape.(0) l.init_typ in
    mkpri l |> Array.map copy_primal' |> update l';
    l'

  let run x l =
    let m = Mat.row_num l.w in
    let n = Arr.numel x / m in
    let x = Maths.reshape x [| n; m |] in
    let y = Maths.((x *@ l.w) + l.b) in
    y

  let to_string l =
    let wm = Array.fold_left (fun a b -> a * b) 1 l.in_shape in
    let wn = l.out_shape.(0) in
    let bn = l.out_shape.(0) in
    let in_str = Owl_utils_array.to_string string_of_int l.in_shape in
    Printf.sprintf
    " FullyConnected : tensor in:[*,%s] matrix out:(*,%i)\n"
    in_str
    l.out_shape.(0)
    ^ Printf.sprintf " init : %s\n" (Init.to_string l.init_typ)
    ^ Printf.sprintf " params : %i\n" ((wm * wn) + bn)
    ^ Printf.sprintf " w : %i x %i\n" wm wn
    ^ Printf.sprintf " b : %i x %i\n" 1 bn
    ^ ""

  let to_name () = "fullyconnected"
end
```

MaxPool2D Module

```
module MaxPool2D = struct
  type neuron_typ =
    { mutable padding : padding
    ; mutable kernel : int array
    ; mutable stride : int array
    ; mutable in_shape : int array
    ; mutable out_shape : int array
    }

  let create padding kernel stride =
    { padding; kernel; stride; in_shape = [| 0; 0; 0 |]; out_shape = [| 0;
    0; 0 |] }

  let connect out_shape l =
    assert (Array.(length out_shape = length l.in_shape));
    l.in_shape.(0) <- out_shape.(0);
    l.in_shape.(1) <- out_shape.(1);
    l.in_shape.(2) <- out_shape.(2);
    let out_cols, out_rows =
      Owl_utils_infer_shape.calc_conv2d_output_shape
        l.padding
        l.in_shape.(0)
        l.in_shape.(1)
        l.kernel.(0)
        l.kernel.(1)
        l.stride.(0)
        l.stride.(1)
    in
    l.out_shape.(0) <- out_cols;
    l.out_shape.(1) <- out_rows;
    l.out_shape.(2) <- out_shape.(2)

  let copy l = create l.padding l.kernel l.stride

  let run x l = NN.max_pool2d l.padding x l.kernel l.stride
```

```
let to_string l =
  let padding_s =
    match l.padding with
    | SAME -> "SAME"
    | VALID -> "VALID"
  in
  Printf.sprintf
    " MaxPool2D : tensor in:[*,%i,%i,%i] out:[*,%i,%i,%i]\n"
    l.in_shape.(0)
    l.in_shape.(1)
    l.in_shape.(2)
    l.out_shape.(0)
    l.out_shape.(1)
    l.out_shape.(2)
  ^ Printf.sprintf " padding : %s\n" padding_s
  ^ Printf.sprintf " kernel : [%i; %i]\n" l.kernel.(0) l.kernel.(1)
  ^ Printf.sprintf " stride : [%i; %i]\n" l.stride.(0) l.stride.(1)
  ^ ""

  let to_name () = "maxpool2d"
end
```

AvgPool2D Module

```
module AvgPool2D = struct
  type neuron_typ =
    { mutable padding : padding
    ; mutable kernel : int array
    ; mutable stride : int array
    ; mutable in_shape : int array
    ; mutable out_shape : int array
    }

  let create padding kernel stride =
    { padding; kernel; stride; in_shape = [| 0; 0; 0 |]; out_shape = [| 0;
    0; 0 |] }
```

```
let connect out_shape l =
  assert (Array.(length out_shape = length l.in_shape));
  l.in_shape.(0) <- out_shape.(0);
  l.in_shape.(1) <- out_shape.(1);
  l.in_shape.(2) <- out_shape.(2);
  let out_cols, out_rows =
    Owl_utils_infer_shape.calc_conv2d_output_shape
    l.padding
    l.in_shape.(0)
    l.in_shape.(1)
    l.kernel.(0)
    l.kernel.(1)
    l.stride.(0)
    l.stride.(1)
  in
  l.out_shape.(0) <- out_cols;
  l.out_shape.(1) <- out_rows;
  l.out_shape.(2) <- out_shape.(2)

let copy l = create l.padding l.kernel l.stride

let run x l = NN.avg_pool2d l.padding x l.kernel l.stride

let to_string l =
  let padding_s =
    match l.padding with
    | SAME -> "SAME"
    | VALID -> "VALID"
  in
  Printf.sprintf
    " AvgPool2D : tensor in:[*,%i,%i,%i] out:[*,%i,%i,%i]\n"
    l.in_shape.(0)
    l.in_shape.(1)
    l.in_shape.(2)
    l.out_shape.(0)
    l.out_shape.(1)
    l.out_shape.(2)
```

```
        ^ Printf.sprintf " padding : %s\n" padding_s
        ^ Printf.sprintf " kernel : [%i; %i]\n" l.kernel.(0) l.kernel.(1)
        ^ Printf.sprintf " stride : [%i; %i]\n" l.stride.(0) l.stride.(1)
        ^ ""

  let to_name () = "avgpool2d"
end
```

UpSampling2D Module

```
module UpSampling2D = struct
  type neuron_typ =
    { mutable size : int array
    ; mutable in_shape : int array
    ; mutable out_shape : int array
    }

  let create size = { size; in_shape = [| 0; 0; 0 |]; out_shape = [| 0;
  0; 0 |] }

  let connect out_shape l =
    assert (Array.(length out_shape = length l.in_shape));
    l.in_shape.(0) <- out_shape.(0);
    l.in_shape.(1) <- out_shape.(1);
    l.in_shape.(2) <- out_shape.(2);
    l.out_shape.(0) <- l.in_shape.(0) * l.size.(0);
    l.out_shape.(1) <- l.in_shape.(1) * l.size.(1);
    l.out_shape.(2) <- out_shape.(2)

  let copy l = create l.size

  let run x l = NN.(upsampling2d x l.size)

  let to_string l =
    Printf.sprintf
      " UpSampling2D : tensor in:[*,%i,%i,%i] out:[*,%i,%i,%i]\n"
      l.in_shape.(0)
      l.in_shape.(1)
      l.in_shape.(2)
```

```
      l.out_shape.(0)
      l.out_shape.(1)
      l.out_shape.(2)
    ^ Printf.sprintf " size : [%i; %i]\n" l.size.(0) l.size.(1)
    ^ ""

  let to_name () = "upsampling2d"
end
```

Dropout Module

```
module Dropout = struct
  type neuron_typ =
    { mutable rate : float
    ; mutable in_shape : int array
    ; mutable out_shape : int array
    }

  let create rate = { rate; in_shape = [||]; out_shape = [||] }

  let connect out_shape l =
    l.in_shape <- Array.copy out_shape;
    l.out_shape <- Array.copy out_shape

  let copy l = create l.rate

  let run x l =
    let a = _f (1. /. (1. -. l.rate)) in
    let b = NN.(dropout ~rate:l.rate x) in
    Maths.(a * b)

  let to_string l =
    let in_str = Owl_utils_array.to_string string_of_int l.in_shape in
    let out_str = Owl_utils_array.to_string string_of_int l.out_shape in
    Printf.sprintf " Dropout : in:[*,%s] out:[*,%s]\n" in_str out_str
    ^ Printf.sprintf " rate : %g\n" l.rate

  let to_name () = "dropout"
end
```

GaussianDropout Module

```
module GaussianDropout = struct
  type neuron_typ =
    { mutable rate : float
    ; mutable in_shape : int array
    ; mutable out_shape : int array
    }

  let create rate = { rate; in_shape = [||]; out_shape = [||] }

  let connect out_shape l =
    l.in_shape <- Array.copy out_shape;
    l.out_shape <- Array.copy out_shape

  let copy l = create l.rate

  let run x l =
    let s = shape x in
    let sigma = Stdlib.sqrt (l.rate /. (1. -. l.rate)) in
    let a =
      match primal' x with
      | Arr _ -> Arr.gaussian ~sigma:(A.float_to_elt sigma) s
      | _ -> failwith "owl_neural_neuron:gaussiandropout:run"
    in
    Maths.(x * (a + _f 1.))

  let to_string l =
    let in_str = Owl_utils_array.to_string string_of_int l.in_shape in
    let out_str = Owl_utils_array.to_string string_of_int l.out_shape in
    Printf.sprintf " GaussianDropout : in:[*,%s] out:[*,%s]\n" in_
    str out_str
      ^ Printf.sprintf " rate : %g\n" l.rate

  let to_name () = "gaussian_dropout"
end
```

AlphaDropout Module

```
module AlphaDropout = struct
  type neuron_typ =
    { mutable rate : float
    ; mutable in_shape : int array
    ; mutable out_shape : int array
    }

  let create rate = { rate; in_shape = [||]; out_shape = [||] }

  let connect out_shape l =
    l.in_shape <- Array.copy out_shape;
    l.out_shape <- Array.copy out_shape

  let copy l = create l.rate

  let run x l =
    (* parameters of affine transformation *)
    let alpha = 1.6732632423543772848170429916717 in
    let scale = 1.0507009873554804934193349852946 in
    let p = -.alpha *. scale in
    let a = ((1. -. l.rate) *. (1. +. (l.rate *. (p ** 2.)))) ** -0.5 in
    let b = -.a *. p *. l.rate in
    let s = shape x in
    let mask =
      match primal' x with
      | Arr _ -> Arr A.(bernoulli ~p:(A.float_to_elt (1. -. l.rate)) s)
      | _ -> failwith "owl_neural_neuron:alphadropout:run"
    in
    let p = _f p in
    let a = _f a in
    let b = _f b in
    let x = Maths.((x * mask) + (p * (_f 1. - mask))) in
    Maths.((a * x) + b)

  let to_string l =
    let in_str = Owl_utils_array.to_string string_of_int l.in_shape in
    let out_str = Owl_utils_array.to_string string_of_int l.out_shape in
```

```
    Printf.sprintf " AlphaDropout : in:[*,%s] out:[*,%s]\n" in_str out_str
    ^ Printf.sprintf " rate : %g\n" l.rate

  let to_name () = "alpha_dropout"
end
```

Flatten Module

```
module Flatten = struct
  type neuron_typ =
    { mutable in_shape : int array
    ; mutable out_shape : int array
    }

  let create () = { in_shape = [||]; out_shape = [||] }

  let connect out_shape l =
    let o = Array.fold_left (fun a b -> a * b) 1 out_shape in
      l.in_shape <- Array.copy out_shape;
      l.out_shape <- [| o |]

  let copy _l = create ()

  let run x l = Maths.reshape x [| (shape x).(0); l.out_shape.(0) |]

  let to_string l =
    let in_str = Owl_utils_array.to_string string_of_int l.in_shape in
    Printf.sprintf " Flatten : in:[*,%s] out:[*,%i]\n" in_str l.out_
    shape.(0)

  let to_name () = "flatten"
end
```

Slice Module

```
module Slice = struct
  type neuron_typ =
    { mutable in_shape : int array
    ; mutable out_shape : int array
    ; mutable slice : int list list
    }
```

```ocaml
  let create slice = { in_shape = [|||]; out_shape = [|||]; slice }

  let connect out_shape l =
    assert (List.length l.slice <= Array.length out_shape);
    (* Calculate the output shape based on input and slice *)
    l.in_shape <- Array.copy out_shape;
    l.out_shape <- Owl_utils_infer_shape.slice out_shape l.slice

  let copy l = create l.slice

  let run x l = Maths.get_slice ([] :: l.slice) x

  let to_string l =
    let in_str = Owl_utils_array.to_string string_of_int l.in_shape in
    let out_str = Owl_utils_array.to_string string_of_int l.out_shape in
    let slice_str =
      List.mapi
        (fun i l ->
           let s = List.map string_of_int l |> String.concat "; " in
           Printf.sprintf "%i:[%s]" i s)
        l.slice
      |> String.concat " "
    in
    Printf.sprintf " Slice : in:[*,%s] out:[*,%s]\n" in_str out_str
    ^ Printf.sprintf " Axes : %s\n" slice_str

  let to_name () = "slice"
end
```

Add Module

```ocaml
module Add = struct
  type neuron_typ =
    { mutable in_shape : int array
    ; mutable out_shape : int array
    }

  let create () = { in_shape = [|||]; out_shape = [|||] }
```

```
let connect out_shapes l =
  Array.iter (fun s -> assert (s = out_shapes.(0))) out_shapes;
  l.in_shape <- Array.copy out_shapes.(0);
  l.out_shape <- Array.copy out_shapes.(0)

let copy _l = create ()

let run x _l =
  let n = Array.length x in
  (* at least two inputs *)
  assert (n > 1);
  let acc = ref x.(0) in
  for i = 1 to n - 1 do
    acc := Maths.(!acc + x. (i))
  done;
  !acc

let to_string l =
  let in_str = Owl_utils_array.to_string string_of_int l.in_shape in
  let out_str = Owl_utils_array.to_string string_of_int l.out_shape in
  Printf.sprintf " Add : in:[*,%s] out:[*,%s]\n" in_str out_str

let to_name () = "add"
end
```

Mul Module

```
module Mul = struct
  type neuron_typ =
    { mutable in_shape : int array
    ; mutable out_shape : int array
    }

  let create () = { in_shape = [||]; out_shape = [||] }

  let connect out_shapes l =
    Array.iter (fun s -> assert (s = out_shapes.(0))) out_shapes;
    l.in_shape <- Array.copy out_shapes.(0);
    l.out_shape <- Array.copy out_shapes.(0)
```

```
let copy _l = create ()

let run x _l =
  let n = Array.length x in
  (* at least two inputs *)
  assert (n > 1);
  let acc = ref x.(0) in
  for i = 1 to n - 1 do
    acc := Maths.(!acc * x. (i))
  done;
  !acc

let to_string l =
  let in_str = Owl_utils_array.to_string string_of_int l.in_shape in
  let out_str = Owl_utils_array.to_string string_of_int l.out_shape in
  Printf.sprintf " Multiply : in:[*,%s] out:[*,%s]\n" in_str out_str

let to_name () = "mul"
end
```

Dot Module

```
module Dot = struct
  type neuron_typ =
  { mutable in_shape : int array
  ; mutable out_shape : int array
  }

let create () = { in_shape = [||]; out_shape = [||] }

let connect out_shapes l =
  (* for dot neuron, two matrices must have [*,m][m,n] shape *)
  let m = out_shapes.(1).(0) in
  let n = out_shapes.(1).(1) in
  assert (m = out_shapes.(0).(1));
  l.in_shape <- [| m; n |];
  l.out_shape <- [| n |]

let copy _l = create ()
```

```
let run x _l =
  assert (Array.length x = 2);
  Maths.(x.(0) *@ x.(1))

let to_string l =
  let m = l.in_shape.(0) in
  let n = l.in_shape.(1) in
  Printf.sprintf " Dot : in:[*,%i] [%i,%i] out:[*,%i]\n" m m n n

let to_name () = "dot"
end
```

Max Module

```
module Max = struct
  type neuron_typ =
    { mutable in_shape : int array
    ; mutable out_shape : int array
    }

  let create () = { in_shape = [||]; out_shape = [||] }

  let connect out_shapes l =
    Array.iter (fun s -> assert (s = out_shapes.(0))) out_shapes;
    l.in_shape <- Array.copy out_shapes.(0);
    l.out_shape <- Array.copy out_shapes.(0)

  let copy _l = create ()

  let run x _l =
    let n = Array.length x in
    (* at least two inputs *)
    assert (n > 1);
    let acc = ref x.(0) in
    for i = 1 to n - 1 do
      acc := Maths.(max2 !acc x. (i))
    done;
    !acc
```

```
  let to_string l =
    let in_str = Owl_utils_array.to_string string_of_int l.in_shape in
    let out_str = Owl_utils_array.to_string string_of_int l.out_shape in
    Printf.sprintf " Max : in:[*,%s] out:[*,%s]\n" in_str out_str

  let to_name () = "max"
end
```

Concatenate Module

```
module Concatenate = struct
  type neuron_typ =
    { mutable axis : int
    ; mutable in_shape : int array
    ; mutable out_shape : int array
    }

  let create axis = { axis; in_shape = [||]; out_shape = [||] }

  let connect out_shapes l =
    let s0 = out_shapes.(0) in
    let _d = ref 0 in
    Array.iter
      (fun s1 ->
        Array.iteri
          (fun i d -> if i + 1 <> l.axis then assert (d = s0. (i)) else _d
          := !_d + d)
          s1)
      out_shapes;
    l.in_shape <- Array.copy s0;
    l.out_shape <- Array.copy s0;
    (* should not concatenate along batchs axis *)
    assert (l.axis > 0);
    l.in_shape.(l.axis - 1) <- -1;
    l.out_shape.(l.axis - 1) <- !_d

  let copy l = create l.axis
```

```
let run x l =
  let n = Array.length x in
  (* at least two inputs *)
  assert (n > 1);
  let acc = ref x.(0) in
  for i = 1 to n - 1 do
    acc := Maths.(concat ~axis:l.axis !acc x. (i))
  done;
  !acc

let to_string l =
  let in_str =
    Owl_utils_array.to_string
      (fun i -> if i = -1 then "*" else string_of_int i)
      l.in_shape
  in
  let out_str = Owl_utils_array.to_string string_of_int l.out_shape in
  Printf.sprintf " Concatenate : in:[*,%s] out:[*,%s]\n" in_str out_str
  ^ Printf.sprintf " axis : %i\n" l.axis
  ^ ""

let to_name () = "concatenate"
end
```

Embedding Module

```
module Embedding = struct
  type neuron_typ =
    { mutable w : t
    ; mutable init_typ : Init.typ
    ; mutable in_dim : int
    ; mutable in_shape : int array
    ; mutable out_shape : int array
    }

  let create ?inputs in_dim out_dim init_typ =
    let i =
      match inputs with
```

```
    | Some i -> i
    | None -> 0
  in
  { w = Mat.empty 0 0
  ; init_typ
  ; in_dim
  ; in_shape = [| i |]
  ; out_shape = [| i; out_dim |]
  }

let connect out_shape l =
  assert (Array.(length out_shape = 1));
  l.in_shape.(0) <- out_shape.(0);
  l.out_shape.(0) <- out_shape.(0)

let init l =
  let m = l.in_dim in
  let n = l.out_shape.(1) in
  l.w <- Init.run l.init_typ [| m; n |] l.w

let reset l = Mat.reset l.w

let mktag t l = l.w <- make_reverse l.w t

let mkpar l = [| l.w |]

let mkpri l = [| primal l.w |]

let mkadj l = [| adjval l.w |]

let update l u = l.w <- u.(0) |> primal'

let copy l =
  let l' = create l.in_dim l.out_shape.(1) l.init_typ in
  mkpri l |> Array.map copy_primal' |> update l';
  l'

let run x l =
  let x = primal' x |> unpack_arr in
  let s = A.shape x in
```

```ocaml
    let m, n = s.(0), s.(1) in
    let y = A.one_hot l.in_dim (A.reshape x [| m * n |]) in
    let y = Maths.(Arr y *@ l.w) in
    Maths.reshape y [| m; n; l.out_shape.(1) |]

  let to_string l =
    let wm, wn = l.in_dim, l.out_shape.(1) in
    Printf.sprintf
    " Embedding : matrix in:(*,%i) out:(*,%i,%i) \n"
    l.in_shape.(0)
    l.out_shape.(0)
    l.out_shape.(1)
    ^ Printf.sprintf " init : %s\n" (Init.to_string l.init_typ)
    ^ Printf.sprintf " in_dim : %i\n" l.in_dim
    ^ Printf.sprintf " params : %i\n" (wm * wn)
    ^ Printf.sprintf " w : %i x %i\n" wm wn
    ^ ""

  let to_name () = "embedding"
end
```

APPENDIX F

Actor System for Distributed Computing

F.1 MapReduce Engine

Interface

```
(*
 * Actor - Parallel & Distributed Engine of Owl System
 * Copyright (c) 2016-2018 Liang Wang <liang.wang@cl.cam.ac.uk>
 *)

(* Data Parallel: Map-Reduce module *)

val init : string -> string -> unit

val map : ('a -> 'b) -> string -> string

val map_partition : ('a list -> 'b list) -> string -> string

val flatmap : ('a -> 'b list) -> string -> string

val reduce : ('a -> 'a -> 'a) -> string -> 'a option

val reduce_by_key : ('a -> 'a -> 'a) -> string -> string

val fold : ('a -> 'b -> 'a) -> 'a -> string -> 'a

val filter : ('a -> bool) -> string -> string

val flatten : string -> string

val shuffle : string -> string
```

```
val union : string -> string -> string

val join : string -> string -> string

val broadcast : 'a -> string

val get_value : string -> 'a

val count : string -> int

val collect : string -> 'a list

val terminate : unit -> unit

val apply : ('a list -> 'b list) -> string list -> string list ->
string list

val load : string -> string

val save : string -> string -> int
```

Server

```
(*
 * Actor - Parallel & Distributed Engine of Owl System
 * Copyright (c) 2016-2018 Liang Wang <liang.wang@cl.cam.ac.uk>
 *)

(* Data Parallel: Map-Reduce server module *)

open Actor_types

(* the global context: master, worker, etc. *)
let _context = ref (Actor_utils.empty_mapre_context ())

let barrier bar = Actor_barrier.mapre_bsp bar _context

let _broadcast_all t s =
  let bar = Random.int 536870912 in
  StrMap.iter (fun _k v -> Actor_utils.send ~bar v t s) !_context.workers;
  Bar
```

```ocaml
let run_job_eager () =
  List.iter (fun s ->
    let s' = List.map (fun x -> Actor_dag.get_vlabel_f x) s in
    let bar = _broadcast_all Pipeline (Array.of_list s') in
    let _ = barrier bar in
    Actor_dag.mark_stage_done s;
  ) (Actor_dag.stages_eager ())

let run_job_lazy x =
  List.iter (fun s ->
    let s' = List.map (fun x -> Actor_dag.get_vlabel_f x) s in
    let bar = _broadcast_all Pipeline (Array.of_list s') in
    let _ = barrier bar in
    Actor_dag.mark_stage_done s;
  ) (Actor_dag.stages_lazy x)

let collect x =
  Owl_log.info "%s" ("collect " ^ x ^ "\n");
  run_job_lazy x;
  let bar = _broadcast_all Collect [|x|] in
  barrier bar
  |> List.map (fun m -> Marshal.from_string m.par.(0) 0)

let count x =
  Owl_log.info "%s" ("count " ^ x ^ "\n");
  run_job_lazy x;
  let bar = _broadcast_all Count [|x|] in
  barrier bar
  |> List.map (fun m -> Marshal.from_string m.par.(0) 0)
  |> List.fold_left (+) 0

let fold f a x =
Owl_log.info "%s" ("fold " ^ x ^ "\n");
  run_job_lazy x;
  let g = Marshal.to_string f [ Marshal.Closures ] in
  let bar = _broadcast_all Fold [|g; x|] in
  barrier bar
```

```
  |> List.map (fun m -> Marshal.from_string m.par.(0) 0)
  |> List.filter (function Some _x -> true | None -> false)
  |> List.map (function Some x -> x | None -> failwith "")
  |> List.fold_left f a

let reduce f x =
  Owl_log.info "%s" ("reduce " ^ x ^ "\n");
  run_job_lazy x;
  let g = Marshal.to_string f [ Marshal.Closures ] in
  let bar = _broadcast_all Reduce [|g; x|] in
  let y = barrier bar
  |> List.map (fun m -> Marshal.from_string m.par.(0) 0)
  |> List.filter (function Some _x -> true | None -> false)
  |> List.map (function Some x -> x | None -> failwith "") in
  match y with
  | hd :: tl -> Some (List.fold_left f hd tl)
  | [] -> None

let terminate () =
  Owl_log.info "%s" ("terminate #" ^ !_context.job_id ^ "\n");
  let bar = _broadcast_all Terminate [||] in
  let _ = barrier bar in ()

let broadcast x =
  Owl_log.info "%s" ("broadcast -> " ^ string_of_int (StrMap.cardinal !_
context.workers)     ^
  let y = Actor_memory.rand_id () in
  let bar = _broadcast_all Broadcast [|Marshal.to_string x []; y|] in
  let _ = barrier bar in y

let get_value x = Actor_memory.find x

let map f x =
  let y = Actor_memory.rand_id () in
  Owl_log.info "%s" ("map " ^ x ^ " -> " ^ y ^ "\n");
  let g = Marshal.to_string f [ Marshal.Closures ] in
  Actor_dag.add_edge (to_msg 0 MapTask [|g; x; y|]) x y Red; y
```

```
let map_partition f x =
  let y = Actor_memory.rand_id () in
  Owl_log.info "%s" ("map_partition " ^ x ^ " -> " ^ y ^ "\n");
  let g = Marshal.to_string f [ Marshal.Closures ] in
  Actor_dag.add_edge (to_msg 0 MapPartTask [|g; x; y|]) x y Red; y

let filter f x =
  let y = Actor_memory.rand_id () in
  Owl_log.info "%s" ("filter " ^ x ^ " -> " ^ y ^ "\n");
  let g = Marshal.to_string f [ Marshal.Closures ] in
  Actor_dag.add_edge (to_msg 0 FilterTask [|g; x; y|]) x y Red; y

let flatten x =
  let y = Actor_memory.rand_id () in
  Owl_log.info "%s" ("flatten " ^ x ^ " -> " ^ y ^ "\n");
  Actor_dag.add_edge (to_msg 0 FlattenTask [|x; y|]) x y Red; y

let flatmap f x = flatten (map f x)
  let union x y =
  let z = Actor_memory.rand_id () in
  Owl_log.info "%s" ("union " ^ x ^ " & " ^ y ^ " -> " ^ z ^ "\n");
  Actor_dag.add_edge (to_msg 0 UnionTask [|x; y; z|]) x z Red;
  Actor_dag.add_edge (to_msg 0 UnionTask [|x; y; z|]) y z Red; z

  let shuffle x =
  let y = Actor_memory.rand_id () in
  Owl_log.info "%s" ("shuffle " ^ x ^ " -> " ^ y ^ "\n");
  let z = Marshal.to_string (StrMap.keys !_context.workers) [] in
  let b = Marshal.to_string (Random.int 536870912) [] in
  Actor_dag.add_edge (to_msg 0 ShuffleTask [|x; y; z; b|]) x y Blue; y

let reduce_by_key f x =
(* TODO: without local combiner ... keep or not? *)
  let x = shuffle x in
  let y = Actor_memory.rand_id () in
  Owl_log.info "%s" ("reduce_by_key " ^ x ^ " -> " ^ y ^ "\n");
  let g = Marshal.to_string f [ Marshal.Closures ] in
  Actor_dag.add_edge (to_msg 0 ReduceByKeyTask [|g; x; y|]) x y Red; y
```

```
let join x y =
  let z = Actor_memory.rand_id () in
  Owl_log.info "%s" ("join " ^ x ^ " & " ^ y ^ " -> " ^ z ^ "\n");
  let x, y = shuffle x, shuffle y in
  Actor_dag.add_edge (to_msg 0 JoinTask [|x; y; z|]) x z Red;
  Actor_dag.add_edge (to_msg 0 JoinTask [|x; y; z|]) y z Red; z

let apply f i o =
  Owl_log.info "%s" ("apply f ... " ^ "\n");
  let g = Marshal.to_string f [ Marshal.Closures ] in
  let o = List.map (fun _ -> Actor_memory.rand_id ()) o in
  let x = Marshal.to_string i [ ] in
  let y = Marshal.to_string o [ ] in
  let z = Actor_memory.rand_id () in
  List.iter (fun m -> Actor_dag.add_edge (to_msg 0 ApplyTask [|g; x; z;
  y|]) m z Red) i;
  List.iter (fun n -> Actor_dag.add_edge (to_msg 0 NopTask [|z; y|]) z n
  Red) o; o

let load x =
  Owl_log.info "%s" ("load " ^ x ^ "\n");
  let y = Actor_memory.rand_id () in
  let bar = _broadcast_all Load [|x; y|] in
  let _ = barrier bar in y

let save x y =
  Owl_log.info "%s" ("save " ^ x ^ "\n");
  let bar = _broadcast_all Save [|x; y|] in
  barrier bar
  |> List.map (fun m -> Marshal.from_string m.par.(0) 0)
  |> List.fold_left (+) 0

let init m context =
  _context := context;
  (* contact allocated actors to assign jobs *)
  let addrs = Marshal.from_string m.par.(0) 0 in
  List.map (fun x ->
```

```
    let req = ZMQ.Socket.create !_context.ztx ZMQ.Socket.req in
    ZMQ.Socket.connect req x;
    let app = Filename.basename Sys.argv.(0) in
    let arg = Marshal.to_string Sys.argv [] in
    Actor_utils.send req Job_Create [|!_context.myself_addr; app;
    arg|]; req
  ) addrs |> List.iter ZMQ.Socket.close;
  (* wait until all the allocated actors register *)
  while (StrMap.cardinal !_context.workers) < (List.length addrs) do
    let _i, m = Actor_utils.recv !_context.myself_sock in
    let s = ZMQ.Socket.create !_context.ztx ZMQ.Socket.dealer in
    ZMQ.Socket.connect s m.par.(0);
    !_context.workers <- (StrMap.add m.par.(0) s !_context.workers);
  done
```

Client

```
(*
 * Actor - Parallel & Distributed Engine of Owl System
 * Copyright (c) 2016-2018 Liang Wang <liang.wang@cl.cam.ac.uk>
 *)

(** Data Parallel: Map-Reduce client module *)

open Actor_types

(* the global context: master, worker, etc. *)
let _context = ref (Actor_utils.empty_mapre_context ())

let barrier bar = Actor_barrier.mapre_bsp bar _context

let shuffle bar x z =
  List.mapi (fun i k ->
    let v = Actor_utils.choose_load x (List.length z) i in
    let s = if StrMap.mem k !_context.workers then
      StrMap.find k !_context.workers
    else (
      let s = ZMQ.Socket.(create !_context.ztx dealer) in
      let _ = ZMQ.Socket.(set_identity s !_context.myself_addr;
```

```
  connect s k) in
        let _ = !_context.workers <- StrMap.add k s !_context.workers in
        let _ = ZMQ.Socket.set_send_high_water_mark s Actor_config.high_
        warter_mark in
        s ) in
      Actor_utils.send ~bar s OK [|Marshal.to_string v []|]
  ) z

let process_pipeline s =
  Array.iter (fun s ->
    let m = of_msg s in
    match m.typ with
    | MapTask -> (
        Owl_log.info "%s" ("map @ " ^ !_context.myself_addr);
        let f : 'a -> 'b = Marshal.from_string m.par.(0) 0 in
        List.map f (Actor_memory.find m.par.(1)) |> Actor_memory.add
        m.par.(2)
      )
    | MapPartTask -> (
        Owl_log.info "%s" ("map_partition @ " ^ !_context.myself_addr);
        let f : 'a list -> 'b list = Marshal.from_string m.par.(0) 0 in
        f (Actor_memory.find m.par.(1)) |> Actor_memory.add m.par.(2)
      )
    | FilterTask -> (
        Owl_log.info "%s" ("filter @ " ^ !_context.myself_addr);
        let f : 'a -> bool = Marshal.from_string m.par.(0) 0 in
        List.filter f (Actor_memory.find m.par.(1)) |> Actor_memory.add
        m.par.(2)
      )
    | FlattenTask -> (
        Owl_log.info "%s" ("flatten @ " ^ !_context.myself_addr);
        List.flatten (Actor_memory.find m.par.(0)) |> Actor_memory.add
        m.par.(1)
      )
```

```
| UnionTask -> (
    Owl_log.info "%s" ("union @ " ^ !_context.myself_addr);
    (Actor_memory.find m.par.(0)) @ (Actor_memory.find m.par.(1))
    |> Actor_memory.add m.par.(2)
  )
| ReduceByKeyTask -> (
    Owl_log.info "%s" ("reduce_by_key @ " ^ !_context.myself_addr);
    let f : 'a -> 'a -> 'a = Marshal.from_string m.par.(0) 0 in
    Actor_memory.find m.par.(1) |> Actor_utils.group_by_key |> List.map
    (fun (k,l) ->
      match l with
      | hd :: tl -> (k, List.fold_left f hd tl)
      | [] -> failwith "error in reduce"
    )
    |> Actor_memory.add m.par.(2)
  )
| JoinTask -> (
    Owl_log.info "%s" ("join @ " ^ !_context.myself_addr);
    (Actor_memory.find m.par.(0)) @ (Actor_memory.find m.par.(1))
    |> Actor_utils.group_by_key |> Actor_memory.add m.par.(2)
  )
| ShuffleTask -> (
    Owl_log.info "%s" ("shuffle @ " ^ !_context.myself_addr);
    let x = Actor_memory.find m.par.(0) |> Actor_utils.group_by_key in
    let z = Marshal.from_string m.par.(2) 0 in
    let bar = Marshal.from_string m.par.(3) 0 in
    let _ = shuffle bar x z in
    barrier bar
    |> List.map (fun m -> Marshal.from_string m.par.(0) 0 |> Actor_
    utils.flatten_kvg)
    |> List.flatten |> Actor_memory.add m.par.(1);
  )
| _ -> Owl_log.info "%s" "unknown task types"
) s
```

```
let service_loop () =
  Owl_log.debug "mapre worker @ %s" !_context.myself_addr;
  (* set up local loop of a job worker *)
  try while true do
    let i, m = Actor_utils.recv !_context.myself_sock in
    let bar = m.bar in
    match m.typ with
    | Count -> (
        Owl_log.info "%s" ("count @ " ^ !_context.myself_addr);
        let y = List.length (Actor_memory.find m.par.(0)) in
        Actor_utils.send ~bar !_context.master_sock OK [|Marshal.to_
        string y []|]
        )
    | Collect -> (
        Owl_log.info "%s" ("collect @ " ^ !_context.myself_addr);
        let y = Actor_memory.find m.par.(0) in
        Actor_utils.send ~bar !_context.master_sock OK [|Marshal.to_
        string y []|]
        )
    | Broadcast -> (
        Owl_log.info "%s" ("broadcast @ " ^ !_context.myself_addr);
        Actor_memory.add m.par.(1) (Marshal.from_string m.par.(0) 0);
        Actor_utils.send ~bar !_context.master_sock OK [|||]
        )
    | Reduce -> (
        Owl_log.info "%s" ("reduce @ " ^ !_context.myself_addr);
        let f : 'a -> 'a -> 'a = Marshal.from_string m.par.(0) 0 in
        let y =
          match Actor_memory.find m.par.(1) with
          | hd :: tl -> Some (List.fold_left f hd tl)
          | [] -> None
        in
        Actor_utils.send ~bar !_context.master_sock OK [|Marshal.to_
        string y []|];
        )
```

```ocaml
  | Fold -> (
      Owl_log.info "%s" ("fold @ " ^ !_context.myself_addr);
      let f : 'a -> 'b -> 'a = Marshal.from_string m.par.(0) 0 in
      let y =
        match Actor_memory.find m.par.(1) with
        | hd :: tl -> Some (List.fold_left f hd tl)
        | [] -> None
      in
      Actor_utils.send ~bar !_context.master_sock OK [|Marshal.to_
      string y []|];
    )
  | Pipeline -> (
      Owl_log.info "%s" ("pipelined @ " ^ !_context.myself_addr);
process_pipeline m.par;
      Actor_utils.send ~bar !_context.master_sock OK [||]
    )
  | Terminate -> (
      Owl_log.info "%s" ("terminate @ " ^ !_context.myself_addr);
      Actor_utils.send ~bar !_context.master_sock OK [||];
      Unix.sleep 1; (* FIXME: sleep ... *)
      failwith ("#" ^ !_context.job_id ^ " terminated")
    )
  | Load -> (
      Owl_log.info "%s" ("load " ^ m.par.(0) ^ " @ " ^ !_context.
      myself_addr);
      let path = Str.(split (regexp "://")) m.par.(0) in
      let b =
        match (List.nth path 0) with
        | "unix" -> Actor_storage.unix_load (List.nth path 1)
        | _ -> failwith "Load: unknown system!"
      in
      Actor_memory.add m.par.(1) [ b ];
      Actor_utils.send ~bar !_context.master_sock OK [||]
    )
```

```
    | Save -> (
        Owl_log.info "%s" ("save " ^ m.par.(0) ^ " @ " ^ !_context.
        myself_addr);
        let path = Str.(split (regexp "://")) m.par.(0) in
        let c =
          match (List.nth path 0) with
          | "unix" -> Actor_storage.unix_save (List.nth path 1) (Actor_
          memory.find m.par.(| _ -> failwith "Save: unknown system!"
        in
        Actor_utils.send ~bar !_context.master_sock OK [|Marshal.to_
        string c []|]
      )
    | _ -> (
        Owl_log.info "%s" ("Buffering " ^ !_context.myself_addr ^ " <- " ^
        i ^ " m.bar : "
        Hashtbl.add !_context.msbuf m.bar (i,m)
      )
  done with Failure e -> (
    Owl_log.warn "%s" e;
    ZMQ.Socket.(close !_context.master_sock; close !_context.myself_sock);
    Pervasives.exit 0 )

let init m context =
  _context := context;
  !_context.master_addr <- m.par.(0);
  (* connect to job master *)
  let master = ZMQ.Socket.create !_context.ztx ZMQ.Socket.dealer in
  ZMQ.Socket.set_send_high_water_mark master Actor_config.high_warter_mark;
  ZMQ.Socket.set_identity master !_context.myself_addr;
  ZMQ.Socket.connect master !_context.master_addr;
  Actor_utils.send master OK [||!_context.myself_addr|];
  !_context.master_sock <- master;
  (* enter into worker service loop *)
  service_loop ()
```

F.2 Parameter Server Engine

Interfaces

```
(*
 * Actor - Parallel & Distributed Engine of Owl System
 * Copyright (c) 2016-2018 Liang Wang <liang.wang@cl.cam.ac.uk>
 *)

(* Model Parallel: Parameter server module *)

open Actor_types

(* context type, duplicate from Actor_types *)
type param_context = Actor_types.param_context

type barrier =
  | ASP     (* Asynchronous Parallel *)
  | BSP     (* Bulk Synchronous Parallel *)
  | SSP     (* Stale Synchronous Parallel *)
  | PSP     (* Probabilistic Synchronous Parallel *)

(** core interfaces to parameter server *)

val start : ?barrier:barrier -> string -> string -> unit
(** start running the model loop *)

val register_barrier : ps_barrier_typ -> unit
(** register user-defined barrier function at p2p server *)

val register_schedule : ('a, 'b, 'c) ps_schedule_typ -> unit
(** register user-defined scheduler *)

val register_pull : ('a, 'b, 'c) ps_pull_typ -> unit
(** register user-defined pull function executed at master *)

val register_push : ('a, 'b, 'c) ps_push_typ -> unit
(** register user-defined push function executed at worker *)

val register_stop : ps_stop_typ -> unit
(** register stopping criterion function *)
```

```
val get : 'a -> 'b * int
(** given a key, get its value and timestamp *)

val set : 'a -> 'b -> unit
(** given a key, set its value at master *)

val keys : unit -> 'a list
(** FIXME: reture all the keys in a parameter server *)

val worker_num : unit -> int
(** return the number of workders, only work at server side *)
```

Server

```
(*
 * Actor - Parallel & Distributed Engine of Owl System
 * Copyright (c) 2016-2018 Liang Wang <liang.wang@cl.cam.ac.uk>
 *)

(* Model Parallel: Parameter server module *)

open Actor_types

(* the global context: master, worker, etc. *)
let _context = ref (Actor_utils.empty_param_context ())

let _param : (Obj.t, Obj.t * int) Hashtbl.t = Hashtbl.create 1_000_000

(* default schedule function *)
let _default_schedule = fun _ -> [ ] (** TODO: fix scheduler ... *)

let _schedule = ref (Marshal.to_string _default_schedule [
Marshal.Closures ])

(* default pull function *)
let _default_pull = fun updates -> updates

let _pull = ref (Marshal.to_string _default_pull [ Marshal.Closures ])

(* default stopping function *)
let _default_stop = fun _ -> false

let _stop = ref (Marshal.to_string _default_stop [ Marshal.Closures ])
```

```
(* default barrier function *)
let _default_barrier = Actor_barrier.param_bsp

let _barrier = ref (Marshal.to_string _default_barrier [
Marshal.Closures ])

let update_steps t w =
  let t' = Hashtbl.find !_context.worker_step w in
  match t > t' with
  | true -> (
    Hashtbl.replace !_context.worker_busy w 0;
    Hashtbl.replace !_context.worker_step w t;
    Hashtbl.add !_context.step_worker t w )
  | false -> ()

let _get k =
  let k' = Obj.repr k in
  let v, t = Hashtbl.find _param k' in
  Obj.obj v, t

let _set k v t =
  let k' = Obj.repr k in
  let v' = Obj.repr v in
  match Hashtbl.mem _param k' with
  | true -> Hashtbl.replace _param k' (v',t)
  | false -> Hashtbl.add _param k' (v',t)

let _broadcast_all t s =
  StrMap.iter (fun _k v -> Actor_utils.send ~bar:!_context.step v t s) !_
  context.workers;
  !_context.step

let terminate () =
  let _ = _broadcast_all Terminate [|||] in
  Unix.sleep 1 (** FIXME: change to BSP *)

let service_loop () =
  Owl_log.debug "parameter server @ %s" !_context.myself_addr;
  (* unmarshal the schedule and pull functions *)
```

```
let schedule : ('a, 'b, 'c) ps_schedule_typ = Marshal.from_string !_
schedule 0 in
let pull : ('a, 'b, 'c) ps_pull_typ = Marshal.from_string !_pull 0 in
let barrier : ps_barrier_typ = Marshal.from_string !_barrier 0 in
let stop : ps_stop_typ = Marshal.from_string !_stop 0 in
(* loop to process messages *)
try while not (stop _context) do
  (* synchronisation barrier check *)
  let t, passed = barrier _context in !_context.step <- t;
  (* schecule the passed at every message arrival *)
  let tasks = schedule passed in
  List.iter (fun (worker, task) ->
    let w = StrMap.find worker !_context.workers in
    let s = Marshal.to_string task [] in
    let t = Hashtbl.find !_context.worker_step worker + 1 in
    let _ = Hashtbl.replace !_context.worker_busy worker 1 in
    Actor_utils.send ~bar:t w PS_Schedule [|s|]
  ) tasks;
  if List.length tasks > 0 then
    Owl_log.debug "schedule t:%i -> %i workers" !_context.step (List.
    length tasks);
  (** wait for another message arrival *)
  let i, m = Actor_utils.recv !_context.myself_sock in
  let t = m.bar in
  match m.typ with
  | PS_Get -> (
      Owl_log.debug "%s: ps_get" !_context.myself_addr;
      let k = Marshal.from_string m.par.(0) 0 in
      let v, t' = _get k in
      let s = to_msg t' OK [| Marshal.to_string v [] |] in
      ZMQ.Socket.send_all ~block:false !_context.myself_sock [i;s]
    )
  | PS_Set -> (
      Owl_log.debug "%s: ps_set" !_context.myself_addr;
      let k = Marshal.from_string m.par.(0) 0 in
```

```
        let v = Marshal.from_string m.par.(1) 0 in
          _set k v t
        )
      | PS_Push -> (
          Owl_log.debug "%s: ps_push" !_context.myself_addr;
          let updates = Marshal.from_string m.par.(0) 0 |> pull in
          List.iter (fun (k,v) -> _set k v t) updates;
          update_steps t i
        )
      | _ -> Owl_log.debug "unknown mssage to PS"
  done with Failure e -> (
    Owl_log.warn "%s" e;
    terminate ();
    ZMQ.Socket.close !_context.myself_sock )

let init m context =
  _context := context;
  (* contact allocated actors to assign jobs *)
  let addrs = Marshal.from_string m.par.(0) 0 in
  List.map (fun x ->
    let req = ZMQ.Socket.create !_context.ztx ZMQ.Socket.req in
    ZMQ.Socket.connect req x;
    let app = Filename.basename Sys.argv.(0) in
    let arg = Marshal.to_string Sys.argv [] in
    Actor_utils.send req Job_Create [|!_context.myself_addr; app;
    arg|]; req
  ) addrs
  |> List.iter ZMQ.Socket.close;
  (* wait until all the allocated actors register *)
  while (StrMap.cardinal !_context.workers) < (List.length addrs) do
    let _i, m = Actor_utils.recv !_context.myself_sock in
    let s = ZMQ.Socket.create !_context.ztx ZMQ.Socket.dealer in
    ZMQ.Socket.set_send_high_water_mark s Actor_config.high_warter_mark;
    ZMQ.Socket.connect s m.par.(0);
    !_context.workers <- (StrMap.add m.par.(0) s !_context.workers);
  done;
```

```
(* initialise the step <--> work tables *)
StrMap.iter (fun k _v ->
  Hashtbl.add !_context.worker_busy k 0;
  Hashtbl.add !_context.worker_step k 0;
  Hashtbl.add !_context.step_worker 0 k;
) !_context.workers;
(* enter into master service loop *)
service_loop ()
```

Client

```
(*
* Actor - Parallel & Distributed Engine of Owl System
* Copyright (c) 2016-2018 Liang Wang <liang.wang@cl.cam.ac.uk>
*)

(* Model Parallel: Parameter client module *)

open Actor_types

(* the global context: master, worker, etc. *)
let _context = ref (Actor_utils.empty_param_context ())

(* default push function *)
let _default_push = fun _worker_id _vars -> []

let _push = ref (Marshal.to_string _default_push [ Marshal.Closures ])

let _get k =
  let k' = Marshal.to_string k [] in
  Actor_utils.send ~bar:!_context.step !_context.master_sock PS_Get [|k'|];
  let m = of_msg (ZMQ.Socket.recv ~block:true !_context.master_sock) in
  Marshal.from_string m.par.(0) 0, m.bar

let _set k v t =
  let k' = Marshal.to_string k [] in
  let v' = Marshal.to_string v [] in
  Actor_utils.send ~bar:t !_context.master_sock PS_Set [|k'; v'|]
```

```
let update_param x t =
  (* update multiple kvs, more efficient than set *)
  let x' = Marshal.to_string x [] in
  Actor_utils.send ~bar:t !_context.master_sock PS_Push [|x'|]

let service_loop () =
  Owl_log.debug "parameter worker @ %s" !_context.myself_addr;
  (* unmarshal the push function *)
  let push : 'a -> ('b * 'c) list -> ('b * 'c) list = Marshal.from_string
  !_push 0 in
  (* loop to process messages *)
  try while true do
    let _i, m = Actor_utils.recv !_context.myself_sock in
    let t = m.bar in
    match m.typ with
    | PS_Schedule -> (
        Owl_log.debug "%s: ps_schedule" !_context.myself_addr;
        !_context.step <- (if t > !_context.step then t else !_
        context.step);
        let vars = Marshal.from_string m.par.(0) 0 in
        let updates = push !_context.myself_addr vars in
        update_param updates t
      )
    | Terminate -> (
        Owl_log.debug "%s: terminate"!_context.myself_addr;
        Actor_utils.send ~bar:t !_context.master_sock OK [|||];
        Unix.sleep 1; (* FIXME: sleep ... *)
        failwith ("#" ^ !_context.job_id ^ " terminated")
      )
    | _ -> ( Owl_log.debug "unknown mssage to PS" )
  done with Failure e -> (
    Owl_log.warn "%s" e;
    ZMQ.Socket.close !_context.myself_sock;
    Pervasives.exit 0 )
```

```
let init m context =
  _context := context;
  !_context.master_addr <- m.par.(0);
  (* connect to job master *)
  let master = ZMQ.Socket.create !_context.ztx ZMQ.Socket.dealer in
  ZMQ.Socket.set_send_high_water_mark master Actor_config.high_warter_mark;
  ZMQ.Socket.set_identity master !_context.myself_addr;
  ZMQ.Socket.connect master !_context.master_addr;
  Actor_utils.send master OK [|!_context.myself_addr|];
  !_context.master_sock <- master;
  (* enter into worker service loop *)
  service_loop ()
```

F.3 Peer-to-Peer Engine

Interfaces

```
(*
 * Actor - Parallel & Distributed Engine of Owl System
 * Copyright (c) 2016-2018 Liang Wang <liang.wang@cl.cam.ac.uk>
 *)

(* Peer-to-Peer Parallel *)

open Actor_types

(** start running the model loop *)
val start : string -> string -> unit

(** register user-defined barrier function at p2p server *)
val register_barrier : p2p_barrier_typ -> unit

(** register user-defined pull function at p2p server *)
val register_pull : ('a, 'b) p2p_pull_typ -> unit

(** register user-defined scheduler at p2p client *)
val register_schedule : 'a p2p_schedule_typ -> unit
```

```
(** register user-defined push function at p2p client *)
val register_push : ('a, 'b) p2p_push_typ -> unit

(** register stopping criterion function at p2p client *)
val register_stop : p2p_stop_typ -> unit

(** given a key, get its value and timestamp *)
val get : 'a -> 'b * int

(** given a key, set its value at master *)
val set : 'a -> 'b -> unit
```

Server

```
(*
 * Actor - Parallel & Distributed Engine of Owl System
 * Copyright (c) 2016-2018 Liang Wang <liang.wang@cl.cam.ac.uk>
 *)

(* Peer-to-Peer Parallel: Server module *)

open Actor_types

(* the global context: master, worker, etc. *)
let _context = ref (Actor_utils.empty_peer_context ())

let _param : (Obj.t, Obj.t * int) Hashtbl.t = Hashtbl.create 1_000_000

(* buffer of the requests and replies of pulling model parameters *)
let _plbuf : (Obj.t, Obj.t option) Hashtbl.t = Hashtbl.create 1_000

(* default pull function *)
let _default_pull _ updates = updates

let _pull = ref (Marshal.to_string _default_pull [ Marshal.Closures ])

(* default barrier function *)
let _default_barrier = fun _ -> true

let _barrier = ref (Marshal.to_string _default_barrier [
Marshal.Closures ])
```

```
(* routing table module *)
module Route = struct

  (* FIXME: given ONLY 30-bit address space *)
  let _space = 2. ** 30. |> int_of_float

  let hash x = Hashtbl.hash x

  let distance x y = (x - y + _space) mod _space

  let add addr sock =
    if Hashtbl.mem !_context.spbuf addr = false then Hashtbl.add !_context.
    spbuf addr 0;
    !_context.workers <- (StrMap.add addr sock !_context.workers)

  let exists addr = StrMap.mem addr !_context.workers

  let connect addr =
    let sock = ZMQ.Socket.create !_context.ztx ZMQ.Socket.dealer in
    ZMQ.Socket.set_send_high_water_mark sock Actor_config.high_warter_mark;
    ZMQ.Socket.set_identity sock !_context.myself_addr;
    ZMQ.Socket.connect sock addr;
    sock

  let furthest x =
    let d = ref min_int in
    let n = ref "" in
    List.iteri (fun _i y ->
      let d' = distance (hash y) x in
      if d' > !d then ( d := d'; n := y )
    ) (StrMap.keys !_context.workers @ [!_context.myself_addr]);
    !n

  let furthest_exclude x l =
    let addrs = StrMap.keys !_context.workers @ [!_context.myself_addr]
      |> List.filter (fun x -> not (List.mem x l))
    in
    let d = ref min_int in
    let n = ref "" in
```

```
  List.iteri (fun _i y ->
    let d' = distance (hash y) x in
    if d' > !d then ( d := d'; n := y )
  ) addrs;
  !n

let nearest x =
  let d = ref max_int in
  let n = ref "" in
  List.iteri (fun _i y ->
    let d' = distance (hash y) x in
    if d' < !d then ( d := d'; n := y )
  ) (StrMap.keys !_context.workers @ [!_context.myself_addr]);
  !n

let nearest_exclude x l =
  let addrs = StrMap.keys !_context.workers @ [!_context.myself_addr]
    |> List.filter (fun x -> not (List.mem x l))
  in
  let d = ref max_int in
  let n = ref "" in
  List.iteri (fun _i y ->
    let d' = distance (hash y) x in
    if d' < !d then ( d := d'; n := y )
  ) addrs;
  !n

let forward nxt typ msg =
  let s = StrMap.find nxt !_context.workers in
  Actor_utils.send ~bar:!_context.step s typ msg

let init_table addrs =
  (* contact initial random peers *)
  Array.iter (fun x ->
    let s = connect x in
    let _ = add x s in
    Actor_utils.send s P2P_Ping [|!_context.myself_addr|];
  ) addrs;
```

```
    (* contact nodes of fixed distance *)
    let myid = hash !_context.myself_addr in
    let _ = Array.init 30 (fun i ->
      let d = 2. ** (float_of_int i) |> int_of_float in
      let a = (myid + d) mod _space in
      let n = nearest_exclude a [!_context.myself_addr] in
      if String.length n <> 0 then
        let s = Marshal.to_string a [] in
        forward n P2P_Join [|!_context.myself_addr; s|]
    ) in ()

end

let _get k =
  let k' = Obj.repr k in
  let v, t = Hashtbl.find _param k' in
  Obj.obj v, t

let _set k v t =
  let k' = Obj.repr k in
  let v' = Obj.repr v in
  match Hashtbl.mem _param k' with
  | true -> Hashtbl.replace _param k' (v',t)
  | false -> Hashtbl.add _param k' (v',t)

  let _allocate_params x y =
  let x = Route.hash x in
  let y = Route.hash y in
  let l = ref [] in
  Hashtbl.iter (fun k v ->
    let h = Obj.obj k |> Route.hash in
    if (Route.distance y h) < (Route.distance x h) then l := !l @ [(k,v)]
  ) _param; !l

let _shall_deliver_pull () =
  let ready = ref true in
  Hashtbl.iter (fun _k v ->
```

```
    match v with Some _ -> () | None -> ready := false
  ) _plbuf;
  if !ready = true then (
    let s = Hashtbl.fold (fun _ v l ->
      match v with
      | Some v -> let k,v,_t = Obj.obj v in l @ [(k,v)]
      | None -> l
    ) _plbuf []
    in
    let s = Marshal.to_string s [] in
    Actor_utils.send !_context.master_sock OK [|s|];
    Hashtbl.reset _plbuf
  )

let _barrier_control barrier pull =
  let updates = List.map Obj.obj !_context.mpbuf in
  if barrier _context = true then (
    pull _context updates |> List.iter (fun (k,v,t) -> _set k v t);
    !_context.mpbuf <- [];
    if !_context.block = true then (
      Actor_utils.send ~bar:!_context.step !_context.master_sock OK [||];
      !_context.block <- false
    )
  )

let _update_step_buf addr step =
  if Hashtbl.mem !_context.spbuf addr = true then (
    let step = max step (Hashtbl.find !_context.spbuf addr) in
    Hashtbl.replace !_context.spbuf addr step
  )
  else Hashtbl.add !_context.spbuf addr step

let _notify_peers_step () =
  List.iter (fun k ->
    Route.forward k P2P_Ping [|!_context.myself_addr|]
  ) (StrMap.keys !_context.workers)
```

```
let _process_timeout () =
  _notify_peers_step ();
  Owl_log.debug "%s: timeout" !_context.myself_addr

let service_loop () =
  Owl_log.debug "%s: p2p server" !_context.myself_addr;
  let barrier : p2p_barrier_typ = Marshal.from_string !_barrier 0 in
  let pull : ('a, 'b) p2p_pull_typ = Marshal.from_string !_pull 0 in
  (* loop to process messages *)
  ZMQ.Socket.set_receive_timeout !_context.myself_sock (1 * 1000);
  try while true do
  (* first, wait and process arriving message *)
  try let i, m = Actor_utils.recv !_context.myself_sock in (
    match m.typ with
    | P2P_Connect -> (
        Owl_log.debug "%s: p2p_connect %s" !_context.myself_addr m.par.(0);
        let addr = m.par.(0) in
        !_context.master_addr <- addr;
        !_context.master_sock <- Route.connect addr
      )
    | P2P_Ping -> (
        Owl_log.debug "%s: p2p_ping %s" !_context.myself_addr m.par.(0);
        let addr = m.par.(0) in
        if Route.exists addr = false then Route.(connect addr |> add addr)
      )
    | P2P_Join -> (
        Owl_log.debug "%s: p2p_join %s" !_context.myself_addr m.par.(0);
        let src = m.par.(0) in
        let dst = Marshal.from_string m.par.(1) 0 in
        let next = Route.nearest_exclude dst [src] in
        if next = !_context.myself_addr then (
          if Route.exists src = false then (
            let s = Route.connect src in
            let _ = Route.add src s in
            Actor_utils.send s P2P_Ping [|!_context.myself_addr|]
          );
```

```
    (* oh, hello neighbour, maybe take my model *)
    if Route.hash src = dst - 1 then (
    let next = Route.furthest_exclude dst [src; !_context.myself_
    addr] in
    if String.length next <> 0 then
      Route.forward next P2P_Ping [|src|];
      let h = _allocate_params !_context.myself_addr src in
      let s = Marshal.to_string h [] in
    Owl_log.debug "params: %s ===> %s size:%i" !_context.myself_
    addr src
      (String.Route.forward src P2P_Copy [|s|]
    )
  );
    if next <> !_context.myself_addr && String.length next <> 0 then
      Route.forward next P2P_Join m.par;
  )
| P2P_Copy -> (
    Owl_log.debug "%s: p2p_copy" !_context.myself_addr;
    let h = Marshal.from_string m.par.(0) 0 in
    List.iter (fun (k,v) ->
      match Hashtbl.mem _param k with
      | true -> Hashtbl.replace _param k v
      | false -> Hashtbl.add _param k v
    ) h
  )
| P2P_Get -> (
    Owl_log.debug "%s: p2p_get" !_context.myself_addr;
    let k = Marshal.from_string m.par.(0) 0 in
    let next = Route.(hash k |> nearest) in
    match next = !_context.myself_addr with
    | true -> (
            (* FIXME: what if i cannot find the k *)
            let v, t = _get k in
            let s = Marshal.to_string (k, v, t) [] in
            Actor_utils.send !_context.master_sock OK [|s; next|]
    )
```

449

```
      | false -> Route.forward next P2P_Get_Q m.par
  )
| P2P_Get_Q -> (
      Owl_log.debug "%s: p2p_get_q" !_context.myself_addr;
      let k = Marshal.from_string m.par.(0) 0 in
      let next = Route.(hash k |> nearest) in
      match next = !_context.myself_addr with
      | true -> (
          let v, t = _get k in
          let s = Marshal.to_string (k, v, t) [] in
          let addr = m.par.(1) in
          let next = Route.(hash addr |> nearest) in
          Route.forward next P2P_Get_R [|s; addr|]
          )
      | false -> Route.forward next P2P_Get_Q m.par
  )
| P2P_Get_R -> (
      Owl_log.debug "%s: p2p_get_r" !_context.myself_addr;
      let addr = m.par.(1) in
      let next = Route.(hash addr |> nearest) in
      match next = !_context.myself_addr with
      | true -> Actor_utils.send !_context.master_sock OK m.par
      | false -> Route.forward next P2P_Get_R m.par
  )
| P2P_Set -> (
      Owl_log.debug "%s: p2p_get" !_context.myself_addr;
      let k, v, t = Marshal.from_string m.par.(0) 0 in
      (* check whether this is from the local client *)
      let t = if t < 0 then (
        let s = Marshal.to_string (k, v, !_context.step) [] in
        m.par <- [|s|]; !_context.step
      ) else t
      in
      let next = Route.(hash k |> nearest) in
      match next = !_context.myself_addr with
```

```
  | true -> !_context.mpbuf <- !_context.mpbuf @ [Obj.repr (k, v, t)]
  | false -> Route.forward next P2P_Set m.par
)
| P2P_Push -> (
    Owl_log.debug "%s: p2p_push" !_context.myself_addr;
    Marshal.from_string m.par.(0) 0
    |> List.iter (fun (k,v) ->
      let next = Route.(hash k |> nearest) in
      match next = !_context.myself_addr with
      | true -> !_context.mpbuf <- !_context.mpbuf @ [Obj.repr (k, v,
        !_context.step)]
      | false -> (
          let s = Marshal.to_string (k, v, !_context.step) [] in
          Route.forward next P2P_Set [|s|]
      )
    )
  )
| P2P_Pull -> (
    Owl_log.debug "%s: p2p_pull" !_context.myself_addr;
    Marshal.from_string m.par.(0) 0
    |> List.iter (fun k ->
      let next = Route.(hash k |> nearest) in
      match next = !_context.myself_addr with
      | true -> (
          let v, t = _get k in
          Hashtbl.add _plbuf (Obj.repr k) (Some (Obj.repr (k,v,t)))
        )
      | false -> (
          let y = Marshal.to_string k [] in
          let s = [|y; !_context.myself_addr|] in
          Route.forward next P2P_Pull_Q s;
          Hashtbl.add _plbuf (Obj.repr k) None
        )
    );
    _shall_deliver_pull ()
  )
```

```
| P2P_Pull_Q -> (
    Owl_log.debug "%s: p2p_pull_q %s" !_context.myself_addr m.par.(1);
    let k = Marshal.from_string m.par.(0) 0 in
    let next = Route.(hash k |> nearest) in
    match next = !_context.myself_addr with
    | true -> (
        let v, t = _get k in
        let s = Marshal.to_string (k, v, t) [] in
        let addr = m.par.(1) in
        let next = Route.(hash addr |> nearest) in
         Route.forward next P2P_Pull_R [|s; addr|]
      )
    | false -> Route.forward next P2P_Pull_Q m.par
  )
| P2P_Pull_R -> (
    Owl_log.debug "%s: p2p_pull_r %s" !_context.myself_addr m.par.(1);
    let addr = m.par.(1) in
    let next = Route.(hash addr |> nearest) in
    match next = !_context.myself_addr with
    | true -> (
        let k, v, t = Marshal.from_string m.par.(0) 0 in
        Hashtbl.replace _plbuf (Obj.repr k) (Some (Obj.repr (k,v,t)));
         _shall_deliver_pull ()
      )
    | false -> Route.forward next P2P_Pull_R m.par
  )
| P2P_Bar -> (
    Owl_log.debug "%s: p2p_bar" !_context.myself_addr;
    !_context.block <- true;
    !_context.step <- !_context.step + 1;
    _notify_peers_step ();
  )
| _ -> Owl_log.error "unknown mssage type"
);
```

```
    (* second, update the piggybacked step *)
    if i <> !_context.master_addr then _update_step_buf i m.bar;
    (* third, check the barrier control *)
    _barrier_control barrier pull;
    (* fourth, in case the process hangs *)
    with Unix.Unix_error (_,_,_) -> _process_timeout ()
  done with Failure e -> (
    Owl_log.warn "%s" e;
    ZMQ.Socket.close !_context.myself_sock )

  let init m context =
    _context := context;
    (* contact allocated peers to join the swarm *)
    Marshal.from_string m.par.(0) 0 |> Route.init_table;
    (* enter into server service loop *)
    service_loop ()
```

Client

```
(*
 * Actor - Parallel & Distributed Engine of Owl System
 * Copyright (c) 2016-2018 Liang Wang <liang.wang@cl.cam.ac.uk>
 *)

(* Peer-to-Peer Parallel: Client module *)

open Actor_types

(* the global context: master, worker, etc. *)
let _context = ref (Actor_utils.empty_peer_context ())

(* default schedule function *)
let _default_schedule = fun _ -> [ ]

let _schedule = ref (Marshal.to_string _default_schedule [
Marshal.Closures ])

(* default push function *)
let _default_push = fun _ _ -> []

let _push = ref (Marshal.to_string _default_push [ Marshal.Closures ])
```

```
(* default stopping function *)
let _default_stop = fun _ -> false

let _stop = ref (Marshal.to_string _default_stop [ Marshal.Closures ])

let _get k =
  let k = Marshal.to_string k [] in
  let s = [|k; !_context.master_addr|] in
  Actor_utils.send !_context.master_sock P2P_Get s;
  let _, m = Actor_utils.recv !_context.myself_sock in
  let _k, v, t = Marshal.from_string m.par.(0) 0 in
  v, t

let _set k v =
  let s = Marshal.to_string (k, v, -1) [] in
  Actor_utils.send !_context.master_sock P2P_Set [|s|]

let _push_model params =
  let s = Marshal.to_string params [] in
  Actor_utils.send !_context.master_sock P2P_Push [|s|]

let _pull_model params =
  List.map (fun k -> let v, _ = _get k in (k,v)) params

let _pull_model_batch params =
  let s = Marshal.to_string params [] in
  Actor_utils.send !_context.master_sock P2P_Pull [|s|];
  let _, m = Actor_utils.recv !_context.myself_sock in
  let kvs = Marshal.from_string m.par.(0) 0 in
  kvs

let _barrier () =
  Actor_utils.send !_context.master_sock P2P_Bar [||];
  let _, m = Actor_utils.recv !_context.myself_sock in
  !_context.step <- m.bar

let service_loop () =
  Owl_log.debug "p2p_client @ %s" !_context.master_addr;
  (* unmarshal the schedule and push function *)
  let schedule : 'a p2p_schedule_typ = Marshal.from_string !_schedule 0 in
```

```
  let push : ('a, 'b) p2p_push_typ = Marshal.from_string !_push 0 in
  let stop : p2p_stop_typ = Marshal.from_string !_stop 0 in
  (* loop to process messages *)
  try while not (stop _context) do
    schedule _context
    |> _pull_model
    |> push _context
    |> _push_model
    |> _barrier
  done with Failure e -> (
    Owl_log.warn "%s" e;
    ZMQ.Socket.close !_context.myself_sock;
    Pervasives.exit 0 )

let init _m context =
  _context := context;
  (* re-initialise since it is a new process *)
  !_context.ztx <- ZMQ.Context.create ();
  !_context.master_addr <- context.myself_addr;
  let _addr, _router = Actor_utils.bind_available_addr !_context.ztx in
  !_context.myself_addr <- _addr;
  !_context.myself_sock <- _router;
  (* set up local p2p server <-> client *)
  let sock = ZMQ.Socket.create !_context.ztx ZMQ.Socket.dealer in
  ZMQ.Socket.set_send_high_water_mark sock Actor_config.high_warter_mark;
  ZMQ.Socket.set_identity sock !_context.myself_addr;
  ZMQ.Socket.connect sock !_context.master_addr;
  !_context.master_sock <- sock;
  Actor_utils.send !_context.master_sock P2P_Connect [|!_context.
  myself_addr|];
  (* enter into client service loop *)
  service_loop ()
```

Bibliography

[1]. Martín Abadi, Paul Barham, Jianmin Chen, Zhifeng Chen, Andy Davis, Jeffrey Dean, Matthieu Devin, Sanjay Ghemawat, Geoffrey Irving, Michael Isard, et al. Tensorflow: A system for large-scale machine learning. In *12th {USENIX} symposium on operating systems design and implementation ({OSDI} 16)*, pages 265–283, 2016.

[2]. Amr Ahmed, Mohamed Aly, Joseph Gonzalez, Shravan Narayananmuthy, and Alexander Smola. Scalable inference in latent variable models. *WSDM*, pages 123–132, 2012.

[3]. Istemi Ekin Akkus, Ruichuan Chen, Ivica Rimac, Manuel Stein, Klaus Satzke, Andre Beck, Paarijaat Aditya, and Volker Hilt. Sand: Towards high-performance serverless computing. In *2018 USENIX Annual Technical Conference (USENIX ATC'18)*, pages 923–935, 2018.

[4]. Tal Ben-Nun and Torsten Hoefler. Demystifying parallel and distributed deep learning: An in-depth concurrency analysis. *ACM Computing Surveys (CSUR)*, 52(4):1–43, 2019.

[5]. Yoshua Bengio, Nicolas Boulanger-Lewandowski, and Razvan Pascanu. Advances in optimizing recurrent networks. In *2013 IEEE international conference on acoustics, speech and signal processing*, pages 8624–8628. IEEE, 2013.

[6]. Keith Bonawitz, Hubert Eichner, Wolfgang Grieskamp, Dzmitry Huba, Alex Ingerman, Vladimir Ivanov, Chloe Kiddon, Jakub Konecny, Stefano Mazzocchi, H Brendan McMahan, and Others. Towards federated learning at scale: System design. *arXiv preprint arXiv:1902.01046*, 2019.

© Liang Wang, Jianxin Zhao 2023
L. Wang and J. Zhao, *Architecture of Advanced Numerical Analysis Systems*,
https://doi.org/10.1007/978-1-4842-8853-5

[7]. H. Brendan McMahan, Eider Moore, Daniel Ramage, Seth Hampson, and Blaise Agüera y Arcas. Communication-efficient learning of deep networks from decentralized data. *Proceedings of the 20th International Conference on Artificial Intelligence and Statistics, AISTATS 2017*, 54, 2017.

[8]. Sebastian Caldas, Sai Meher Karthik Duddu, Peter Wu, Tian Li, Jakub Konečný, H. Brendan McMahan, Virginia Smith, and Ameet Talwalkar. LEAF: A Benchmark for Federated Settings. *NeurIPS*, pages 1–9, 2018.

[9]. Jianmin Chen, Xinghao Pan, Rajat Monga, Samy Bengio, Google Brain, Mountain View, Rafal Jozefowicz, and San Francisco. Revising distributed synchronous SGD. *ICLR'17*, pages 1–10, 2017.

[10]. Tianqi Chen, Thierry Moreau, Ziheng Jiang, Lianmin Zheng, Eddie Yan, Haichen Shen, Meghan Cowan, Leyuan Wang, Yuwei Hu, Luis Ceze, et al. TVM: An automated end-to-end optimizing compiler for deep learning. In *13th USENIX Symposium on Operating Systems Design and Implementation (OSDI 18)*, pages 578–594, 2018.

[11]. Minsik Cho and Daniel Brand. MEC: Memory-efficient convolution for deep neural network. In *International Conference on Machine Learning*, pages 815–824. PMLR, 2017.

[12]. James Cipar, Qirong Ho, Jin Kyu Kim, Seunghak Lee, Gregory R Ganger, Garth Gibson, Kimberly Keeton, and Eric Xing. Solving the straggler problem with bounded staleness. In *Presented as part of the 14th Workshop on Hot Topics in Operating Systems*, 2013.

[13]. Daniel Crankshaw, Xin Wang, Guilio Zhou, Michael J Franklin, Joseph E Gonzalez, and Ion Stoica. Clipper: A low-latency online prediction serving system. In *14th USENIX Symposium on Networked Systems Design and Implementation (NSDI 17)*, pages 613–627, 2017.

[14]. Henggang Cui, James Cipar, Qirong Ho, Jin Kyu Kim, Seunghak Lee, Abhimanu Kumar, Jinliang Wei, Wei Dai, Gregory R Ganger, Phillip B Gibbons, et al. Exploiting bounded staleness to speed up big data analytics. In *2014 USENIX Annual Technical Conference (USENIX ATC'14)*, pages 37–48, 2014.

[15]. Wei Dai, Abhimanu Kumar, Jinliang Wei, Qirong Ho, Garth Gibson, and Eric P Xing. High-performance distributed ml at scale through parameter server consistency models. In *Twenty-Ninth AAAI Conference on Artificial Intelligence*, 2015.

[16]. Yu-Hong Dai and Yaxiang Yuan. A nonlinear conjugate gradient method with a strong global convergence property. *SIAM Journal on optimization*, 10(1):177–182, 1999.

[17]. Jeffrey Dean and Sanjay Ghemawat. MapReduce: Simplified data processing on large clusters. *Communications of the ACM*, 51(1):107–113, 2008.

[18]. Ulrich Drepper. What every programmer should know about memory. *Red Hat, Inc*, 11:2007, 2007.

[19]. Moming Duan, Duo Liu, Xianzhang Chen, Renping Liu, Yujuan Tan, and Liang Liang. Self-Balancing Federated Learning with Global Imbalanced Data in Mobile Systems. *IEEE Transactions on Parallel and Distributed Systems*, 32(1):59–71, 2021.

[20]. John Duchi, Elad Hazan, and Yoram Singer. Adaptive subgradient methods for online learning and stochastic optimization. *Journal of machine learning research*, 12(7), 2011.

[21]. Reeves Fletcher and Colin M Reeves. Function minimization by conjugate gradients. *The computer journal*, 7(2):149–154, 1964.

[22]. Ross Girshick. Fast R-CNN. In Proceedings of the IEEE international conference on computer vision, pages 1440–1448, 2015.

[23]. Ross Girshick, Jeff Donahue, Trevor Darrell, and Jitendra Malik. Rich feature hierarchies for accurate object detection and semantic segmentation. In *Proceedings of the IEEE conference on computer vision and pattern recognition*, pages 580–587, 2014.

[24]. Xavier Glorot and Yoshua Bengio. Understanding the difficulty of training deep feedforward neural networks. In *Proceedings of the thirteenth international conference on artificial intelligence and statistics*, pages 249–256. JMLR Workshop and Conference Proceedings, 2010.

[25]. Kazushige Goto and Robert A van de Geijn. Anatomy of high-performance matrix multiplication. *ACM Transactions on Mathematical Software (TOMS)*, 34(3):1–25, 2008.

[26]. Andreas Griewank and Andrea Walther. *OCaml Scientific Computing: Functional Programming in Data Science and Artificial Intelligence*. Undergraduate Topics in Computer Science. Springer Cham, 2022.

[27]. Kaiming He, Georgia Gkioxari, Piotr Dollár, and Ross Girshick. Mask R-CNN. In *Proceedings of the IEEE international conference on computer vision*, pages 2961–2969, 2017.

[28]. Kaiming He, Xiangyu Zhang, Shaoqing Ren, and Jian Sun. Deep residual learning for image recognition. In *Proceedings of the IEEE conference on computer vision and pattern recognition*, pages 770–778, 2016.

[29]. Magnus R Hestenes and Eduard Stiefel. Methods of conjugate gradients for solving. *Journal of research of the National Bureau of Standards*, 49(6):409, 1952.

[30]. Qirong Ho, James Cipar, Henggang Cui, Jin Kyu Kim, Seunghak Lee, Phillip B. Gibbons, Garth A. Gibson, Gregory R. Ganger, and Eric P. Xing. More effective distributed ML via a stale synchronous parallel parameter server. In *Advances in Neural Information Processing Systems*, 2013.

[31]. Kohei Honda, Vasco T Vasconcelos, and Makoto Kubo. Language primitives and type discipline for structured communication-based programming. In *European Symposium on Programming*, pages 122–138. Springer, 1998.

[32]. Kevin Hsieh, Aaron Harlap, Nandita Vijaykumar, Dimitris Konomis, Gregory R. Ganger, Phillip B. Gibbons, and Onur Mutlu. Gaia: Geo-distributed machine learning approaching LAN speeds. *Proceedings of the 14th USENIX Symposium on Networked Systems Design and Implementation, NSDI 2017*, pages 629–647, 2017.

[33]. Diederik P Kingma and Jimmy Ba. Adam: A method for stochastic optimization. *arXiv preprint arXiv:1412.6980*, 2014.

[34]. Mu Li, David G. Andersen, Jun Woo Park, Alexander J. Smola, Amr Ahmed, Vanja Josifovski, James Long, Eugene J. Shekita, and Bor Yiing Su. Scaling distributed machine learning with the parameter server. In *Proceedings of the 11th USENIX Symposium on Operating Systems Design and Implementation, OSDI 2014*, 2014.

[35]. Xiangru Lian, Yijun Huang, Yuncheng Li, and Ji Liu. Asynchronous parallel stochastic gradient for nonconvex optimization. In *Advances in Neural Information Processing Systems*, 2015.

[36]. Xiangru Lian, Ce Zhang, Huan Zhang, Cho-Jui Hsieh, Wei Zhang, and Ji Liu. Can decentralized algorithms outperform centralized algorithms? A case study for decentralized parallel stochastic gradient descent. *arXiv preprint arXiv:1705.09056*, 2017.

[37]. Anil Madhavapeddy, Richard Mortier, Charalampos Rotsos, David Scott, Balraj Singh, Thomas Gazagnaire, Steven Smith, Steven Hand, and Jon Crowcroft. Unikernels: Library operating systems for the cloud. *Acm Sigplan Notices*, 48(4):461–472, 2013.

[38]. Yaron Minsky, Anil Madhavapeddy, and Jason Hickey. *Real World OCaml: Functional programming for the masses*. O'Reilly Media, Inc., 2013.

[39]. Stephen L Moshier. Cephes math library. *See www.moshier. net*, 2000.

[40]. Yurii Nesterov. A method for unconstrained convex minimization problem with the rate of convergence o $(1/k^2)$. In *Doklady an USSR*, volume 269, pages 543–547, 1983.

[41]. Feng Niu, Benjamin Recht, Christopher Re, and Stephen J. Wright. Hogwild!: A lock-free approach to parallelizing stochastic gradient descent. *NIPS'11 Proceedings of the 24th International Conference on Neural Information Processing Systems*, pages 693–701, 2011.

[42]. Adam Paszke, Sam Gross, Francisco Massa, Adam Lerer, James Bradbury, Gregory Chanan, Trevor Killeen, Zeming Lin, Natalia Gimelshein, Luca Antiga, et al. PyTorch: An imperative style, high-performance deep learning library. *Advances in neural information processing systems*, 32:8026–8037, 2019.

[43]. Shaoqing Ren, Kaiming He, Ross Girshick, and Jian Sun. Faster R-CNN: Towards real-time object detection with region proposal networks. *Advances in neural information processing systems*, 28:91–99, 2015.

[44]. Alexander Sergeev and Mike Del Balso. Horovod: fast and easy distributed deep learning in TensorFlow. *arXiv*, 2017.

[45]. Ravi Sethi. Complete register allocation problems. *SIAM journal on Computing*, 4(3):226–248, 1975.

[46]. Konstantin Shvachko, Hairong Kuang, Sanjay Radia, Robert Chansler, et al. The hadoop distributed file system. In *MSST*, volume 10, pages 1–10, 2010.

[47]. Jeffrey Mark Siskind and Barak A. Pearlmutter. Perturbation confusion and referential transparency: Correct functional implementation of forward-mode AD. In *Implementation and Application of Functional Languages—17th International Workshop, IFL'05*, pages 1–9, Dublin, Ireland, September 2005.

[48]. Benoit Steiner, Chris Cummins, Horace He, and Hugh Leather. Value learning for throughput optimization of deep learning workloads. In *Proceedings of Machine Learning and Systems*, volume 3, pages 323–334, 2021.

[49]. Pierre Vandenhove. Computer vision in OCaml & computation graph optimisation. *Internship Report, OCaml Labs*, 2018.

[50]. Philip Wadler. Linear types can change the world! In *Programming concepts and methods*, volume 3, page 5. Citeseer, 1990.

[51]. Liang Wang. Owl: A general-purpose numerical library in ocaml. *arXiv preprint arXiv:1707.09616*, 2017.

[52]. Liang Wang, Ben Catterall, and Richard Mortier. Probabilistic synchronous parallel. *arXiv preprint arXiv:1709.07772*, 2017.

[53]. Liang Wang, Sotiris Tasoulis, Teemu Roos, and Jussi Kangasharju. Kvasir: Scalable provision of semantically relevant web content on big data framework. *IEEE Transactions on Big Data*, 2(3):219–233, 2016.

[54]. Eric P Xing, Qirong Ho, Pengtao Xie, and Dai Wei. Strategies and principles of distributed machine learning on big data. *Engineering*, 2(2):179–195, 2016.

[55]. Da Yan, Wei Wang, and Xiaowen Chu. Optimizing batched winograd convolution on GPUs. In *Proceedings of the 25th ACM SIGPLAN symposium on Principles and Practice of Parallel Programming*, pages 32–44, 2020.

[56]. Lian-Zhong Yang. Solution of a differential equation and its applications. *Kodai Mathematical Journal*, 22(3):458–464, 1999.

[57]. Matei Zaharia, Mosharaf Chowdhury, Michael J. Franklin, Scott Shenker, and Ion Stoica. Spark: Cluster computing with working sets. *Proceedings of the 2nd USENIX conference on Hot topics in cloud computing*, 2010.

[58]. Wei Zhang, Suyog Gupta, Xiangru Lian, and Ji Liu. Staleness-aware async-SGD for distributed deep learning. *arXiv preprint arXiv:1511.05950*, 2015.

[59]. Shuxin Zheng, Qi Meng, Taifeng Wang, Wei Chen, Nenghai Yu, Zhi-Ming Ma, and Tie-Yan Liu. Asynchronous stochastic gradient descent with delay compensation. In *Proceedings of the 34th International Conference on Machine Learning-Volume 70*, pages 4120–4129. JMLR. org, 2017.

Index

A

Activation function, 126, 127, 131

Actor distributed engine
    barrier control methods, 252–256
    composing, OWl, 249, 250
    definition, 245
    framework, 249
    map-reduce, 245, 246
    parameter server module, 246, 248
    synchronization methods, 254

Actor system
    MapReduce engine, 423–428, 430–434
    parameter server engine, 435–442
    peer-to-peer engine, 442–455

Adagrad and RMSprop methods, 93

Adagrad method, 91

Adam optimizer, 92

add_node function, 128

add_scalar function, 154

adjoint function, 72

adjval function, 73

alcotest framework, 281, 291

Algodiff.gradhessian function, 98

Algodiff module, 51, 107, 109, 155, 156

Algorithmic differentiation (AD), 5, 51
    Algodiff module, 51, 52
    APIs, 70, 72, 73, 75
    computation, 53
    core modules, 352–356, 358
    data types, 53, 58–60
    definition, 49
    forward/reverse modes, 54–58

    graph converter, 358, 359, 361
    graph utility, 80, 81
    lazy expression, 78
    module design, 79
    Ndarray module, 81–84
    operations, 61, 62
    operator building, 325–334, 336–352
    operators
        Mat, 63
        rules, 63–65, 68
        SISO, 66, 69
    perturbation confusion/tag, 76, 77

Amazon Lambda, 234

Arithmetic Logic Unit (ALU), 15

Arr.add_ function, 303

Artificial Intelligence (AI), 1, 191, 233

Asynchronous barrier method, 265

Asynchronous Parallel (ASP), 253

Automated Empirical Optimization of
        Software (AEOS), 42–47

B

backward function, 132

Barrier control mechanisms, 245, 252,
        260, 263

Basic Linear Algebra Subprograms
        (BLAS), 293

Batch module, 100

Bigarray module, 9, 218

Builder module, 83

Bulk Synchronous Parallel (BSP), 253, 262

C